# Tone Poem for the Deaf

## Amity at Law

Brad Lancaster

Library of Congress Cataloguing in Publication Data:
Lancaster, Brad.
*Tone Poem for the Deaf: Amity at Law*
Includes epitomes of core texts
Includes bibliography

ISBN 978-0-9986435-6-4

Published by:
Saint George's Hill Press
17503 10th Avenue N.E.
Shoreline, Washington 98155

First Printing: 2025

This book is printed in Times New Roman font.

Printed in the United States of America

## PRIMUS

For dear, not-so-tall friend, Joe Shaub,
He of big laugh and enormous heart.
Joseph clubbed my thick skull
with an odd theory of law,
until it transformed
my law practice,
worldview,
and, last,
me.

## SECUNDUS

For Harvard Law Professor, Dean Roscoe Pound (1870-1964),
Who told it like it was, and still is, in his brave 1906 essay,
*"The Causes of Popular Dissatisfaction*
*With the Administration of Justice,"*
Which talk the ABA tried to suppress.
For Pound, pointed and blunt,
Told the Bar NOTHING
They wanted to hear
Or tolerate, at all.
Emphatically.
No morsel,
Not a jot,
Iota, or
Bit.
∞

## FIRST EPIGRAPHS

"I hold every man a debtor to his profession; from the which as men of course do seek to receive countenance and profit, so ought they of duty to endeavor themselves, by way of amends, to be a help and ornament thereunto. This is performed in some degree by the honest and liberal practice of a profession, when men shall carry a respect not to descend into any course that is corrupt and unworthy thereof, and preserve themselves free from the abuses wherewith the same profession is noted to be infected: but much more is this performed if a man be able to visit and strengthen the roots and foundation of the science itself; thereby not only gracing it in reputation and dignity, but also amplifying it in profession and substance."

Francis Bacon
Preface
*The Elements of the Common Lawes of England*
1630

"Are we moving towards an age of colossal organizations and collective institutions, or will the desire of innumerable people for small, manageable, personal relationships be satisfied?"

Dietrich Bonhoeffer
*Letters and Papers from Prison*, 299
May 1944

'I have something important to say; I shall have you hear it, and I shall let you know it: the design for eternity, a way / of life as it should be and of passing a lifetime at peace."

"The Loyalist Instruction"
Reign of Senwosret III
*Literature of Ancient Egypt, 173*
~1,950 B.C.

# TABLE OF CONTENTS

## PROLOGUE

### Tone Poem[1] for the Deaf

Many years now I have declined to address the Bar.[2] Reform sounds implausible, even corny. Who would listen if I spoke? The offer to aspire together presupposes collegiality conspicuously absent from my relations with many lawyers. Sowing hope in the field of law yields a harvest of discord. Rationality flowers in soils of shared values, that elusive and earthy "we" eerily absent from life in law.[3] The task of waking American jurisprudence, even locally, seems a windmill at which only a Quixote might tilt. So, I have said nothing, and practiced, and grieved.[4] Grief should end. Joy, or at least forgetfulness, in the normal course, surmounts tragedy. Rhapsodies, once mired in muds of melancholy, should lilt free to drown the dirge.

My legal despondence, however, lingers, its dark flame fanned by the withering sirocco of court houses. Disputing legatees claw for testamentary cash. Pyrotechnic dissolutions, detonated upon babies, fragment childhoods and lacerate attachment.[5] Parents forget their young, lusting after intimate vengeance. With Solomonic logic, the time of minors is sundered, like bucks and bills, as divorce booty. None among criminals, their victims, lawyers, law enforcement, prosecutors, judges, or parole

---

[1] A "tone poem" is a single movement of orchestral music, which illustrates in sound a non-musical theme or sentiment. In this book, the musical themes are a sharp trill at the Bar's insensitivity to the social carnage it fosters, and a somber dirge that the Bar spurns amity as the profession's core rationale, preferring combat metaphors and pugilistic spectacles.

[2] The "Bar" is a metonym for the institutions of law and associations of lawyers. The term particularly refers to the physical partition in some courtrooms that segregates members of the public from direct participants (such as lawyers and claimants).

[3] From my vantage, much of American life has misplaced its sense of communal solidarity. We are much degraded by this loss. If flourishing coexistence stands nowhere near the apex of our values, how could we cherish friendship? How can we value one another? To hear some we tend to ignore, many indigenous thinkers assert: All flourishing is mutual.

[4] About a quarter century ago, while contemplating whether to enter law school, I wrote admonitions to myself. One read: "Law is a mess. Just practice. Don't fix. They'll punish you for trying. Swallow your idiosyncrasy. Just hide." I find, now decades later, I can no longer restrain myself. Apparently, I surrender to old age and hubris (or, possibly, dementia, or, as my spouse might insert, grumpiness).

[5] See **Epitome 6: Karen, *Becoming Attached*.**

officers, when candid, views their system as remotely adequate. Some believe that judicial retribution wounds society so deeply that it is hardly preferable to self-help vendetta. Attorney entrepreneurs sell injury-outrage to juries, their windfalls funded by everyman's insurance. Juries are sidestepped by plea bargains that hardball prosecutors zing at society's errant members, enforcing ill-born statutes, bequeathing jails frothing with struck-out felons, often convicted by uncriticized evidence. Incarcerated, cellmates teach amateurs the professional standards of larceny. We transform drug dabblers into hardened menaces. The jury trial itself wanders far from principled fact-finding, inching ever closer to rootless theater for an audience of bored locals. Courts mandate rules which those same courts decline to enforce, emboldening corrupt lawyers while hobbling diligent ones. Fairness is hijacked. In my subterranean heart, and in that of many attorneys, a magma plume of frustration simmers just beneath our carefully-manicured topography. Our inwardness is a Yellowstone hot spot, awaiting some triggering seismism to erupt. Some disagree. Those are not paying attention to themselves or me. My tone poem is lost upon their dead ears. Even as I speak, most dysphoria lingers unspoken.[6] So, grief endures.

One cannot expect systemic change. When the alarm of first stampeders over a cliff rings back through the onrushing herd, there ensues yet greater haste to the brink. Lawyers, ever obsessive-compulsive, sense something awry in their ceaseless hand washing. They feel an urge to give their digits yet another thorough metaphorical scrub. Confronted with law's shortcomings and misdirection, the legal community proffers what it knows: more distinctions, another rule, more procedure, another tax, more this, another that. Scrub, scrub, scrub. The more we offer is more of the same.

Roscoe Pound called this fix-it sentiment "tinkering." Fixes that are too little, too late, to matter. Nugatory emendations. Fixes that compound problems, rather than resolve them. Most law workers scarcely consider that we might restructure our life together. We might reorganize our inwardness. We might seek and become something fundamentally better. We seem incapable of even attempting those conversations.[7]

Most judges are good people working hard, making tough decisions. Their tough decision-making is part of our problem. Most attorneys are good people working hard, advocating intelligently. Their intelligent advocacy is part of our problem. Have we been seduced? Character, the homely but chaste cousin of that painted looker, law, dies an uncourted spinster. Shall we rediscover deeper truths and begin

---

[6] You may think me prone to clinical depression. Neither that, nor its weak sister, situational depression, are characteristic. I prefer to think that I *see* the law. I believe you *see* the law as well. The experience for me is somber and often painful. Which is not to say that I am never depressed.

[7] I have mulled, at some length, deliberated societal and personal change in others of my works. Those pages address conversations we need to have, must have, should have, but don't. See my political morality effort, Lancaster, *Cull: Choosing Well*, and a comedy: Lancaster, *Analyzing Justitia*.

afresh, in our courts, in our culture? Can we abandon at least some laws in favor of a resurgent bloom of self-restraint? Can we fashion some better way to relate to one another than as strangers? Is friendship still an option? A dispirited voice inside me laments,

*The answer is "No."*

Fundamental change waits, not bouts of cheerful collaboration, but, rather, disturbing derailments of disasters and demolitions.[8]

The Oracle at Delphi declared Socrates the wisest man in the world for knowing he knew nothing. The old gadfly spent his days pressing questions, living provisionally, and savaging the haunch of Athenian normalcy. Socrates never knew. For him, uncertainty broadcast the virtue of epistemological humility. Lao Tzu advocated letting people rule themselves from below, intuitionally ferreting the Way. To his lawyers and kings, Lao Tzu advocated non-action, abandoning coercion, recognizing that inherent contradictions riddle truth. Verity is ever a ratty fabric.

But we attorneys spit out Socrates and the Taoist masters as might we spew rancid meat. We **know**. We **act**. American jurisprudence springs from opulence of purported knowledge, erected upon dunes of oft-unexamined supposition.[9] The word "jurisprudence" means the wisdom of law. Is law wise? Our halls of law tackle fathomless problems. Court rooms ring with din barked by people more studious than educated. Those women and men execute plans and remove obstacles, intervening from above, making themselves a sorrow to Lao Tzu. Attorney "knowledge" is a concrete that defies jackhammers, grieving Socrates.[10] Attorney suppositions, ever

---

[8] The restorative justice movement, focused mostly on criminal activity and victim restoration, has been yammering away at courts and their denizens for many decades. Still, efforts to redirect jurisprudence have had little (but not no) effect. See Zehr, *The Little Book of Restorative Justice*, 74-76. David Gil chastens me. He says: "Moving toward structurally just societies by nonviolent, rather than violent means—the only strategic mode likely to be effective—requires transformation of status quo-reproducing consciousness into status quo-challenging critical consciousness. . . . When people speak and act in accordance with 'normal' expectations, they reinforce, by implication, the existing social order and its 'common sense' consciousness. On the other hand, when people's words and actions 'transgress' the ranges of 'normal' communications and behaviors, by questioning and challenging the status quo, they create opportunities for reflection and for the emergence of critical consciousness on the part of others with whom they interact." Gil, "Toward a 'radical" paradigm of restorative justice," 508-509. As you can tell, I have concluded that I should speak, transgressing normal legal communications and behaviors.

[9] "The main thrust of lawyer's legal history, then, is to pervert the real function of history by reducing it to the pathetic role of justifying the world as it is." Morton Horowitz, "The Conservative Tradition in the Writing of American Legal History," 281 (criticizing the legal history of Roscoe Pound).

[10] Edmund Cahn, in his introduction to Frank's *Courts on Trial*, tells this parable of the mentation of lawyers: "For a long time, Mr. Lex had been annoying his family and neighbors with an obsessive conviction that he was not a living man but a corpse. It was the premise of all his conversations. Nothing could convince him that he was still alive; whatever others might say, he knew absolutely that he was a corpse. At last, his family insisted that he see a doctor. At the doctor's office, Mr. Lex explained that—despite everyone's refusal to acknowledge the obvious—the man they saw before them was not alive but a corpse. The doctor reasoned with him for about an hour. Finally, wearied of Lex's obduracy, the doctor asked, 'Will you at least admit that a corpse cannot bleed?' Lex replied, 'Yes, that is true.' Whereupon

shifting yet masked, castrate needful change. We peer to the past, to precedent. Attorney action dismays and disappoints; its rudiment is coercion. Attorney mindsets induce skeptical politicking where spin savages scruples. Our juridical administration lies locked in a thousand minds too exhausted to learn ignorance-in-principle. Our courtrooms are peopled by humans too jaded to ask what would happen if we did nothing, if we let matters unfold and resolve themselves. Jurisprudence trundles onward, suspecting its futility, but hawking its necessity. We attorneys have transmuted community healing, once the task of our profession, into for-profit mega-corporation cash grab. Socrates and Lao Tzu weep.

So why break silence? Why indeed. To what end?[11]

Perhaps there is some point. The hoary medieval walls of our imported English jurisprudence trap a horde of uncomprehending litigants, and, perhaps, more than a few attorneys clutching after sanity.

As to the litigants, who suffer the misfortune of paying the invoice, financial and emotional, for our misguided system, they may find relief in hearing it said, "Peace is banished from courtrooms." Perhaps, then, litigants can file their encounter with courts in that mental bin which contains road rage, bar fights, beserk shooters, and war. Jeremiah, an eighth century B.C. Jewish prophet, criticized his "lawyers." He said, "They have healed the wound of the people lightly, saying 'Peace, peace,' where

---

the doctor took a scalpel and cut Lex lightly across the hand so that the blood came pouring forth. Then he looked inquiringly at Lex, only to hear him exclaim, 'Imagine, a corpse can bleed, after all!'" Cahn, "Introduction" in Frank, *Courts on Trial*, x.

[11] It is my intention in this book to offer non-frivolous views that are warranted by existing law or a good faith argument for the extension, modification, or reversal of existing law or the establishment of new law. One can find similar language in Washington's or the federal court's Civil Rule 11, or MRPC 3.1. The American Bar Association's Model Rules of Professional Conduct (MRPC) assert: "As a public citizen, a lawyer should seek improvement of the law, access to the legal system, the administration of justice and the quality of service rendered by the legal profession. As a member of a learned profession, a lawyer should cultivate knowledge of the law beyond its use for clients, employ that knowledge in reform of the law and work to strengthen legal education. . . . A lawyer should be mindful of deficiencies in the administration of justice and of the fact that the poor, and sometimes persons who are not poor, cannot afford adequate legal assistance." (MRPC Preamble, §6.) When guiding lawyers with regard to client advice, the ABA counsels, "[W]hen a matter is likely to involve litigation, it may be necessary . . . to inform the client of forms of dispute resolution that might constitute reasonable alternatives to litigation." (MRPC 2.1, Comment 5.) MRPC 8.3 requires lawyers to report lawyer or judicial ethical violations if they raise "substantial question[s] as to that lawyer's honesty, trustworthiness, or fitness as a lawyer." (Washington's RPC 8.3 makes the obligation to report the misdeeds of others discretionary, rather than mandatory.) I find final refuge for speaking in an admonition of MRPC Preamble §7: "[A] lawyer is also guided by personal conscience and the approbation of professional peers. A lawyer should strive to attain the highest level of skill, to improve the law and the legal profession and to exemplify the legal profession's ideal of public service." George Bernard Shaw said: "The salvation of the world depends on the men who will not take evil good-humouredly, and whose laughter destroys the fool instead of encouraging him." Shaw, *Quintessence of Ibsenism*, 186.

Washington Supreme Court Chief Justice, Steven González asserts: "Disagreement is healthy, using your voice is healthy. We can do it respectfully, but it's important that we speak honestly, directly, with no gaslighting. This is about truthfully and forthrightly addressing the challenges we face. The challenges are serious." González and Mansfield, "Working Toward a Just Court," 44.

there is no peace. Were they ashamed when they committed abomination? No, they were not at all ashamed; they did not know how to blush."[12] I do not blush in courtrooms. I see no others blushing either. I do, however, feel redness creep up my neck, late at night, when assessing my part in the day's legal tumult. At the border of sleep's limbo, distress and humiliation gnaw. I suffer, as do many of my colleagues, courtroom chagrin.

As to the attorneys who may share my concerns, who are taxed as officers of courts in the coin of equanimity, they may find solace in hearing Cicero say, "Laws damage us." *Summum ius, summa iniuria.*[13] Perhaps, then, we can set aside our denial and be reconciled to our role in the suffering that our legal dynamic creates. We might whisper that other, better ways to arrange ourselves may exist. We who share these concerns might even talk face-to-face; the timid among us could email; those agoraphobic or inarticulate could text or tweet. In the end, breaking silence may help rescue my own sanity, which is always at issue. And perhaps peril awaits your equipoise as well. I occasionally doubt your stability. I lie when I say "occasionally."

My singing voice is crap. I am better lip-synching Gregorian chant than crooning Taylor Swift. So, I sound scratchy, out of tune to ears accustomed to a different register and catchier rhythm. My jeremiad rings doleful. Still, I harbor, in a secluded vestibule of my heart, more hope than my words trumpet. I write to invite you to peek in my seldom-revealed closet. For I know you hide such a covert closet as well.

I bray my lament. I sing this *tone poem for the deaf.*[14]
You clap trembling hands over tortured ears.
You resist my ragged rendition.
I sympathize utterly.
So once did I.
Years ago.
Then…

---

[12] *Jeremiah* 6:14-15 (Revised Standard Version).

[13] Cicero, *De Officiis*, Book I, X, 33. Free translations of this Latin saw might be: "The more law we make, the more injury we cause," or "Maximum justice is the greatest injury."

[14] Deafness may be congenital or acquired, partial or complete. All deafness is not physiological; some suffer aural incapacity for psychological reasons. Metaphorical deafness (that is, acquired partial psychological inattention) may emerge from religious conviction, inveterate opposition, exhaustion, ill-marriage, or hubris. Life at law would seem to be another of the syndrome's risk factors.

## SECOND EPIGRAPHS

"My aim and purpose have been to show that the various forms of liability known to modern law spring from the common ground of revenge."

Oliver Wendell Holmes, 1881
*The Common Law*, 33.

ᴥ

"[A] court-less, litigation-less, legal profession is unimaginable. . . . It is essential to remember Aristotle's warning to distinguish between the desirable and the possible. We should avoid suggestions, however delightful, which lack all practicality."

Jerome Frank, 1970
*Courts on Trial*, 11, 424

ᴥ

"Revenge and its modern outgrowth, punishment, belong to the past of legal history."

Roscoe Pound, 1906
*Causes of Popular Dissatisfaction with the Administration of Justice*, 338

ᴥ

"Do not seek revenge. Do not cause revenge to be sought against you."

"The Instruction of 'Onchsheshonqy"
*Ancient Egyptian Literature,* 511
After 332 B.C.

ᴥ

"For never can true reconcilement grow
Where words of deadly hate have pierced so deep."

John Milton, 1674
*Paradise Lost*
Book IV

ᴥ

"All that I saw I cannot well relate:
So lengthy is my theme, that oftentimes
My words are insufficient for the fact."

Dante Alighieri
*The Divine Comedy*
Inferno, Canto 4

CS

"Shut not your doors to me proud libraries,
For that which was lacking on all your well-fill'd shelves,
yet needed most, I bring.
Forth from the war emerging, a book I have made,
**The words of my book nothing, the drift of it everything.**
A book separate, not link'd with the rest nor felt by the intellect,
But you ye untold latencies will thrill to every page."

Walt Whitman
"Shut Not Your Doors"
*Leaves of Grass*, Inscriptions, 18
(Emphasis added)

CS

"It's extraordinary the way the whole quality of our existence can be changed by altering the words in which we think and talk about it. We float in language like icebergs."

Aldous Huxley
*After Many a Summer Dies the Swan*
326 (Mr. Propter)

CS

"Law is the business to which my life is devoted, and I should show less than devotion if I did not do what in me lies to improve it, and, when I perceive what seems to me the ideal of its future, if I hesitated to point it out and to press toward it with all my heart."

Oliver Wendell Holmes, 1920
*Collected Legal Papers,* 194

CS

"You've offended the Miss Gunns, I'm sure."
"What have I done, child?" said Priscilla, in some alarm.
"Why, you asked them if they minded about being ugly—you're so very blunt."
"Law, did I? Well, it popped out: it's a mercy I said no more, for I'm a bad un to live with folks when they don't like the truth."

George Eliot, 1861
*Silas Marner*, 95
*The Lammeter sisters,*
*Nancy and Priscilla*

# INTRODUCTION

## AMITY OR ENMITY

Why law? *Law is how we cope with those who are not our companions.* What is law? [15] *Law is the "or else" by which we strong-arm strangers we fear or fear we might fear.* By what agglomeration of ideas do we justify law? *Sit in a courtroom and listen. Hear yourself talk to clients. All revolves around effective delivery of recompense.* What alternatives exist that might supplant law? *Have a beer with friends at a tavern or pay attention to a neighbor's family at dinner. Plumb how they govern themselves.* Should thoughtful people support law as a theory of human relations? *Not to the extent there exist better alternatives.* What are the outcomes of laws, as compared to the outcomes of irenic[16] approaches to human self-organization? *Law produces* **coercive class competitors**. *Irenic approaches produce* **collaborative consensual companionships**. Can amity[17] supplant law? *Possibly, if we humans reorganize ourselves.* Might law atrophy? *Law trends toward an abrupt conclusion. In courtrooms, we see late-stage social metastasis as the cancer, loneliness, kills its*

---

[15] Here we have the jumping off point of H.L.A. Hart's famous meditation. To the question, "What is law?" Hart answers that law is something different from but related to orders backed by threats, different from but related to moral obligation, and different from but related to rules. Hart, *The Concept of Law*, 1, 13. Hart admits that his deliberation creates nothing concise enough to constitute an answer to the question. In fact, Hart denies that his purpose is to define law. Hart, *The Concept of Law*, 16-17.

Being a relative simpleton, I answer less subtly than Hart. *Lawyers address conflict.* They may reduce conflict's intensity. They may help clients avoid conflicts altogether by carefully-drawn agreements and prudent advice. Life at law is only marginally a philosophical or rhetorical endeavor. In its gut, law is deeply interpersonal. Compassion is more relevant to life at law than erudition or courtroom eloquence. If lawyers were carpenters, our timber would be social structures and our chisels frank conversation. Karl Llewellyn, in his primer for law students, said: "What, then, is this law business about? It is about the fact that our society is honeycombed with disputes. . . . This doing of something about disputes, this doing of it reasonably, is the business of law. And the people who have the doing in charge, whether they be judges or sheriffs or clerks or jailers or lawyers, are officials of the law. What these officials do about disputes is, to my mind, the law itself." Llewellyn, *The Bramble Bush*, 2-3.

[16] The root of irenism/irenic derives from εἰρήνη, Attic Greek for "fasten together" or, metaphorically, "peace." I kidnap the idea of "irenism" from its Reformation usage. Narrowly, "irenism" is a coinage absent from the English dictionary. Irenist theologians pondered issues of faith in a conciliatory and collaborative manner, often seeking to reconcile divergent faith communities to one another. Other theologians, of pugnacious preference, grappled theological questions polemically, savoring debate and intellectual warfare.

[17] "Amity" is "friendly relationship." Its synonyms are friendship, friendliness, harmony, harmoniousness, understanding, accord, cooperation, companionship, amicableness, goodwill, cordiality, warmth, or concord. An antonym of "amity" is "enmity," which means "a feeling of active opposition to someone or something." Synonyms are hostility, animosity, antagonism, friction, antipathy, animus, acrimony, bitterness, rancor, resentment, aversion, bad feeling, ill will, bad blood, hatred, loathing, and odium.

*host.*[18] What might amity look like? *Hark back to that tavern and dinner table.* What different agglomeration of ideas might justify amity as the core organizing principle of lawyers? *One could look to this book or the books it epitomizes to begin an answer.* Are compelling irenic ideas available? *We shall see.* If so, what are those amicable ideas? *Patience, please.*

**A primary purpose of this book is to induce you[19] to inspect the outcomes your labors create in you, your clients, your workmates, courts, and human society. This book invites you to re-construct law as something other than the common law.[20]** Can we start afresh, fabricating rules and skills that restore friendship, that nurture communities, that address communal problems and those of their members? What happens to you and your people as a result of the acts you undertake in your profession at law? I suggest that *how* one practices law deeply affects her clients' expectations and the adequacy of their outcomes. At what do you aim? For what do you hope?[21] What, empirically, is the moral outcome of your legal interventions into the lives of your neighbors? Do you find yourself saying to your clients, "I

---

[18] Humankind's essential sociality echoes through history. One finds the concept in foundational Brahmanist literature, in several Biblical books, in Plato and Aristotle (and probably in Socrates as well, judging by his actions—he was, however, too preoccupied with knowing nothing to say so), in the Stoics, and in the American student radicals of the 1960s. Tom Hayden wrote: "*Human relationships* should involve fraternity and honesty. Human interdependence is contemporary fact; human brotherhood must be willed, however, as a condition of future survival and as the most appropriate form of social relations. . . . Loneliness, estrangement, isolation describe the vast distance between man and man today." Hayden, *Port Huron Statement* of the Students for a Democratic Society, June 15, 1962.

[19] I assume you work professionally in some cubbyhole of law, or have interest in such endeavors.

[20] **Throughout this book, I use the term "common law" expansively. The scope of common law exceeds what judges do in courtrooms. Common law includes statutory intrusions of legislatures and the administrations of executives and the corrective opinions of courts of appeal. The cultures of America also invade the court process, delivering both its subject matter and its players, mixing that whipped blend of interactive governmental action that is the common law.**

**An objector prefers that I carefully differentiate common law (courts) from statutory law (legislatures), and both from enforcement (executive actions). I decline this approach. I find courts to be first among equals, as branches of government go (or so *Marbury v. Madison* asserts). Everywhere courts intrude and are intruded upon, willy-nilly. Acts of American government are not judicial or legislative or executive acts alone, but rather a froth of all three (and other cultural inputs), a generally-coercive goo liberally slathered upon the body politic. The buck (and the slathering) stops at Supreme Court benches (contrary to Harry Truman's imaginations). I liken segregating these law-inputs by branch to separating bananas from raspberries in a well-shredded smoothie. To abruptly shift metaphors, the common law system, if it were an omelet, would contain everything in the fridge, but still be an omelet.**

[21] Edmund Burke puts a sobering face on the suburban practitioner. He said lawyers are "obscure provincial advocates, of stewards of petty local jurisdictions, country attornies, notaries, and the whole train of the ministers of municipal litigation, the fomenters and conductors of the petty war of village vexation." They "are habitually meddling, daring, subtle, active, of litigious dispositions and unquiet minds." Burke, *Reflection on the Revolution in France*, page 42-43 (of 250). Burke, in 1790, speaks of humbler members of the Third Estate in France's nascent, post-revolution national assembly. Perhaps, however, Burke is prescient, peering down law's primordial gut, glimpsing practitioner essence.

know this is miserable. I know it is counterproductive and stupid expensive. But it is the way things are done at law"?

This sentiment, this excuse, this prevarication that shunts responsibility from the practitioner to the system, betrays a fundamental misstep. We say,[22] "I am a professional. I did not invent this system. I do not even approve this system. I just fill a role. I am a technician, not an engineer. The duty of fundamental legal reform lies with others—with the Washington Supreme Court, or with the county judges, or with academics, or with the American Bar Association. Not with me." So we say. So we feel. Yet, it is not so. To be a professional means to take responsibility for the system in which one participates.[23] Bluntly, when Washington's legal system causes suffering, I caused it. Or, better, you and I did. Or, most frankly, we all did. It is entirely possible to conform fastidiously to Washington's Rules of Professional Conduct and still participate in legal proceedings that savage participants. I speak not of errant proceedings. I speak of proceedings in which due process is provided, in which the rules of court prevail, in which civility dominates, in which all professionals perform competently. We sometimes have trouble seeing deficiencies in our own time and context, but recognize defects in historical distance. Think of Homer Plessy's ejection from a whites-only train car,[24] or Carrie Buck's involuntary sterilization,[25] or Dred Scott's stillborn citizenship,[26] or Fred Korematsu's compulsory lingering at Manzanar concentration camp,[27] or the thousands of indigenous dead along the Trail of Tears, an American ethnic cleansing in breach of stacks of treaties approved by Congress. The United States Supreme Court found, in a breathtaking act of cowardice, that it lacked authority to enjoin Georgia from taking Cherokee land without compensation.[28] Even apart from great missteps such as those that abused Homer or

---

[22] I have said, to my chagrin.

[23] Conrad G. Brunk, "Professionalism and Responsibility in the Technological Society," 1985 *Conrad Grebel Review*, Waterloo, Ontario, Canada: 60-75. Brunk argues for an Ethic of Conscientious Professionalism. He believes legal professionals, as well as other sorts of professionals, "must be prepared to take the difficult step of conscientious refusal to participate in the system or in aspects of the system. This is not an easy thing to do, because it almost always implies great personal sacrifice, including often the loss of professional standing in the eyes of one's colleagues, and even banishment from the profession." (Brunk, Professionalism, 73).

[24] *Plessy v. Ferguson*, 163 U.S. 537 (1896).

[25] *Buck v. Bell*, 274 U.S. 200 (1927).

[26] *Dred Scott v. Sandford*, 60 U.S. (19 How.) 393 (1856).

[27] *Korematsu v. United States*, 323 U.S. 214 (1944).

[28] Andrew Jackson, as President of the United States, vigorously enforced the Indian Removal Act of 1830, Pub. L. 21-148, leading to the many-tendrils of the Trail of Tears, in which (mostly) eastern seaboard indigenous tribes were forcibly evicted across the Mississippi River to the region that now is Oklahoma. Jackson was a self-made slaver and plantation owner, opponent of abolition, who sought to extend slavery into the new western states. Jackson also opposed creation of the Second Bank of the United States. In an

Carrie or Dred or Fred or Cherokees, litigation harms litigants and litigators. There is the post-secondary stress of unrelenting nastiness. There are the astounding financial burdens of courtroom process. There is the hidden tax on the weal of society by diversion of zeal from constructive remediations to pugilistic spectacles. Litigants never win. Even winners lose. We like to say to ourselves, "I did not argue *Korematsu*. I do not set the fee structure for Seattle lawyers. I conduct myself ethically in every matter. I litigate cooperatively, without rancor or pettiness. I am what lawyers are supposed to be—principled advocates for clients in conflict." I say, It is not so.

Hannah Arendt sat through and wrote about the trial of Adolph Eichmann in Israel. Eichmann, a Nazi officer, had organized transportation for Europe's Jews to Hitler's ghettos and death camps. Eichmann's argument was simple and familiar: *I did nothing wrong. I killed no Jew. I do not even harbor ill-will toward Jews. I was assigned a task. I performed that task as well as I was able. I was a tiny cog in a great machine for which I bear no personal responsibility. You are wrong to condemn me for doing my duty in time of war. I did not design the Final Solution. I do not approve the Final Solution. My superiors would have executed me for refusing their orders.* Arendt observed that, to the end, Eichmann never recognized that what he did was wrong. So, too, the other actors, who were not on trial in Jerusalem. None claimed responsibility. In the end, Arendt writes, evil is banal—pedestrian, hidden in plain sight.[29] Conscientious people set themselves a task, effect horrific evil, and each blames some person other than himself or herself. Great evils, when one learns the excuses of all participants, are the act of No One in particular. Death by bureaucracy. Evil by committee. For lawyers, this boils down to procedural due process bereft of substantive due process.[30] It tempts some to the tedious performative tinkering by which we desperately wish we might improve our hobbled system of law.

---

irony, Jackson's face now graces the twenty-dollar bill, issued by the federal government, which likeness, as I write this sentence, hides in my wallet. Why do we honor such a man? As for the U.S. Supreme Court's evasions of responsibility, see *Cherokee Nation v. Georgia*, 30 U.S. (5 Pet.) 1 (1831). For that court's complicity in stealing Indian lands, see *Johnson v. M'Intosh*, 21 U.S. 543 (1832).

[29] Arendt, *Eichmann in Jerusalem*, 287.

[30] Behind and beneath rules of civil procedure crowd many values that procedural rules aim, silently, to assure. These are rights many of us take for granted, though some of them are not mentioned in constitutions: the right to marry, to create and rear children, to decline to make children, to exist without unwarranted governmental intrusion (privacy), to travel, to relate to weird people, to do nothing, to invent new musical instruments and play them, to invent values, some of which may come to be protected by procedural due process, though they are utterly novel. None knows the exact boundaries of the values protected by court rules. When high courts make decisions about the extent of protections for unexpressed (or constitutionally-explicit) values, they shift the protected territory of these substantive due process rights. Justice Thomas and the Trump Court labor to shrink those boundaries. Previous courts have expanded the scope of these rights. The bottom line is this: one who raises issues concerning substantive due process seeks to insure that the rules of civil procedure protect those values worth defending—neither more nor less. Substantive due process considers what rights should be protected. Procedural due process considers what rules should govern deprivation of those valued rights.

When all was said, Eichmann's judges condemned him to death. After many appeals for clemency, Eichmann was hung, his body cremated, and the ashes scattered outside Israeli territory in the Mediterranean Sea by the Israeli Navy.

I do not liken Washington Superior Courts to the Final Solution. I do not assert that non-dissenting Washington lawyers are "little Eichmen."[31] Our evils are less extravagant, and generally less fatal, than Germany's World War II obsession. Our practitioner morality is not so brain dead as Eichmann's, who denied responsibility for participating in unparalleled crime. But we Washington lawyers find solace in Eichmann's self-defense. It rings sweet. We emulate Eichmann, seldom knowing we do so. Thus, we err. Washington's defects of justice remain our problems to solve. In this book, I frame such a solution, if not in expansive detail, then more modestly as a map or summary, or, at worst, a suggestion.

> IN ITS DEEP LOGIC, THE COMMON LAW REMAINS COMPETITIVE, CLASSIST, AND COERCIVE.

When one reads ancient codes, say, the Babylonian *Code of Hammurabi*,[32] one finds, all a-jumble, criminal laws, rules of judicial conduct, civil rules, economic regulations, cultic observances, and moral exhortation. Hammurabi's code built on predecessors, lost to history, moldering bodies of law, long interred in Mesopotamian muds.[33] Hammurabi's penalty for non-compliance was generally death, though occasionally amputations or hefty fines sufficed.[34] An errant middle-class surgeon might have his hands cut off if his scalpel injured a patient in the fertile crescent.[35] There lie risks in every occupation, but one is glad not to be Hammurabi's physician. Baldly, the *Code of Hammurabi* stated a class structure: *amelu* (patricians), *muskinu* (landless freemen), and *ardu* (slaves). It surprises none that *amelu* fare better than *ardu* in the Babylonian code. For Hammurabi's

---

[31] We lawyers may, however, be an inert sludge that clogs arteries that might otherwise nourish the heart of law.

[32] Hammurabi ruled Mesopotamia from 1795 to 1750 B.C.

[33] The *Code of Ur-Nammu* (~2,100 B.C.), the oldest extant legal code, was almost lost. It is fractured, and its legibility fragmentary. This code derives from Mesopotamia, and is written in Sumerian. This code also jumbles criminal and civil matters, and like the Code of Hammurabi, departs from the Babylonian governing principle of "eye for an eye, tooth for a tooth." Bodily injuries merit compensation in money. Perjury in a civil matter results in money penalties equal to the value of the suit in which one lied. As expected, serious crimes merit death.

[34] Roscoe Pound reports of the English penal system: "All crimes of any consequence were once felonies punishable with death." Pound, *The Spirit of the Common Law*, 103.

[35] *The Code of Hammurabi*, Section 218.

Mesopotamia, law was everywhere about classes in competition within a coercive regime. That is what "law" meant in Babylon.

In reading modern codes, say, the *Revised Code of Washington*, one finds much the same, and much that is different.[36] Our slaves have been freed. Some among their descendants languish, however, near the rotting bottom of our economic heap, joined by persons who are unproductive, diseased, and uneducated. Our codes are less jumbled.[37] Our bourgeois middle-classers have rights guaranteed by written constitutions. These muddlers need their rights. Our amelu, kings of computers and mass sales and video games and airplanes, still roll in the dough that our labor kneads. The upper crust can no longer own us. But we remain fungible excrescence to the lords of society. Our penalties have migrated from executions and dismemberments to fines and incarcerations.[38]

But the underlying competitive-classist-coercive rationale of law gushes on, unabated. Learned Hand warned: "I must say that, as a litigant, I should dread a lawsuit beyond almost anything else short of sickness and of death."[39] The regime is little else but prettified enmity. Prisons bulge. Annually, we Americans consign millions of inmate life-years to unproductive loitering at public expense.[40] Class structure lingers in Washington's statutes. Facially, our laws pander to democratic sentiment; egalitarian mumblings abound. The change of tone, however, is only word-deep. Elites still control commoners' lives and well-being. To steal much from many merits a white collar slap on the hand, or, occasionally, praise. To steal a pittance from the neighborhood convenience store merits years-long lock-up at the glower of a nonplussed jury. If one examines the rolls of the incarcerated, black and Hispanic and male and mentally-ill faces predominate, far exceeding their demographic shares. The cause might be offenders' misbehavior; it might be raw prejudices of class and sex and race and mental status; it might be all. Our statutes seem positively compassionate, when laid syllable-for-syllable beside Hammurabi's. But the deep logic, the driving force, of law, even enlightened leading-edge Washington law, remains competitive and classist and coercive.[41]

---

[36] I speak of the RCW because I have some familiarity with it. But any state's code, or any nation's code, would suffice.

[37] Washington's probate statute, however, may approximate Hammurabi-esque degree of disorder.

[38] Mostly—not so much in Mr. Trump's Terre Haute death row (2016-2020), where America has again done unconscionable things to people who have done unconscionable things (and, all too often, to those who have not committed the crimes of which they were convicted).

[39] Hand, "The Deficiencies of Trials to Reach the Heart of the Matter," 89, 105.

[40] Some seem to welcome this outcome with unaccountable glee.

[41] David Gil argues that societies meet inherent needs (food and sex, meaningful social relations in a supportive community, meaningful work, trust and security, self-actualization, and spirituality) and perceived needs (socially-constructed ciphers for needs). When perceived needs poorly track our inherent

Is competitive coercive classism necessary?[42] Perhaps we lack alternatives. Many so assert. Human behavior lacks reliable self-restraint, they pessimize. We implant sharp incisors and crushing molars in the State's jaw. The worst among us our State gnaws: to restrain crimes, to give pause to imitators, to tip our hat to justice.[43] So goes the juridical liturgy that many chant. Surely, these argue, we better prosper when our Ted Bundies and Hillside Stranglers languish in solitary cells. The worst among offenders we kill outright, or take scant notice as they murder one another. We fear much. So, we warn those who would fan our fears that their depredations will not go unanswered. It is a lie. Many crimes in fact go unpunished, even undiscovered. Yet the lie comforts us. The lie is an essential crutch for a limping society. Hobbled, we grit our teeth. Steely, we trudge on, re-enacting the errors our parents and their parents committed generations ago. Quietly, suffering unspoken trepidation at the incompetence of our system of jurisprudence, we arm up. We bristle with guns at home, even on hips. Self-defense runs amok. Still, we gape, astonished, when mentally unstable or sociopathic persons go berserk, slaughtering us with the "defensive" weapons we sold them.

Internationally, law lacks teeth. So again, we arm up. A prudent nation trembles, wholly prepared to rain unimaginable violence upon any who might harm, or even slander, its people. The law of nations is big dog eats little dog. Much blood drips from all jowls. But, so the tale goes, better to be a big dog. America has drunk this particular bitter cup to its dregs. We sigh relief when Osama bin Laden has an American hole in his head and his sons have perished of Seal-team bullets. Yet these vengeance murders resurrected not a single victim of the Twin Towers mass murder. Our trembling waxes when we imagine angry, immoderate men possessing nuclear devices. No reasonable person wishes to live in such a world. All fear. Justifiably, we fear.

---

needs, people can pursue ends that poorly serve them. Gil styles cultures with scant overlap between inherent and perceived needs "false consciousness," following Mannheim's 1936 work, *Ideology and Utopia*. Gil, "Toward a 'radical' paradigm' of restorative justice," 500.

[42] Many would argue that common law is indispensable. Though no fan of judicial proceedings, Jerome Auerbach admits, "When disputants cannot be reconciled litigation structures the melodrama of human conflict within a precise set of procedures for its resolution. Legal ritual, especially at its most compulsive levels of due process, can contain explosive emotions. Society benefits from the formal processing of disputes that otherwise might erupt in public violence or private vengeance. . . . The idea of a society without courts and lawyers inspires trepidation." Auerbach, *Justice without Law?,* vii.

[43] Our criminal justice system purports to have purposes: to **incapacitate** the criminal propensities of those incarcerated, to **deter** the unsavory predilections of those not incarcerated, to **rehabilitate** the willing incarcerated, to **punish** ill-behavior, and when an incarcerated person is released, and to tax their incomes for the benefit of victims in the name of **restitution**.

So, following the rationale of competitive coercive classism, we jail millions of our fellows,[44] and spend trillions on a nuclear arsenal[45] that can never be deployed. Put this way, we sound insane, or at least aggressively neurotic. Our incarcerations fail to reduce crime (some, wrongly, argue otherwise[46]). Our weapons of mass destruction have not forestalled wars, nor have they blunted ravening among bad faith actors for thermonuclear devices.[47]

So, both at home and abroad, we tolerate competitive coercive classism. Inflated people coerce deflated minions to unchosen countries, workplaces, institutions, and jails. In courtrooms and law offices we legal professionals grease the cogs of that engine. Most of us heave a sigh of relief to be unshackled from minimum wage occupations doing doleful drudgery. In the evening, finally home, we try not to think too much about our day's tasks. We have family to love and pickleballs to doink and dinner to eat and Netflix to watch. We are, understandably, too pooped to engage much soulish spelunking. That is understandable, but perhaps not optimal.

> IN ITS DEEP LOGIC, AMITY INVITES CONSENSUAL COLLABORATIVE COMPANIONSHIPS.

What might we find, were we to shake off our doldrums? What if, instead of litigating and arbitrating, we labored as mightily to avoid litigation altogether? What if, instead of "defending clients' rights," we strove to improve relationships among the alienated

---

[44] Zakaria, Fareed, "Incarceration Nation," *Time* 179, No. 13 (April 2, 2012): [unable to recover page reference]. Zakaria reports that six million Americans were under "correctional supervision" in 2012.

[45] Current estimates put total spending on United States nuclear weapons in excess of ten trillion dollars since 1940. The United States currently spends $2.19 million per hour updating and maintaining our nuclear arsenal. https://www.nationalpriorities.org/cost-of/nuclear-weapons/ (By 2025, this page has been removed from the internet). One is not, then, surprised to find no spare cash to staff courthouses, pave streets, provide health care, educate children, or balance the federal budget.

[46] Recently, Texas and New Jersey have reformed their incarceration policies, leading to reductions in crime and incarcerations. California reduced its prison population by twenty-three percent; violent crime fell by twenty-one percent. http://www.huffingtonpost.com/entry/proof-mass-incarceration-doesnt-reduce-crime_us_56255cfbe4b08589ef489a3d.

[47] Despite our coercive ethos (or, as Pinker argues, because of it), human society has become much less violent than it was 10,000 years ago. See Pinker, *Better Angels of Our Nature: Why Violence Has Declined.* If you think violence has not declined, Pinker will convince you otherwise (as did he me). You can find Pinker's *Better Angels* epitomized in the second volume of my two-volume work, *Cull*, which is titled *Cull: Epitomes*, at page 365. But read Pinker himself. Pinker attributes diminution of global violence to five factors: state restraint of violence (coercion), lawful trade, female values, sympathy expansion, and rational thinking. See Pinker's tenth chapter: On Angel's Wings. I disagree with Pinker about the beneficial effects of State coercion. The attempts of States to quash violence results in police officers and courts responding in kind to the violence of violent perpetrators. Hence, the black lives matter movement. None can coerce others to live amicably. Amity has a different root and genealogy.

and heal their community ruptures? Instead of fires of recompense might we seek to kindle amity? Might we find that redirected effort could fundamentally improve our outcomes? For our clients? For us? For our colleagues? For our city? For our culture? Dare we hope, for the world?

Some lawyers conduct facets of this amity experiment in their law practices. Some divert clients to mediations and therapists, when such efforts promise progress. Some teach with care the unwanted outcomes of coercive solutions. Some speak about the psychological and relational causes of conflict, before describing remedies a judge might offer. Some take the "counselor" part of their job description to heart, diminishing their role as "advocate." Some collaborate, promising no litigation will issue from their offices in a conflicted matter. Such approaches are called, mostly by detractors, "alternative dispute resolution." Rather, these bashful peacemakers tremble at the edge of amity, an alternative theory of justice. Such lawyers embrace, or begin to do so, a different understanding of the work of lawyers. They seek, not incisive advocacy before impartial decision-makers, but relational healing for people with divergent, but not necessarily incompatible, interests. They seek amity in relationship, not mere recompense in money. Money judgments remain a cipher for enmity that lurks in courthouse shadows. Those who aim at amity mortar bricks in a new edifice, a redirected jurisprudence. They seek to midwife irenea. They bind the wounds of battered communities. They seek to reconstitute law. Amity aims to restore equilibrium to conflict-shocked communities and their members. Amity makes friends of putative enemies. Amity abandons coercion in favor of collaboration on common problems. Amity recognizes that we all participate in the dysfunctions of our errant members, whose troubles cannot be dispatched by penalties and incarcerations.

The theory of amity-at-law is this. Courtrooms enact competitive classist coercion. Classism glosses over human differentiation. Each human is unique, and deserves consideration in his or her oddness. Every situation has never before occurred in the history of the universe; we should address its idiosyncrasies. Coercion breeds eventual retaliation. Coercion, as the womb of vendetta, is the enemy of amity. Statutes savage social sodality.[48] Cooperation exceeds competition. Humans are happier and more productive when collaborating. They even live longer. Competition lusts for heroes and exuberances. Most of our mettles are not such. We are dull. We dodge pugilists. We plod. We value peace within, between, and around us. We long for amity.[49]

---

[48] "Sodality" means "brotherhood, companionship." The term is sometimes used of Catholic lay charitable groups.

[49] I do not wish to overstate the antithesis between mainstream common law processes and amity-at-law. In courthouses, much collaboration occurs (plea bargains, referrals to therapeutic courts, hallway horse-trading, and so forth). Perhaps, if proponents of the common law system were more forthcoming about the level of cooperation within that system, amity might find a warmer welcome among law people.

Irenists urge every lawyer, and every human: find an alternative to litigation. The outcome of courtrooms, and the attitudes that enliven those halls of law, pervert our sociality like an undiagnosed wasting disease. We ask: How did we come to be so angry and alienated? How did gun violence and perpetual wars run amok. At least one fragment of the answer is: By venerating law, the common law.[50]

You may disagree. You may not know what I am talking about. Or you may think me, and those of my ilk, daft. My request is this. So much is at stake, can you pause to consider the possibility that there may be a better way to resolve social and interpersonal conflict than what happens in courtrooms, than what happens at law? Do you have an inkling that impartial judicial decision-makers are not all that impartial?[51] Have you noticed that judicial findings of fact often diverge from those rudiments asserted by disputing parties? Can you see that our prudential argumentation before those high benches is not all that prudent or rational? Can you acknowledge that we would take a step toward a better future if we stopped redistributing money among contestants, and paused to listen and knit the torn fabric of injured communities? Can you spend some hours deliberating whether courts might be relegated to a seldom-visited backwater in restoring injured members? Might courts recede, becoming the appendix of our body politic, often troublesome and seldom useful. Might amity rush over the sands of human disputes like a tsunami of well-being?[52]

The path from litigation to amity may hold some (possibly painful) introspective demolition. We all change, and often complain in the process. The critical question is this: do our changes trend in a direction we approve? Is the social universe we fabricate one in which we wish to dwell? Or would you rather escape what we have made? Our culture deems the coercive ethos of law normal, even necessary, and certainly unavoidable. Coercion is what we learned in law school. It is what we do,

---

See Snedker, *Therapeutic Justice*, 42. Most cases settle (belatedly, on the courthouse steps). And some effort is made to divert conflicts to shuttle mediations and arbitrations, which amount to litigation lite. Insurance companies resist litigation, seeing it as a insufferable cash sinkhole. The presence of limited collaborative efforts in common law courts, however, does not gainsay the serious misdirection of common law theory.

[50] A friend commented that I seem to assert that the common law generates all social ills. This I do not believe. Our society suffers many generative diseases, such as overpopulation and escapist drug intoxication and moral indolence and lax education and gun frenzy, to name but a few. Though I do not lay all ills at the feet of court process, I do deem courts responsible, as one player among many, for the distressing dysfunctions of American society, and a prime purveyor of the pugilist theory of society.

[51] In the Navajo circle, a form of conflict resolution, the "judge" is called a "keeper." His or her role is not to pretend impartiality, but rather to participate vigorously. The keeper's core qualification is that he or she cares equally about all the participants. Stuart and Pranis, "Peacemaking circles," 128.

[52] Perhaps the tsunami metaphor misses the mark. The process of making irenic changes will certainly be slow and require many years, even if most attorneys adopted amicable priorities. Courts will remain important, chewing, as they do, the gristly torn tendons of money-manic combatants, a concoction often churned by salivating sociopaths. And peacemaking alternatives will sound, probably for centuries, like inarticulate mumbo-jumbo to ears accustomed to the din of battle frenzy and cash-clawing clients.

primarily, at work. We addicted many require a remedy with a moral dimension and some measure of chastisement. A fearless moral inventory, a change of values, apology, commitment to make amends, and a pledge to do no further harm would well-serve the purveyors of American justice.[53]

Some choose changes. I did. Those reversals I clumsily engaged. They proved nonetheless effective. One can practice law without fostering litigation. One can stop litigating altogether. One can divert frenzied clients from courtrooms, describing their defects and the merits of a different approach. One may mediate; one may negotiate; one may draft conflict-avoiding agreements. One may redirect most clients[54] from vengeance to healing. One listens, so far as she is able. One empathizes, to the extent of his limited capacity. One builds bridges and imagines futures. In short, lawyers may collaborate with clients to foster amity. I am certain each of you does at least some of these tasks, often with much finer delicacy than I might ever muster. For me, friends helped in abandoning litigation. Authors provided cognitive superstructure. I had to muster some fiscal courage[55] the first day I told a telephonic inquirer, "Sorry, I do not do litigation work. I can help you resolve your conflict, but I decline to slug it out in court for you. I believe, win or lose, litigation is bad for you and your family and your opponent. It is also bad for me and my colleagues and judges and court staff. If you want that sort of work done, I will refer you to a competent practitioner who, for no good reason I can discern, still chooses to litigate for people."

Amity courses within us, a river, sometimes unrecognized, flowing from every human heart. Only you can discover and paddle that irenic soulish stream. In your life. In your work.

If you will.

Will you?

---

[53] Though many would reject the theological undertow of Twelve Step theory, such programs accurately capture the essence of how one effects deep internal change in oneself. If you are interested in making such a change of course, you might mull the admonitions of Appendix B to this book.

[54] Say, more than ninety percent.

[55] Or madness.

## CHAPTER 1

### COMMON LAW SKETCHED

Our judge delivered her oral decision. Black robes swished as she bustled out. This hellish divorce trial had raged for eleven days, spread, due to senseless wrangling and jammed dockets, over ten weeks. Exhausted, opposing counsel and I rocked back in our courtroom swivels, sore from their dead padding and torn upholstery. Counsel glared at me, war-weary: "The one upside here is that I will never have to see you again, you corrupt turd."[56] I searched for something appropriate to say, then settled on the truth. I growled, "Back at you," without a smile, without making eye contact. In her defense, opposing counsel was suffering cancer. For me, I offer no excuse.

I came to law mid-life. After the bar exam, I drafted a philosophy of legal practice. One part reads: "Courts exist to end intractable conflicts and should be the forum of last resort. Litigation benefits no one except attorneys. Litigated solutions necessarily involve coercion, forcing unchosen change on unwilling participants. The results dismay. When litigation cannot be avoided, courtesy and candor must temper advocacy. Ethical probity and personal trustworthiness are the essence of practicing law." In the mud of client frenzy, I found this, like every aspiration, easier to say than do. An unholy alliterative trinity of ambition and anger and angst crowded my heart, hobbling its better impulses. I came to law to help. I came to law to serve. I saw that most often I achieved neither. That recognition, though painful, launched a journey that has occupied the last twenty years of my practice of law.

Morality inquires after the impact our choices bear for those affected. In small communities, say under 150 members, morality governs. Laws prove pointless, for folkways, shared sentiment, affection, friendship, reciprocal caring, the possibility of personal criticism, and persistent familiarity render "proclamations of universal applicability" strange impositions. Amity has its reasons, unknown to law.

---

[56] A kind editor has asked where lay the root of my corrupt "turdity." This I have pondered. I am aware of no ethical breaches in my representation of my client or courtroom demeanor (but this state of mind might be nothing more than a weary testament to the persistent blindness which denial induces). Perhaps opposing counsel rankled that I represented my client, about whom one might justifiably harbor refractory moral distaste (I do). Or perhaps opposing counsel blustered because she did not get from the bench all she had promised her client. Perhaps she shared my distemper being in that courtroom with these particular clients. My reservation about these speculations on the nature of my turdity is that I largely get off the hook in each. That is, I escape turd-free. That seems unlikely. Our polite little war was hell. Neither of our clients deserved the consideration they received.

Relationships rule. One knows everyone, and all their various interrelations. The "rules of amity," if they can be called such, mutate to the member and moment at hand, in an interpersonal manner that laws cannot imitate. For members of a community share a mind. No one needs to invent and impose commonalities. Those already exist. Such small groups choose, not by unanimity, but by consensus. Dissenters retain their reservations, and interject them when new moments beckon. Dissents are cherished, for, often, dissenters' reservations prove prescient. Law has no natural place in small human communities. As Jerold Auerbach put it, "[L]aw begins where community ends."[57] Law governs bloated aggregations of strangers. The State emerges from strangers coercing one another. Law chooses losers in this ceaseless fratricide; but even winners lose. Amity soothes injury among friends. Amity's adherents resolve conflict by means that preserve, rather than sunder, relationships. Law arm-twists unknown others to conform. Law assumes citizens to be disconnected individuals. Law "elevates personal greed above mutual need."[58] Amity massages communities waiting birth or healing. Amity associates. Law dissociates.[59]

---

[57] Auerbach, *Justice Without Law?*, 5.

[58] Auerbach, *Justice Without Law?*, 13.

[59] At the behest of Thomas Andrews, a law professor (now retired) and valued friend, I attempt to capture the essence of the rules of amity at Appendix A of this book. I am unsuccessful in that effort, because, as I have said, the rules of amity cannot be "taken alive," and so are "un-zoo-able." Amity is mutable and mutating. These rules squirmed loose from my grip. The rules of amity dwell in that deep evolutionary logic which values adaptability over consistency. Still, the rules of amity say something intelligible, if one allows that the something is also simultaneously errant. Metaphorically, amity massages human systems with heartfelt intrusions, while law dissects conflict cadavers with the dull scalpel of antagonism. The rules of amity are better practiced than written.

Few Americans live any longer in communities numbering no more than 150.[60] Life at the Dunbar number[61] seems a fantastical dream, if we imagine supplanting States with small anarchic communities.[62]

We, in our American matrix, hardly know our neighbors, though most often neither are we hostile. We inhabit lives insulated from others, for the vast majority are strangers, and so, untrusted. Henry Maine argues that such is the constant refrain of society progressing from tending herds to building cities: a movement from family obligations toward contracts with individuals with whom we lack intimate connections.[63] Among strangers, morality loses its referent. Shared values leak away. We know little of our impact on others, and so are ill-positioned to offer evaluation. We

---

[60] Though all of us, in fact, live in just such communities, embedded within our broader anonymous and fear-drenched contexts. Those of us possessed of a modicum of health dwell in reading clubs and churches and businesses and soccer teams and gymnasia and extended families. We live in community, though our togetherness consists in pockets of interpersonal warmth hunkered in a frozen wasteland of societal alienation. Every community suffers from the inclement chill of its anti-personal context.

Perhaps I overstate. We each dwell in overlapping contexts. One high, one low. In **high-context** settings, one knows her companions and shared communal rules. Togetherness is valued. Group well-being trumps solo achievement. Communication may consist in a raised eyebrow or a cough. People live as members of a community. In **low-context** settings, one is demoted to individuality. Communications are express, detailed, and lengthy, for one cannot assume shared experience or histories or educations. Commitment to the shared mass of unknown others pales by comparison to the relationships of our high-context communities. We who live in modern States (if we are healthy), experience both high- and low-contexts, and are proficient at both modes of communication. See Hall, *Beyond Culture*. I thank my friend, Gary Bloom, retired therapist and thoughtful human, for connecting me to these thoughts. Gary has stoically suffered through review of each of my books. Seneca would marvel. Email correspondence from Gary Bloom to author, dated August 25, 2025.

[61] Robin Dunbar, *How Many Friends Does One Person Need?,* 24, 26. Dunbar argues that when human social groups exceed 150 members, they must form hierarchical structures and impose impersonal rules to remain viable and efficient. Excess numbers (over 150) overwhelm the human ability to sustain relationship. We slide toward anonymity. See also Dunbar, *Friends*, at Chapter 2.

[62] Fundamental social change proves difficult, but not impossible. 200 cities in southern Europe and South America have adopted *City of Children* transformations. Francesco Tonucci says: "The city has become hostile to its own inhabitants, unsupportive and lacking in hospitality. . . . [T]he city has been thought, planned and evaluated, taking as a parameter an average citizen with the characteristic of an adult, man and worker, and that corresponds to the strong voter. In this way, the city has lost the non-adult citizens, non-men and non-workers, second-class citizens, with fewer rights or without them. . . . [Our] proposal is, therefore, to replace the average citizen, adult, man and worker with the *child*. . . . It is assumed that when the city is more suitable for children, it will be more suitable for all." Tonucci, *City of Children*, 11-14. Perhaps one should not write off the possibility of restructuring modern societies to communities of 150 persons. I have written of this possibility at length in Lancaster, *Cull: Choosing Well.*

[63] Maine, *Ancient Law*, 163-165. "The movement of progressive societies has been uniform in one respect. Through all its course it has been distinguished by the gradual dissolution of family dependency [which Maine calls "Status"] and the growth of individual obligation in its place. The individual is steadily substituted for the Family, as the unit of which civil laws take account. . . . Starting, as from one terminus of history, from a condition of society in which all the relations of Persons are summed up in the relations of Family, we seem to have steadily moved towards a phase of social order in which all these relations arise from the free agreement of individuals. . . . [T]he movement of the progressive societies has hitherto been a movement *from Status to Contract*" (emphasis in original). The inevitability of progress toward individualism that Maine envisions seems positively Hegelian, or even predestinarian, in the Calvinist sense.

lean on law to protect us from the horde—the unknown, unknowable many. We gulp relationship from our loved ones, often overwhelming them with our terrible thirst. Our tribes are chosen interest groups or family. We sip a watery, mostly tasteless nectar from sub-personal spigots of relationship, that is, from emails and Facebook and tweets. We seem headed to nestling in the artificial embrace of machine intelligence, having debrided dead relations and ruptured rapport with our messy organic companions. We embrace Zoom ghosts and make kissy-noises toward our cameras.

What impact does relation-starved living have? Does our inwardness shrivel? Do we find ourselves empathy-crippled? Are we less able to engage than we might be if we lived in a richer social environment? Does sympathy falter? Is life really nothing more than veiled war?

Jonathan Glover considers our relations with strangers at their extreme—in lethal combat. In war, State kills State.[64] The war-dead, being always actual human corpses, constitute collateral damage in this mythic struggle of ideas and oligarchic egos. War distills relationless relating. Those who are not friends pose risks. In Glover's treatment of war morality in the twentieth century[65], one recognizes a cousin of our courtroom engagements and their quagmires. Litigation enacts quiet little wars. Hoary ideas and low-frequency vocabulary replace bullets and IEDs. Courtroom carnage is social and financial, not physical and deafening. But battlefields and courtrooms share their psychological toll. Post-traumatic stress gushes, afflicting all. We lawyers, well-intentioned as we often are, may be little more than tacticians in the soulless assaults of stranger upon stranger. I asked myself, Does Glover's description of increasing depersonalization in lethal technology track the social outcomes of American courtrooms? Is life at law simply bloodless bellicosity? When I litigate, am I merely a mercenary, a hack-for-hire with an educational battle-axe?[66]

---

[64] Murray Rothbard styles the State a societal parasite that rules by violence and, produces nothing of value, feeding itself by coercion. The State marauds in a miasmatic myth, pretending be to a social service organization. Rothbard was an unvarnished libertarian, possessed of many objectionable, and sometimes silly, sentiments. Rothbard, *Anatomy of the State*, 11. Yet here we should consider whether Rothbard has something useful to contribute on the subject of law. Does the common law create social goods beyond those that succor conditions of its own survival? Rothbard concludes his little tract: "Of all the numerous forms that governments have taken over the centuries, of all the concepts and institutions that have been tried, none has succeeded in keeping the State in check. The problem of the State is evidently as far from solution as ever. Perhaps new paths of inquiry must be explored, if the successful, final solution of the State question is ever to be attained." Rothbard, *Anatomy of the State*, 44.

[65] I epitomize Glover's *Humanity: A Moral History of the Twentieth Century*, at Epitome 1.

[66] I do not assert that there exists no place for courthouses and formal procedures in a well-structured society. We are occasionally troubled by people of such extravagant bad faith or sociopaths of such ugly predilections that, with respect to these bad actors, raw coercion may prove the only viable path to preserving social well-being. I do assert that most human conflicts are not exigent, and should be addressed by non-legal (not illegal) processes. This assertion is not even news. Always, most dust-ups among neighbors are resolved informally or by low-formality means (tolerating, avoiding, ignoring, moving, negotiating, gossiping, fencing, ineffectual incantations, or the salve of people: pastors, therapists, coaches, principals, grandmothers, barkeeps, friends, or trusted non-lawyer professionals).

## THE COMMON LAW

To speak intelligibly of the "law" about which I have reservations, I must describe the common law as elaborated by its proponents.[67] The common law emerges from British history.[68] The Isle suffered repeated invasions.[69] Its kinglets resisted, but warred with one another as often as invading hordes. Ultimately, one dominated: Æthelstan (died 927 A.D.), called by his vassals Betwalda, king over other kings. Æthelstan partially subjected his rivals, making of them lords and vassals, to whom he granted lands and from whom he extracted armies and tribute. Over time, landed classes dominated all things political, adopting a trans-generational juridical structure for managing human society. Its core thrust lay in keeping aristocratic property secure from starving hordes, and incrementally (glacially) improving matters (around the 13th century A.D.) for lords and, very occasionally, even for underlings. England rooted herself, unlike Rome and its written codes, in "immemorial unwritten traditions.'[70]

Beginning from an admittedly deficient root, the medieval courts of law and equity heard cases and rendered judgments, diverting trial-by-combat from fields to

---

[67] This cartoon of the common law is written, without too much research or historical hand-wringing, from materials available in the cereal aisle of the intellectual grocery store we all shop.

[68] The common law is second-tier jurisprudence. The primordial first tier, which is primitive law, consisted in whatever means might prevent us from slaughtering one another to oblivion. "In primitive law the end is simply to keep peace. The legal order is a peaceable order at whatever cost, and in consequence whatever serves to divert private vengeance and prevent private war is an instrument of justice. In this beginning law is no more than a body of rules by which controversies are adjusted peaceably. At first, therefore, it attempts nothing more than to furnish the injured a substitute for revenge." Pound, *The Spirit of the Common Law*, 85. At the second tier, in which the common law resides, a more stifling rule emerges, one that seeks to preserve the status quo, and thereby to repress altogether those pesky irritants that give rise to bloodletting in the first place. Amity would, then, be a third tier jurisprudence. Amity asks people not just to attenuate primordial self-help bloodletting (Tier one: brutal countermeasures), not just to submit their torrent of conflicts and unbridled egos to an ordered process (Tier two: courts and civil/criminal procedure), but to rebuild torn communities and character-restrain fury (Tier three: amity and Klatches). I will speculate on Klatching at chapter 3 of this work.

[69] According to Blackstone, Romans, Picts (northeastern Scots), Danes, and Saxons intruded. Blackstone, *Commentaries on the Laws of England*, Book IV, §402, page 264.

[70] The most ancient root of Rome's law lay in the Twelve Decemviral Tables. Since this root was written, it is subject to analysis. Henry Sumner Maine opines that written codes, like that of Rome, offered protection against "the frauds of the privileged oligarchy and also against the spontaneous depravation and debasement of the national institutions." Maine, *Ancient Law*, 1, 17. The civil law jurisdictions follow Rome's example. When common law becomes published, Maine argues that it more closely resembles the theory of Roman codes.

William Blackstone attributes the origin of an *unwritten* judicial tradition to Britain's Druids, who, it appears, never wrote their instructions. Blackstone, *Commentaries on the Laws of England*, Book IV, §401, page 263.

courtrooms.[71] Courtroom winners had their "rights" defended by community coercion. Those who lost incurred "duties," again enforced by community coercion. Most conflicts were pedestrian; they fell into the usual scheme and were disposed accordingly. But a few presented unusual facts or questions never before considered ("matters of first impression"). Judges pondered, then rendered decisions about law pertaining to these odd circumstances. In some cases, those decisions seemed provident to other judges, who adopted them as the "rule." Subsequent cases would be disposed by reference to the rule ("precedent").[72] Occasionally, a rule would itself be replaced or adjusted or ignored ("overturned").[73] Kings issued decrees. Judges enforced regal edicts ("law courts"). Other judges, often from ecclesiastical benches ("courts of equity"), criticized the law benches and focused, rather, on fairness. The *Magna Carta* (1215 A.D.) granted English barons some paltry rights against their kings.[74] Slowly, consensus emerged among the (landed, white, male, educated, urban) courts. When agreement spread, some judge-made rules became "common," and were entitled to judicial deference in factually similar cases (*stare decisis*).[75] That

---

[71] Jerome Frank assesses litigation: "Yet, for the most part, a law-suit remains a sort of sublimated, regulated brawl, a private battle conducted in a court-house." Frank, *Courts on Trial*, 7.

[72] *Stare decisis* is not, however, of ancient origin. "Legal historians widely agree that before the eighteenth century there was no firm doctrine of *stare decisis* in English common law. Indeed, it may not have been firmly established until sometime in the nineteenth century." Gerald Postema, "Philosophy of the Common Law," page 489, which is Chapter 15 of Coleman and Shapiro, *The Oxford Handbook of Jurisprudence and Philosophy of Law*. Karl Llewellyn said that "precedent consists in an official doing over again under similar circumstances substantially what has been done by him or his predecessor before." That is, the judge is doing what she habitually does. Llewellyn, *The Bramble Bush*, 70. Precedent acts to restrain and guide judges. Not so legislatures. Llewellyn said "in comparison to courts the legislature is a horse without a halter." Llewellyn, *The Bramble Bush*, 88.

Steven González, 58th chief justice of the Washington Supreme Court (appointed to a four year term in 2021), our court of last resort, asserts: "I think that attorneys as a class tend to be conservative. I'm not talking about party politics "Conservative." I mean conservative with a small c—incremental in change, reticent to address or change things, focused on tradition. Our very method of education is to look at precedent. We are walking into the future backward, looking back to where we've been, trying to predict what we're going to stumble over next. That's not a great way to walk. Try walking through the forest backward: 'There's a stump there, maybe there will be another.' Perhaps we need to peep over our shoulder a little bit and try to see what's coming and be willing to make some bigger changes and not be quite so afraid of that." González and Mansfield, "Working Toward a Just Court," 43.

[73] "The order in law is of decisions by the lawyers' committees that we call appellate courts, and these decisions frequently are ill informed, outmoded, and ignoble." Posner, *The Problems of Jurisprudence*, 261.

[74] The *Magna Carta* became a template for American jurisprudence—in its essence, law cabins its sovereign to benefit minions. The individual citizen has claims against her sovereign, not only duties to that head.

[75] Though *stare decisis* governs the decisions of inferior courts in common law jurisprudence, the issue is oppositely decided in civil law jurisdictions. In those civil realms, the law code, created by the legislature, governs all. Judges merely apply the code to specific instances. Pound says, "All the nineteenth-century codes in Continental Europe, except the German Civil Code of 1896, go upon the theory that judicial decisions shall have no authority beyond the cases in which they are rendered and that there can be no authoritative interpretation by anyone except the legislature itself." The French Civil Code went

is, those cases became "precedents." Revolutions and Parliament and monarchical overreaching drove further innovations. Nautical technologies bequeathed Britain her Empire. Parliament aggregated powers, and occasionally remediated matters constructively, a fact with which the common law judges had to contend. Put to the task of applying the gist of statutes to the dramas of humanity, judges became "interstitial legislators,"[76] filling in blanks that hobbled statutes. The powers of the Crown blossomed, flush with wealth pilfered from colonies, but, over a long period, ceded an increasing number of prerogatives to the House of Commons. England exported common law to its colonies and protectorates. The reach of common law grew global, but not universal.

A penchant for revolution became fashionable. The divine right of kings seemed wrong. America demanded its United States from George III, but did not jettison England's common law.[77] Those American States drove neighbors who would keep the Crown north to Canada, but kept others who would cling to their slaves in the bosom of the nascent country, so sowing seeds of sedition deep in American soil. France took a different tack. Its Parisian revolution encouraged disastrous efforts to revise everything at once. The *Republique*'s dreams collapsed into bilious despotisms and stacks of beheaded partisans, which bloodletting ended after strongman Napoleon and his terrible wars drove guillotining Jacobins[78] from history's stage.

Edmund Burke (1729-1797), a Dubliner with a London armchair, dissected the heady French Revolution with a whetted conservative scalpel. In 1790, he lamented those "destroying at their pleasure the whole original fabric of their society; hazarding to leave to those who come after them, a ruin instead of an habitation." Fearing repugnant French attitudes might leak across the Channel and sully British and Irish minds, Burke growled, "By this unprincipled facility of changing the state as often, and as much, and in as many ways as there are floating fancies or fashions, the whole chain of continuity of the commonwealth would be broken. No generation could link with the other. Men would become little better than the flies of a summer."[79] Society

---

further: "Judges are forbidden, when giving judgment in the cases which are brought before them, to lay down general rules of conduct or decide a case by holding it was governed by a previous decision." Pound opines that these strict rules have been relaxed, and there was, at Pound's time, a truncated form of common law in the European civil jurisdictions. Pound, *The Spirit of the Common Law*, 180.

[76] So Oliver Wendell Holmes so styled the judicial work product in his dissent to *Southern Pacific Company v. Jensen*, 244 U.S. 205, 221 (1917): "I recognize without hesitation that judges do and must legislate, but they can do so only interstitially; they are confined from molar to molecular motions."

[77] This, despite the trend of the time to harbor "prejudice against all things English." Pound, *The Spirit of the Common Law*, 6.

[78] The Jacobins called themselves "The Society of the Friends of the Constitution." Beware of friends of constitutions, wherever they trouble the nose with autocratic odors. (This sentiment was written upon Mr. Trump's improbable return to the Presidency.)

[79] Edmond Burke, *Reflections on the Revolution in France*, 99.

is a social contract, "a partnership not only between those who are living, but between those who are living, those who are dead, and those who are to be born. Each contract of each particular state is but a clause in the great primæval contract of eternal society, linking the lower with the higher natures, connecting the visible and invisible world, according to a fixed compact sanctioned by the inviolable oath which holds all physical and all moral natures, each in their appointed place."[80]

To revise law apace, much less mutating the levers of power themselves, toppled society. So Burke warned. France was proof. Men who ignore life's complexities, styling themselves geniuses and their ideas incontestable, invite disaster. Common law offers refuge—a creeping, but reliable, scheme for societal adaptation.[81] That is Burke's anthem. The bellwether of common law is human existence, with all its troubles and stumbles, not grand undertakings or lofty schemes. Society progresses, in Burke's view, not by ingenious political systems, but by tiny steps wrought from one man's conflict with another. So delimiting the purview of law, one assures incremental change in a conservative matrix. The common law, in its origin, is a chain novel; one judge writes the first chapter, another the second, and so forth.[82] Generation by generation, century by century, creeping adaptation fits society's rules to its mutating circumstances. Tradition, for Burke, was all. And no locale in the British political landscape more deeply reflected Burkean conservatism than the common law courts of the British realm.[83]

The critical question that underlies the rudiments of law is this: What steps might one take to preserve social order? By social order, one contemplates "an absence, more or less complete, of violence, a state of affairs in which people are relatively safe from physical attack. . . . [S]ocial order lies in the day-to-day predictability of social life. There is social order, on this account, to the extent that most of the time people do not have their expectations upset."[84] Members will be idiosyncratic. The

---

[80] Edmond Burke, *Reflections on the Revolution in France*, 101. David Brooks styles Burkean disposition to be one of reverence for tradition and suspicion of radical change. Brooks, "The Republican Collapse," at A25.

[81] Francis Bacon, in considering the reform of common law traditions, said: "The work, which I propound, tendeth to pruning and grafting the law, not to plowing up and planting it again; for such a remove I should hold indeed for a perilous innovation." Bacon, *Elements of the Common Laws of England*, 369.

[82] So Ronald Dworkin styles the process of common law's development. Dworkin, *Law's Empire*, 228-250. Arthur Corbin alleges that over one entrance to the Yale Law School quadrangle stands this inscription: "The Law Is a Living Growth, Not a Changeless Code." Corbin, Preface, *v*, in Cardozo, *The Growth of the Law*.

[83] With the possible exception of the monarchy itself. Cynics might suggest that Burkean conservatism existed to forestall societal change generally.

[84] Taylor, *Community, Anarchy, and Liberty*, 44, 48.

common law asks each to prune herself to fit society's mold, or, at a minimum, to moderate one's divergences from the status quo.[85] As a society, how might we preserve practices and attitudes to avoid kindling widespread resentments, while simultaneously adapting to mutating circumstances and preferences? "Law must be stable and yet it cannot stand still. . . . Thus the legal order must be flexible as well as stable. It must be overhauled continually and refitted continually to the changes of the actual life in which it is to govern."[86]

So, how does a society effect the constant overhaul of law? The common law urges (agreeing with Burke) that no person peers so deeply into human affairs as to be able to prescribe law's contours. Rather, judges decide cases, and those but one at a time. Judges do not create common law; they discover it. Common law subsists in the habits and customs and morality of the people. Judges recognize and give voice to the contours of that shared life. The proponent of common law believes that wisdom emerges from the decisions of many judges all acting without coordination, other than that provided by reading some opinions of other judges.[87] There lurks a ghost in the machine[88] of common law, one that jostles law's cogs to mysteriously elicit from uncoordinated activity a relatively-coherent legal landscape.[89] Further, Edward Coke

---

[85] "The standards of the law are standards of general application. The law takes no account of the infinite varieties of temperament, intellect, and education which make the internal character of a given act so different in different men. It does not attempt to see men as God sees them, for more than one sufficient reason. In the first place, the impossibility of nicely measuring a man's powers and limitations . . . [W]hen men live in society, a certain average of conduct, a sacrifice of individual peculiarities going beyond a certain point, is necessary to the general welfare." Holmes, *The Common Law*, 86.

[86] Pound, *Interpretations of Legal History*, 1.

[87] "Most of these [legal] rules have never been deliberately invented but have grown through a gradual process of trial and error in which the experience of successive generations has helped to make them what they are. In most instances, therefore, nobody knows or has ever known all the reasons and considerations that have led to a rule being given a particular form." Hayek, *The Constitution of Liberty*, 225.

[88] This metaphor, "ghost in the machine," derives from Gilbert Ryle's *A Concept of Mind* (1949), where, in critique of Descartes' mind-body dualism, the mind-soul is a spectral invader, governing the human body without being part of it. The metaphor has gained cultural currency as a description of unexpected functioning of a system or results contrary to a system's design. For the majority of the lifespan of common law, a widespread mythology asserted that the rules of common law were not created by legislatures and courts, but "discovered" by them hiding in plain sight in the life of the people. This notion blushes the cheek of even the most credulous observer of courts.

[89] Andrew Spiropoulos notes the relevance to common law practice of the Condorcet Jury Theorem (wisdom-of-crowds theory), which argues that the probability of a decision being right is proportional to the number of persons in the decisional group. Since common law precedents aggregate the views of thousands of jurists, and perhaps millions of people, living and dead, its accuracy nears 100%. Spiropoulos, "A Critique of Common Law Constitutionalism," 192. Spiropoulous prefers **common law constitutionalism** over its primary challengers in constitutional interpretation: first, **Originalism** (a judge decides constitutional meaning by asking, What did this passage mean to the man, now long dead, who wrote it?, thereby necessitating that every judge be also an historian, and condemning that judge to imposition of his own preferences, since the paucity of available historical materials is likely to leave her with no originalist answer to her question) (Spiropoulos at 185-187), and, second, **Moral-Philosophical interpretation** (a judge weighs issues in light of the best moral and philosophical and sociological information available,

(1552-1634), who is perhaps the very person of the common law, argued that the common law governs all else. "[W]hen an Act of Parliament is against common right and reason, or repugnant, or impossible to be performed, the common law will control it, and adjudge such Act to be void."[90] Indeed, Coke asserted that even the king is in no position to judge cases. Coke earned the ire of James I when he disputed royal authority to interfere in cases at law (*Fuller's Case*[91], 1607-1608), for the common law was the supreme law of the land; kings have no right to interject.

Without fundamental change, societies ossify.[92] They lose relevance. Excess fundamental change may, however, liquefy a society, leaving no purchase by which to bind members to one another. Such societies slosh and lose coherence. How might one balance a society's competing needs for continuity and adaptation?

The common law gives a clear, if unsatisfying, answer. The common law grumbles: None knows what changes are needed. None knows how much change is too much change. So, be cautious. Be very cautious.[93] The human mind is not so capacious as to conceive workable reforms; only monstrous dislocations emerge. Thus, courts retreat from programs to procedure and timid incrementalism.[94] The common

---

structuring decisions to protect critical rights, even when not protected by traditional legal theories, again condemning the judge to imposition of her own preferences given the complexity and scope of the available relevant material) (Spiropoulos at 184-185). In my view, Spiropoulos's common law constitutionalism leaves little room for innovation and experimentation, condemning American society to forever linger in the gloom of yesteryear's misconceptions. Spiropoulos says, "What is most important is that judges rely on every source of legal reasoning that justifies their decisions to vindicate existing practices and traditions." Spiropoulos at 190. I argue that there is nothing sacred or preferable about traditions where promising alternatives exist. If we dare not try new recipes, we shall be forever doomed to yesterday's mouldering porridge.

[90] Lobban, "The common law mind in the age of Sir Edward Coke," 20.

[91] In *Fuller's Case* (1607), Sir Nicholas Fuller, member of Parliament and a barrister, induced Sir Edward Coke to agree that the crown was subject to judicial orders concerning ecclesiastical prisoners. Fuller had defended much-disfavored Puritans against persecution of the Star Chamber and Court of High Commission, for which hubris Fuller was expelled from Parliament. He was later re-elected, served in the opposition throughout, and remained a member of Parliament until his death in 1620.

[92] When repeatedly I spoke at city council meetings on behalf of adapting my hometown's zoning code to permit homeless encampments, an opponent rose to snarl, giving voice to the other pole. She said, "Homeless people. I don't want to see them. I don't want to hear them. And I definitely do not want to smell them." When the council voted, NIMBY (not in my back yard) sentiment prevailed—unanimously. I slunk home, silenced.

[93] Friedrich Hayek, a libertarian darling and the smaller-government economist of Ronald Reagan and Margaret Thatcher, put it: "[A] successful free society will always in a large measure be a tradition-bound society." Hayek, *The Constitution of Liberty*, 122. Hayek cites Chief Justice Hale (17$^{th}$ century): "Long experience makes more discoveries touching conveniences or inconveniences of laws than is possible for the wisest council of men at first to foresee. And that those amendments and supplements that through the various experiences of wise and knowing men have been applied to any law must needs be better suited to the convenience of laws, than the best invention of the most pregnant wits not aided by such a series and tract of experience." Hayek, *The Constitution of Liberty*, 114.

[94] This is not to say that American government lacks facilities for planning change. Legislatures should fill this role, though often they dither in their charge. Constitutions balance aspiration with

law contemplates no particular configuration of society. It seeks not to improve society, but only to keep it from spinning apart into bloodbaths of warring constituencies. Centripetal forces, such as expectations of constancy or fear of change or external threats, pull society's members together toward their usual configuration. Centrifugal forces, such as member dissensus or environmental change or technological innovation may loosen society's grip, and fling open doors for revised habits, structures, or mores. The common law prescribes that only one safe approach exists to balance continuity with adaptation: the litigated dispute. One makes a decision about specific litigants in their specific conflict.[95] Common law seeks to avoid architecture altogether, rather framing social order one tiny brick at a time, without really knowing what sort of abode it creates. What one should fear, the proponents of common law argue, is not the decisional chaos that common law imposes, but rather gross societal truncations that attend efforts at more generalized reform.[96] Edmund Burke's lamentation upon French guillotines lingers, haunting the night sweats of common law judges.[97]

---

continuity. When constitutional and legislative agencies sputter, we see executives stumble into the breach, pens whipping out orders to keep the boat of society afloat. But, in this book, I speak of common law, which is what happens in courtrooms and in the offices of those licensed to address the bench. What *courts* do is apply common law, or create some. They also do a fair bit of statutory interpretation and interstitial legislating. Courts are corrected in their vagaries by legislatures and executives (and their own appellate branches). Courts correct the other branches right back, and claim the final word as the ultimate exponent of constitutional interpretation.

[95] "The life of the law has not been logic; it has been experience. The felt necessities of the time, the prevalent moral and political theories, intuitions of public policy, avowed or unconscious, even the prejudices which judges share with their fellow-men, have had a good deal more to do than the syllogism in determining the rules by which men should be governed. The law embodies the story of a nation's development through many centuries, and it cannot be dealt with as if it contained only the axioms and corollaries of a book of mathematics. In order to know what it is, we must know what it has been, and what it tends to become." Holmes, *The Common Law*, 5. Focus upon individual litigants and their personal rights makes of the common law a hyper-individualistic regime. Lost in the shuffle are the needs of the many, who lack inclination or resources to defend non-individual concerns. Perhaps class action suits and federal multi-district litigation and mass tort actions swim against the tide of judicial individualism, but only marginally. Communal concerns frequently find no home in courts, for the bench can hardly grasp who in large groups is the petitioner and who the defendant. These group wrongs are frequently inchoate or blurry, and liabilities run multiple directions.

[96] "The law did not begin with a theory. It has never worked one out. The point from which it started and that at which I shall try to show that it has arrived, are on different planes. In the progress from one to the other, it is to be expected that its course should not be straight and its direction not always visible." Holmes, *The Common Law*, 63.

[97] I am not privy to what specters trouble judicial REM cycles, so I indulge literary license. However, absent fairly neurotic apprehension about rampant change, it is difficult to account for the profoundly cautious pace of common law adaptation. The juridical legion seems bent upon *stare decisis* at all costs. Is our togetherness really so fragile? Or does precedential lock-step betray cloying terror of reversal, wincing at the prospect of appellate disapprobation? Precedent is the practice of letting the past hamstring the future. Of course, the persons and circumstances that constituted that past have themselves passed. The precedent-follower reiterates a rule of decision of a case long sunk in history's bogs, until someone rich enough to appeal persuades a higher court to supersede the precedent. Does it serve the interests of the

What is more, proponents of common law argue that no person is positioned to criticize that process. We are all embedded in tradition-laden contexts, which contexts are the product of events more numerous than any person might grasp, of influences exceeding human comprehension, and of histories which have been mostly lost in time's bramble. Ignorance disqualifies us as reformers. We do well if we adequately decide a case that is actually before us, with live humans reporting what they actually experienced, and documents, authenticated by those who created them, sitting in front of us. To expect more of humans is to flatter. Experience teaches our limitations. Our legal structures must reflect appropriate humility. Hayek puts it:

> The same considerations apply even more where our conduct will directly affect not ourselves but others and where our primary concern, therefore, is to adjust our actions to the actions and expectation of others so that we avoid doing them unnecessary harm. Here it is unlikely that any individual would succeed in rationally constructing rules which would be more effective for their purpose than those which have been gradually evolved; and, even if he did, they would not really serve their purpose unless they were observed by all. We have thus no choice but to submit to rules whose rationale we often do not know, and to do so whether or not we can see that anything important depends on their being observed in the particular instance. The rules of morals are instrumental in the sense that they assist mainly in the achievement of other human values; however, since we only rarely can know what depends on their being followed in the particular instance, to observe them must be regarded as a value in itself, a sort of intermediate end which we must pursue without questioning its justification in the particular case."[98]

So, the common law makes past conflicts a template for future disputes. One does—no, one *must* do—what has been customary (precedent). Those critical customs are English, or, by adoption, American. Can one discover a common morality, a common experience of living, in a multi-cultural agglomeration of hundreds of millions? Or does common law rudder itself by that morality and experience most akin to those inhabiting its benches? Is the common law: White law? Black law? Native law? Rich law? Poor law? Middle class law? Christian law? Secular law? Shariah law? Even Coke's Britain of four million mostly parochial folk was not so monolithic

---

poorer ninety percent of Americans to have our judicial rules created in response to the interests and conflicts that accompany immense wealth—the collisions of yachts and corporate fratricides?

[98] Hayek, *The Constitution of Liberty*. 128. Hayek sometimes conflates the evolution of common law principles with the process by which moral rules guide us. Morality reduces instances of necessary coercion as a population self-restrains its excesses and foolishness. Hayek, *The Constitution of Liberty*, 123.

as he portrayed it. If one doubts this, ask the Celts and Scots and Irish and Puritans and Welsh and Catholics.

When new questions arise, inquiries emerging from technological innovation or immigration or cultural shifts, common law obligates judges to analogize to what has come before. Dead hands claw from grave soil to rankle the ankle of the living jurist and litigant. Even when moribund, even when pertinent circumstances have been forgotten, the common law resists. Judges must innovate meagerly. If law were an art, its mode would be minimalist.[99] Common law must be so constrained, for, according to its proponents, citizens wallow in barely-restrained bloodlust. And every judge is very nearly too dim for her tasks at bench. Any view that departs this grim assessment threatens, according to common law, cataclysm.[100]

So, common law drags its feet. Legislatures may innovate and aspire. But common law douses legislative flames with trembling terror of all things novel. Executives may order and arrange. But common law doubts every governor's insight, predicting gouts of unforeseen miseries. Must law be ever behind? Was yesterday so delectable that we should hunger for its left-overs every day for the next decade or century?[101]

This, then, is the common law. Constitutions constitute. Judges judge, making rules. Legislatures legislate, imposing statutes within a judge-made framework. Executives execute, doing what they imagine conforms to the rules judges and representatives have fashioned. Each branch of government makes law. Each defers to the others (mostly). All restrain one another, correcting lurches of the other branches (so they assert), proposing where proposals seem warranted. The complex batter, whipped by roiling endeavors of society, seems never quite ready for the oven. This is the common law.

I turn to criticisms of American common law.[102] These are not my criticisms, though each seems to me true. I would change law at its fundament, divert law from

---

[99] Artistic minimalism asserts that each such work creates a world of its own; exterior forces ought not be dragged into its aesthetic. The mode works from a delimited palate, and calls to mind Stoic (or monkish Buddhist) promotion of lifestyle simplicity.

[100] "[T]he doctrine of *stare decisis* seems to mean that certainty outweighs justice: Let certainty be achieved though injustice be done and the heavens fall. Since to follow precedents will presumably produce certainty, some courts say that they feel obligated to consecrate their former blunders." Frank, *Courts on Trial*, 267.

[101] "[L]aw is often in very truth a government of the living by the dead. . . . The law does not respond quickly to new conditions. It does not change until ill effects are felt; often not until they are felt acutely." Pound, *Causes of Popular Dissatisfaction with the Administration of Justice,* 341.

[102] Lawrence Friedman calls the much-reformed American legal system "a patchwork of power, a rug made of rags." He further styles our federal system of decentralized power the "warlord system in American politics and law." Friedman, *A History of American Law*, 660.

enmity to amity, as I have said. But one must hear critique of the common law, not from my squeaky mouth, but from the deep baritones of famous proponents. For my critique does not stick until the reader recognizes that common law as a theory does, and always has, suffered rudimentary dysfunctions.[103] Do not heed me. Hear the salvos of Coke and Bacon and Blackstone and Story and Pound, each a common law proponent. Then hear some squawkings of recent (and mostly living) detractors.

---

[103] In Hebrew scriptures, one finds an assault upon law (*Torah*) by the prophetic tradition (*Nevi'im*), which complains of its heartless imprecision and its elevation of form over substance. For example, consider Isaiah 58, in which Israel proffers its fasting as adequate obedience to Yahweh's laws. The prophet responds that the fast God chooses is deeper: avoiding wickedness, freeing prisoners, sharing with the needy, clothing the naked. This is obedience, a heartfelt conformity that exceeds rote compliance with Toranic laws.

In Greek mythology, Justicia was born of Mother Chaos and Father Power, presumably to make of humans something better than either parental god could manage. Justicia has not fared well in her charge, it would seem.

Thomas Aquinas (1225-1274 A.D.), author of *Summa Theologica*, addresses law in Questions 90-108. At Reply 4 to Question 92, Aquinas asserts that tyrannical laws are not laws at all, but perversions of law. The Angelic Doctor therefore opens the door to all manner of criticism of laws. He further argues, at the second article of Question 97, that human laws should be changed but only when "conducive to the common weal." Aquinas warns: "But, to a certain extent, the mere change of law is of itself prejudicial to the common good: because custom avails much for the observance of laws, seeing that what is done contrary to general custom, even in slight matters, is looked upon as grave. Consequently, when a law is changed, the binding power of the law is diminished, in so far as custom is abolished. Wherefore human law should never be changed, unless, in some way or other, the common weal be compensated according to the extent of the harm done is this respect. . . . Wherefore the jurist says that in establishing new laws, there should be evidence of the benefit to be derived, before departing from a law which has long been considered just." Aquinas, *Summa Theologica*, Question 97. Aquinas's timid view dovetails neatly with Burkean conservatism.

## CHAPTER 2

### COMMON LAW SCRUTINIZED

One might style common law the whipping boy[104] of society's critics. The rationale goes, *Society brims with problems, and we citizens are the root of society. Since we decline to excoriate ourselves, vexation is best directed at courts.* This rationale disappoints. Our communal perversities bubble up from psychic muds deeper than law. Nevertheless, law (in the American circumstance, the common law) remains a target. Robert Kagan said: "[T]he American political system, . persistently venerates courts and the rule of law but just as persistently derides the rule of lawyers, judges, and legal excess."[105] Fusillades, one after another, pummel.[106] Roscoe Pound said, "Dissatisfaction with the administration of justice is as old as law. . . . [A]s long as there have been laws and lawyers, conscientious and well-meaning men have believed that laws were mere arbitrary technicalities, and that the attempt to regulate the relations of mankind in accordance with them resulted largely in injustice."[107]

The assault on law is of ancient provenance, for some flaws of law lie in its germ, not in any particular historical incarnation. Regardless what law one chooses, if its rule is of general application, that rule will inflict injustice under some circumstances. For circumstances differ intrinsically. Regardless what punishments are meted, those penalties work hardships of differing magnitude depending upon whom they sanction. For humans differ intrinsically. Law cuts cookies. Regardless the shape of dough

---

[104] A "whipping boy" in early modern Europe, was a commoner educated alongside a prince. When the prince faltered in his studies, the whipping boy suffered the lashes which the prince had earned. For it was unbecoming that a mere tutor should thrash a royal. Courts catch the hell that society should sling at itself, but won't.

[105] Kagan, *Adversarial Legalism*, xvi.

[106] Consider the derogations of common law in twentieth century academic critiques of critical legal theory (law enshrines values and discriminations, and cannot be meaningfully distinguished from politics), feminist jurisprudence (law must be deconstructed from the perspective of the female sex; Catharine McKinnon argues: "Liberal legalism is a medium for making male dominance both invisible and legitimate by adopting the male point of view in law at the same time as it enforces that view on society." McKinnon, *Toward a Feminist Theory of the State*, 237), or law-and-economics analysis (which applies economic theory and method to interpreting legal structures, emphasizing efficiency).

[107] Pound, "The Causes of Popular Dissatisfaction with the Administration of Justice," 337.

with which one begins, law lops off all the unwanted bits—all cookies uniform after baking. Objections of these sorts complain bitterly of the pigeon-holing law indulges to reach its results. One pares away idiosyncrasy. One lumps Swiss chocolate peppermint gelato and coco-berry banana crunch and orange pomegranate sherbet into the category "ice cream," losing much by categorization. Such broadsides denigrate law itself. Their gist recommends anarchy.[108] Global arguments against law are not the sort I am making in this book.[109] I do not here advocate for abolition of law,[110] but rather for American law to adopt a more adequate fundament.

---

[108] Not the now-prevalent use of the word "anarchy" which disparages criminals with megaphones in the grip of adolescent ill-restraint, but rather the "anarchy" of political theory, the sense that there exist (or may exist) communities with governing principles more internalized, less coercive, and better-suited to humans. That is, polity without government (an oxymoron). William Godwin elaborates a political anarchy (*Political Justice*). Robert Nozick toys with political anarchy, but retreats to a minimalist libertarianism (*Anarchy, State, and Utopia*). Michael Taylor perhaps best articulates political anarchy (*Community, Anarchy, and Liberty*); he is not, however, hopeful about the prospects of such a politics, at least in the near future.

[109] I have made those arguments elsewhere. See Lancaster, *Cull: Choosing Well*, at Part IV, §9 (especially §9.2). In that two volume work, I ask whether we cannot create a manner of living with one another that bestows meaning, one that is more deeply interpersonal. I ask whether the common law helps or hinders us in that purpose. I include a portion of my epitome of portions of my book, *Cull: Choosing Well*, in Chapter 3 of this book.

William Godwin speaks of the role of law in society in a manner I find compelling. I have summarized Godwin's *Political Justice* (1796), Volume II, Book VII, Section 8 ("Of Law") as follows:

> "All countries rely on laws to set the standard by which criminality is judged. Law, however, has problems. Laws pile one upon the next. They do so because every human action is unique. Law exists to shoehorn unlike-cases into like-categories. To pursue this approach with persistence promises to fill the world with tedious books. All this serves to make law uncertain, which cuts against the very purpose for which laws were first created. Law presumes, wrongly, to predict what men should do under circumstances that have not yet occurred. So, law tends to mental stagnation, and presumes permanence where there is none and uniformity in a world of universal idiosyncrasy. Law, as an institution, is pernicious. Lawyers, as men of their circumstance, are driven toward dishonesty. All societies should abandon law in favor of right reason determining a course of action in the light of existing circumstances. Some object that when men decide matters, rather than law, we become subject to those deciders' passions. Law offers no refuge from this problem. The only remedy lies in unshackling men, bidding them to reason and decide for themselves. We must trust men to care for themselves. Their judges will rise to what is required of them. So too juries. They will apportion according to the actual merits of circumstances and persons. Ultimately, law is the minion of coercion. Law perishes as coercion vanishes."

[110] For we shall no time soon become a population dwelling in human-sized groups (<150 persons), which social structure would obviate law altogether (as I have argued elsewhere: *Cull: Choosing Well*, at §§ 9-10). Not all would agree. Leidloff, speculating on revising our shared Western culture, contemplates just such a diminution in social scope from millions to tens. We need groups of tribal size and comprehensible expanse. Leidloff, *The Continuum Concept*, 141. Aristotle finds that ten people do not constitute a polis, but that a hundred thousand cannot constitute a polis, since the polis is the seedbed of friendship. Aristotle, *Nichomachean Ethics*, 180 (1170b). Aristotle goes so far as to say that friendship is community, and that our social relations mirror our relationship to ourselves. Aristotle, *Nichomachean Ethics*, 182 (1171b). Thomas Jefferson, reflecting on what he had learned from observing how the American Constitution functioned, advised that we form "wards" in which every man is engaged in making choices about his most local and pressing concerns. "[T]he whole is cemented by giving to every citizen, personally, a

Practitioners of common law have long lamented its inadequacies, and often in terms that sound eerily familiar to critics of our own era.[111]

## Edward Coke[112] (1600)

Edward Coke, though an avatar of the common law, nevertheless expressed concerns about its structure. Coke asserts that he wrote his many volumes of case *Reports,* so that "all the Judges and Justices in all the several parts of the Realm, might, as it were, with one Mouth in all mens Cases pronounce one and the same Sentence,"[113] evidencing concern that the multiplicity of minds involved in the common law process leads to inconsistent and inequitable outcomes. The imperfections of case reports leave diverse opinions clashing and persistent doubts lingering. Coke further laments that the common law, even in 1600,[114] had reached unmanageable bulk. He said: "And in Troth if Judges should set down all Reasons and Causes of

---

part in the administration of public affairs." Jefferson, *Writings*, 1400 (*Letter to Samuel Kercheval*, July 12, 1816).

[111] Lon Fuller offers an allegory of a king creating a legal system. Fuller teaches that such jurisprudential endeavors collapse in eight ways: "[T]here are in this enterprise, if you will, eight distinct routes to disaster. The first and most obvious lies in a failure to achieve rules at all, so that every issue must be decided on an ad hoc basis. The other routes are: (2) a failure to publicize, or at least to make available to the affected party, the rules he is expected to observe; (3) the abuse of retroactive legislation, which not only cannot itself guide action, but undercuts the integrity of rules' prospective in effect, since it puts them under the threat of retrospective change; (4) a failure to make the rules understandable; (5) the enactment of contradictory rules or (6) rules that require conduct beyond the powers of the affected party; (7) introducing such frequent changes in the rules that the subject cannot orient his action by them; and, finally, (8) a failure of congruence between the rules as announced and their actual administration." Fuller, *The Morality of Law*, 39.

[112] Though Edward Coke (whose name is unaccountably pronounced "Cook") may claim fame, he was no moral exemplar. Though hard-working, Coke must thank his first wife, Bridget, mother of ten of his children and manager of his extensive household, for the time Coke found for his extensive writing. His primary works are *Reports*, summaries and rumination on court cases, and his *Institutes of the Lawes of England*. His prose has been panned as dry, crabbed, verbose, pedantic, narrow-minded, and quaint. Yet, Coke's importance is unquestioned. After Coke and Francis Bacon contested for the hand of Liz Hatton, a skirmish which Coke won (she bore Coke two additional daughters, according to his mortuary stone), Coke harbored a grudge against Bacon. The two devolved into trite fulminations. Once given a copy of Bacon's *Novum Organum*, Coke wrote childish insults in its margins. Bacon believed that the scandal which drove Bacon from the public scene was a plot of Coke's invention. Others note that as a prosecutor, Coke sought conviction by every means in his power, including distortion of medieval precedents; Coke was arrogant and brutal and insulted parties in open court. As a prosecutor, Coke tortured those accused of crimes (as was common, though illegal, in his day). He lied when confronted, denying his torment of the King's subjects. Coke amassed a fortune by purchasing estates with clouded title. These problem titles he would clear, then sell at great profit. His wealth grew so expansive that the King put a stop to it. Coke "had already as much land as it was proper a subject should possess." Johnson, Cuthbert William, *The Life of Sir Edward Coke*, Vol. 1, page 25.

[113] Coke, *Reports, Part III*, Preface.

[114] In 1600, the population of England was approximately four million. Today, England's population is approximately fifty-six million.

their Judgments within every Record, that immense Labour should withdraw them from the necessary Services of the Common-wealth, and their records should grow to be like *Elephantini libri* of infinite Length, and in mine Opinion lose somewhat of their present Authority and Reverence." Yet case reports without judicial rationales illuminate nothing. So, common law founders upon its inner logic. Only cases are creditable law-work. Yet, cases proliferate. Their number, and the diverse rules they inspire, inundate lawyers. Sheer expanse beclouds common law. None masters it.

**Francis Bacon (1600)**

Consider Francis Bacon's complaints, near the end of his life:

> Certain it is, that our laws, as they now stand, are subject to great incertainties, and the variety of opinion, delays and evasions; where of ensueth,(1) That the multiplicity and length of suits is great; (2) that the contentious person, is armed, and the honest subject wearied and oppressed; (3) that the judge is more absolute; who, in doubtful cases, hath a greater stroke and liberty; (4) that the chancery courts are more filled, the remedy of law being often obscure and doubtful; (5) that the ignorant lawyer shroudeth his ignorance of law, in that, doubts are frequent and many; (6) that men's assurances of their lands and estates by patents, deeds, will, are often subject to question, and hollow; and many the like inconveniences."[115]

Bacon identifies aspects of the common law, more than 420 years ago, that troubled him enough to record: uncertainty,[116] judicial dissensions, delay, failing to address matters directly, too many suits, inadequate speed in processing cases, empowering the unscrupulous while shackling the honest, judicial overreach, insufficient leniency, obscurity, incompetent lawyers, and rendering expectancies in property insecure. Bacon also notes there exist other deficiencies he has declined to address. Bacon elsewhere prescribed: "Laws are made to guard the rights of the people, not to feed the lawyers. The laws should be read by all, known to all. Put them into shape, inform them with philosophy, reduce them in bulk, give them into every man's hand."[117] Bacon proposes four core changes: 1) Statutes addressing vanished circumstances should be retired and no longer printed; 2) Unused statutes should be

[115] Bacon, *Elements of the Common Laws of England*, in a chapter on "Compiling and Amendment of the Laws of England," Volume 4, 366. Published 1630 posthumously (Bacon died in 1626 A.D.).

[116] "There is such an accumulation of statutes concerning one matter, and they so cross and intricate, as the certainty of law is lost in the heap." Bacon, *Elements of the Common Laws of England*, in a chapter on "Compiling and Amendment of the Laws of England," 367.

[117] From a public speech on 26 February 1593.

repealed; 3) Penalties should be more lenient; and 4) Duplicative statutes should be simplified and published as one.[118] The common law presents a tangle to be sorted, a bramble to be pruned. At the time Bacon's pen scratched his paper, the planet held fewer than 600 million humans, four million of whom dwelt in England and Wales.

**William Blackstone (1765)**

Blackstone's *Commentaries* were, by their existence, a criticism of the common law. Blackstone's purpose lay in restating the tangled skein of common law[119] in a straightforward manner understandable to the public, in imposing some rationale that penetrated the arcana of its body of decisions. His four volumes of commentary praise the common law, in Blackstone's view, for its solid foundations, its extensive plan, and elegant proportion. Still, British common law suffered defects, mostly due to ravages of time and the amendments of less-than-stellar reformers. Blackstone never lays out his criticisms in tabular form. He makes no list. But one derives his concerns from his text. Blackstone laments the common law's fractionated historical origins, its tendency over time to accumulate "excrescences" which would be better excised, its harsh criminal penalties, the common law's gravitational attraction to the halls of monied lords to the disregard of the liberties of everyday citizens,[120] and its propensity for becoming incomprehensible to the people it is intended to govern. Blackstone would have the common law codified so that commoners might read the common law in its "pristine simplicity and vigour,"[121] shorn of foreign and historical embellishments.

**Joseph Story (1821)**

On September 4, 1821, in Boston, Joseph Story delivered an anniversary address to colleagues of the Suffolk County Bar Association, next door to Boston. After execrating the listless and ill-adapted laws of kings, Story praised the gradual adaptation that characterizes the common law. He styled his topic the analysis of the state of the

---

[118] Bacon, *Elements of the Common Laws of England*, in a chapter on "Compiling and Amendment of the Laws of England," Volume 4, 373-374.

[119] Blackstone calls England's common law a "noble pile." Blackstone, *Commentaries on the Common Laws of England*, §436, page 285.

[120] Blackstone concludes his Commentaries: "The protection of the liberty of Britain is a duty which [the nobility and members of Parliament] owe to themselves, who enjoy it; to their ancestors, who transmitted it down; and to their posterity, who will claim at their hands this, the best birthright, and noblest inheritance of mankind." Blackstone, *Commentaries on the Laws of England*, Book IV, §436, page 285.

[121] Blackstone, *Commentaries on the Laws of England*, Book IV, §411, page 269.

common law, and its future prospects and necessary improvements.[122] Story's paean upon the adequacies of American common law, which borders on the florid, contains a counter-melody both darker and critical.

Story finds that the federative logic of our national and state constitutions renders uniformity in law impossible.[123] Despite attempts to abridge the common law for the sake of comprehension, it remains so voluminous that the ablest minds cannot master it, despite lifetimes of study.[124] "[T]he administration of justice [when federal law is added to state laws] is there filled with perplexities, that strain the human mind to its utmost bearings."[125]

Fundamental improvement of the law awaits better education of judges and lawyers. Story puts it: "[T]he principal improvements must arise from a more thorough and deep laid juridical education, a more exact preparatory discipline, and a more methodical and extensive range of studies."[126] Story goes so far as to call the pleadings of practitioners slovenly, and given to "perpetual mistakes in grammatical construction, or of a gross and unclassical style of composition." So egregious are these defects that "one is at a loss to know at what point the pleadings aim, or whether they aim at any."[127]

Despite its defects, Story praises the common law as "cautious and unwearied exertions of a succession of wise men through a long course of ages, withdrawing every case, as it arises, from the dangerous power of discretion, and subjecting it to inflexible rules, extending the dominion of justice and reason, and gradually contracting within the narrowest possible limits the domain of brutal force and of arbitrary will."[128]

**Roscoe Pound (1906)**

On August 29, 1906, Roscoe Pound offered a keynote address to the annual convention of the American Bar Association, from the rostrum in the Minnesota House of Representatives, where the association was then assembled. His speech was titled

---

[122] Story, *Address to Suffolk Bar*, 3.

[123] Story, *Address to Suffolk Bar*, 13.

[124] Story, *Address to Suffolk Bar*, 24.

[125] Story, *Address to Suffolk Bar*, 25.

[126] Story, *Address to Suffolk Bar*, 26.

[127] Story, *Address to Suffolk Bar*, 27.

[128] Story, *Address to Suffolk Bar*, 33.

"The Causes of Popular Dissatisfaction with the Administration of Justice."[129] Not all such popular dissatisfactions found just cause in the defects of law. The citizenry itself suffered deficiencies. Pound cites Owen Wister, who growled: "The unthinking sons of the sage brush ill tolerate anything which stands for discipline, good order and obedience; and the man who lets another command him they despise. I can think of no threat more evil for our democracy, for it is a fine thing diseased and perverted, namely, the spirit of independence gone drunk."[130]

Still, much popular dissatisfaction with American justice Pound laid to the account of the common law and the lawyers who practice it.

Pound's first complaint lay in the observation that law creates one set of rules for the rich, and another for the poor. Such complaints cross borders. No modern legal system escapes this broadside. Monied interests are set a legal table from which the poor are forbidden any morsels. Petty causes, the sort that trouble normal people, get short shrift from courts. These persons lack not only the fee for an attorney, but even the price of admission in the filing fee. In courthouses, some such become *pro se* litigants who gum the work of judicial calendars.

Pound's second complaint is that law is delayed. Pound found there exists an "inevitable difference in rate of progress between law and public opinion."[131] The public grows frustrated that law lags their consensus. Pound notes that common law "discovers" public sentiment, and so, of course, cannot conform to what has yet to form or settle. So, bygone sentiments govern those whose perspectives have evolved. "[L]aw is often in very truth a government of the living by the dead."[132] Pound notes that law responds glacially to change. Often, law's dysfunction must become acute before needful change prevails.

---

[129] Pound claimed to be limiting his comments to civil cases. It is not difficult, however, to perceive implications of his words for matters criminal. Chief Justice Warren Burger, in the keynote address to a 1976 conclave of the American Bar Association, on the seventieth anniversary of Pound's address, noted that Pound's thoughts met with hostility from the ABA. Rather than undertake deep revision of the justice system which Pound advocated, the ABA settled for tinkering, of which outcome Pound himself had warned. Berger, "Agenda for 2000 A.D.—A Need for Systematic Anticipation," in *The Pound Conference: Perspectives on Justice in the Future*, 23. Yet the "tinkering" proposals of the Pound Conference of 1976 were hardly inconsequential: establish neighborhood justice centers, spread small claims courts widely, divert appropriate cases to arbitration, sunset administrative agency rules to require review, decriminalize some morals crimes, limit professional malpractice claims, remove courts from non-adversarial matters, find deterrents to illegal police search and interrogation procedures, correct and sanction civil discovery abuse, revise class action rules, limit use of juries, eliminate federal diversity jurisdiction, make legal services available to all, improve the selection of judges, and establish a federal data collection agency concerning judicial administration. Pages 301-336.

[130] Pound, "The Causes of Popular Dissatisfaction with the Administration of Justice," 342.

[131] Pound, "The Causes of Popular Dissatisfaction with the Administration of Justice," 340.

[132] Pound, "The Causes of Popular Dissatisfaction with the Administration of Justice," 341.

A third complaint laments the rampant individualism of the common law.[133] A case consists of one individual (or several) confronting another (or several). Combatants struggle without input from the many outside their conflict who are affected by the outcome of the clash. So, the needs of communities are ignored, while the rumbling of aggressive monied interests find welcome and accommodation. Law presumes that individuals rise to protect themselves. But such is seldom the case. Normal people lack time and funds to squander on legal philandering. They must work and sleep and raise children. Only the rich have leisure for time-squandering contests.

Pound iterated, with substantial vehemence, his fourth complaint; he inveighed against "the sporting theory of justice."[134] By this, Pound points a finger at "contentious procedure, which turns litigation into a game."[135] Pound said:

> The sporting theory of justice . . is so rooted in the profession in America that most of us take it for a fundamental legal tenet. . . . So far from being a fundamental fact of jurisprudence, it is peculiar to Anglo-American law; and it has been strongly curbed in modern English practice. . . . The idea that procedure must of necessity be wholly contentious disfigures our judicial administration at every point. It leads the most conscientious judge to feel that he is merely to decide the contest, as counsel present it, according to the rules of the game, not to search independently for truth and justice.[136]

Adversarial excesses lead to "error seeking," lack of finality, and the "slaughterhouse of reputations." Lawyers, engaged in the game of judicial jousting, seek errors (or even plant them) to facilitate appellate review, which keeps client hackles raised, and corrals the additional fee for review litigation. When appeal seems likely, little effort is wasted ending disputes at the trial level. And the contentious spirit leads to excessive grubbing after ugly facts about witnesses, which aspersions are dredged to disparage the witness before juries or judges. Hence, we have Pound's reference to

---

[133] Pound links the individual character of our jurisprudence to its adversarial excesses. Pound says: "[O]ur legal tradition . . is characterized by an extreme individualism. . . . Its respect for the individual makes procedure, civil and criminal, ultra-contentious, and preserves in the modern world the archaic theory of litigation as a fair fight, according to the canons of the manly art, with a court to see fair play and prevent interference. Moreover it is so zealous to secure fair play to the individual that often it secures very little fair play to the public." Pound, *The Spirit of the Common Law*, 13.

[134] Pound attributes the aphorism to Professor Wigmore.

[135] Pound, "The Causes of Popular Dissatisfaction with the Administration of Justice,"343.

[136] Pound, "The Causes of Popular Dissatisfaction with the Administration of Justice,"344.

social-regard meat-packing. Pound believes adversarial tilting derogates law, making citizens doubt law's beneficent purposes. In the end, law abets lawlessness.[137]

Pound's fifth complaint concerns litigant use of judicial process for political purposes. Courts are the final word in interpretation of law. Courts are positioned to shut down executive initiatives, and to lay low legislative innovations. When they do so, courts act at the behest of individuals or corporations possessed of sufficient excess funds to bring suits, which, if won, give the litigant his purpose without the difficulties of swaying executives and electing legislative majorities. So, courts, the least accountable branch of government, can be thrust into the role of arbiters of societal progress, and a short cut to political influence.

Pound complains also, a sixth complaint, of law's lack of philosophical foundation. Whoever might offer such a foundation is promptly shouted down.[138] Law's rudiment shifts in the mouth of each speaker. Is law sociological, economic, natural, arbitrary, fixed, or fluid, a profession, an institution, a bulwark, a threat? The answer depends upon who stands at the podium. Lacking bellwethers, law wobbles. Pound put it: "[A]nother phase of the great game; a citation match between counsel, with a certainty that diligence can rake up a decision somewhere in support of any conceivable proposition."[139] When the canon supports every proposition, no philosophy can describe it. Litigants are stranded in a desert very dry, with no indication in which direction waters lie.

Pound rattles off a few brief, but no less weighty, complaints. These complaints are pedestrian and universal, and Pound declines to further elaborate them, beyond listing them.

Seventh, law lacks certainty. No lawyer can settle definitively upon any given rule. The rule may have changed yesterday. The lawyer may have misconstrued the rule. Worst, a court may ignore a disfavored rule, daring an appeal of its ruling, but confident your little client cannot muster funds for such proceedings.

Eighth, law is confused, which derives from the "incompleteness inherent in all case law."[140]

---

[137] Pound, "The Causes of Popular Dissatisfaction with the Administration of Justice,"345.

[138] An outcome this author expects, second only to being utterly ignored.

[139] Pound, "The Causes of Popular Dissatisfaction with the Administration of Justice,"347. Oliver Wendell Holmes weighs in on this problem, assessing the mutating nature of common law rules: "The customs, beliefs, or needs of a primitive time establish a rule or a formula. In the course of centuries the custom, belief, or necessity disappears, but the rule remains. The reason which gave rise to the rule has been forgotten, and ingenious minds set themselves to inquire how it is to be accounted for. Some ground of policy is thought of, which seems to explain it and to reconcile it with the present state of things; and then the rule adapts itself to the new reasons which have been found for it, and enters on a new career. The old form receives a new content, and in time even the form modifies itself to fit the meaning which it has received." Holmes, *The Common Law*, 8.

[140] Pound, "The Causes of Popular Dissatisfaction with the Administration of Justice,"347.

Ninth, law has grown to such proportions as to be unmanageable, even to lawyers, who waste time attempting to make sense of it all.[141]

Pound's tenth complaint targets archaic court procedures. Pound cites uncertainty, as well as delay and expense, as causes of public dissatisfaction. Worst, from the public's view, is courts deciding cases on "points of practice, which are the mere etiquette of justice."[142] Such defects have made avoiding the courts a business imperative.[143] Pound laments that normal people lack access to courts: "[T]aking the country as a whole, it is so obvious that we have almost ceased to remark it, that in petty causes, that is with respect to the everyday rights and wrongs of the great majority of an urban community, the machinery whereby rights are secured practically defeats rights by making it impracticable to assert them when they are infringed."[144] Pound further seeks consolidation of duplicative courts, which lead to substantial waste of resources. And Pound laments "lavish granting of new trials," which squanders scarce judicial resources.

Pound's eleventh complaint is composite. The jurist notes lack of public interest in the justice system, the decline of morals which puts courts to tasks for which it is ill-suited,[145] political intrusions into the court system, the transmutation of the role of lawyer from professional to tradesperson, [and] misguided press reports of judicial

---

[141] Benjamin Cardozo cites the American Law Institute's criticisms of American common law (1924): "lack of agreement on the fundamental principles of the common law; lack of precision in the use of legal terms; conflicting and badly drawn statutory provisions; attempted distinction between cases where the facts present no distinction in the legal principles applicable; the great volume of recorded decisions; ignorance of judges and lawyers; the number and nature of novel legal questions." Cardozo notes: "Of all these causes, the weightiest, I fancy, is the multiplication of decisions. . . . This danger, great as it has always been, grows greater every day as mass and maze increase." Cardozo, *The Growth of the Law*, 3-5.

[142] Pound, "The Causes of Popular Dissatisfaction with the Administration of Justice,"347. Elsewhere, Pound recounts a lawyer's tale from western Massachusetts of 1861: "[I]n a prosecution for malicious injury to real estate, the case was that a wooden pump had been taken out of a well in mere wanton mischief. Counsel contended that there was no malicious injury to real estate since the land was not injured and the pump itself was personalty so that the complaint should have been for malicious injury to personal property. To show this he argued that if a pump were realty there would have to be a conveyance by deed of sale every time one was sold. The magistrate was duly impressed and discharged the accused, but, being a conscientious man, proceeded to draw up a new complaint for malicious injury to personal property, upon which the accused were re-arrested and put upon trial. Thereupon the same counsel cited authorities, which were unanimous and conclusive, that the pump in the well and annexed thereto for permanent use was a fixture and so not personal property. The justice could not deny the force of these decisions and was obliged to discharge the accused upon this charge also, so that they escaped. But, we are told, the magistrate enjoyed the joke upon himself as much as the rest of us. In fact . . . many of these legal trials at the time were looked upon as huge jokes." Pound, *The Spirit of the Common Law*, 125-126.

[143] I became acquainted with a successful operator of car dealerships in the Puget Sound region. I inquired about his business philosophy. He responded, "I always tell my customers the truth. And I never take them to court. I just pay the unhappy ones, and then sell another car."

[144] Pound, *The Spirit of the Common Law*, 132.

[145] "Law is the skeleton of social order. It must be 'clothed upon by the flesh and blood of morality.'" Pound, *The Causes of Popular Dissatisfaction with the Administration of Justice*, 352.

proceedings."[146] Together, these complaints point to a process of dumbing down citizens, lawyers, and courts. Our common law jurisprudence suffers the death of a thousand cuts.

Twelfth, Pound complains that an elected judiciary lies too close to our political maelstrom, and may lack the analytical and philosophical skills that common law demands.[147]

Finally, Pound castigates half-hearted reforms. Lawyers are inclined to reform themselves by nibbling bits of law that are already moribund. The result is tinkering, which fixes nothing while generating an illusion of reform.[148] **"The right course is not to tinker** with our courts and with our judicial organization in the hope of bringing about particular results in particular kinds of cases at a sacrifice of all that we have learned or ought to have learned from legal and judicial history. It is rather to provide **a new set of premises, a new order of ideas** in such form that the courts may use them and develop them into a modern system by judicial experience of actual causes."[149]

In the end, Pound recurs to the common law, despite its defects. "[T]here are inherent limitations on what may be achieved through law and inherent limitations upon the efficacy of effort in conscious lawmaking; that for the greatest part law must always be found through application of reason to causes as they arise and the testing of principles in their actual operation; that laws are not like clothes to be thrown off

---

[146] "[T]he average press reports distract attention from the real proceedings to petty tilts of counsel, encounters with witnesses and sensational by-incidents." Pound, *The Causes of Popular Dissatisfaction with the Administration of Justice*, 352.

[147] Pound puts it: "The institution of an elective judiciary, holding for short terms, which prevails in so many of our jurisdictions, does not give us courts adequate to such a task [of revising law to its changed circumstances]. Indeed, the illiberal decisions of which complaint was made so widely at the beginning of the twentieth century were largely, one might say almost wholly, the work of popularly-elected judges." Pound, *The Spirit of the Common Law*, 7.

[148] Jerome Frank thinks one has no alternative but to perform a "first-hand study of removable evils in the all-too-human conduct of court-house government," and to ameliorate those ills. Frank, *Courts on Trial*, 218. I respond that such has been tried. Reforming courts has failed. We should invent boldly, and dare new strategies in managing human conflict.

I note that the word "tinker" might lead one to believe all such reforms are feigned or underwhelming. Pound may have thought this, but it is not so. Some modern tinkerings are large incursions into the common law, seeking to effect serious remediations. Consider, for example, efforts to alleviate the fractionated individualism of law by class action suits, federal multi-district litigation, and mass tort suits. My complaint is not that tinkering is unserious, but that it is misdirected. Once tinkered, the common law nevertheless remains classist, coercive, and conflictual.

[149] Pound, *The Spirit of the Common Law*, 165 (emphasis added). As mentioned above, on the occasion of the seventieth anniversary of Pound's Minnesota address, Chief Justice Warren Burger admitted that Pound would have viewed post-1906 legal reform activities as no more than tinkering. See *supra*, footnote near the beginning of Pound's critique of the common law.

and replaced, but, like language, are so intimately a part of all we do that development of the traditional materials will always be the chief agency of growth." [150]

**Contemporary Criticisms**

The population of the planet has exploded since 1906. In that year, approximately 1.7 billion humans inhabited Earth.[151] Technologies have raced, as have human numbers. Law followed suit, growing enormously in both volume and scope. Robert Kagan notes that "private litigation to enforce federal statutes grew from a rate of 3 per 100,000 population in 1967 to 13 by 1976, to 21 by 1986, to 29 in 1996."[152] Predictably, criticisms of law have also multiplied, like rabbits in fat years. Small wonder, for law has sought to load upon the bent medieval spine of common law the freight of a world no longer sparse or feudal.

I offer a table, for the reader's convenience, summarizing criticisms of common law by core proponents of that common law (three English, two American). The last column contains criticisms of others, not all of whom are proponents of American common law, but nevertheless critics who adopt all those reservations expressed by Coke, Bacon, Blackstone, Story, and Pound.[153] I attempt to sketch a few of these perspectives, and to describe some amendments to the common law system that some critics might prefer.

Please be clear, however, that the prescriptions of these critics are not solutions I advocate. These reforms are expressions of what Pound disparages as "tinkering." These proposals mistake law's problems as errors of policy or management or culture, not a deficient rudiment. If all reforms these critics advocate were fully implemented, we would have a better system, but that improved format would still be competitive, classist, and coercive.[154] That meliorated system of law would still generate a regime of animosity, and, in its worst incarnation, a jurisprudence of enmity. Law devolves,

---

150 Pound, *The Spirit of the Common Law*, 165.

151 And the planet then was dramatically over-populated. Now, at 8.0 billion (471% of our 1906 numbers), we have entered a realm approved only by those who are not paying attention (which seems to include almost everyone). Which of our many problems would not be alleviated by a reduction of the human population to one billion (the human population in 1800)? I have argued for this reduced population in *Cull: Choosing Well*, Sections 1.13.1 and 7.16 and 8.3.2.

152 Kagan, *Adversarial Legalism*, 58. That is an increase in private litigation of 9.67 times over the course of a mere twenty-nine years.

153 The critical articles and bibliography are voluminous. I make no attempt to survey these, and pretend no global comprehension of them.

154 Anthony D'Amato says that legal rules are "a potential means for one person to use the legal system to gain something forcibly from another person." D'Amato, "Legal Certainty," 16.

in its core rationale, toward vendetta. Law sweeps the dust-ups of human relating under rugs, where emotional grime aggregates and festers. Law does not clean. Law does not disinfect. Law does not mend. American law blurts a verdict, then declares the matter decided. Parties are seldom convinced.

When a selection of the litany of contemporary criticisms has been explored, I turn at Chapter 3 to discuss, as Pound proposed, a new fundament and better sort of ideas to guide law's development.[155] That root I organize under the rubric "amity."

## CRITICISMS OF COMMON LAW

| COKE 1600 | BACON 1600 | BLACKSTONE 1765 | STORY 1821 | POUND 1906 | CURRENT |
|---|---|---|---|---|---|
| Inconsistent | Incertain | Uncertain | Non-uniform | Uncertain | Confused |
| Diverse | Dissension | Fractionated | Discordant | Discretionary | Scattered |
| | Obscure | Incomprehensible | Perplexing | Archaic | Elitist |
| Elephantine | Bloated | | Labyrinthine | Bulky | Metastatic |
| | Severe | Harsh | | Coercive | Coercive |
| | Adversarial | | | Adversarial | Adversarial |
| | Discretionary | | Slovenly | Unprincipled | Vapid |
| | | | | Impersonal | Pessimistic |
| | | | | Ill-judged | Ill-judged |
| | | | | | Juried |
| | Overreach | | | Political | Partisan |
| | Bad faith | | | | Corrupt |
| | Overwhelmed | | | Crowded | Under-funded |
| | Legal fees | | | Expensive | Inaccessible |
| | | | | Lawyer trade | Oligarchic |
| | | | | Duplicative | Duplicative |
| | | Monied | | Wealth Biased | Wealth Agent |
| | | Fanciful | | Legal fictions | Deeming |
| | | | | | Jurispathic |
| | Delayed | | | Behind | Delayed |
| | | | | Tinkered | Misdirected |
| | | | | | Unresponsive |
| | | | | | Hidebound |
| | | | | | Untailored |
| | | | | Individualist | Anti-communal |
| | | | | | Pathogenic |
| | | | | | Monetized |
| | | | | | Racist |
| | | | | | Misogynistic |
| | | | | | Epistemologically Naive |

(These broadsides are not all the extant criticisms of common law. I do not attempt to portray each in intensive detail. Seldom do I pursue threads of rebuttal to these broadsides. I seek to demonstrate that non-frivolous critique of the common law reaches all tributaries of its expanse, that many critics are persons of standing in the legal

155 As Roscoe Pound called his solution to the problem of half-measure tinkering, recourse to "a new set of premises, a new order of ideas." Pound, *The Spirit of the Common Law*, 165.

community, and that their lamentations mirror those that rumble in the reader's own reflective moments.)

**Some argue the common law is:**

A. CONFUSED, SCATTERED, ELITIST, AND METASTATIC. Four related complaints about common law predominate. Each pertains to concerns about process. First, common law is **confused** (or inconsistent or uncertain or non-uniform, as proponents assert). No one who reads cases comes away, despite the brilliance of particular jurists, with clarity about the rules being applied.[156] Each case states some rule, and invites an appeal, evasion, or obfuscation. The next case does the same. Advocates make distinctions, evoke subtleties.[157] Lawyers clench their brains to parse coherence. Then a subsequent case arrives. Short-lived coherence crumbles, inviting more frontal lobe gymnastics. For this is the case method. Legal rules mutate. Uncertainty prevails. Cognitive constipation predominates. Law, one assumes, began thousands of years ago to mitigate ambiguity and lend regularity and promote equity. But law has ended sowing confusion. I tell every client who contemplates putting her matter before a judge or jury that I, quite literally, have no idea how her cause will turn out.[158] Benjamin Cardozo said, "Law as a guide to conduct is reduced to the level of mere futility if it is unknown and unknowable."[159]

Much of the practice of law concerns evading laws. Not knowing what rules apply, the prudent actor seeks paths that altogether dodge legal strictures, or ameliorate their impacts. Global cocaine dealing comes to look not all that different from international banking or stock arbitrage. The virtuous need no laws, the vice-ridden scoff, and the masses cower, uncomprehending, in the shadow of law. So law is pointless or skirted or feared. Uncertainty leads to a market in opinion. If one wants to know what is right to do, ask a lawyer. If you disdain that lawyer's answer, find a different lawyer. Eventually, you will exhume a lawyer who mumbles the sentiment you prefer.

---

[156] Jeremy Bentham (in 1789) said: "[A]s uncertainty is of the very essence of every particle of law so denominated [as civil law] (for the instant it is clothed in a certain authoritative form of words it changes its nature, and passes over to the other denomination [penal law]) hence it is that a great part of the law in being in such countries remain uncertain and incomplete. What are those countries? To this hour, every one on the surface of the globe." Bentham, *The Principles of Morals and Legislation*, 335.

[157] Ronald Lansing colorfully styled the lawyer penchant for fine distinctions as divining matters as "different as mud and wet dirt." Lansing, *Juggernaut*, 82.

[158] Some reader now sniffs, "That is because you are a crappy lawyer, Lancaster." That critic is wrong, not in his evaluation of my skills, but in his baseless optimism concerning his own predictive capacity.

[159] Cardozo, *The Growth of the Law*, 3.

Certainly, we lament these features of our circumstance. Yet, there are potent reasons to think that legal uncertainty is irremediable. It may be the case that we cannot undertake repairs to make of law some passable rules for living that help normal people. Circumstances, technologies, people, social structures, climates, genetics, and divergent values all mutate. Law cannot keep up. Because law is perpetually dated, settling questions no longer bearing directly upon life's cutting edge, we puzzle. The common law asks us to impose yesterday's solutions upon emerging events, leaving us always with a mismatch in varying degrees of severity. That confuses. And confusion renders law unreliable.

Confusion as to applicable rules emerges directly from the common law process. In the United States, thousands of judges process cases, applying rules or making new ones. They are jurists of some comprehension or lack of it, some skill or lack of it, some devotion or lack of it. These judicial persons race or limp toward no agreed end, no particular form of society. So, cacophony ensues. Multiplicity of voices, a menagerie of perspectives, a tangle of decisions: the result is **scattered** (or diverse, dissented, fractionated, discordant, or discretionary, as proponents assert). How could uniformity emerge from this decisional welter? The system relies on precedent to bridle judicial eccentricity. But evading precedent to achieve preferred outcome is a judicial sport. Courts limit precedents to their facts, or declare them inapposite, or seize an obscure point to divert unhappy precedent into happier channels. Ultimately, precedent serves as fodder for further fractionation of rules. The common law ends as a welter.[160]

Of necessity, then, the common law becomes **elitist** (or obscure, incomprehensible, perplexing, archaic, as proponents assert). Grasping after its slippery rules, its mazed procedures, its endless arcana—these duties fall to deeply indoctrinated slices of society. These lords of law are hardly normal people. They finish college and then spend years more getting a graduate degree, followed by yet further years of apprenticeship in the sweat shops of corporate law or self-study in the back rooms of sole practices or "publish or perish" regimes of academe. Because law is fragmented, only the gifted dare its interpretation.[161] These puzzlers flail about, disgorging their thousand page hornbooks, and

[160] Acknowledging the muddled welter of case law, significant effort has been invested by ALI and others to dim the din. Restatements and model codes, and the work product of the Commissioners on Uniform State Laws attempt remediation. These efforts themselves are subject to multiple editions.

[161] Debating the meaning of the word "home" for tax deduction purposes, the Circuit court found that for the purposes of the case under consideration, a taxpayers home was her place of business. In the concurrence of District Judge Keeton, one finds this gem: "[I]t is a distinct disadvantage of a body of law that it can be understood only by those who are expert in its terminology. Moreover, needless risks of misunderstanding and confusion arise, not only among members of the public but also among professionals who must interpret and apply a statute in their day-to-day work, when a word is given an extraordinary meaning that is contrary to its everyday usage." *Hantzis v. Commissioner*, 638 F.2d 248 (1st Cir.), *cert. denied*, 452 U.S. 962 (1981).

esoteric treatises, and innumerable law review articles. These are their attempts to wrangle the flailing firehose of case law that gushes from America's appellate fire hydrant.

So, law grows. Each appellate decision contributes to the cancer.[162] Law has **metastasized** for thousands of years.[163] In a comprehensive law library, millions of pages burden shelves. Each page tells a little tale of coercion. The pages are of ghastly number. Nobody knows the law. Law is a lake in a rain-drenched region, shores beyond the horizon, inestimable in volume, flooding by the hour. The lake of law cannot be swallowed, or even adequately tasted. So, law grows balkanized. One knows this bay, another that beach. Law's regions are poorly (if at all) coordinated. None knows, even in broad overview, the world's law. Were some genius to catch a glimmer, she would be just one star soaring over endless fields of earthen clods. I see no stars.[164] American lawyers are selected, by dint of law school admissions and coursework demands, for quick wits and attention to detail. None, however, is smart enough.[165]

Lawyers are psychologically and vocationally addicted to laws and coercions. If one complained to a lawyer about law's unmanageable volume, that lawyer might propose a law against further laws. If she were truly serious, she might make violations of the anti-law law a crime. Drenched in the cloudburst deluge of common law and the spawn of legislatures, lawyers perform rain dances.

Anthony D'Amato[166] offers careful analysis of the phenomenon of legal certainty. He asserts: "Legal certainty decreases over time. Rules and principles

---

[162] I analogize to cancer because, like the metabolic dysfunction, law grows without plan, ultimately to deliver termination to its host. The process of its growth can, therefore, be likened to metastasis.

[163] To give some sense of proportion, the United States Code (federal law) contains 23,000 pages. The Code of Federal Regulations (CFR), its interpretive administrative regulations, contains 175,496 pages (as of 2013). The Internal Revenue Code (a part of the United States Code) contains 3.4 million words contained in 7,500 fine print pages. (These numbers may be apocryphal because no lawyer has the patience to endure counting the pages of such material.) Kagan reports that from 1987 to 2017, the federal tax code increased in length by 300%. Kagan, *Adversarial Legalism*, 62. Google's AI, on which one should never rely heavily, says: "it is not possible to provide a single, reliable number for the total published cases in the U.S." The same doubtable source reports that in 2023, a total of 68.5 million new cases were filed in state and federal courts.

[164] For, alas, I am a clod.

[165] "A glance at the volumes of rules contained in the Code of Federal regulations should convince the most ardent positivist of the self-defeating nature of runaway rulemaking. Only the most spurious kind of certainty is produced—the feeling that, with all the verbiage, the 'law' must have an answer to every question. In fact, the verbiage creates intractable problems of organization and indexing, with many areas overlapping others. No one can be certain when finding a rule that there does not exist some other rule, perhaps poorly indexed, that directly contradicts it." D'Amato, "Legal Certainty," 23.

[166] Anthony D'Amato (d. 2018) taught for thirty-seven years in Northwestern's Pritzker School of Law. His academic focus concerned ethics and human rights. D'Amato authored more than twenty books and 110 articles. D'Amato received his law degree from Harvard University, where he served as editor of

of law become more and more uncertain in content and in application because legal systems are biased in favor of unravelling those rules and principles." Critically, D'Amato finds that the facts lead to a deflating conclusion: "[T]he tendency toward increasing uncertainty in the law is inexorable." [167] When a client asks what the law says, she is asking for a professional assessment of what a judge would do to address the dispute she suffers. If the rule to be applied is relatively favorable to the client, the lawyer might tell her that she has a 0.9 chance of prevailing. If the rule bodes ill for the client, her attorney might give her a 0.1 likelihood of winning. In both of these cases, the rule applicable to the client's circumstance is relatively clear. If the lawyer's assessment, however, finds a 0.5 chance of the outcome the client seeks, then the lawyer has no idea what will happen if the matter lands before a judge. This last is what D'Amato means by legal uncertainty. The more rules of a 0.5 sort, the less certain will be the client's ability to predict an outcome of her dispute.

So, why does D'Amato conclude that growing legal uncertainty is intrinsic to the common law? Might judges not discipline themselves to be more clear and concise in their language? He answers "no." The problem is not judicial sloppiness, at least not solely. The common law process involves inherent fractionation. A court establishes a rule, a 0.9 or 0.1 sort of rule that offers reasonable certainty. The legislature tweaks that rule. So, now the rule is a holding plus a statutory gloss (and so becomes a 0.7 rule). A subsequent court shifts interpretation of the glossed holding by a clever counter-example that captures the fancy of many judges. A ham-fisted appellate court mangles both the rule and the statute and the gloss (now a 0.6 rule). A further trial court cleans up the mess, but fails to detect that it has now punted the original holding far from its original destination. It has been years, after all, since that antique original rule. The rule has descended to the 0.5 region. None fathoms the outcome of the rule's application.[168] And so, the bramble grows, well-watered by judicial ambition,[169] and

---

the Harvard Law Review. He studied also at Columbia University, where he received his Ph.D. When D'Amato taught at Wellesley College (1960s), Hillary Clinton served as one of D'Amato's student researchers.

[167] D'Amato, "Legal Uncertainty," 1.

[168] The concept of "contract" poses an example. Here we have a concept rudimentary to much of law. One learns in the tutelage of the learned that a "contract" consists in an offer, an acceptance, and mutual consideration. In reading the law of contracts, one finds "contracts" that suffer no offer, no acceptance, nor any consideration. Exceptions have ground the concept to a nub, and then pinched off the nub. When a client asks me "What is a contract?" I answer with a shrug and a wink. It is symptomatic of law's uncertainty that the word "probably" infests lawyer diction.

[169] D'Amato says that judges, sometimes unawares, desire recognition, which attention arrives more readily on wings of invention than plodding competence. Hence, there exists pressure to distinguish precedents, to recognize issues of first impression, to innovate while pretending to clarify, or to become in one way or another socially visible. D'Amato, "Legal Uncertainty," 10-11.

scholarly need to publish,[170] and client urgencies lathered in plenteous cash.[171] Note that each intervenor believes its work alleviates previous inadequacies or injustices. Yet, all the "improvements" to the rule serve only to make the rule harder to understand and less useful. The tangle sprouts, ever more uncertain, ever more confused, more elitist, more metastatic.[172]

When we lack certainty (that is, rules of the 0.9 or 0.1 sort), none is able to plan activity to conform to them. Lawyers do not know how a matter might turn out, for judges cannot fathom the applicable rule. When, then, a judge decides, she may do as she pleases. We become a society of judicial discretion, not a realm of law. Our courts cease to be *de jure*, becoming instead *ad hoc*. Trial

---

[170] The academe rewards new theories and criticisms of old ones over competent restatements. "New theories which cast doubt upon the soundness of existing case law tend to get published more easily and disseminated more widely than do restatements." D'Amato, "Legal Uncertainty," 11.

[171] "[J]udges dislike ruling totally for one side and giving the losing party nothing. Like all human decisionmakers, they tend to try to compromise disputes. They dislike sending someone away from court with the feeling that the judicial machinery has been wholly unresponsive." D'Amato, "Legal Uncertainty," 13. Judge Higginbotham in *Zenith Radio Corp. v. Matsushita Elect. Indus. Co*., 402 F. Supp. 251, 262 (E.D. Pa. 1975) says: "Until these motions were briefed and argued, I had never before witnessed at close range a Dionysian intoxication with the creation of intellectual chaos and confusion where none need exist. Defendants' written and oral arguments have amply filled that prior gap in my experience. Throughout the proceedings on these motions, defense counsel have sought earnestly to prove themselves the Lamont Cranstons [an anti-hero of the fictional superhero crimefighter, the Shadow] of our common profession, that is, lawyers endowed with a singular ability to cloud men's minds." Beclouded minds suffer fogs of uncertainty.

[172] This problem has long been recognized. Aristotle notes that rules will not bear the freight we load upon them. No rule can be framed that admits no exceptions (hence, the need for equity). Each exception itself admits exceptions. This inexorable process encrusts its rule. In the end, every rule loses itself in a wilderness overrun with organic layers of exceptions and re-interpretations. Weediness renders the rule's gist null. One might conclude that no rule survives the intrinsic eccentricity of human members and their plights. We prove too complex to be corralled within demarcating verbal fences.

For those who savor exquisite detail, I cite Aristotle: "The source of the difficulty is that equity, though just, is not legal justice, but a rectification of legal justice. [4] The reason for this is that law is always a general statement, yet there are cases which it is not possible to cover in a general statement. In matters therefore where, while it is necessary to speak in general terms, it is not possible to do so correctly, the law takes into consideration the majority of cases, although it is not unaware of the error this involves. And this does not make it a wrong law; for the error is not in the law nor in the lawgiver, but in the nature of the case: the material of conduct is essentially irregular. [5] When therefore the law lays down a general rule, and thereafter a case arises which is an exception to the rule, it is then right, where the lawgiver's pronouncement because of its absoluteness is defective and erroneous, to rectify the defect by deciding as the lawgiver would himself decide if he were present on the occasion, and would have enacted if he had been cognizant of the case in question. [6] Hence, while the equitable is just, and is superior to one sort of justice, it is not superior to absolute justice, but only to the error due to its absolute statement. This is the essential nature of the equitable: it is a rectification of law where law is defective because of its generality. In fact this is the reason why things are not all determined by law: it is because there are some cases for which it is impossible to lay down a law, so that a special ordinance becomes necessary. [7] For what is itself indefinite can only be measured by an indefinite standard. . . ." Aristotle, *Nichomachean Ethics*, Book 5, Section 10: 3-7.

judges may rule either way, or no way. So too courts of appeal. Jurisprudence peels its veneer of rationality, and dons the habit of roulette wheels.

D'Amato asks why this pattern of increasing uncertainty is not apparent to all lawyers. He argues that most lawyers cherish deep psychological investment in the notion that their activities contribute to societal stability and smooth functioning of the legal universe. To see D'Amato's point about inherent uncertainty, one needs to examine the evidence from an odd perspective, in a manner that may prove unsettling to many attorneys. D'Amato calls this unsettled perspective "a gestalt shift."[173] Where such shifts occur, evidence absorbs an altered patina. "The same evidence that once seemed to render the law more detailed and precise will instead appear to demonstrate law's muddiness." Thus, D'Amato's argument recommends a change of paradigm.[174] Lawyers might look past their need to believe in the ameliorative effect of their law work, and gaze upon the underbelly of its functioning: its uncertainty, which devolves from confusion as to the meaning of its rules, from the scattering which the application of many minds (some fleet, some dim) generates, from its elite interpreters who stand as keepers of sacred mysteries for the ruck, from the metastatic growth of precedents and corrective measures to address the shortcomings of those mutating rules.

D'Amato suggests purgatives. He doubts his prescriptions would make law certain. His hope is more modest. D'Amato suggests his remedies might slow law's inexorable slide toward 0.5-edness.

1. Codification

Law might be codified. This solution to legal confusion is as old as law itself. One extracts from extant practices and judicial habits the entire law of a region, rendering it in a written form accessible to many and immune to judicial vagaries and wandering. The Code of Hammurabi (~1750 B.C.) selected provisions from among earlier codes of the city-states of Mesopotamia for those the Babylonian king preferred. It weeded the Euphrates bramble. The Twelve Roman Decemviral Tables (449 B.C.) codified the welter of extant laws in the fractured kingdoms of Italy to form a code that became the basis of law in the Empire for a thousand years. The Code of Justinian (565 A.D.) selected relevant precedents and statutes from among

[173] D'Amato, "Legal Uncertainty," 3. In footnote 13, D'Amato cites Thomas Kuhn, *The Structure of Scientific Revolutions*, at 112: "Therefore, at times of revolution, when the normal-scientific tradition changes, the scientist's perception of his environment must be re-educated—in some familiar situations he must learn to see a new gestalt." The idea is that one may organize a whole of many parts in more than one way, in more than one shape or gestalt.

[174] D'Amato, "Legal Uncertainty," 4.

the Roman corpus and served another thousand years as the legal skeleton of Byzantium. The Napoleonic Code (1804 A.D.) selected provisions from among the codices of neighbor states to guide French jurisprudence.[175] Codes remove judges from the law. The judge applies law, but does not create it. So, to propose, as D'Amato suggests, that common law jurisdictions codify is to suggest that we abandon the common law altogether, selecting in its place something more like the civil law traditions of Europe.[176]

Codes, however, fail to clarify. These contain difficult terms (such as reasonable, sufficient, due, and good faith) that will be interpreted as they are applied. Judges, though evicted from making laws, find themselves back in business, despite codification. Language, and so law, wriggles from its codified cage. Slippery terms infest all law.[177]

Wittgenstein argued that verbal indeterminacy lies in the root of language. Words arrive in piles. Each leans on many others for meaning. Individually, words are empty. One learns language by watching others play with the piles (language games).[178] Common law jumbles the piles and extracts or adds words, potentially in every case. Nevertheless, common law pretends that it does no jostling, but only plays the game (precedent).

2. Weeding

D'Amato suggests "delegalization" as an approach that might relieve problems associated with the common law's uncertainty. If a rule has no application, or has grown pointless, repeal that law. Then outdated or ill-conceived laws can no longer pose a danger to the uninformed citizen. But there lies a danger of exacerbating uncertainty in this approach. If one may say of any law that it might be weeded out, then does this not cast a pall of equivocation over every law? D'Amato argues that many ill-begotten laws

---

[175] Upon investigation, it would appear that code-making has occupied most civilizations, each tailoring a set of laws adapted to its own people and region.

[176] American common law addresses codification by oxymoronic conjunction of legislative and judicial functions. Every State, and the Union as well, harbors a legal code, for example the Revised Code of Washington, or the United States Code. Yet these codes are subject to interpretation by judges. The common law itself has become written, stated in the cascade of reported cases, and so is more code-like, in being written, than was the oral judge-law of Druidical England. Yet the common law has become a concourse for extensive dialogue between the judicial and legislative branches of government. Legislatures enact statutes to correct those common law precepts they deem offensive. Judges interpret away, or overrule outright, statutes they deem unwise or unconstitutional.

[177] When Napoleon learned of the publication of the first commentary on his Civil Code of France, he exclaimed, "My code is lost!" D'Amato, "Legal Uncertainty," 22, citing J. Merryman, *The Civil Law Tradition* 62 (1969).

[178] Wittgenstein, *Philosophical Investigations*, 23-25.

emerge from legislative attempts to address specific, often horrific, events. "Throwing more words at a problem usually makes it worse."[179]

3. Non-Rule Decision-Making

Non-rule decision-making entails entering the fact patterns and decisional rules of cases in an area of law into a database. By an approved algorithm, a computer would compare facts of a current case and facts most closely analogous of previous cases, and then state the rule(s) applicable to the conflict being adjudicated. In this manner, the legal system might depart the debates of attorneys and judges about conflicted rules. Courts would be limited to factual determinations. These human excisions from the legal process might create uniformity and speed matters to decision. But they would, according to D'Amato, fix the common law in its aspect at the time of the computer algorithm's fabrication.[180] Also, though D'Amato does not consider this, it seems a forlorn enterprise to vacate this most human of events[181] of human decision-makers.

4. Imposing Practical Reasonableness

A commission (the Case Revision Commission) might be created which amends case and statutory law rules of decision that appear to be outliers with respect to existing rules. One might seek to align applicable legal rules to the normal sense of practical reasonableness, which non-pathological persons share.[182] The point of early amendment is to avoid entrenching odd precedents in the human skein, which creates an obligation to stay the course of a decision once persons have reasonably relied upon that precedent.[183] In the American system, such a commission would constitute a super-legislature, which, if it existed, would compound the uncertainty of law (and require amendment of constitutions). Any law, no matter how entrenched,

---

[179] D'Amato, "Legal Uncertainty," 26-27.

[180] D'Amato, "Legal Uncertainty," 28.

[181] That is, the community's assessment of its members' behavior.

[182] If in fact most people do share these rudiments. D'Amato believes that practical reasonableness coincides with natural law, and attributes this idea to Finnis, *Natural Law and Natural Rights*, 100-127 (1980). Constitutional barriers emerge, because such a commission would be exercising powers granted to all three branches of government, and so be operating in a supra-constitutional role.

[183] Think of the durability of the contributory negligence rule in tort law, long after it had been superseded by the comparative negligence regime in the estimation of lawyers and judges. Public reliance may have been one argument for retaining the rule. Washington's tormented relationship to the contributory negligence rule, and its period of retention of both theories, well-describes the pressures created by precedent that should be superseded. Contributory negligence as a bar to plaintiff's recovery was finally resolved by the contributory fault statute of 1974: RCW 4.22.

> might be transmogrified by the Case Revision Commission. One weighs the damage against benefits, without discerning any potent conviction that such an innovation might help.
>
> D'Amato contemplates another approach to conforming law to common sense realism: changing, not the law, but the populace. Popular views concerning the rules of law might be adjusted, say by extensive education in civics. If the citizenry better understood law's functioning, then its perceptions of law's value might rise and expectations might be more realistic, leading to greater legal certainty. D'Amato believes that such changes would have to begin in law schools. If in the teaching of law there was less rule-mongering and more attentive deliberation of the values underlying our attempts to resolve disputes peacefully, then D'Amato anticipates that lawyers might lead the public toward a better place. Citizens would know more of moral reasoning and learn an appreciation for finer points of issues implicated by human conflicts. But he pessimizes. "Law school education today seems to be heading in precisely the wrong direction." Law schools "teach a law that has lost its moorings, that drifts on a sea of verbiage." Where prevalent attitudes obtain, "Law school becomes training in how to generate attorney's fees."[184]

D'Amato is not hopeful about his proposals. He admits: "My proposals at best might constitute a holding action against the entropic forces of legal uncertainty."[185] D'Amato's proposals are the very stuff to which Pound's complaint of tinkering pertains: well-intentioned mini-reforms with no promise of fixing law's fundamental problems.

D'Amato doubts the certainty of legal rules. But uncertainty in law suffers another even more devastating flaw. Court judgments emerge from rules applied to *facts*. To those troubled by courthouse uncertainty, the fact-finding regime of courts screams for scrutiny. Jerome Frank[186] argues that judicial fact-finding piles the judge's or jury's own subjectivity upon the subjective reports of live witnesses. In

---

[184] D'Amato, "Legal Uncertainty," 31-32.

[185] D'Amato, "Legal Uncertainty," 33.

[186] Jerome Frank (1889-1957) was a lawyer, academic, Chairman of the Securities and Exchange Commission in the Roosevelt administration, and judge on the United States Second Circuit Court of Appeals. Frank wrote the appellate opinion on the Julius and Ethel Rosenberg espionage conviction, affirming the trial court and its imposition of the death sentence (though privately, he urged the trial court to avoid the death sentence). Frank, with Karl Llewellyn, advocated for legal realism, which viewpoint admitted the gaps and uncertainty of law. Frank was known for the inordinate length of his opinions. A clerk, objecting to a sixty-five page opinion, slashed that opinion to one-half page, and laid the sixty-five page original and the one-half page condensation on Frank's desk. Frank appended the clerk's effort to the end of the opinion.

the end such fact-finding amounts to no more than informed guesses about what happened in that part of the past that bears on the conflict before the court. Hence, Frank finds judicial fact-finding defective, and recommends "fact skepticism."[187] The past is past, and none can disinter it. Trial fodder consists in testimony, documents, and expert opinion. When a witness testifies, she states what she remembers, which perception has been winnowed by forgetfulness, misperception, bias, inventive gap-filling, and possible perjury. The judge or jury becomes witness to the demeanor of the witness, and suffers the same sort of perception problems concerning the witness's account. So, "subjectivity [is] piled on subjectivity."[188] Documentary evidence often requires witness testimony to set it in its proper perspective, and subjectivity again charges through that open gate. Finally, a court may hear an expert opine. Once again, all one hears in the expert's words is the subjective assessment of one person, though, on a good day, that assessment may be a studious and well-reasoned perception. The past itself fled in time's torrent. We are stuck with history, a human account, distorted to tell a tale the speaker prefers.

We must add to the uncertainty of facts from witnesses, documents, and experts, the likelihood of competing evidence. The finder of fact hears alternative theories of the case, with similar, but divergent, tales attached. Bits are strung together variously. More than one tale is told. In what sense does a jury unearth events of the past by selecting between alternative versions of the novels that opposing counsels proffer? To add to the jumble, testimony may be mumbled or confused or duplicative. And each shred of evidence may contain, swirling in its guts, its own ambiguities and latent improbabilities.

Finally, we must add to the uncertainty of judicial facts the propensity of some fraction of the Bar to fabricate evidence or put words in the mouths of witnesses.[189] Aside from such misbehaviors, jurors may select a lawyer's version of facts for irrelevant reasons: one likes her looks, or finds he reminds the juror of someone famous, or he dresses stylishly, or she is kind to the victim's family. Interposing spurious factors into the fact-finding enterprise discredits the process as a whole. Facts, so discovered, settle as a fuzz of fumbling. Applying legal rules to discredited facts results in injustice, just as surely as adopting inane rules works inequities.

So, Frank argues that human fallibility pervades judicial fact-finding, and adversarial skirmishes leave finders of fact deeply influenced by words that were no part of the evidence. Hence, the observer of courts arrives at Frank's "fact-skepticism."

---

[187] Frank, *Courts on Trial*, viii.

[188] Frank, *Courts on Trial*, 22.

[189] I wish I could say professional prevarications are unlikely, but, in my experience, they are anything but infrequent. They issue from the mouths of those so inclined like hordes of startled starlings.

Rule fractionation added to fact-skepticism leads one to a conclusion difficult to evade: None knows what will happen when a matter comes before judge or jury. So, the common law is confused and confusing.

**Some argue the common law is:**

B. COERCIVE, ADVERSARIAL, VAPID, AND PESSIMISTIC. Four related complaints about common law criticize its culture.

Law **coerces**. Law forces unwilling participants to acts they fervently reject—to pay someone undeserving, to sit in a jail cell with rancid companions, to be more fair to a spouse than that person deserves, to see or not see one's children, to stand by impotently while bad faith actors ravage, to let electoral minorities dominate because they skewed electoral rules in bad faith, or to watch the worse cause prevail because on a given day that opponent lied more persuasively than you managed to tell the truth. The bottom line in every court case is this shrill arm-twisting imperative: *Do what I want or a judge will compel you to do what I want.*[190] Every law, every judicial order presumes that, once enacted, non-compliance merits penalties. Law gulps whole the punch bowl of coercion.[191] As such, judicial process insures simmering retribution and eventual retaliation, having ended each case in something other than peace.[192] Litigated

[190] Thomas Paine, in his fanciful tale of man's coalescence into societies, imagines that the first public guidance was enforced by nothing more than public finger-wagging. But men discover that considerations of virtue lack sufficient gravity to organize the world, and so government is born for man's freedom and security. Paine, *Common Sense*, 252-253.

[191] "Do you know how they make [the common law]? Just as a man makes laws for his dog. When your dog does anything you want to break him of, you wait until he does it and then beat him. This is the way you make law for your dog, and this is the way judges make laws for you and me. They won't tell a man beforehand. . . . the French had had enough of this dog-law; they are turning it as fast as they can into statute law, that everybody may have a rule to go by." Bentham, *The Works of Jeremy Bentham* 235 (1843), cited in D'Amato, "Legal Uncertainty," at footnote 69. Yankah calls Bentham's characterization a "crude picture of the law," because Bentham fails to account for the authoritative and normative functions of law. In its normative function, law tells people not only what the government requires of them, but also how they ought to behave. In its authoritative function, law tells people that, though there may exist other rationales for behavior, when law speaks, that is the end of the conversation. Yankah says, "Simply put, the law takes the position that when it tells a person what to do, he had better darn well do it." Yankah, "The Force of Law," 1195-1196. I do not take the normative and authoritative functions of law to differ in any important way from its coercive countenance. As a normative proposition, law says you ought to do this, but murmurs under its breath, "or I will beat you." As an authoritative proposition, law says its rationales are final, but mumbles under its breath, "and if you argue otherwise, I will crush you." When coercion slips in the front door of a human relationship, good faith and cooperation bolt out the back.

[192] The federal judiciary and state bar associations appear none too fastidious about the manner in which the system censures its errant members. A study of prosecutorial misconduct in federal trials for five states revealed that, where prosecutorial misconduct was identified, sanctions were imposed in less than two percent of such cases. Center for Prosecutor Integrity, "Epidemic of Prosecutor Misconduct," Appendix B. Innocence Project's rate of DNA exoneration indicates that perhaps thousands of persons are wrongly convicted and incarcerated, violating their constitutional liberty rights. The misconduct saga grows ever more sordid as one descends from judges to prosecutors to police. Police brutality, especially

conflicts survive judicial resolution, and flare when one prods their banked coals. Conversations that might create better-functioning agreements are crushed. Ekow Yankah asserts that "coercion is inherent to the very nature of the law. Without understanding coercion, one misses a defining characteristic of the law. Thus, one cannot delineate the social phenomenon known as the law without accounting for its coerciveness."[193] Yankah would seem to be right, if one takes what can be seen in courtrooms as the measure of law. Law, the common law, coerces. Legal normativity brandishes a club. If law lacked coercion, it would, according to most lawyers, have no greater standing than those expectations grandmothers impose on dinner table etiquette.

Law, by its cudgel, takes from one person (a defendant) what another seeks (a plaintiff), invoking powers most often banal (fines or therapies) but sometimes extravagant (incarcerations or death). Some lawyers ask whether the only rule for societal order consists in robbing one man of liberty to assure that of another. Do we sort pedestrian conflicts of the poor with rules established to deter sociopaths and protect millionaires? Is coercion overinclusive, lumping traffic infractions and jilted lovers into a system built to restrain ravening trainwrecks of human personality? For untold millennia, humans survived without governments or coercive legal systems.[194] These primitives lacked modern coercive finesse.[195] Raised eyebrows and sniffs sufficed for peripatetic tribes clinging to the fringe of survival. Theirs was a normative system in which human social bonds proliferated and which provided pressures toward conformity more subtle than threats, yet also more compelling. The survival of any leaned upon the wholehearted

---

excesses aimed at people of color, is staggering in proportion. Hence, the recent calls for defunding the police. Robin D. G. Kelley (black historian and, at the time of writing, professor of American Studies and Ethnicity at University of Southern California) wrote of his own experiences of police brutality, and concluded (in the year 2000, decades before the George Floyd unrest): "What needs to change is the role of the police and their relationship to urban communities of color. The colonial mentality, rooted in slavery and imperialism, that has structured the entire history of policing in urban American needs to be overturned. Indeed, I would go so far as to propose the complete dismantling of police departments (and consequently the entire criminal justice system) as we know it. Perhaps we might return to the long-standing radical proposal for community-based policing. Imagine institutions for public safety restructured along nonmilitary lines and run by elected community boards! I am not simply proposing that community members be employed to do the work of policing; rather, I am suggesting that the very job itself be reinvented." Kelley, "Slangin' Rocks . . Palestinian Style," in Nelson, *Police Brutality*, 51.

[193] Yankah, "The Force of Law," 1214. Ekow N. Yankah is a professor of law at Cardozo School of Law. He has written on issues of political obligation and theories of punishment, and has expertise in voting rights and election law. Professor Yankah is a board member of the Innocence Project.

[194] Coercive systems emerged with the dawn of agriculture, an invention necessitated by our habit of overpopulating. When human groups exceed 150 members (the Dunbar Number), some become strangers. The interpersonal social control system erodes. When all but a few are strangers, law and its coercions find a home in the empty space between persons.

[195] Though one suspects that those cohesive small groups found unpleasant ways to deal with dissenters who scoffed at communal weal.

participation of all. Members protected the group because in doing so one protected oneself and those one loved. Certainly, an unrestrained sociopath would be dealt death, but probably by exclusion from the community, not by execution.[196]

Because of its essential coercion, law constantly butts against demands for justification. Those sanctioned find law's impositions despicable. So, law ends up barricaded, defending itself from assaults all around. Philosophy's best minds opine, offering this or that explanation. Few offer no justification at all. Yet, might it be the case that, in fact, no adequate defense of legal compulsion exists?[197] No one seeks justification for the peaceful activities of members building their communities. None demands explanation for neighbors sharing a meal together or kicking their soccer ball. No lips flap or tongues wag when a town puts itself back together after storms pummel. Is it not true that law requires justification simply (and only) because law coerces? Absent coercion, law would be a book proposing a normative path to prosperity. Absent coercion, law might transmit lucid ideas from one community to another. None would then seek justification for law. All would just say, "Welcome. And thanks." But because law coerces, it sows injustice and vendetta. We all would certainly like to have it

---

[196] Which sentence of excommunication likely amounted to death by hands other than those of the ejecting community or by jaws seeking an easy meal.

[197] Some argue that Western culture has grown more flexible and tolerant as its populations have grown. Gays marry. Millions think that "black lives matter." Most hope that no Islamist will suffer discrimination. Crime flags. Murder falls. Steven Pinker advises well. Engage commerce, hear women, enforce laws, increase sympathy (read novels), and promote rationality. Those who credit Pinker hope we careen (perhaps unintentionally) toward rampant peace. See Pinker, *Better Angels of Our Nature*. I am glad for good outcomes, whenever they occur. Pinker is right that violence has, historically, declined. Pinker fails to identify why, given all the effort, violence nevertheless persists. Coercion is effective, but short-sighted. We coerce "improvements," ignoring the backlash and sequels. After compulsion, all but the most timid among us sucks a seed of retaliation, an emotional imperative to do the doer. Such is the nature of insult. Victims bury relational mines where coercers saunter. Detonations maim. Coercers become victims, and lay their own mines. Where does coercion end? Shall we coerce ever more deeply? Shall every person be watched and prodded and punished into wider submissions, each intrusion more intimate than the last? Will not the circle of vendetta lash ever more deeply our culture and children? The dry well of coercion slakes no cooperative thirst. Coercion stanches those springs of activity that would otherwise become collaborations, poisoning trust. Can one compel tolerance? Can one force caring? Compassion blossoms from quiet listening, not rants. Trust is a seedling that roots only in clement weather. *See* our culture. We dwell senselessly near the border of the horrid. Suicide is up. Anomie is up. American mass murders have become pedestrian. Loneliness is a raging plague. Children starve (usually elsewhere). Homelessness swells like a tumor in society's intestines. We seem to have no answer for sociopaths on rampages. We lack words to deter people who breed heedlessly. Antipathy freezes Congress. Presidents dither, even indulge crimes. The Pentagon lusts after yet one more war. We invoke martial murder with practiced ease, but gape, astonished, when hated by the survivors of our targets. Americans seem no longer to believe in America. Public confidence in our institutions gutters. I suggest a reason for this collapse of confidence: our groundless faith in compulsion. Coercion is an ethical *cul de sac*. The only way out is to go back to the beginning and take a different path. Pinker missed that. I thank Michael Loges and the Witless Protection Program participants for the conversation, on February 6, 2016, that led to this footnote.

explained why we need our system of coercive sanctions.[198] Why is coercion the template for resolution of every public conflict?

Another much-maligned feature of common law's culture is its **adversarial** essence.[199] At common law, private parties and their advocates define issues, choose courts, select opponents, and drive the cases brought before benches and juries. Judges hear what parties have to say, which amounts to listening to what the parties' lawyers have to say. The theory goes like this: *Each party is motivated to ably argue on its own behalf, adducing arguments it deems maximally persuasive. A rational and impartial decision-maker, that is, a judge or jury, identifies which proponent prevails in this contest of ideas. Rational outcomes guarantee justice, and promote consistency among various legal outcomes.* "[A]dversarial legalism can meaningfully be called the American way of law."[200]

Such was the Enlightenment ebullience of the American system, riding a wave of confidence that human rationality might, by science or philosophy, penetrate all things social, physical, and mental. Optimistic Americans hoped in the potency of rational deliberation; the nation's founding literati were enthusiasts. Post-modern developments, however, dimmed the nation's trust in reason's efficacy. Psychological investigations demonstrated that rationality serves emotional preference in an instrumental manner. One justifies what one prefers. Seldom do humans prefer what has been to them rationally justified, if they suffer a

---

198 One obvious reason we need coercive law is to deter extravagant predations by bad faith actors and sociopaths. I take up that issue later is this work. Suffice it to say, for now, that some diminished measure of coercion would endure even in a society committed to amity at law.

199 Read the *Rules of Civil Procedure* or the *Rule of Professional Conduct* again, with fresh eyes. Are these systems not aimed solely at adversarial litigation, and, in fact, at litigation of the sort conducted by large law firms? Note the haughty sniffs thrown at non-adversarial resolution of human conflicts.

200 Kagan, *Adversarial Legalism*, 16. Robert A. Kagan is a professor of political science at University of California Berkeley, where he teaches jurisprudence and public law. Professor Kagan studied law at Columbia Law School, and received his Ph.D. in sociology from Yale University.

That adversarial excess is common does not mean it is well-received. Abraham Lincoln, himself a litigator, laments in oft-cited notes: "Discourage litigation. Persuade you neighbors to compromise whenever you can. Point out to them how the nominal winner is often a real loser—in fees, expenses, and waste of time. As a peacemaker the lawyer has a superior opportunity of being a good man. There will still be business enough. . . . Never stir up litigation. A worse man can scarcely be found than one who does this. Who can be more nearly a fiend than he who habitually overhauls the register of deeds in search of defects in titles, whereon to stir up strife, and put money in his pocket? A moral tone ought to be infused into the profession which should drive such men out of it." Lincoln, Fragment July1, 1850, in the *Collected Works of Abraham Lincoln*.

Chief Justice Warren Burger noted: "For many claims, trial by adversarial contest must, in time, go the way of the ancient trial by battle and blood. Our litigation system is too costly, too painful, too destructive for a truly civilized people." Cited in Wilets and Imoukhuede, "A Critique of the Uniquely Adversarial Nature of the U.S. Legal, Economic and Political System and its Implications for Reinforcing Existing Power Hierarchies," 341.

contrary sentiment.[201] If rationality is so conceived, trials prove to be, not deliberative assessment of facts, but shouting matches subject to a rarefied aesthetic. The courtroom spectacle becomes, not legal scientists teasing out the happenstance of history and applying normative morality, but saloon toughs brawling with weaponized educations. Rules of evidence twist to rhetorical torque, keeping judges and juries from knowing what happened. The adversarial contestant's goal is "throwing pepper in the eyes of a surgeon when he is performing an operation."[202] Adversaries tell not what happened but the fable a litigant prefers his judge or jury should hear. Pervasive lying means the case is won by the preponderance of the perjury.

Robert Kagan warns that "adversarial legalism," as he terms America's rampant litigious ethos, bears critical virtues, not only vices. These virtues Kagan identifies as:

- Encouraging new types of legal claims,
- Providing a viable counterpoint to systemic bias, pandering, and capricious decisions in governments,
- Prodding recalcitrant agencies to action,
- Breaking some political deadlocks,
- Offering a deterrent to corporate sociopathy and government neglect by publicizing their defects.[203]

The many sins of adversarial legalism are familiar to the reader, since they echo those many criticisms I have considered so far. Kagan notes these flaws:

- Inefficiency,
- Inordinate cost,
- Complexity,
- Unpredictability,

---

[201] The scientific community may pose a counter-example, since its members are committed ideologically to provisionality and empirical results. Still, science seems to progress one funeral at a time, despite the commitment of its devotees to evidence. Younger, more flexible minds take up new paradigms, reshuffling the known and investigating new unknowns. Hence, youths usher core innovations. A counterfact: the average age of Nobel prize winners is fifty-eight. (But the Nobel prize is often awarded for research completed decades earlier.)

[202] Frank, *Courts on Trial*, 85.

[203] In support of his contention that adversarial litigation has upside benefits, Kagan tells of litigation's role in reforming Alabama's prisons. In the fall of 1971, responding to an inmate petition detailing horrific medical neglect of incarcerated Alabamans, Judge Frank Johnson, U.S. District Court for the Middle District of Alabama, compelled Alabama state prisons to undertake twenty-four steps to improve medical care. Judge Johnson then moved on to ameliorate prison violence, overcrowding, substandard meals, and overzealous punishments, finding all to be cruel and unusual punishments. Ever a bulwark of Southern racism, George Wallace, took the issue to the Court of Appeals, but lost. Kagan reports that "by 1990, state prisons in forty-one states were operating under court orders," as were one-third of all large county jails. Kagan, *Adversarial Legalism*, 23-25.

- Deterring meritorious claims and fostering unworthy ones,
- Inspiring defensive tactics,
- Encouraging ugly social relations,
- Gumming the cogs of government and industry, and
- Political conflict.[204]

One must not, Kagan argues, discard adversarial legalism for its faults, because one then forfeits its benefits. It is folly to "cripple adversarial legalism without providing effective alternatives."[205] Despite Kagan's concern about dismantlement, he memorably ridicules adversarial litigation: "American adversarial legalism is like a professional baseball slugger who leads the league in magnificent home runs—but who also misses routine plays in the outfield, often arrives late to the game, and commands such a large salary that many fans can't afford to come to the ballpark."[206]

The ugly aspects of litigation are not lost on most attorneys. "Finding ways to avoid litigation is the stock in trade of most practicing lawyers."[207] Most lawyers seldom conduct trials. Such process remains so costly and uncertain that only high rollers risk the approach. So, even if tried cases reached rational results, that fact would matter little, since none but a tiny fraction of cases will ever be heard by a judge or jury. In contested civil litigations, fewer than two percent reach trial before a judge or jury.[208] Litigants with meritorious claims or defenses settle to avoid the expense, uncertainty, and emotional brutality of trial. Parties that can afford better counsel, tolerate delays, and cope with uncertainty and

---

[204] To illustrate his point that adversarial litigation creates significant downside complications, Kagan tells the story of dredging the Oakland, California, harbor. Oakland's port needed deeper harbor channels to accommodate new, larger container ships. The Port petitioned to dredge in the 1970s at a cost of $2 per cubic yard. Congress funded the project in 1986. Non-stop lawsuits ensued, in constant seesaw between courts and regulatory agencies. The port was finally dredged, as planned, in 1995. The cost per cubic yard for disposal was more than $20 per cubic yard. These sums do not reflect the cost of full-on litigation among citizen, fishery associations, governmental agencies, and port authorities, or the costs of testing and reporting in support of those litigants for a period of eight years. Kagan, *Adversarial Legalism,* 30-33.

[205] Kagan, *Adversarial Legalism*, 4-5, 26-29.

[206] Kagan, *Adversarial Legalism*, 38.

[207] Kagan, *Adversarial Legalism*, 39. One should note, also, the effect of liability insurance on the court system. The result of insuring matters is that disputes concerning liabilities of various sorts are frequently driven into mandatory arbitration, thereby sidestepping the court system. I have been in mandatory arbitrations. These differ from courtrooms only marginally in substance, and not at all in their adversarial ethos. Arbitrations are common law lite.

[208] Galanter and Frozena report the steady decline in civil trials, both bench and jury, over the last fifty years. The writers ask (but do not conclude) whether the trial is headed to extinction. None seems able to describe a scenario in which the civil trial might again find vigor. Glanter and Frozena, "The Continuing Decline of Civil Trials in American Courts," 28.

disparagement force those less resilient into compulsory settlements.[209] Most one-time litigants simply lack the stamina to endure civil pre-trial procedures and trial.[210] In federal criminal cases, less than two percent of cases go to trial. Litigation makes "the American criminal trial a distinctively inefficient method of deciding disputes—a method so complex and costly that it has become a relatively uncommon event."[211] Resolution of criminal matters falls to plea bargaining, in which prosecutors overcharge, then bargain away their surplusage, to achieve conviction without systematic testing of inculpatory or exculpatory evidence. In both civil and criminal matters, the promise of determinations issuing from an impartial finder-of-fact proves illusory. Outcomes follow wealth more closely than factual merit. Where lies truth-finding in these summary processes? Where justice?[212]

Matters are worse yet for common law overall. The grist that feeds the mill of common law is cases tried before courts, then appealed. If only the rich suffer trials, if only the rich can afford appeals, then case law addresses only those issues that trouble the well-heeled.[213] Law wanders far from the concerns of normal people, coming in the end to address only the dilemmas of aristocrats and political action committees.[214]

Kagan contrasted American legalism to European systems, where fact-finding is judge-driven and contests much less expensive. Lawyers do not drive the process, but assist judicial fact finding. In the United States, Kagan found that our systems encourage adversarial litigation by suppressing alternative institutions and approaches. "American adversarial legalism arises from political traditions and legal arrangements that provide incentives to resort to adversarial legal weapons. Put another way, American adversarial legalism arises from the

---

209 Kagan, *Adversarial Legalism*, 122-123.

210 And aggressive lawyering seeks to identify those fragile parties and drive them, by means of oppressive procedure, to settlement.

211 Kagan, *Adversarial Legalism*, 94.

212 Kagan reports that lawyer professional codes in Netherland and England strongly enjoin adversarial tilting, rather emphasizing the "search for objective truth." Americans with civil legal needs are much more likely than citizens of Netherlands or the United Kingdom to "lump it," declining to seek legal advice at all in order to avoid the known downsides of litigation culture. Kagan, *Adversarial Legalism*, 137, 143.

213 In criminal prosecutions, it is prosecutors who are "rich," working with many colleagues in well-funded, deeply-established organizations.

214 Roscoe Pound complains: "[I]n petty causes, that is with respect to the everyday rights and wrongs of the great majority of an urban community, the machinery whereby rights are secured practically defeats right by making it impracticable to assert them when they are infringed." Pound, *The Spirit of the Common Law*, 132.

relative absence of institutions that effectively channel contending parties and groups into other ways of resolving disputes."[215] American adversarial litigation perseveres because Americans distrust bureaucracies and prefer fragmented authority.[216] There exist erosions of the adversarial ethos in American law—mandatory arbitration clauses (which bypass the court system in favor of private adjudications), and court-mandated mediations (which admit *sub silentio* that parties, rather than judges, can better resolve their marital or probate disputes), and those branches of repetitive torts that have been lopped off for determination by administrative agencies (such as worker's compensation or lemon law administrative hearings).

So, to draw together Kagan's conclusions, America should not quash adversarial litigation, despite its failings, until the country has allowed alternative institutions and dispute-resolution approaches to root, flourish, and evolve.

Some assert that the depredations of American adversarial process have leaked into the United States culture generally. Two law professors argue:

> The uniquely adversarial nature of the United States legal system, rooted in the medieval English system of "trial by battle," has replicated itself in almost all aspects of American society, distinguishing the United States from even its common law counterparts that shared the genesis of their legal systems in English "trial by battle." Even resolution of basic Constitutional concepts is subject to battles between parties, rather than a proactive determination by a Constitutional court as can be found in many other legal systems. . . . These adversarial methods of not only resolving disputes but also creating policy outcomes tends to perpetuate existing power hierarchies: those with power and the "tools of battle" accompanying it are better able to compete in such a context.[217]

---

[215] Kagan, *Adversarial Legalism*, 41. Kagan reports the saga of attempting administrative resolution of routine bankruptcies. A 1970 bill, based on the report of a congressional commission, advocating a sub-judicial bankruptcy bureaucracy, was opposed by lawyers, members of Congress, consumer advocacy groups, American Bankers Association, National Consumer Finance Association, Department of Justice, organized labor, and other politically-influential persons. The bill died. The opponents just did not trust a new federal bureaucracy to be competent. Kagan, *Adversarial Legalism*, 145. Hence, Kagan's assertion that we cannot temper adversarial litigation if we refuse to allow less-combative alternatives to germinate. See the discussion of the "jurispathic" nature of the common law below.

[216] Kagan, *Adversarial Legalism*, 285.

[217] Wilets and Imoukhuede, ""A Critique of the Uniquely Adversarial Nature of the U.S. Legal, Economic and Political System and its Implications for Reinforcing Existing Power Hierarchies," 379. Others concur. Judge Marvin Frankel laments the adversarial excesses he has observed, and promotes changes to the rules of professional conduct and civil procedure (changes that have subsequently been adopted). He appreciates the growing role of mediation, as a non-adversarial conflict resolution format. He ruminates on lawyer-less tribunals. Frankel, *Partisan Justice*, 117ff. Julie Macfarlane (Canadian Professor of Law at University of Windsor) joins the chorus of legions who find no place for "zealous advocacy" in modern legal practice, but rather advocate for settlement and practice a different ethic. Macfarlane calls such

Another professor concludes: "[S]cholars have criticized modern adversarialism for the ways it teaches people to act toward each other. Although I share some of the critics' views regarding the incivility of lawyers, I am more concerned that the rhetoric and structure of adversarial discourse prevent not just better and nicer behavior, but more accurate and open thinking. A culture of adversarialism, based on our legal system, has infected a wide variety of social institutions."[218]

What alternative institutions might encourage non-litigious resolution of conflicts? In the 1990s, Britain perceived itself to have a nasty litigation problem. On April 26, 1999, the English Parliament adopted a revised Civil Procedure Code expressly aimed at suppressing adversarial excess. This code emerged from the Woolf Inquiry. Lord Harry Woolf, who has been a British peer, barrister, and judge, was appointed to oversee a five month inquiry (which turned into two years) into the processes of the common law system. Woolf found that British common law suffers inordinate expense, painful slowness, and vast complexity, in addition to favoring some litigants over others. As a result, the common law system inhibits access to justice and is, overall, inefficient and ineffective.[219]

Woolf's proposals addressed excesses of Britain's adversarial litigation by two means. First, he shifted the management of civil cases from lawyers to the courts themselves, more closely mirroring the style of civil case management in civil law jurisdictions, such as France and Germany.[220] Those systems style their judicial role as inquisitorial. Judges identify case issues, narrow them, and impose time schedules. Lawyers assist the bench. Second, Woolf proposed that legal culture shift fundamentally toward cooperation between parties and their counsels. Woolf seeks to adjust the rules of procedure in such a manner as to reduce incentives for adversarial excess, and punish those who decline to alter their approach to law. Evaluations of the effects of the Woolf reforms have been

---

practitioners the "new lawyer." Macfarlane, *The New Lawyer: How Settlement is Transforming the Practice of Law*, 243ff.

[218] Menkel-Meadow, "The Trouble with the Adversary System in a Postmodern, Multicultural World," 10-11.

[219] Vorrasi, "England's Reform to Alleviate the Problems of Civil Process," 361.

[220] Woolf asserted this was not an effort to abandon adversarial litigation in favor of an inquisitorial approach, but rather an attempt to extract the procedural elements of inquisition in order to render its process less complex, less expensive, and more rapid, rendering trial a genuine venue of last resort. Vorrasi, "England's Reform to Alleviate the Problems of Civil Process," 361.

generally positive, and the climate of adversarial tilting in England and Wales has cooled considerably.[221]

I offer a selection of Lord Woolf's fifty conclusions about the adversarial problems of British courts:

- *Adversarial Excess*: "4. Without effective judicial control, the adversarial process is likely to encourage an adversarial culture and to degenerate into an environment in which the litigation process is too often seen as a battlefield where no rules apply. In this environment, questions of expense, delay, compromise and fairness may have only low priority. The consequence is that expense is often excessive, disproportionate and unpredictable; and delay is frequently unreasonable." *The bilateral zero-sum game of litigation encourages scorched earth stratagems, and counsels weaponize each rule for strategic advantage.*
- *Judicial Non-Enforcement of Standards.* "6. It is often said that the existing rules and practice directions contain the solution to the present problems, if only litigation were to be conducted in accordance with them. But the present system does not ensure this. Instead the rules are flouted on a vast scale." *When judges decline to censure unpermitted acts of litigators, then bad acts proliferate and good faith compliance with the rules is punished. The compliant litigator finds herself hogtied by rules others ignore with impunity. The incentives trend in all the wrong directions.*
- *Metastatic Discovery.* "10. The scale of discovery, at least in the larger cases, is completely out of control. The principle of full, candid disclosure in the interests of justice has been devalued because discovery is pursued without sufficient regard to economy and efficiency in terms of the usefulness of the information which is likely to be obtained from the documents disclosed." *When no outside controls govern factual inquiry, discovery expands to fill the chasm of fearful counsel's imagination.*
- *Financial Preclusion.* "13. Excessive cost deters people from making or defending claims. A number of businesses have told me that it is often cheaper to pay up, irrespective of the merits, than to defend an action. For individual litigants the unaffordable cost of litigation constitutes a denial of access to justice." *Costs beyond the means of normal people lock the courthouse doors to those potential claimants or defendants. In effect, the judicial system says "Petty matters do not matter."*

[221] Vorrasi, "England's Reform to Alleviate the Problems of Civil Process," 379-387.

*The net effect of widespread cost-preclusion is a flood of* pro se *parties bumbling their way through the system, again reducing efficiency*

- *Dilatory Processing.* "30. Delay is an additional source of distress to parties who have already suffered damage. It postpones the compensation or other remedy to which they may be entitled. It interferes with the normal existence of both individuals and businesses." *Delay is often strategically determinative; delay defeats the weak by attrition—death by a thousand "buts."*[222]

Woolf prescribes a host of ameliorations, which he calls a "new landscape." These United Kingdom changes fall under the following headings: Litigation will be avoided whenever possible, litigation will be less complex, the timescale of litigation will be shorter and more certain, the cost of litigation will be more affordable, more predictable, and more proportionate to the value and complexity of individual cases, and parties of limited financial means will be able to conduct litigation on a more equal footing.[223]

As tinkering goes, Lord Woolf's enterprise impresses. He would remake judges into inquisitorial case managers,[224] admonish lawyers to play fair and care about more than their financial benefit and punish them when they fail to comply, categorize cases so that small matters get substantial consideration, mandate discovery controls, and insist that experts be neutral as between parties and only one

---

[222] Woolf, "Civil Justice in the United Kingdom," 710-715. I present only five of Woolf's fifty items, but perhaps five among his most important points.

[223] Woolf, "Civil Justice in the United Kingdom," 722-724.

[224] Ellen Sward compares the values of adversarial (common law) and inquisitorial (European civil law) systems. Adversarial adjudication leaves judges to assess pre-packaged (by advocates) presentations of which the judge knows little or nothing. Its values emphasize individualism and claimant pro-activity. Sward says: "But individualism untampered by communitarian values can lead to unremitting selfishness, including an utter lack of concern for the consequences of one's action." Sward, "Values, Ideology, and the Evolution of the Adversary System," 311. Judges as inquisitors, on the other hand, investigate with the help of party counsels. They examine witnesses; they narrow the scope of disputes. The inquisitorial judge represents the community in its resolution of the dispute. Hence, then needs of society enter into every resolution. Sward concludes: "Adversarial ideology has failed. The adversary system is transforming itself into a more inquisitorial, less individualistic methodology even as apologists debate the various justifications for adversarial adjudication. . . . The less individualistic, more communitarian ethic that is reflected in the transformation should be recognized and encouraged. That recognition may entail abandoning adversarial ideology, but a focus on our goals and values is more helpful in evaluating and modifying our adjudicatory system than any rigid ideology could be." Sward, "Values, Ideology, and the Evolution of the Adversary System," 355.

King County in Washington State has recently innovated in family law, creating an elective "informal trial" system for determining family and dissolution matters. The change shifts such adjudications from the common law approach toward an inquisitorial model. The judge reviews all documents, and examines the proponents of the documents presented. The only witnesses allowed are the parties and *guardian ad litem* (if one has been appointed), and only the bench asks witnesses questions. No interruptions are allowed; cross-examinations of witnesses by the parties or their counsels are not permitted. If an expert is needed, only one is appointed. *King County Local Family Law Rule 23: Informal Family Law Trials.*

per case. Yet, for the purposes of this book, post-Woolf Britain's common law still suffers a system that is coercive, classist, and darkly competitive—just less so.

A third cultural misgiving finds the common law **vapid**.[225] Other proponents seize on elements of that evaluation by calling law unprincipled, slovenly, or discretionary. Law drones on and on, regulating minutiae, missing the momentous. Life, which law presumes to guide, exudes vim and mystery. Yet, law shuffles along, trying to make the best of a bad situation. Having lost its feeling, law lionizes mere functioning.[226] Law, if it were to have value, would brim with humanity's values. Instead, law excises exuberance and pares precocity. Common law is a grim aunt, babysitting mankind with a nasty little switch in her hand.

Common law cannot avoid vapidity. Law reduces citizens to units that sometimes grate upon one another disturbingly. Persons disappear, substituted by uniform wan doppelgangers.[227] Disturbance is prohibited. So, law intervenes, short-circuiting the natural processes of reconciliation. Instead, law offers the thin gruel of trial and judgments, where eminent strangers, oddly dressed, sort the conflicts of people they do not know.[228] Statutes render citizens, who are

---

[225] The word "vapid" means offering nothing of great interest, banal, flat, dull, stale, or lacking flavor, zest, interest, animation, or spirit.

[226] Albert Schweitzer found ours a lawless period. Statutes proliferate, but confidence in law is a smoldering ruin. Law, where vital, is simply humanity codifying itself. Law loses vitality when it abandons its universal rationale: reverence for life. Schweitzer, *The Philosophy of Civilization*, 81-82 (Part II, Preface).

[227] Is not this transformation of the human into units one component of our policing problems? The perpetrator is drained of personhood, becoming a "problem" to be disposed. In the grip of law, policing degenerates from community relations toward trash management.

[228] In the decades before Washington Territory became a State, people in its predecessor territory undertook to become "lawful." The tale is a sad one: In 1847, in the Oregon Territory, in the area of Wai-il-at-pu (not far from today's Walla Walla, Washington), the medical mission of Marcus and Narcissa Whitman was attacked. Both Whitmans and twelve others were murdered by assailants supposed to be natives of the Cayuse tribe. After a time, to prevent retributive war against their people (which numbered no more than 850), the Cayuse people offered up five of their own as perpetrators. Despite an abject dearth of reliable testimony (all eyewitnesses had been killed), their jury found the Cayuse prisoners guilty. No court of appeals had yet been organized. Judge Orville C. Pratt imposed a sentence of death by hanging for each of the five natives. Four days later, the hangings were enacted simultaneously on a gibbet specially constructed for the purpose. Many gathered to watch this public spectacle. Ronald Lansing, speaking as a fictional narrator, tells the story of those who watched: "I looked into the faces of those who stayed on. I thought to see faces satisfied, hearts made good. But it was not so. It was not the look of pity, either. It was a different look, hard to cipher. I had seen that look before. And then it came to me. It was the look of a hunter standing over the carcass of his quarry after a long day's track—a stare that took the place where hunt had been. In 1845, seven years before the hanging, folks here made a choice at Champoeg. Joe Meek had called out, 'All in favor of an Organization, follow me!' Settlers went to Meek's side and took the first step toward civilized ways. Here, seven years later, with Territory government at hand and trials fit and proper, five souls hanged under a new order of ways to come. It was what folks wanted, what it had all been for, but not without forsaking. That was the look I saw—forsaking. Not rejoicing, not pitying. It was regret for the passing on old ways. Each step away from wild country makes the heart

multi-form and wild, into lowing, gentle, numbered herds. In this sense, law seeks to make bewildering human diversity legible to administrators.[229] Bureaucracy needs units it can find. Law cuts up the land you live on, and, if you are lucky and diligent, allocates you a chunk. Law tells you where you can and cannot walk. Law specifies what is yours, what is others', and what belongs to governments. In its worst incarnations, law controls your thoughts. Law renders people as one renders fat into useable products—under low, but persistent, heat. Locked in its rut, law squints at humankind through medieval glasses. Law conceives disputes over internet data access in a rubric fabricated by English lords to deal with starving peasants who swiped the occasional wild boar from hunting stock. Having reduced humans to evanescent ciphers, law's pronouncements induce yawns. Zing drains; life's luxurious crop of detail withers in the worrisome whittling of legal pigeon-holing. Vapid. Ever so vapid. Ever more vapid.

Vapidity hides an underground connection to law's negativity. At root, law **pessimizes**. Law indulges scowling schadenfreude.[230] Law perceives society's members as hordes of isolated cretins much inclined to antisocial outrages. Law fashions punishments sufficiently draconian to deter any who dare scoff. In its dire, Hobbesian assessment of human sensibilities, law entirely ignores the essential gregariousness and cooperation of humans.[231] When humans gather in numbers, one anticipates remarkable peace and collaboration, often startlingly creative. Law, however, finds no room for celebration. Every silver lining must don its stormy cloud. Someone, somewhere in that crowd is likely to err. Law must ferret out that person and stigmatize him or her. Law expresses our fears in their most dark and anxious intrusions. Law's pessimism lies not as a lesion upon its skin, but deep in jurisprudential bones.[232] Humans behold themselves,

---

heavy with forsaking." Lansing, *Juggernaut*, 98. The Cayuse, when they murdered the Whitmans, imposed their own law: a medicine man whose patients died must be executed. The juggernaut of which Lansing writes is the steam-rolling arrival of America's common law in the Oregon Territory.

[229] James Scott styles government an attempt to standardize people and their circumstances for ease of management and control. Scott, *Seeing Like a State*, 2, 183.

[230] A borrowed German term for "pleasure derived from the misfortune of others."

[231] See **Epitome 4: Keltner, *Born to be Good***. Keltner argues that mankind is not as Hobbes portrayed it. Humans are, rather, gregarious and cooperative. They degenerate toward war only when compelled to dwell in untenable circumstances. Arthur Schopenhauer offers counterpoint to Keltner's happy view, a grim view consonant with much of common law. Schopenhauer, venting his moral skepticism, says: "The thousands that throng before our eyes, in peaceful intercourse each with the other, can only be regarded as so many tigers and wolves, whose teeth are secured by a strong muzzle. Let us now suppose this muzzle cast off, or, in other words, the power of the state abolished; the contemplation of the spectacle then to be awaited would make all thinking people shudder." Schopenhauer, *The Basis of Morality*, 74, 121. Men are born to rapacity, though some few find compassion persuasive, Schopenhauer argues. All are unable to change their stripes.

[232] Thomas Andrews, a law professor emeritus at University of Washington School of Law, takes a more positive view of law. He styles much of law as facilitation of relationships among persons, property,

in the mirror of law, not as moral, kind, empathetic, sympathetic, cooperative creatures inclined to help, anxious to create. Rather, the reflection people suffer at law portrays a species whose lives are "solitary, poor, nasty, brutish, and short,"[233] awash in ignorance, and much inclined to outrageous misconduct. We are, according to law, reluctantly social, and quick to abandon society's needs.[234] Law's tale of humanity fixates upon the sociopath[235] to the neglect of society's massively-more-numerous conformers and cooperators and creators.

Law's grim assessment of human predilections trends toward self-fulfillment. People watched with suspicion feel diminished; their dysphoria erupts in just the sort of misbehavior for which law so studiously scans. Distrusted people feel depersonalized. The jurisprudence of alienation strips members of individuality, rendering them impersonal placeholders. So, in the end, law's impersonal pessimism midwifes a society about which one can justifiably pessimize.

So, some complain of the common law for its coercive sentiments, its adversarial extravagances, its vapid worldview, and its rabid pessimism.

**Some argue the common law is:**

C. ILL-JUDGED, JURIED, PARTISAN, AND CORRUPT. The common law has always had a problem selecting judges. Where elected, canons of judicial professionalism discourage speaking publicly about one's political opinions; the public, however, needs to know just those prohibited judicial views to

---

and communities. Surely, he is correct; most attorneys would agree with Tom, and disagree with me. Andrews argues that I overstate my case. Nevertheless, I persevere in my view. Thomas Andrews, in private correspondence with the author, July 2016.

[233] [♪] Hobbes, *Leviathan*, 107 (Chapter 13). Thomas Jefferson argues that economic desperation, caused by private or public excesses, leads men to be "glad to obtain subsistence by hiring ourselves to rivet their chains on the necks of our fellow-sufferers. . . . Then begins, indeed, the *bellum omnium in omnia*, which some philosophers observing to be so general in this world, have mistaken it for the natural, instead of the abusive state of man." For the government's part in driving men to despair, its primary error is excessive taxation. Jefferson, *Writings*, 1400-1401 (*Letter to Samuel Kercheval*, July 12, 1816).

[234] Given the debacle of unvaccinated hordes, despite the awful killing-field of COVID-19, one may concede that grim-law has a point as to about half of America.

[235] No society can afford to ignore its sociopaths. Unfettered, they make grave havoc. Every society requires a clear-eyed approach to address the predations of this four to six percent of the human population (more men than women) who are empathy-crippled and moral morons (but often deeply intelligent). Oddly, a sociopath's crimes are not crimes at all, despite their abundance, since the perpetrator lacks the ability to appreciate the moral dimension of his outrageous acts. Sociopaths cannot be rehabilitated by punishment; censure serves only to render the sociopath more sly. Sociopaths suffer mental defect, and so should be treated as we do others whose crippled mentality endangers society. Every sociopath must be assigned permanent watchers; his miscreant impulses should be restrained in the most humane manner possible. We need not wait until the sociopath has committed crimes. Anti-social personality disorder is a psychological malady. We can treat, aggressively, and save our selves the horrors we might otherwise endure.

frame any meaningful vote for a judge. Public ignorance of judicial views results in the election of candidates with familiar names or those who have extensively self-promoted. Lacking meaningful information, voters re-elect incumbents. In Washington State, few judges face competition in re-election; they run unopposed.[236] Where judges are appointed by State executives, voters lose out altogether, and the dangers of nepotism and partisan appointments loom. The bench grows crowded with sycophants and sons-in-law of lame duck governors. A third blended alternative, merit selection,[237] creates a non-partisan commission to weed out unqualified candidates and to recruit highly qualified candidates. The merit candidates are appointed for a period of years, and then face a retention election where voters choose to unseat or retain the jurist. Where judges find their benches by vote of a commission, the judge's elevation appears a meritocratic promotion, but the fact is that partisanship has merely retreated one step, to the appointments of the commissioners and the preparers of slates of judicial candidates.

Regardless the method by which judges are selected, some will be poorly qualified.[238] Judges are people, arriving at their benches with prejudices and histories and personalities and diseases and foibles.[239] Consequently, due to lack of initial qualification or subsequent loss of capacity or

[236] In 2018, 147 judges and justices ran for office; twenty-nine had an opponent. William R. Andersen argues: "[T]he election system for choosing Washington judges is not, in any significant degree, an election system at all. Most Washington judges do not get on the bench by election and elections are rarely used to evaluate sitting judges. Through the quiet adoption of certain practices and customs, citizen voice through elections rarely plays a role." Washington jurists customarily retire mid-term, leaving appointment of a successor to the state governor. Andersen continues, "Problems in the evaluation of sitting judges flow from two sources. First is the surprising fact that most (perhaps 90%) of sitting judges never have to face the voters at all. The second is that even if there is a challenge, inadequate information is available to support informed voter choice." Andersen, "Judicial Selection in Washington—Taking Elections Seriously," 605, 611.

[237] The State of Missouri adopted such a merit scheme for selecting judges in 1940. Missouri's approach has been widely emulated, with some similar form of selection in thirty-eight states (as of 2016).

[238] There comes to mind the confirmation of Trump's nominee to the Eighth Circuit Court of Appeals, Leonard Steven Grasz. Mr. Grasz was judged "not qualified" by the American Bar Association, which went to the trouble to send a letter to that effect to the Senate and testify at his confirmation hearing. In 2017, Grasz was approved for the appellate seat by the Republican majority. I am glad not to be an Iowa appellant.

[239] And sports manias, as well. One superior court judge attempted to continue trial of an errant personal representative (for which hearing the parties had waited six months) because the judge, as he said in an improbable moment of candor, had a killer tee time he desperately did not want to miss. He averred that he was headed toward retirement in the near future. Thankfully.

motivation, some decisions will be **ill-judged**.[240] Shoddy judicial decision-making may increase partisanship, delegitimate the courts, and paint a picture of jurists as mere advocates for cronies.[241] The troubles are not over when the public has managed to seat a competent jurist. If the court system is overtaxed or underfunded, even a competent jurist cannot perform adequately. The result is the same—loss of public confidence, and a boost to those who view the court as just another venue for political barfights.

When a judge is not authorized to make findings of fact, such matters are **juried**. Jurors are selected for qualities that one would never employ, in any other aspect of life, to identify facts and make judgments. Jurors can know nothing of the matter at issue. Jurors must lack personal expertise. Jurors are admonished to follow rules described to them by the bench. So, jurors are either rule-followers (civil yes-men) or persons willing to prevaricate about willingness to follow legal rules (moral munchkins). Fact-finding, by both judges and juries, is the seldom-examined underbelly of our jurisprudence. Peering, the view is not pretty. Surmise stacks upon supposition, spattered with subjectivity.[242]

In every other circumstance of life, where there is quandary or uncertainty, one seeks a decision-maker of deep personal knowledge and wide experience. One has a lump on his chest. He goes to a doctor who knows much of fleshy bumps and what should be done about them. Our car breaks down. We seek a mechanic trained to repair vehicles of the sort we own. Imagine making decisions in a juried manner. Your doctor says, "Well, I know much of lumps like yours. But let's go a different, possibly better, way. I will gather twelve people from the sidewalk outside, none of whom know anything of medicine and nothing about you or your history. I will

---

[240] In an international comparison of removal of judges for their misbehaviors, Volcansec writes: "What is most remarkably apparent from our country-by-country examination is that very few judges are removed from the bench for any reason." Volcansec, *Judicial Misconduct*, 111.

[241] Known colloquially as "home cooking." Not an insignificant problem. Judges are not alone in their deficiencies. The Bar itself is riddled with attorneys given to misconduct or incompetence. We have often asked judges to report such lawyers for discipline, but they comply feebly. See Greenbaum, "Judicial Reporting of Lawyer Misconduct," 538. Jerome Frank said: "I think we have been astonishingly careless in our haphazard method of educating and selecting men to serve as trial judges." Frank, *Courts on Trial*, 224.

[242] Courts also lament racial prejudice imported into the judicial process by jurors. One issue seems critical: jurors unduly credit eye-witness testimony involving cross-racial identifications. SCOWA says: "Racial bias is pervasive in our society, and the ways in which it can impact eyewitness identification are well established. . . . Studies have confirmed the particular impact of cross-racial bias on eyewitness identifications of Black person by white persons: 'One of the oldest and most consistent findings of systematic studies of eyewitness identification is that white Americans are much more likely to mistake one [B]lack person for another than to mistakenly identify members of their own race'." *State v. Butler*, 200 Wn.2d 695, 711 (2022). For further elaboration, see Chief Judge Gonzalez's concurrence in *State v. Butler*.

explain your situation for a few minutes. Then we will let them vote. Your treatment will be whatever the group's majority thinks best." Or your mechanic dials three telephone numbers at random, describes your car's dysfunction, and takes his cue from their views of the matter. You would walk out the door. Is your lump or vehicle of greater value than a respondent's life, freedom, or prosperity?

You object to my characterization. "The jury follows the rules a judge describes for them!" No, they do not. Juries do not obey judges; they hardly understand judges. Jerome Frank, a jurist experienced in jury trials, quotes a colleague Ulman, himself deeply experienced: "'[T]he jury has made the law . . . in . . . direct conflict with the law as laid down by the highest law-making authority of the state' and told to them by the trial judge. 'The jury has substituted its own notion of law of that which the law-books say is the law.'"[243]

Not only do juries distort or ignore their judge's legal instructions, panels also mistake rhetoric for fact. Those who have observed more than a few trials recognize that juries try not the clients, but their lawyers. Trial may boil down to beauty pageant strutting. Lawyers appeal to jurors' vilest prejudices and crudest emotions. Jurors often reward the winsome rhetorician with fealty.[244]

Not only are juries swayed by emotional appeals, not only do juries ignore legal instructions, juries are also hog-tied by impairment of the evidence presented to them. Lawyers are (rightly) concerned that juries will ignore evidence and run with their gut. So a maze of rules inhibits what facts come before the panel at trial. These evidence rules seem reasonable on their surface. But beneath that complex but comprehensible façade lurks deep distrust of jurors. The evidence rules say, "We must keep normal people from making this decision in my courtroom as they make all their other decisions." The rules of evidence exclude just the sort of facts that most people use to guide judgment. For example, hearsay (what others have observed and reported) and prior convictions (bad past acts predict future bad acts) are excluded. So, an image of juries emerges: believing stories that are partial or even false, using those stories to justify prejudices they brought

---

[243] Frank, *Courts on Trial*, 120. Frank and Ulman were discussing the doctrine of contributory negligence, which is a now-gone tort doctrine that any fault in a plaintiff precluded recovery from any defendant. The jurors were, apparently, right when they re-wrote the law in Frank's and Ulman's courtrooms.

[244] "Jurors prefer witnesses and lawyers who are likeable and attractive, both physically and personally. They are more influenced by people they like and who appear to be much like themselves. They prefer witnesses and lawyers who project energy, enthusiasm, and confidence when they testify or argue." Mauet and Easton, *Trial Techniques and Trials*, 19.

into the courthouse from their work-a-day lives, and voting for the lawyer with whom they would most like to have lunch.

Behavioral science, in examining juries, asserts that most people, and hence most jurors, are affective decision-makers. Few prefer problems over people. Few defer conclusions until the relevant facts are in play.

> Affective persons have several common characteristics. First, they are usually emotional and creative, and are more interested in people than problems. They see trials as human dramas, not legal disputes. Second, they use deductive reasoning, which is primarily emotional and impulsive, in which a few premises about how life works and relatively little factual information are used to create "stories" of what probably happened, reach decisions, and attribute cause and blame quickly. Third, once they make decisions, they become committed to them, and they validate their decisions by selectively accepting, rejecting, or distorting later information to "fit" the already reached decisions. This allows them to justify their decisions and believe the decisions are logical and fair.[245]

So, though judicial decisions may be flawed, jury decision-making is far worse. Woe to the person whose fate lies in a jury's perceptions.

But, back to judges. In States where judges are elected, like Washington State, the judiciary is ripe for perceptions of judicial **partisanship**. Though Washington judges are not identified by political party on ballots, their political sentiments emerge once they begin ruling on cases. Perhaps the Supreme Court of the United States sealed the fate of the nation's judiciary by its rancid 2000 decision in *Bush v. Gore*,[246] which effectively handed the Presidency to George W. Bush by vote along party affiliations of the justices. Seven states have gone so far as to elect their judges on ballots in which their political preference is identified. At some level, the common law attempts to address partisan judging. All decisions must conform to legal precedent.[247] Where it is so, judging tastes more of intelligent administration than partisan skullduggery. But then, precedent leads to common law unresponsiveness. Suppressing one problem engenders another—jurisprudential whack-a-mole.

---

[245] Mauet and Easton, *Trial Techniques and Trials*, 14.

[246] *Bush v. Gore*, 531 U.S. 98 (2000).

[247] One fairly doubts, in a post-*Roe* landscape, whether the U.S. Supreme Court adheres to precedent, now that its conservative majority has taken matters into their partisan hands.

One skates down the slippery slope from judicial partisanship to **crime and corruption and misdeeds**. Judges are so seldom censured and enforcement is so tepid that a sitting judge has little to fear from his or her ill-behavior.[248] In Oklahoma, no judge has been publicly disciplined in fourteen years. Thirty-eight states censure judges privately—no public scrutiny allowed.[249] Of all judicial censure, ninety percent is private. Of all censured judges, ninety percent retain their positions. Lest one dismiss these matters as peccadillos, I offer sample anecdotes:

- Alabama judge sentenced an impoverished Black single mother of three to 496 days in jail for non-payment of traffic tickets. Her children were dispersed into the foster care system. One was sexually molested; another was physically abused.
- A Texas judge intruded into a jury deliberation room and pronounced to the panel that God had told him the defendant was innocent.
- A California judge had sex in his chambers with an intern and with an attorney.
- Three Indiana judges got drunk. At 3:00 a.m., they shot at one another. Two were hit. None died. All returned to their benches after suspensions.
- An Alabama judge repeatedly appointed his son as public defender in indigent criminal matters. The son was paid $105,000 over two years. The judge retired from the bench without further investigation or censure.
- Two Pennsylvania judges sentenced juveniles to terms in a private detention center, from which the judges received kickbacks. After investigation of the matter, the criminal records of 2,251 juveniles were expunged.[250]

Closer to home in my little neck of the woods, just north of Seattle, the judge who officiated my wedding was removed for inappropriate contact with minors. The judge who officiated the marriage of dear friends left office for exchanging lenient prostitution sentences for in-chambers sex. Another local judge took drug money for

---

[248] Reuters has compiled court discipline documentation for judges from 2008-2019. https://www.reuters.com/investigates/special-report/usa-judges-data/. Reuter's enterprise has been laborious since they encountered significant resistance among the States to releasing their judicial censure data. California, apparently, was especially reticent.

[249] Washington abolished its private judicial censure system in 1989. Now all judge discipline is conducted in publicly available forums. Consequently, numerous Washington judges are represented in Reuter's catalog of judicial discipline in the United States. I know a few judges on that Washington list.

[250] Berens and Shiffman, "Thousands of U.S. judges who broke laws or oaths remained on the bench." https://www.reuters.com/article/us-usa-judges-misconduct-specialreport/special-report-thousands-of-u-s-judges-who-broke-laws-oaths-remained-on-the-bench-idUSKBN2411WG.

favorable treatment of transport mules. He left the bench when one $10,000 cash payment was left in a paper bag on the judge's chair in his courtroom. That jurist saw jail time. But these are mere anecdotes, and so poorly indicate the scope of the matter.

My point is not to berate these errant souls.[251] May they grope their way toward probity. Nor is it my point to insinuate that most judges are corrupt or terminally stupid. Far from it—in my experience most judges are thoughtful, thorough, principled people, especially when it comes to their work. My point is to note that some judges are frequently out of bounds in a manner that, conjoined with lackluster investigation and private censure, leaves the common law system tarnished and the bench blemished with cretins best relegated to less demanding employments. Bad judges beckon bad outcomes. Bad faith lawyers are emboldened. Straight arrows are discouraged. And every citizen is left to wonder—and doubt. Courts do not want to confront their defects. They suffer magical thinking, as to the efficacy of their rules and sensitivities. Jerome Frank said:

> These [judicial] assertions concerning the efficacy of the legal rules are reached by the wish-route; they derive not from experience but from wishes. They are magical verbal devices for concealing what I have stressed—that one's rights to life, liberty or property are subject to the effect of such variable factors as crooked lawyers, crooked witnesses, mistaken witnesses, absence or death of witnesses, loss of documents, competence of lawyers, mistaken judges, biased judges, inattentive judges, stupid judges, crooked judges, inattentive juries, biased juries."[252]

So, some complain of common law judges for their defective judging, their partisanship, and their corrupt, criminal, or misbegotten acts.[253] Some assert that juries are even worse. The criticism gives one pause.

---

[251] Learned Hand said of judges and judicial discretion: "With all his sins upon him, his self-importance, his ignorance, his bad manners, his impatience, he is all you have got, and I believe he will produce better results if you give him a little more room to roam about." Hand, "The Deficiencies of Trials to Reach the Heart of the Matter," 318.

[252] Frank, *Courts on Trial*, 62. Of the "wish-route" Frank said that one who follows it "make one's wish the father of one's thoughts." Frank, *Courts on Trial*, 59.

[253] Learned Hand said: ""[W]hile I am willing to admit that we upon the bench are lacking in firmness, in learning, in industry and in acumen, you cannot lay it all to us. The administration of justice is a good test of the civilization of the people where it exists; it shows their interest in equity, their freedom to adapt themselves to new conditions and their courage in protecting the weak and controlling the rapacious. It measures the point they have reached in education and in virtue, and how far they are serious in the formal expression of their will." Hand, "The Deficiencies of Trials to Reach the Heart of the Matter," 319.

**Some argue the common law is:**

D. UNDER-FUNDED, INACCESSIBLE, OLIGARCHIC, AND DUPLICATIVE. The common law prescribes an intricate process for deciding thorny factual issues. That process, laden with rules and their many exceptions, proves cumbersome, slow, and fraught with tactical possibilities. Lawyers spend a great deal of time learning and then staying abreast of the morass. In these complexities, lawyers seek advantage for their clients, and derivatively, for themselves. All the while, these attorney machinations are superintended by judges, clerks, court reporters, bailiffs, all of whom need places to sit, work, eat lunch, meet privately, meet publicly, and go to the bathroom. Being a public location in which conflicts are adjudicated, these judicial places can become targets for violence of the disaffected, and so require another horde of screeners, police officers, and administrators, who themselves need places to do their work. The result is a fabulously expensive enterprise. Funded from public coffers,[254] courthouses are strapped, under-staffed, short of room, and suffering unworkable backlogs[255] of waiting cases. So, some complain that the justice system is chronically **under-funded**. Michael Graetz notes that State courts hear more than ninety-five percent of all court cases filed in the United States. He notes: "In 2010, more than forty states cut their courts' funding. In most states, courts received 10 to 15 percent less funding in the years 2008 through 2011 than they did in 2007."[256] With years-long delay in hearing cases, corporations and the wealthy take their causes to mediators and private arbiters, leaving the state court system to cope with *pro se* divorces and criminal jury trials. A two-tier system has emerged, one well-funded and efficient and private, but limited to the rich.[257]

---

[254] And so, subject to the vagaries of political infighting, and the venom of disaffected legislators.

[255] After the mess that the COVID pandemic created, gigantic backlogs of cases have grown wholly unmanageable. In King County, some 4,800 felony criminal trials await adjudication (May 2022).

[256] Graetz, "Trusting the Courts: Redressing the State Court Funding Crisis," 97.

[257] Many of the mediation and arbitration firms providing this private court system are staffed by "retired" superior court judges, perhaps more tired of the public system than retired from providing legal services.

Another, broke and backlogged and public, serves the poor.[258] The courts themselves appear incapable of staying the course on ameliorative steps.[259]

---

[258] In 2022, several civil litigants joined their disparate languishing causes, hoping to represent a class that challenged persistent underfunding of Washington State Courts, and the subsequent failure to manage its caseloads promptly. The trial court dismissed the cause for failure to state a cause of action. The appeals court affirmed that decision. The appellate court did not find that the plaintiffs' various causes of action were being timely disposed. Rather, the court leaned heavily on the separation of powers. The legislature is charged with funding state government. The courts have authority (and *only* the courts have such authority) to compel the state legislature to fund the judicial system more generously, but should exercise this power with trepidation, given that such rulings are likely to elicit backlash. The Court of Appeals wrings it hands about "more funding battles, court-packing, jurisdiction stripping, altered methods of judicial selection, and retaliation against the judge(s) who permitted the forced funding. . . . Backlash could affect the judiciary's ability to fulfill its constitutional duties more dramatically than underfunding ever did." *Ralston v. State*, 25, Wn. App. 2d 31, 40-41 (2022). If the courts decline to use their powers to fund their essential duties, why should the legislature dig deeper into our common purse?

[259] For example, Stephen C. González, Chief Justice of Washington's Supreme Court, writes winningly of an improved court system: "A just court would be one where outcomes were not disproportional. Where court participants were both heard and felt like they had been heard. Where everyone believed that the process was fair. It would be one based on research and evidence, not tradition and anecdote. It would be one that's culturally competent and provides language access fully to everyone who needs it, which includes those who don't speak, read, or write the English language, whether they speak a foreign language or whether they are deaf or hard of hearing. That would mean true access to them. It would mean that when you go to the court webpage you can easily find the forms that you need which are in clear, plain, understandable language. It would mean that you could find resources to help you understand if you can't afford a lawyer. It would mean that people whose liberty or substantial rights are at stake would be provided counsel to assist them through the process. It would mean that the judges would provide timely rulings that could be clearly understood and followed. The system that we have, the democracy as a whole, specifically the judicial branch, exists and works only if people are confident that the system is fair. We have work to do to make [sure] everyone believes the system is fair to them." To my surprise, these fine sentiments slipped away from our Chief Justice not long after he gave them voice. Aspiration expired, a dead letter.

Chief Justice González is deeply qualified. His experience, both in and out of the court system, is expansive. He may have (I cannot remember for certain) sat on a RALJ appeal of mine, once long ago. Judge González was fair, prompt, and caring. He has long championed access to justice and supported initiatives that address barriers to the court system. So, one puzzles his recent decision to terminate, with six of his Supreme Court colleagues, the limited license legal technician (LLLT) program. This rule (APR 26) created a class of legal practitioners, less broadly educated than attorneys, but perhaps more competent than most lawyers in family law, where LLLTs are permitted to practice, and substantially cheaper for the consumer. After more than a decade of hard labor on the part of many, the Supreme Court axed the LLLT program in one afternoon, without notice, without public comment, without publicly-stated rationale, and without good faith with the many hundreds of persons who had been building LLLT practices. One suspects that the Court caved to pressure from whiny members of Washington's bar, whose sense of monopolistic entitlement overwhelmed their professional oaths. There appears to have been inordinate fluster about the finances of the program (the LLLT program cost each lawyer licensed to practice in Washington seven dollars annually, according to the Stanford study). But we do not know this was the Court's rationale. For the high court has not explained itself.

Belatedly, the Supreme Court called for public comment, an after-the-fact band-aid on their breach of public trust in acting precipitously. Perhaps the Supreme Court, Chief Justice González included, should repent this gaffe, reinstate the LLLT program, and set about ameliorating its perceived deficiencies. The practice of law is a public trust, not a cash machine for attorneys, nor a guarantor of lawyer prosperity. And the Supreme Court governs the practice of law in Washington. It does not answer to the lawyers of Washington, no matter how clamorous we may be. Rather, lawyers answer to the Court. Perhaps this constitutional arrangement is more aspirational than actual. A troubling rumination....

Not only are state court systems underfunded, but they are also **inaccessible** to most of the public.

> It is a shameful irony that the nation with one of the world's highest concentrations of lawyers does so poorly in making legal services available to its citizens. The U.S. ranks just 109 out of 128 countries in access to justice and affordability of civil legal services, below Zambia, Nicaragua, and Afghanistan. . . . In 2003, Washington State conducted its own civil legal needs study and found that low-income people in Washington State faced more than 85% of their legal problems without assistance from an attorney."[260]

The primary reason associated with lack of legal services was expense.[261] From my own practice experience, I find that expense not only prices out

---

I wrote nine mangled limericks for SCOWA. The high court did not respond, as is appropriate for bad poetry. See Appendix C. For transparency's sake, I state that I know so much about, and am so sorely rankled by, the summary execution of the LLLT program because I followed and supported its adoption for years. My spouse (who works as my paralegal) became the eighth LLLT licensed to practice in Washington. She has since retired from that limited practice of law for reasons other than SCOWA's misdeed.

Solomon and Smith offer insightful analysis of the demise of Washington's LLLT program in their Stanford white paper, *The Surprising Success of Washington State's Limited License Legal Technician Program*, from 2021. In Smith and Solomon's assessment, the demise of the program lay with Washington Supreme Court's lack of will to rebuff an inveterate and raucous (but small) group of motivated monopolists, ever yammering about LLLTs poaching their market share. (Solomon and Smith couched their conclusions in language considerably less blunt.)

260 Solomon, "Surprising Success," 3, citing from the World Justice Project Rule of Law Index, under the factor "people can access and afford civil justice." (The study actually found that 88%, not 85%, of civil legal needs go unmet.) The situation for Washington's poor appears to have changed somewhat. The 2015 update to the 2003 Washington Civil Legal Needs Study indicates that more than 75% of civil legal needs among low-income people are faced without professional legal assistance, though the number of civil legal needs in each family is up 300%, as compared to the 2003 baseline study.

261 One need not wander far afield to encounter the absurd expense of adjudication in adversary proceedings. In Washington State, we have for decades suffered a grifter who found favor with the State's conservatives by promising to beat back taxes and keep car tabs at $30 per year. Regularly, this none-too-gifted con-man, Tim Eyman, raised money for signature-gathering and initiatives. He then paid himself handsomely from the proceeds, obfuscating when confronted. He took kickbacks from signature gatherers and conducted shell-games with financial transfers. Starting in 2012, the State Public Disclosure Commission over time issued twelve subpoenas for documents related to Eyman's public initiatives. Finally in 2017, Washington's attorney general, Bob Ferguson, took Eyman to task, conducting litigation to hold Eyman accountable for his violations of State campaign finance laws. All told, the PDC and AG litigations lasted almost nine years. Eyman destroyed documents pertinent to the case. He dragged his feet. Eyman issued defensive discovery requests, costing yet more hundreds of State hours to comply. Eyman styled his mulish foot-dragging as putting "that dirty dog on the defensive for a change." None of the documents produced by the Attorney General was offered in evidence at Eyman's trial. When things looked bad, Eyman filed for bankruptcy. When the federal court refused to stay the State of Washington's suit against him, Eyman sought to dismiss the bankruptcy proceeding. Ultimately, Eyman was fined $2.6 million and barred from all financial aspects of future political campaigns. Attorney General Ferguson then moved for attorney's fees and costs, to reimburse the State for its expense in suing Eyman, in the amount of $2.8 million. Seven assistant attorneys general spent 9,899.71 hours litigating against Eyman. The case docket contains approximately 1,600 entries. 160 motions in six different courts were required, including almost

low-income clients, but also many middle-class families as well. Even those who are well-to-do, but imagine themselves just work-a-day blokes, frequently decline to pay the steep freight attorneys seek.[262] Regardless whether the obstacle is inability to pay or monetary objection to the fees of counsel, most legal needs are never addressed by an attorney. So, to the extent that one requires counsel to navigate the laws and courts of Washington, its courts are generally inaccessible.[263]

Jerome Frank said: "For the advantage in litigation is necessarily on the side of the party that can 'purchase justice' by hiring private assistance in obtaining evidence when his adversary cannot. Unless we contrive some method to solve the problem I have posed, we must acknowledge that, in a very real sense, frequently we are 'selling justice,' denying it to many under-incomed persons. It should shock us that judicial justice is thus often an upper-bracket privilege."[264]

Unfortunately, I see no shock.

Lacking access, most of the public scrambles for alternative ways to address their various complaints, which disputes are too insubstantial to rise to judicial scrutiny.[265] The great majority of such "petty matters" never receive a lawyer's attention and die unaddressed. Yet, some mechanisms take up the worst of petty offenses: business complaint departments, government complaint channels, Better Business Bureau and other trade associations, legislators' offices,

---

100 oral arguments. Eyman suffered contempt charges, which he declined to purge for more than two years. The case required more than twenty-four depositions, and review of more than 500,000 pages of discovery. Eyman was represented by eight different law firms at various points. Ferguson said, "The State has had to spend thousands of attorney hours answering baseless discovery requests, responding to unfounded motions, and most of all, contending with Defendant Eyman's refusal to comply with his discovery obligations." David Gutman, "Ferguson seeks $2.8M more from Tim Eyman," *Seattle Times*, March 13, 2021.

262 Surely, there lies a deep conjunction between chronic underfunding of the court system, and public perception that our legal system and its operatives are over-priced. Many perceive the common law as a system in which wealthy people engage in bloodless little wars, while the poor are excoriated for public urination and stealing hens from rich barons.

263 In an assessment of public policy issues in dispute resolution, a panel said: "Although the government subsidizes a great deal of the cost of running the courts, their full use requires expensive lawyers and the time of the disputants. These costs mean that courts are generally inaccessible to all but the most wealthy parties. . . . Thus, although courts are vitally important for protecting private rights and concerns, the delay and costs may render them ineffective in discharging this critical duty." From "Paths to Justice: Major Public Policy Issues of Dispute Resolution," 1983, as contained in Riskin and Westbrook, *Dispute Resolution and Lawyers*, 195.

264 Frank, *Courts on Trial*, 95.

265 The Washington Court system added small claims courts to its spectrum of offered services. Small claims courts are a division of county District Court systems in Washington. See RCW 12.40. For humans, the jurisdictional limit is $10,000. For entities, the limit is $5,000. Generally, no attorneys may represent parties, and judges may interview witnesses directly. Causes of action are limited.

neighborhood service centers, non-profit consumer organizations, labor unions, and media complaint venues.[266]

Unchecked **oligarchic**[267] tendency is another worrisome feature of the common law system. The common law system is controlled by judges, and the consumers of judges' labors, the legal profession (and their clients). These consumers are dominated by several truly gigantic law firms. To put such corporate legal consumers in perspective, Kirkland Ellis, which employs 3,025 attorneys, earned more than six billion dollars in 2021; yet, Kirkland Ellis is only the fifth largest employer of attorneys in the United States. Despite these numbers, all told, the legal industry is controlled by a relatively small number of persons, say, just to guess, a hundred thousand. If that number is anywhere near accurate, America's common law system is the least democratic of our government institutions. This fact bumps one toward a further concern: **oligopoly**. Not only do the judges and their large consumers control the practice of law. They also control the business of law.[268] This court-corporations-cabal is the OPEC of common law. 2021 global law fees were $713 billion. United States law fees for 2022 are estimated to be $365 billion. Oligopolies block new entrants (Bar exams and internecine takeovers), increase prices (or fix them), and slow innovation (preferring short term gain). Hundreds of billions of dollars motivate many. But, even in a capitalist economy, there wafts an undemocratic stench about the whole affair.

Others complain the common law system lends itself to **duplicative** efforts. Multiple courts exercise jurisdiction over the same matters. In Washington, some matters could theoretically be heard by municipal courts, district courts, superior courts, or federal district courts. Further, there lies the problem of dual sovereignty. A perpetrator may be prosecuted in State court, and then again prosecuted in federal court for the same offense—retribution redux. An inordinate number of retrials occur, in which the court retraces journeys it has only just aborted.[269] Finally, common law adjudication is duplicative in that its decisions

---

[266] See Nader, *No Access to Law*, for anthropological evaluation of "how Americans actually handle legal problems," xvii. It is the contributors' view that "in most societies of the world where there are viable alternatives, law is not necessarily the most important form of control," referring to societal maintenance of order, xv.

[267] "Oligarchy" denotes control of an institution by a small group of people. "Oligopoly" denotes control of a market by a few participants.

[268] Yes, there are many munchkins like me (and probably you), dotting the legal landscape. Small practice lawyers comprise about sixty percent of all lawyers in Washington State. But we do not seem to be in charge of much of anything, given that our time is depleted not only by law work, but also by our tasks as office janitor, painter, landscaper, bookkeeper, accountant, and occasional plumber.

[269] In King County District Court, as a legal intern prosecutor, I once retried an alleged violator of contractor registration laws three times, only to suffer ultimate dismissal. This was assuredly the result of my incompetence and inexperience, but it was permitted by both the court and my office superiors.

concern individual conflicts. These disputes, observed from the catbird seat of law practice, bear extensive similarities. Often, it would seem only the names and hair styles differ among cases. So, dockets become déjà vu on Groundhog Day. We have long decided that some matters are better handled administratively by hearing examiners in abbreviated procedures. Consider lemon law disputes, industrial injuries, and land use conflicts.[270] Perhaps a much greater use of these summary processes might benefit, and possibly summary processes still more abbreviated might be fashioned.[271]

So, common law procedures are chronically under-funded in a manner that renders them frequently dysfunctional. The intricacies of common law adjudication render it financially inaccessible to most citizens, and repugnant to many who could afford its expense, but decline to do so. The common law suffers disturbing anti-democratic tendencies in both its function and economics, being governed by a tiny group of insiders. And common law adjudication proves senselessly duplicative at multiple levels.

**Some argue the common law is a:**

E. WEALTH AGENT. Not only is wealth maldistributed in the United States. The common law system acts not as impartial arbiter of disputes, but as the active advocate of monied interests. The common law serves as an **agent to wealth**. As Theda Skocpol put it: "What is quite new in recent time is . . . very systematically, that government really responds much more to the privileged than to even middle-income people who vote."[272]

The common law system has been systematically exploited to insure that the rich stay rich, and the poor do not intrude into the wealth gap. Richard Kaplan argues: "[C]oncentration of economic power inevitably corrupts the political process . . . [T]he political process, thus corrupted, spews forth the public policies that protect its patrons, often at the expense of the masses whose votes theoretically sustain that process."[273] The common law system, touting itself to be open to all and just in its every decision, has morphed

---

[270] Perhaps one might consider mandatory mediation or mandatory arbitration requirements to be attempts to shuttle repetitive matters out of courtrooms into faster, less-expensive fora.

[271] And there I go, tinkering. For those embedded in law, the urge to tinker seems irresistible. Still, one frets whether hyper-summary adjudications would in fact eviscerate due process.

[272] Cited in Pazzanese, "The Costs of Inequality," 3. Theda Skocpol is Professor of Government and Sociology at Harvard's Faculty of Arts and Sciences.

[273] Kaplan, "Economic Inequality and the Role of Law," 1987.

into the guard dog of American aristocrats.[274] Think, for example, of the disparities in criminal penalties.[275] When a person of color steals $100 from a bodega while brandishing a toy gun, that person will spend years in jail and be unemployable upon release. When a risk-ready investment banker loses his firm $100 million, and causes the collapse of his organization, the banker may never be charged for his dereliction, will be immediately hired by another firm, and the government may well bail out the crippled firm, since it is too large to fail.[276] The government will certainly bail out the depositors whose savings our cowboy disposed.

Any attempt to describe the prejudicial effect of common law on people who lack substantial wealth would run hundreds of pages. That is not the purpose of this book.[277] But to appreciate the problem, stop and read the boilerplate of the next contract of adhesion with a large corporation that you encounter. If there is a dispute, the consumer loses. Or contemplate tax exemption on 529 education accounts. How many under-funded people have 529 accounts for their children? Or, in Washington, we raise much revenue by a deeply regressive sales tax. Yet, attempts to introduce an income tax meet a deluge of dollars pouring in to defeat the proposal. One may object that these are particularly political issues, not judicial ones. I respond that law and politics are in bed together, like Clarence and Ginny.

Let me pause to describe just one such policy/law complex that serves to keep the rich rich and the poor poor. Estate taxation, wielded boldly, could erase much wealth disparity. But, politically, estate taxes suffer perpetual assault. Every conservative administration aims to reduce or eliminate the estate tax. Hordes of ever-inventive lawyers help wealthy clients evade estate (and other) taxes. As a result, despite the federal estate tax and Washington's estate tax, the wealthy keep most of their boon. When it

---

[274] Rousseau finds legal oppression of the poor to be inevitable and universal. Rousseau, *Emile*, 236.

[275] To tunnel back toward the origins of law (third millennium B.C.), the Code of Hammurabi would seem to be a long meditation on possession, classes (three: patricians, landless persons, and slaves), and the fate of those who dispossess wrongly. For example, theft from a temple (death: Law 6), robbery (death: Law 22), storing corn of others (one gur per five ka: Law 121), divorce (return the dowry: Law 138), bodily injury (broken bone for broken bone: Law 197), slave insolence (cut off slave's ear: Law 282). *Code of Hammurabi*, 29, 31, 39, 41, 49, 56.

[276] "Too big to fail" seems to mean "too big to anger" in a world of unfettered political contributions, unhinged social media, and unmoored news organizations (such as Fox or NewsMax).

[277] Many such books exist. Search for books on "Law and Inequality." Oswald Spengler said: "Law is the property of the powerful. Their law is the law of all." Spengler, *The Decline of the West*, Vol. II, 345. In 1830, a Providence, Rhode Island, widow was jailed for a debt of sixty-eight cents. Friedman, *History of American Law*, 271.

comes to that unfortunate moment when a family member of wealth needs long-term care, there are funds to pay those huge costs.[278]

Middle class families will owe no estate tax. But, for middle class people, the costs of long-term care debilitate. Three or four years of care gobble most people's life savings. Medicaid steps in to prevent starvation only when an elder's funds fall below $2,000. So, for many non-wealthy families, the Medicaid long-term care regime amounts to a 100% estate tax, imposed before death. When publicly-funded long term-care ends at death, nothing is left. If the deceased elder's residence remains, that real property can (and will) be liened for repayment of the much-begrudged long-term care disbursements. So the rich remain rich. And the non-rich retain no legacy to boost their non-rich children.[279]

So, the common law strains to preserve the rich, and should be disparaged for its duplicity.

**Some argue the common law is:**

F. DEEMING AND JURISPATHIC. Some criticize the common law for its fanciful legal fictions. Courts frequently "**deem**" one thing or circumstance to be another. Legal fictions take a matter as true, though it is known to be, actually or probably, false.

Pierre de Tourtoulon said: "The oldest and most essential ideas are nearly all, if not all, fictitious. Marriage is a fictitious purchase and sale, the power of a father is a fictitious master's power, adoption is a fictitious fatherhood. . . . It would not therefore be inaccurate to claim that our reality is simply fiction differentiated, and that at bottom all law is reduced to a series of fictions heaped one upon another in successive layers."[280]

Perhaps fictions persist because they cannot be avoided. Abstract truths travel in metaphor; our deepest thoughts mislead to some degree, trespassing the borders of accuracy. Words chafe at their definitions, restless to ramble. Lon Fuller styles the law's fictions as "words browsing beyond their

---

[278] Nevertheless, I still get a steady trickle of calls from well-heeled children seeking ways to get the government to pay for mom's long term care, without "squandering" mom's ample funds. These enterprising seekers are deeply disappointed when I report Medicaid long-term care restrictions: the $2,000 asset limitation, and the sixty-month look-back period for gifts. I suspect most find counsel more accommodating than me.

[279] Kaplan, "Economic Inequality and the Role of Law," 2002.

[280] Tourtoulon, *Philosophy in the Development of Law*, 387, as cited in Lon Fuller, "Legal Fictions," 391.

traditional pastures."[281] Yet, law might not *revel* in falsehoods; straight talk could prove a condiment making legal fictions more palatable.

In law, fictions hide in every corner. Corporations are persons, though they neither eat nor sleep. Service may be deemed adequate when mailing or publication have no possibility of notifying a litigant. Constructive fraud may be found when the defrauder had no ill intention at all. Constructive trusts emerge where the "trustor" has the very opposite of a beneficial intent. Contracts may be imposed where there was no offer, no acceptance, and no consideration, by muttering the word "quasi-contract." All citizens are assumed to know the law of their land, despite the fact that they do not. Every landholder is presumed to know the contents of the recording office (constructive notice), though I know no person who reads such documents for sport. Contractual consideration suffices if a lone peppercorn (or its mere husk) is offered in support of a contract, though a peppercorn is no consideration at all (nominal consideration).[282] The reasonable person is the measure of all things legal, though one never encounters so prudent a person. And, ignominiously, a slave can be three-fifths of a person, or a wife's legal existence can melt into her husband's (coverture).[283]

Can one expect desirable outcomes from a system so cozy with known falsehood? Perhaps law mostly exploits the roomy elasticity of language, not taking its legal fictions too seriously. Law, however, proves no amiable companion. With the jaw of the State, law tears at competing ideas, rules, and habits.[284]

Humans create many laws by non-formal means. Our endeavors trend toward habits, then grow in their potency as practiced habit becomes a local rule. Adopted by others, our private "rule" grows to a fragment of culture, an affinity group norm. This fragment swims in a sea of similar fragments, like in kind but mostly not well-coordinated with one another. All such local norms evidence perspectives, shapes of life together. Considered together, they form a polynomia, a landscape of many divergent, often contradictory,

---

[281] Fuller, "Legal Fictions," 379.

[282] Most contemporary jurisdictions reject the peppercorn theory because such consideration is not bargained for, and so amounts to the mere pretense of a bargain.

[283] Some judicially deemed facts become noxious to us as we change. Austin called coverture "sheer imbecility," in his *Lectures on Jurisprudence*, 611. Lon Fuller cites a jurisprudential maxim from East Africa: "A woman is a hyena," meaning that she cannot be a party to males-only legal discussion. Fuller, "Legal Fictions," 388.

[284] Jerold Auerbach said: "[O]ur culture is so thoroughly legalized that it is difficult for Americans to imagine how any society could be otherwise organized and justified." Auerbach, *Justice Without Law?*, 11.

rules. Robert Cover calls creative fabrication of norms the "jurisgenerative" aspect of human existence. Being creative, busy humans make rules and shape their lives.

Not all our various non-formal "rules" nestle well with one another. Were it not for coercive powers of the state, these various conflicts would be sorted by social affiliation and compromise and moral toleration and a modicum of forgiveness. But the State coerces. When government finds its cultural polynomia inefficient or immoral or unpopular, it forbids some rules. Government pares polynomic subcultures, seeking to render them compliant and comprehensible and, on a good day, coordinated. Consider the tribes: boarding schools, and reservations, and Christian indoctrination. Robert Cover calls common law courts "**jurispathic**."[285] Courts kill ideas and practices which law disapproves. Law sifts meanings. Law tells us how to think about problems, about our society, even about ourselves. Law's definitions, since they are linked to the coercive power of the state, crowd out other thoughts, other "laws." Courts do not create much law; rather, they exterminate divergent practices.

Robert Cover, in "Nomos and Narrative," put it:

> In an imaginary world in which violence played no part in life, law would indeed grow exclusively from the hermeneutic impulse - the human need to create and interpret texts. Law would develop within small communities of mutually committed individuals who cared about the text, about what each made of the text, and about one another and the common life they shared. Such communities might split over major issues of interpretation, but the bonds of social life and mutual concern would permit some interpretive divergence. I have played out a fantasy to some extent in suggesting that we can see the underlying reality of the jurisgenerative process in the way in which real communities do create law and do give meaning to law through their narratives and precepts, their somewhat distinct nomos. But the jurisgenerative principle by which legal meaning proliferates in all communities never exists in isolation from violence. Interpretation always takes place in the shadow of coercion. And from this fact we may come to recognize a special role for courts. Courts, at least the courts of the state, are characteristically "jurispathic."[286]

[285] Humans *jurisgenerate*, that is, create rules by which to govern their activities, especially those involving others. But law drives out competing rules that cannot be reconciled with its dominant drift. In this sense, law is *jurispathic*. Law quashes divergent theories of conflict resolution.

[286] Cover, "Nomos and Narrative," 40.

Without attempting to do so, courts delimit our thoughts, our self-concepts. We become what courts (and others) expect us to be. For we are pliant, and want to cooperate. And we are also, frequently, short-sighted, since we are willing to sacrifice what should remain dear. The jurispathic itch of courts diminishes our possibilities, discourages experimentation, and renders us dull. Courts have misplaced epistemic humility; the law *knows*.

**Some argue the common law is:**

G. DELAYED, MISDIRECTED, UNRESPONSIVE, HIDEBOUND, AND UNTAILORED. Five related complaints travel as an unwelcome troupe. Before the COVID pandemic, common law courts were **delayed**. Criminals waited their "speedy" trials, bumping civil trials out one to three years. During COVID, criminal trials, which promise face-to-face confrontation with one's accusers, slowed to a trickle. In some jurisdictions, civil matters were simply canceled. Everywhere in the United States, civil matters waited on criminal trials. Often, the courts cannot even estimate when civil matters will be heard. The result appears to be compelled settlement for those who cannot wait years to be heard.[287] In these approaches, courts are **misdirected**. The purpose of courts is to resolve disputes, in the hope that offering a ready forum for resolution, disputants will be diverted from self-help violence. But common law courts seem **unresponsive** to the dilemmas they are creating by dilatory processing. The courts appear to be of a mind to offer a feeble promise: "we will just work harder" as a solution to sluggish case processing. Promises, even earnest ones, have not, and cannot, resolve this problem. We require a different theory.

In due process, the process that is due is what process the courts prescribe. Due process could be abbreviated, moved online, timelines shortened, presentations delimited, and other such tinkering concepts, all the while offering notice and an opportunity to be heard by an impartial decision-maker. But to make such changes, common law courts would have to decide to be responsive. And they decline that task. For these courts are **hidebound**. Their traditions matter more than their task.[288] Their customs

---

[287] Those who cannot wait are often lower-income citizens. These income-strapped complainants take token settlements rather than none.

[288] The high courts are often incapable of frankness about their own work. My least favorite practice in this regard is "confining a case to its facts." Karl Llewellyn says of this practice: "In the extreme form this results in what is known as expressly 'confining the case to its particular facts.' This rule holds only of redheaded Walpoles in pale magenta Buick cars. And when you find this said of a past case you know that in effect it has been overruled. Only a convention, a somewhat absurd convention, prevents flat overruling in such instances. It seems to be felt as definitely improper to state that the court in a prior case was

seem to them inescapable. Nine people in Olympia (that is, the Supreme Court of Washington) could fix these problems in an afternoon.[289] But they will not.

---

wrong, peculiarly so if that case was in the same court which is speaking now. It seems to be felt that this would undermine the dogma of the infallibility of courts. So lip service is done to that dogma, while the rule which the prior court laid down is disemboweled. The execution proceeds with due respect, with mandarin courtesy." Llewellyn, *The Bramble Bush*, 72-73. When a court wishes to stay the course, it claims the doctrine of *stare decisis* prevents diversion. When a court wishes to diverge, it confines the predecessor rule to its facts, or overrules, or, with studied ignorance, pretends to know nothing of the precedent. The term "inapposite" graces many such pages.

The Supreme Court of the United States (SCOTUS) denies such pussyfooting. Its "decisions remain binding precedent until [it] see[s] fit to reconsider them, regardless of whether subsequent cases have raised doubts about their continued vitality." *Hohn v. United States*, 524 U.S. 236, 252-253 (1998). The Supreme Court does not overrule prior opinions sub silentio." Cited in *OneAmerica Votes v. State*, 23 Wn. App 2d 951, 977 (2022).

[289] As SCOWA "fixed" the limited license legal technician program: an axe in an afternoon, without notice, without public input, without due process. But all of this sound and fury would be only another gusher of tinkering.

To put the lie to my assertion, SCOWA has recently approved a nice piece of tinkering (November 14, 2022). It adopted a form of simplified informal trial in family law matters (GR40: Informal Family Law Trials (IFLT)). In such trials, which are undertaken only upon the consent of both parties, cross-examination is excluded (though the judge may ask questions). The rules of evidence are set aside. The bench determines what evidence is admitted, and what weight to give whatever may be admitted. The parties waive appeal rights as to such evidentiary decisions. The result is a bench actively involved in developing the record of these informal trials, as might the bench in a civil-law regime in its inquisitorial mode.

Civil-law adjudication differs significantly from the common law trial. "Modern codes of civil procedure stress that judicial proceedings are public and controlled by the parties. Party control, however, is somewhat tempered by the extensive power of the civil-law judge to supervise and shape the fact-finding process and by the role of the public prosecutor in private actions. In contrast to the progressive unfolding of evidence—under near complete control of the parties—that occurs through the discovery process in the American common-law system, there is no formal civil-law counterpart to discovery. Nor, in most cases, is there any single event that the common-law lawyer would recognize as a trial. Instead, a civil-law civil action is a continuing series of meetings, hearings, and written communications through which evidence is introduced and evaluated, testimony is taken, and motions are made and decided. Initial pleadings are quite general, and the issues are defined at the direction of the judge as the proceedings progress. The civil process tends to be conducted primarily in writing, and the concept of a highly concentrated and dramatic "trial" in the common-law sense is not emphasized. Thus, a lawyer who wishes to question a witness must first submit to the judge and opposing counsel "articles of proof" describing the scope of the potential questions. The witness will be questioned at a later hearing at which the judge will typically ask the questions, often framing or reformulating the issues raised in the case. Cross-examination is uncommon. Instead, opposing counsel's role is to make certain that the record summary of the testimony is complete and correct. The judge supervises the collection of evidence and preparation of a summary of the record on which a decision will be based. Since there is no "pretrial" phase of the proceeding, the evidence is not "discovered" in the sense understood by common-law lawyers. Instead, the parties submit proposed evidence to the judge in writing or at oral hearings, and the judge delivers rulings concerning the relevance and admissibility of evidence. Admissible evidence is presented, for the first and only time, in the final hearing that constitutes the trial. Many of the differences between the common-law and civil-law judicial process may be attributed to the absence of the civil jury." Apple and Deyling, *A Primer on the Civil-Law System*, Federal Judicial Center, 1995: 27.

One wonders if adoption of GR40 is not SCOWA's wan admission that the common law trial is unsuited for adjudicating at least some civil matters.

So, the need for speed and conceptual-procedural inflexibility lead to cookie-cutter solutions. The bench says, "This case seems something like this sort of situation, so I will ignore the case oddities and impose a maybe-good-enough solution."[290] Though the client came to the court to have their matter heard by an intelligent decision-maker, most clients slog down the courthouse steps at day's end having had their round case hammered into a square slot. And they complain, as well they should, that the common law is sub-responsive and **untailored**. If law were clothing, courts stick every litigant with sparse off-the-rack attire.

**Some argue the common law is:**

H. ANTI-COMMUNAL AND PATHOGENIC. Some complain that common law jurisprudence is **anti-communal**. The common law system styles its constituents as individuals. General concerns lack an identifiable complainant, and those suffering common injury lack standing to be heard. Common law courts have sunk all their attention into the bar room brawl as a model of the sorts of injuries that can be suffered. A struck B. C shot D. Such are cognizable injuries, deserving attention. But industries pouring tons of poisons into the atmosphere is punted to legislative or administrative remedies. Such injuries are not justiciable (though environmental laws attempt to make them so). In English heritage countries, common law's essential individualism renders it neglectful of or hostile toward concerns of human communality.

Fixation on justiciability as conflict between individual contestants promotes the adversarial severity of American courts. Jerome Frank said: "I suggest, as an additional partial explanation of the perpetuation of the excessive fighting method of trials, both civil and criminal, the belief in uncontrolled competition, of unbridled individualism."[291] Citizens do not exist with and for one another; we live in competition and latent (or not so latent) antipathy. "If you prosper, I decline. I am going to keep an eye on you," we say, deep in our soul, just as the court system has taught us to say, to feel, to think.

Social psychologist Jonathan Haidt criticizes his own field of study for its focus on WEIRD people. The WEIRD are Western, educated, industrialized, rich, and democratic.[292] Such persons are a tiny fraction of the human population. Study of them yields results of limited applicability. Haidt

---

[290] Is this not the essence of precedent?

[291] Frank, *Courts on Trial*, 92.

[292] Haidt, *The Righteous Mind*, 112.

adopts the pluralistic tripartite ethic of his post-graduate mentor, Richard Shweder. Three ethics better describe the people served by schools and legal systems, and better situates them in a moral context they might recognize.

> The ethic of *autonomy* is based on the idea that people are, first and foremost, autonomous individuals with wants, needs, and preferences. People should be free to satisfy these wants, needs and preferences as they see fit, and so societies develop moral concepts such as rights, liberty, and justice, which allow people to coexist peacefully without interfering too much in each other's projects. . . .
>
> The ethic of *community* is based on the idea that people are, first and foremost, members of larger entities such as families, teams, armies, companies, tribes, and nations. These larger entities are more than the sum of the people who compose them; they are real, they matter, and they must be protected. People have an obligation to play their assigned roles in these entities. Many societies therefore develop moral concepts such as duty, hierarchy, respect, reputation, and patriotism. . . .
>
> The ethic of *divinity* is based on the idea that people are, first and foremost, temporary vessels within which a divine soul has been implanted. People are not just animals with an extra serving of consciousness; they are children of God and should behave accordingly. The body is a temple, not a playground. . . . Many societies therefore develop moral concepts such as sanctity and sin, purity and pollution, elevation and degradation.[293]

The individualism of courts and legal theory distort the worldviews of many, even in American pluralism. Simply, courts insist that everyone has to be WEIRD. Absent a broader perspective, court resolutions will fail because they seem so very strange to those immersed in community ethics or divine ethics.[294] And, frankly, those dissenters are almost everyone. Hence, the court system suffers broad disrepute, since it insists on an individualist ethic many cannot conceive and have no wish to learn.

Nevertheless, our courts tell us that when we have a conflict, we should conduct a simulated *mano a mano* brawl to resolve the problem, then most of us adopt a fisticuffs approach to conflict resolution. The brawling approach of courts comes at a price. Americans suffer deep anxiety and much

---

[293] Haidt, *The Righteous Mind*, 116-117.

[294] Jerold Auerbach said: "Litigation is the all-purpose remedy that American society provides to its aggrieved members. But as rights are asserted, combat is encouraged; as the rule of law binds society, legal contentiousness increases social fragmentation. Auerbach, *Justice Without Law?*, 10.

depression. We live, so we are told, in a culture rife with brawls.[295] Our politicians imagine themselves hired to do war with other legislators. Even our pastimes simulate tribal bloodsport. So, "Keep your fists up. Be ready to strike." Our alert system strains. Stress bubbles. We suffer the attendant ulcers and cancers and panics and lethargy. For courts do not seek merely to ameliorate these unavoidable sequels to fight or flight hormones. Common law courts are a cause of these dysfunctions. The courts are **pathogenic**.[296] Encounters with the court system are bad for clients,[297] worse for judges and court personnel, and terrible for attorneys.[298] The professional toll is exacted in ulcers and alcoholism and depressions and suicides and cynicism. Courts indulge the worst instincts of people in conflict; courts say, "Come. Fight here. It's what we do." Concerning this problem, Learned Hand was optimistic: "And still at times I can have the hope that in America time may at length mitigate our fierce individualism, may teach us the knowledge we so sorely lack that each of us must learn to realize himself more in our communal life whose formal expression is and as I believe will continue to be the law."[299]

---

[295] Our common law courts recognize the prevalence of conflicts in the substrate of our sociality. They, however, seem to ignore the courts' generative role in creating that hostile environment.

[296] "Pathogenic" means "a cause of disease."

[297] Psychiatrist, Larry H. Strasburger, says: "Despite our awareness that lawsuits are an everyday phenomenon, few psychotherapists or litigants are truly prepared for the forces of aggression that are released and sanctioned by our judicial system. Although it may be that we have exchanged swords and cudgels for subpoenas and depositions, an aura of combat continues to hover about the judicial process, and combat produces casualties." Strasburger, "The Litigant-Patient: Mental Health Consequences of Civil Litigation," 203. Strasburger cites a study which finds "those patients who fare best emotionally with litigation are those who (1) set realistic goals; (2) maintain a sense of control of the litigation process; (3) seek out adequate support from at least one significant source (family, therapist, peers, attorney); (4) appreciate and focus energy on restoring the original equilibrium of their lives independent of the litigation process; and (5) adequately acknowledge and grieve the losses inevitably involved even when the litigation has a favorable outcome." Strasburger, "The Litigant-Patient: Mental Health Consequences of Civil Litigation," 206. I dissent from Strasburger. Those litigation clients who fare best emotionally are those whose attorneys share bluntly with clients the risks and expense of litigation (both financial and emotional), and induce their clients to find other ways to resolve their conflicts.

[298] The legal profession is known for the exceptional depression, substance abuse, burnout, secondary PTSD, and suicidal ideation of its practitioners. Detailing these assorted maladies exceeds the scope of this work.

SCOWA has said, in the context of evaluating a bar admission candidate: "Moreover, by falsely equating Stevens' mental health history with his current moral character and fitness to practice law, the Board majority strongly discourages current and future attorneys, and judges from disclosing and seeking treatment for mental health issues, putting them at increased risk for harmful behaviors that are known to plague the legal profession, ranging from alcohol and drug abuse to suicide." *Bar Application of Stevens*, 200 Wn.2d 531, 559-560 (2022).

[299] Hand, "The Deficiencies of Trials to Reach the Heart of the Matter," 320.

I am not so sanguine as sage Hand. Laws aggregate the sentiments and prejudices of legislatures and judges in their mutual cooperations and disparagements. Laws can be, and are, abused (selective enforcement, overzealous career-mongering, lobbied provisions, bad faith impositions, and unintended consequences, to mention a few). Abuses, when conjoined with the live possibility of raw bad lawmaking, make law dangerous. Laws intrude. The data collected to enforce laws degrades privacy. Watched intimacy squirms and cools. Being spied and criticized stifles creativity and free-wheeling experimentation, a sad legacy of jurispathic courts. Non-legal dispute resolution breeds kerfuffle in courts. The legal system scratches that itch.[300] In short, law-driven government threatens human well-being.[301] Can we not fashion a theory of mutual relation less sorely hobbled?[302] Perhaps not. In the realm of law, we act as people of sorely-hobbled imagination.

**Some argue the common law is:**

I. MONETIZED. Some complain that the common law **monetizes** all manner of non-financial values. Law determines a cash award to compensate for negligent death of a child or spouse. The sum expresses symbolic atonement for loss. Such judgments award dollars for dreams crushed in breach of contracts. They assess child support as between parents, which children need attached attention from two or more parents ever so much more than financial clarity. Negative emotions, to courts, have a cash value. When outcomes cannot be monetized, courts may punt, claiming no remedy exists.[303] Judicial monetization teaches Americans a rude, untrue lesson: life boils down to money.

---

[300] "The relentless force of law in modern American society can be measured by its domination, and virtual annihilation, of alternative forms of dispute settlement." Auerbach, *Justice Without Law?*, 15.

[301] Oddly, given the sentiment of her book, one finds Sarah Conly agreeing, to a degree. See Conly, *Against Autonomy*, 148.

[302] Despite this parade of horribles concerning law, if one grants the existence of too many humans in anonymous societies, no reasonable alternative exists. I find much to admire in law. Intelligent people seek to solve important problems. American constitutional law brims with thoughtful adjustments and careful steps forward; tinkering for sure, but well-considered tinkering. A large number of attorneys appear to be genuinely good humans, for whom I cherish great admiration. That said, we can do better. Law could be better, if better focused on meaningful coexistence emerging from a commitment to amity.

[303] In an older Washington case (1929), *McCullough v. McCullough*, an unrelated child, Ruth McCullough, was taken into the home of a family friend, Mrs. Gaudette, on condition that the child be cared for and educated and made legatee of Mrs. Gaudette's Will, to receive the family home and fifty or sixty thousand dollars in cash as well. Ruth's father consented to this arrangement, because Mrs. Gaudette was wealthy, and he was not. Ruth's mother had died when Ruth was thirteen months old. All parties to the arrangement performed, with the exception that Ms. Gaudette failed to make the promised Will in favor of Ruth McCullough. After Mrs. Gaudette's death, Ruth brought suit on the contract to make a Will, breached by Mrs. Gaudette. Justice Main wrote for the court: "If a claim had been filed in probate and rejected and an action brought thereon, it would have been necessary to measure the damages in money.

Courts offer scant guidance to juries assessing such injuries.[304] Yet, this need not be so. Harry Zavos, professor emeritus at Loyola Law School Los Angeles, argues: "We give monetary awards for losses that have no market or monetary value. On the face of it, our system appears to be an irrational self-contradiction. Because there is no monetary scale or metric to which we can appeal to determine whether the amount of an award for any particular noneconomic harm is appropriate or correct, this practice is irrationally arbitrary."[305]

---

To state it otherwise, it would have been necessary to measure the love, affection, and companionship of the father when he gave up the custody and control and all association with his daughter and the love and affection and companionship which the respondent rendered to Mrs. Gaudette during her lifetime. For services of this character the law furnishes no measure of damages."

[304] Juries recently awarded judgments against InfoWars principal, Alex Jones, in the aggregate amount of $1.4 billion to compensate for his perfidy concerning the murders at Sandy Hook Elementary School. Jones inflamed his followers by repeatedly claiming that the Sandy Hook School massacre (Adam Lanza killed twenty school children, six staff, and himself) was a staged hoax, and the bereaved families were "crisis actors." Jones's followers inflicted death threats, harassment, and emotional distress on the families of Sandy Hook victims. By what standard did the jury assess the emotional grief of Sandy Hook parents and loved ones? What conversion metric guided their perceptions? Why was the judgment not one trillion dollars? Why not one thousand?

Zavos, says: "[I]f losses have no monetary equivalents, how can juries determine noneconomic damages that are not arbitrary? In the current system, juries are given no guidance when they are asked to translate nonmonetary losses into monetary damages awards." Zavos, "Monetary Damages for Nonmonetary Losses," 193. Zavos proposes that legislatures should create a scale from the worst nonmonetary losses to the least, on which scale juries would situate the facts of the case they hear. The legislature would assert values for injures at various points on the severity scale.

In 1980, the National Association of Insurance Commissioners offered such a severity scale for medical malpractice personal injuries, in nine degrees:

1. **Emotional only**: Fright, no physical damage.
2. **Temporary insignificant**: Lacerations, contusions, minor scars, rash. No delay.
3. **Temporary minor**: Infections, misset fracture, fall in hospital. Recovery delayed.
4. **Temporary major**: Burns, surgical material left, drug side-effect, brain damage. Recovery delayed.
5. **Permanent minor**: Loss of fingers, loss or damage to organs. Include non-disabling injuries.
6. **Permanent significant**: Deafness, loss of limb, loss of eye, loss of one kidney or lung.
7. **Permanent major**: Paraplegia, blindness, loss of two limbs, brain damage.
8. **Permanent grave**: Quadriplegia, severe brain damage, lifelong care or fatal prognosis.
9. **Death**.

Cited in Radin, "Compensation and Commensurability," 69. Note the demotion of emotional loss and suffering in the commissioners' rating, which is consistent with the *Restatement of Torts 2d.* To create such a severity scale, and to legislatively assign dollar values to various severities of injury, would be worthy tinkering, but, at root, nothing more than tinkering. The core problem lies in our disconnection from one another, our lack of community. We cannot value lives or capacities lost in our fellows, because we value these strangers with whom we live and work weakly, and their suffering cannot be measured in dollars. These strangers are ciphers drifting through a world with which we have wan connection, to which we cherish no heart-felt bond.

[305] Zavos, "Monetary Damages for Nonmonetary Losses," 200. Zavos, however, does not despair. He argues that a scale of severity, with associated dollar values, can rationalize noneconomic injury awards, if not intrinsically, then to the extent that legislative actions can render the outcomes a matter of societal consensus. Still, Zavos acknowledges that "there is no accepted metric—no social convention— regarding the relative severity of noneconomic losses." See Zavos, "Monetary Damages for Nonmonetary Losses," 270.

Zavos tells a winsome tale:

> [O]ne of my professors told a story of how the medieval theologian characterized the philosopher and how the philosopher characterized the theologian. The theologian described the philosopher as the blind man who goes into a pitch dark coal mine to find a black cat that is not there. The philosopher described the theologian as the blind man who goes into a pitch dark coal mine to find a black cat that is not there and comes [out] with a cat. I believe that asking juries—asking fact finders—to translate plaintiffs' noneconomic losses into the correct monetary amount, without providing them with a metric for that translation, is to put them in the position of the philosopher and the theologian. When the jury comes back with the award, it is like the theologian who comes back with the cat.[306]

There exists a substantial literature writhing on the hook of value incommensurability. Much ink is spilled over "value of statistical lives" (VSL), which calculations are driven by the finance of lost working hours. Despite these VSL machinations, the problem persists. One cannot value a life, an actual human existence, in all its wonder and defects, with coin. We all count more than our labors. Other values exist and could be brought to bear. In addition to money, Americans also measure their lives in other human necessities, such as food, drink, shelter, clothing, rest, membership, security, political office, political power, professional office, professional power, kinds of work, leisure, education, kinship, friendship, love, divine approbation, honor and recognition, and sex.[307] A jurisprudence of amity would add these many values to the pot of compensations which might redress social injury. For human life does not boil down to money.[308]

---

[306] Zavos, "Monetary Damages for Nonmonetary Losses," 272.

[307] Michael Walzer argues that human society, as a whole, distributes social goods to its members. Doing so well, without the domination of one sort of social good over others, constitutes complex equality. Each good has its own sphere, and ought not be translated into another, or dominated by another. Walzer takes complex equality to be the essence of a good society. Walzer, *Spheres of Justice*, 3-20. The common law takes money as its beacon, to the detriment of the many other values and compensations of any human society.

[308] Careful thinkers concur. Government's role exceeds that of referee in bloodsport. Chanakya, an Indian teacher whose life bridged the fourth to third centuries B.C., argued that States make happiness. He says that wisdom leads to elder worship, which leads to humility, which leads to control over sense experience, which leads to the State, which leads to wealth, which leads to righteousness, which leads to happiness. Chanakya, *Maxims of Chanakya*, 21-22. One has doubts whether happiness, in fact, results from Chanakya's linear assessment.

Margaret Jane Radin argues that monetizing nonmonetary losses makes some sense, but these are ultimately just incommensurate: "[T]here must be some other way to restore moral balance between the parties than by putting the parties into the status quo ante, which may be irretrievable, or by putting them

**Some argue the common law is:**

J. RACIST. Some complain that the common law is implicitly, and sometimes explicitly, **racist**. By "racism," I mean the theory that inherent traits of identifiable groups or ethnicities render some groups superior to others, and hence deserving of inegalitarian privileges.[309] Such concepts predate our republic, even our constituent colonies. Racist classifications infected the core of our federal constitution. That pestilence sickened America in the 1860s. Six hundred twenty thousand American lives lost, we amended our Constitution to remedy its misbegotten Philadelphia compromise with slave-holders. We proved loath, however, to revise our culture and censure its racist invective. There followed a century of subversive racial tilting, the Jim Crowe regime. The 1950s and 1960s brought remediating legal change. Yet it remains unclear to this day if we will choose to censure our racists and re-educate their children. Many resist. And the implicit racism that sullies the souls of most Americans eludes remedy.[310]

The Washington Supreme Court (SCOWA) and Washington Courts of Appeal (WACA) have, of late, been moderately aggressive in efforts to extirpate elements of implicit racism in Washington courts.

WACA explains explicit and implicit racism:

> Explicit racial bias is consciously held, although the biased person may not be willing to admit to having such bias if asked. . . . Implicit racial bias, however, primarily exists at an unconscious level, such that the biased person is unlikely to be aware that it even exists. This occurs because "[i]t is now socially unacceptable to be overtly racist. Yet we all live our lives with stereotypes that are ingrained and often unconscious, implicit biases endure despite our best efforts to eliminate them."[311]

---

into a state equivalent in value to the status quo ante, which may be unachievable given the fact of incommensurability. As my earlier description of a core noncommodified conception of compensation reveals, I suggest that compensation can symbolize public respect for rights and public recognition of the transgressor's fault by requiring something important to be given up on one side and received on the other, even if there is no equivalence of value possible." Radin, "Compensation and Commensurability," 69. Surely, though, if no equivalence of value is possible, then any award must be in some measure arbitrary.

[309] I have cobbled together this definition from various dictionary entries.

[310] I find my own racism, oft tamped down, to be both elusive and resilient.

[311] *State v. Gutierrez*, 22 Wn.App.2d 815, 820 (2022) (citations omitted), citing *State v. Saintcalle*, 178 Wn.2d 34, 46 (2013). Cited in *State v. Behre*, 193 Wn.2d 647, 663 (2019). Robert Gutierrez challenged his convictions for robbery, assault, firearm possession, and felony harassment in part because at least one juror was biased. WACA ruled that, since the attorneys did not challenge the biased juror, that duty fell to the judge. Her failure to do so was abuse of discretion. A new trial was ordered.

The racism that marginalized groups experience has long found a friend in American common and statutory law. Richard Rothstein writes of residential racial segregation by law:

> Today's residential segregation in the North, South, Midwest, and West is not the unintended consequence of individual choices and of otherwise well-meaning law or regulation but of unhidden public policy that explicitly segregated every metropolitan area in the United States. The policy was so systematic and forceful that its effects endure to the present time. Without our government's purposeful imposition of racial segregation, the other causes—private prejudice, white flight, real estate steering, bank redlining, income differences, and self-segregation—still would have existed but with far less opportunity for expression. Segregation by intentional government action is not *de facto*. Rather is it what courts call *de jure*: segregation by law and public policy.[312]

With respect to indigenous Americans, the United States and its several constituent States have frequently ignored solemn treaty obligations,[313] or used legalities for bad faith interpretation and enforcement of treaties.[314] And it seems easier for SCOWA to wink at its own rules when the offender is indigenous.[315]

---

[312] Rothstein, *The Color of Law*, vii-viii.

[313] Think of Georgia's Cherokees being driven to their Trail of Tears. *Cherokee Nation v. Georgia*, 30 U.S. (5 Pet.) 1 (1831). For SCOTUS's complicity in stealing Indian lands, see *Johnson v. M'Intosh*, 21 U.S. 543 (1832).

In *Rabang*, WACA stated: "State and federal courts have a long and shameful history of ignoring tribal sovereignty, and we will not add to that history today." *Rabang v. Gilliland*, 23 Wn.App.2d 375, 386 (2022) (The Nooksack tribe evicted a disenrolled tribal tenant from off-reservation trust land; tenants appealed to Whatcom County Superior Court, which dismissed because the Nooksack Tribe, not Washington State, has subject matter jurisdiction).

[314] Consider WACA's admission: "We agree that much of the historical mistreatment of indigenous peoples in this country has been a product of racial prejudice." (page 263). (in a case finding the Cowlitz Tribe lost its aboriginal fishing rights for failure to get its treaty negotiations up to snuff 160 years ago). *State v. Simmons,* 23 Wn.App.2d 250 (2022).

[315] SCOWA recently declined to resentence a Black juvenile murderer on the basis of plenteous tortured reasoning (and the heinousness of the defendant's crime). The dissenters offered the better reasoning.

**Gonzalez Dissent**: "We must strive to do better as we know better. This effort is what marks the evolving standards of decency that mark the progress of a maturing society. . . . All too often we have decided that some disfavored group is not due the full protections our founding documents' promise. We have shrugged our robed shoulders at cruelties embodied in law. We know that trial judges in our own state are more likely to sentence harshly in election years." *State v. Anderson*, 200 Wn.2d 266, 293 (2022) (Gonzalez dissent) (citations omitted; internal quotation marks omitted).

**Yu Dissent**: "This is the court that once routinely affirmed criminal convictions of Native people for lawfully exercising their treaty-protected fishing rights, issuing opinions that were 'supported in theory by ingenious reasons and excuses' but 'based in fact upon the strength of the violator and the weakness of the violated.' . . . These opinions should be a sobering reminder that sometimes the State—and this court—

In the wake of George Floyd's murder (May 25, 2020) and the civil unrest that ensued through that hot, virus-laden summer, SCOWA issued a letter to the judiciary and the legal community, signed by all nine members. Their June 4, 2020, letter stated, in part:

> We continue to see racialized policing and the overrepresentation of black Americans in every stage of our criminal and juvenile justice systems. Our institutions remain affected by the vestiges of slavery: Jim Crow laws that were never dismantled and racist court decisions that were never disavowed.
>
> The legal community must recognize that we all bear responsibility for this on-going injustice, and that we are capable of taking steps to address it, if only we have the courage and the will. . . . [W]e must also recognize that this is not how a *justice* system must operate. Too often in the legal profession we feel bound by tradition and the way things have 'always' been. We must remember that even the most venerable precedent must be struck down when it is incorrect and harmful. The systemic oppression of black Americans is not merely incorrect and harmful; it is shameful and deadly.[316]

To its credit, SCOWA is taking its admonitions to heart. In case after case, the high court has been addressing racism in jury venires, in the selection of

---

can be 'the violator.'" *State v. Anderson*, 200 Wn.2d 266, 313 (2022) (Yu, concurring in dissent) (citations omitted).

[316] SCOWA letter to the judiciary and the legal community, dated June 4, 2020. This text was published in its entirety in *Dependency of Q.S.*, 22 Wn. App. 2d 586, 619-620 (2022). Of SCOWA's letter the WACA bench opined: "Presumably the protests surrounding the deaths of George Floyd, Breonna Taylor, and Ahmaud Arbery, the false accusations of Karens against African American males and the many corporate pronouncements supporting Black Lives Matter prompted the Supreme Court's letter. Many unnecessary deaths of Black men and women have occurred since the summer of 2020. . . . Nothing has changed in all Washington court levels since the Supreme Court's June 2020 open message about racial injustice. The racism inherent in our court system and the child dependency system continues." *Dependency of Q.S.*, 22 Wn. App. 2d 586, 617-619 (2022). So egregious is the racism of the criminal system, that SCOWA now takes judicial notice of its scourge. SCOWA has said: "It goes without saying that the criminal legal system disproportionately affects the poor and people of color . . . No citation to authority is necessary to support the claim that people of color are disproportionately targeted by the criminal justice system." *State v. Waits*, 200 Wn.2d 507, 521 (2022) (citations omitted). In my view, scrubbing Washington's legal system of its explicit and implicit racism will take decades (or longer). Racist attitudes have seeped to our innermost recesses and privacies.

juries,[317] in the language of criminal prosecutors and civil defense counsels,[318] and in deficient racial awareness from the bench.[319]

Justice Montoya-Lewis, for a unanimous SCOWA, said:

> Our legal system is based on the premise of judicial neutrality, procedural fairness, and equal treatment. We know our system has not lived up to its promises, even as we have affirmed our commitment to them. The legal system is made up of people—lawyers, judges, jurors, and others—and it shares in our human strengths and weaknesses. All of us have the capacity to push our system closer to the ideals and promises of justice; we also have the ability to continue to perpetuate harm. To turn our system squarely toward fairness requires conscious effort and honesty when we fail.
>
> Courts take a step toward achieving greater justice when the people who comprise them comprehend the legacy of injustices built into our legal systems, actively work to prevent racism before it occurs, and also recognize how our participation in these systems may reify them. One way judges can do so is to ensure that we bring reality into sharp focus in our legal analysis. When a new trial is sought on the ground that racial bias affected the verdict, the facts must be viewed through the lens of an objective observer who is aware "implicit, institutional, and unconscious biases, in addition to purposeful discrimination, have influenced jury verdicts in Washington State." *Berhe*, 193 Wn.2d at 665. In a hearing based on prima facie evidence that racial bias possibly affected the verdict, the court must presume that it did and the party seeking to uphold the verdict must prove how it did not. If they cannot prove that racial bias was not a factor, that verdict is fundamentally incompatible with substantial justice.[320]

---

[317] "Regardless of the defendant's race, studies have shown that '[d]iverse juries have longer deliberations, discuss more case facts, make fewer inaccurate statements, and members are more likely to correct inaccurate statements. In short, jury and jury pool diversity impact the equity and justice of jury verdicts. Wash. Sup. Ct. Gender & Just. Comm'n, 2021: How Gender and Race Affect Justice Now: Final Report 131 (Sept. 2021) (2021 Gender Justice Study)." *Personal Restraint of Rhone,* 23 Wn.App.2d 307, 324 (2022).

[318] Concerning civil defense counsel's use of subtle signals in speaking to a jury, SCOWA said: "Racial bias can affect a verdict even when it is not the product of intentional misconduct by the prevailing party or jury. 'Not all appeals to racial prejudice are blatant. Perhaps more effective but just as insidious are subtle references. . . . Coded 'dog whistle' language impermissibly allows the speaker to appeal to racial bias and then excuse that behavior by arguing that they did not intend to say anything racist. *Henderson v. Thompson*, 200 Wn.2d 417, 432-433 (2022) (citation omitted).

[319] For a judicial spanking, see *Henderson v. Thompson*, 200 Wn.2d 417, 440 (2022).

[320] *Henderson v. Thompson*, 200 Wn.2d 417, 445-446 (2022). The *Behre* citation is *State v. Berhe*, 193 Wn.2d 647 (2019).

*Behre*'s brave rule flips the usual regime on its head, and may generate a great host of retrials. Perhaps there exists no less disruptive remedy to evils so deeply entrenched. Judging by my own heart, some elements of the problem are intractable.

Of purging racial bias in juries, Mikah K. Thompson argues that racial bias in juries is so prevalent that nothing short of a truth-and-reconciliation process[321] will suffice for commencing repair:

> Social science research has made clear that a majority of Americans carry some level of subconscious or implicit bias against racial minorities and that this bias manifests itself in the application of racial stereotypes. These stereotypes can influence many aspects of the jury's functions. Until courts and legislatures are willing to craft safeguards that will address the impact of bias head-on, the jury system will continue to be infiltrated with bias.
>
> I believe that the first step in ridding the jury system of racial bias is to tell the truth about the prevalence and effect of bias. . . . I acknowledge that these truths may make us uncomfortable, but the truth and reconciliation process tells us that we can heal only after we have sat in the discomfort.[322]

*De jure* segregation (more plainly, government racism) will test us. Implicit racism divides us, not only politically, but also in our deep personal recesses. Rothstein concludes his volume on government racism: "Undoing the effects of *de jure* segregation will be incomparably difficult. To make a start, we will first have to contemplate what we have collectively done and, on behalf of our government, accept responsibility."[323] That would be a beginning. The harder work lingers in our psyches.

---

[321] I describe the truth and reconciliation process in the next chapter.

[322] Thompson, "Bias on Trial," 1244-1245. Mikah K. Thompson is an associate professor of law at University of Missouri-Kansas City.

[323] Rothstein, *The Color of Law*, 217. Unfortunately, de jure discrimination does not end at racial and ethnic bias. Laws are used to exclude citizens experiencing homelessness. WACA, in a case involving discriminatory zoning in Puyallup, Washington, says: "We recognize that local governments, when faced with a requirement that they exercise discretion as to whether and how to site day use centers and overnight shelters for people experiencing homelessness, may be tempted to make the locality an unappealing place for them to settle. In recent years, many local governments have shifted toward policies that penalize people experiencing homelessness, perhaps hoping that they will choose another place to live. For example, a national survey found that between 2006 and 2016, the number of 'city-wide bans on camping in public increased by 69 percent; city-wide bans on begging increased by 43 percent; city-wide bans on standing around increased by 88 percent; and bans on sitting or lying down increased by 52 percent.' Sara K. Rankin, *Punishing Homelessness*, 22 New Crim. L. Rev. 99, 109-110 (2019). Bans on sleeping in vehicles increased by 143 percent in that same period. *Id.* At 110." The conservative super-majority at the United States Supreme Court (2024) has been no help whatsoever, and has re-authorized de jure discrimination against people who are homeless.

**Some argue the common law is:**

K. MISOGYNISTIC.[324] Some complain that the common law is sexist in a way best described as **misogynistic**. Blatant sexism[325] may be in retreat, especially as women command a larger role in the cogs of law. We see emphasis (feeble though it may be) on equal pay for equal work, and efforts to believe female victims of male violence, and promoting women to pinnacle corporate roles. Women dominate the Washington Supreme Court.[326] Women occupy a more potent position in American culture than a generation ago—not equal, but less unequal.[327]

Still, many women find their place in society skewed and diminished. Some complaints strike at deep roots of common law. Kate Manne calls the moral arm of sexist thought "misogyny," to mince no words.[328] In Manne's view, misogyny is not so much a psychological state as a social control function.[329] Misogyny

---

[324] I and my retrograde gender views were introduced to Kate Manne, whose bias studies figure prominently in this section, by Sue Morgan, a friend and colleague, in the course of our Witless Protection Program readings and discussions. I thank her, for helping change my mind, if not my many ingrained habits.

[325] The word "misogyny" is of recent provenance (mid-seventeenth century), but its sentiment is not. Aristotle said: "[T]he male is by nature superior, and the female inferior; and the one rules, and the other is ruled; this principle, of necessity, extends to all mankind." Aristotle, *Politics*, 17. John Stuart Mill, before English women received the right to vote, countered: "That the principle which regulates the existing social relations between the two sexes—the legal subordination of one sex to the other—is wrong in itself, and now one of the chief hindrances to human improvement; and that it ought to be replaced by a principle of perfect equality, admitting no power or privilege on the one side nor disability on the other." Mill, *The Subjection of Women*, 133. Of Mill's text, Catharine McKinnon asserted: "John Stuart Mill's *The Subjection of Women*, published in 1869, remains the most compelling, sympathetic, subtle, perceptive, consistent, coherent, complex, and complete statement of the liberal feminist argument for women's equality." McKinnon, *Toward a Feminist Theory of the State*, 41.

[326] In October 2022, SCOWA comprises seven women and two men. All those SCOWA justices who ran for re-election in 2022 were unopposed.

[327] Perhaps we regress toward blatant and legal sexism, given the SCOTUS decision to unwind *Roe* and its progeny, tossing the fate of reproductive freedom into snarling pit of State legislative dogfights. In some States, women appear to be headed into that dark place where an ability to bear children precludes alternative or additional identities a woman might adopt. To SCOTUS Justice Alito, the womb, not the brain, would seem the preeminent female organ. It remains to be seen whether the women of America (who are its voting majority) will repudiate the high court's excursion into religious imposition and the party that supports theological prohibitions.

[328] Manne asserts that misogyny is not merely a psychological defect of individuals, which she calls the "naïve conception." Rather, misogyny inheres in societal and legal norms, and concerns our togetherness, more than our aloneness. To Manne, misogyny is less an opinion than a subliminal expectation. Misogyny does not entail that one hates all women, but rather that one hates some women reliably. Manne, *Down Girl*, 32, 49.

[329] Manne, *Down Girl*, 20.

serves "to uphold patriarchal order."[330] She styles the thought forms of misogyny as psychic strangulation, which suffering leads some women to self-silence. The ensuing self-preserving acquiescence of females Manne calls "smothering."[331] Patriarchal order, having vanquished its opponent, seizes the narrative and quashes alternative stories. The threatened patriarchal male growls: "The story will be what I insist, or else."

Near the essence of misogyny, according to Manne, are asymmetrical moral support roles.[332] Men are "tacitly deemed entitled to rely for nurturing, comfort, care, and sexual, emotional, and reproductive labor" from the women in their worlds. Women are obligated to provide "feminine coded goods and services"[333] to men, and suffer if they fail to do so. Social censure for failing to provide such resources to men abounds (allegations of lack of caring, unwarranted power grabs, and lack of moral trustworthiness). At the fringes, violence, even lethal assaults, are a potential sanction. Disparagements slash like swords, sundering the self-confidence of allegedly power-hungry, corrupt, self-absorbed women.[334]

---

[330] Manne, *Down Girl*, 13. Manne thinks sexism is one of many systems of domination. Others are racism, xenophobia, classism, ageism, ableism, homophobia, transphobia, and so forth. I would add assaults upon those who are homeless or obese.

[331] Manne, *Down Girl*, 3-4.

[332] Manne, *Down Girl*, xv. Recognition of this asymmetry in provision of social goods is not new. George Bernard Shaw, in 1891, said: "An overwhelming majority of such marriages as are not purely *de convenance* are entered into for the gratification of that [sexual] appetite either in its crudest form or veiled only by those idealistic illusions which the youthful imagination weaves so wonderfully under the stimulus of desire, and which older people indulgently laugh at. This being so, it is not surprising that our society, being directly dominated by men, comes to regard Woman, not as an end in herself like Man, but solely as a means of ministering to his appetite. The ideal wife is one who does everything that the ideal husband likes, and nothing else. Now to treat a person as a means instead of an end is to deny that person's right to live. And to be treated as a means to such an end as sexual intercourse with those who deny one's right to live is insufferable to any human being. Woman, if she dares face the fact that she is being so treated, must either loathe herself or else rebel. . . . The sum of the matter is that unless Woman repudiates her womanliness, her duty to her husband, to her children, to society, to the law, and to everyone but herself, she cannot emancipate herself. . . . A whole basketful of ideals of the most sacred quality will be smashed by the achievement of equality for women and men." Shaw, *The Quintessence of Ibsenism*, 23,26, in a chapter called "The Womanly Woman."

A critic, in the rag *Truth*, snipes at Shaw (and Ibsen): "The sexless. . . The unwomanly woman, the unsexed females, the whole army of unprepossessing cranks in petticoats. . . Educated and muck-ferreting dogs. . . Effeminate men and male women. . . They all of them—men and women alike—know that they are doing not only a nasty but an illegal thing. . . . A wave of human folly." Shaw, *The Quintessence of Ibsenism*, 54.

[333] Manne, *Down Girl*, 130.

[334] The "incel" extremist fringe asserts that their involuntary celibacy (hence, the tag "incel") derives from unjustifiably privileged women refusing to engage sexually with incels. Incel ideology asserts that incels are doomed to sexless existence due to their genetic shortchange in life's lottery. Fatalism leads to despair, which incels call the "black pill." Some incels advocate rape and murder of Stacys (sexually active, attractive women). Department of Homeland Security and the Secret Service judge incel misogynistic extremism a domestic terror threat. The Southern Poverty Law Center places incel fora in the "male supremacist ecosystem" and lists such as hate groups. See https://en.wikipedia.org/wiki/Incel. A hero to

These emotional weapons "police and enforce social roles, and extract moral goods and resources from such women."[335]

Misogyny, according to Manne, swings a moral hammer in support of legal and cultural sexism.

> Sexism should be understood primarily as the 'justificatory' branch of a patriarchal order, which consists in ideology that has the overall function of *rationalizing* and *justifying* patriarchal social relations. . . . So sexist ideology will often consist in assumptions, beliefs, theories, stereotypes, and broader cultural narratives that represent men and women as importantly different in ways that, if true and known to be true, or at least likely, would make rational people more inclined to support and participate in patriarchal social arrangements. . . . Overall, sexism and misogyny share a common purpose—to maintain or restore a patriarchal social order.[336]

Misogyny supports "exonerating narratives," by which Manne means stories that subtly (or not so subtly) stoke concern for the well-being of men accused by women.[337] The tale of male misbehavior mutates. The perpetrator resisted urges poorly, but understandably. His female accuser complains from ignoble motives.

---

incels, Elliot Rodger murdered several women and men in a Santa Barbara rampage (Isla Vista killings of 2014) which Rodger styled as the Day of Retribution for his lifelong sexual drought. Rodger's autobiography/manifesto (*My Twisted World: The Story of Elliot Rodger*) declares that he is a living god, superior to the human race. Women plague the earth, and must be quarantined, then starved to death, as a pestilence. In Rodger's imagination, sexuality would be abolished over time, and the few retained breeding females left would be hidden in a baby lab. https://www.documentcloud.org/documents/1173808-elliot-rodger-manifesto.

[335] Manne, *Down Girl*, xvi.

[336] Manne, *Down Girl*, 79-80. To complain about cultural and legal impediments to female aspiration is well-warranted. Within the bounds of what is ethical, women and girls should be free to do whatever they want whenever they are able. I detect in some feminist reasoning revulsion at the idea that there exist biological and behavioral differences between men-boys and women-girls. Manne, in critique of patriarchal sexism, puts this line of reasoning thus: "If certain social differences between men and women could hardly be otherwise, then is it worth the effort to try to combat them?" (at page 79). She thinks that the effort is warranted. And I agree. However, as Simon de Beauvoir said: "Woman simply *are not* men." de Beauvoir, *the Second Sex*, xlii. In an earlier work, I have listed a series of purported facts which, if borne out, would indicate that women and men are indeed substantially different at their biological and behavioral root. I argue: "Men are not women. Women are not men. Neither are hermaphrodites. As a species, we are sexed. Neither sex can survive independently of the other. We dwell in sexual complementarity. Feminist identity politics has bowdlerized all conversation about our sexual dimorphism. That we are sexed seems, to this author, both patent and worth deliberation. That, at the margins, our sexuality and genders are multiple, mixed, and muddled also seems patent. With humans, one size does not fit all. Nor one sex. We should talk about our differences. To fail to do so is both silly and, possibly dangerous." Lancaster, *Cull: Choosing Well*, 160. See Section 6.6.7 of *Cull* (pp. 257-260) for the full, though brief, discussion.

[337] Manne, *Down Girl*, 179.

When it comes to giving evidence in courts, misogyny authorizes "testimonial injustice." Subordinate group members lack credibility as compared to higher ranked individuals. Accusing women fail to achieve the "epistemic status of *knowers*."[338] The accuser labors under a presumption that she is less competent and less trustworthy than she ought to be, and she should, therefore, not be believed. For a jury (or the public), the mental labor required to confront one's patriarchal milieu dwarfs the moral evasions demanded to disbelieve one credible accuser. Hence, the socially-disabled victim is disparaged, then repudiated.

In its most transparent exonerating story, misogyny expresses itself in what Manne calls "himpathy." Men who prey sexually are presumed, even by many women, to be good "at heart." The rapist is credited over against female accusers, for which Manne coins the term "herasure."[339] The alchemical agent of this odd role reversal is "excessive sympathy sometimes shown toward male perpetrators of sexual violence."[340] At law, this sometimes manifests in trials which blame the rape victim and discount the rapist's predation. Manne asserts we are so immersed in misogynistic murk that we, as a culture, have difficulty perceiving our anti-woman bent. For misogyny is banal, hiding in plain sight, ubiquity so familiar as to have grown invisible. Just as the anti-Semitism of Adolf Eichmann was invisible to him (and many others), though he kept the *Sondersüge* (special trains) jammed with Jews headed to smokes of Auschwitz-Birkenau. This, Hanah Arendt called the "banality of evil."[341] In the end, Kate Manne is

---

[338] Manne, *Down Girl*, 186.

[339] Manne, *Down Girl*, 209.

[340] Manne, *Down Girl*, 197. The confirmation hearings of SCOTUS Associate Justice Brett Cavanaugh come to mind. Accusation of attempted rape against the jurist failed to derail his appointment. Cavanaugh received **himpathy**. Christine Blasey Ford suffered **herasure**.

[341] Arendt, Eichmann in Jerusalem, 252. Arendt says: "Adolf Eichmann went to the gallows with great dignity. He had asked for a bottle of red wine and had drunk half of it. . . . He walked the fifty yards from his cell to the execution chamber calm and erect, with his hands bound behind him. . . . He was in complete command of himself, nay, he was more: he was completely himself. Nothing could have demonstrated this more convincingly than the grotesque silliness of his last words. He began by stating emphatically that he was a *Gottgläubiger*, to express in common Nazi fashion that he was no Christian and did not believe in life after death. He then proceeded: 'After a short while, gentlemen, *we shall all meet again*. Such is the fate of all men. Long live Germany, long live Argentina, long live Austria. *I shall not forget them.*' In the face of death, he had found the cliché used in funeral oratory. Under the gallows, his memory played him the last trick; he was 'elated' and he forgot that this was his own funeral. It was as though in those last minutes he was summing up the lesson that this long course in human wickedness had taught us—the lesson of the fearsome, word-and-thought-defying *banality of evil*. . . .

The trouble with Eichmann was precisely that so many were like him, and that the many were neither perverted nor sadistic, that they were, and still are, terribly and terrifyingly normal. . . . that this new type of criminal . . . commits his crimes under circumstances that make it well-nigh impossible for him to know or to feel that he is doing wrong." Arendt, *Eichmann in Jerusalem*, 252, 276.

not hopeful about making inroads against misogyny: She is "pretty pessimistic about reasoning with people to get them to take misogyny seriously."[342]

So, some find both positive law, and its attendant patriarchal culture, a misogynistic embarrassment and an unexpunged taint upon the common law.

**Some argue the common law is:**

L. Epistemologically Naïve. The common law derives from medieval England. Naïve realism prevailed at the common law's inception.[343] Epistemologically, to the naïve realist, things are as they seem, creating perceptions common to all adequate observers. Common sense perceptions put the perceiver in direct touch with the thing observed, and so are not only reliable, but further inquiry is both unnecessary and possibly dangerous. To the common sense realist, disputes about perceptions emerge from disregard for careful inspection. Truth, once ferreted, is unitary and intrinsically persuasive.

Adversarial trial theory is rooted in common sense realism. Truth is out there, to be grasped. But we are muddled about what truth is and where it hides. So courts toss out unreliable evidence and inference. From behind the smoky cinders of torched uncertainty, Truth peeks out for all to behold. Judgment is rendered. If twelve jurors (or one trained judge) agree concerning a matter, how could that perception be wrong? Such is the truth about truth in the common law.

Empirical studies of the psychology of judges and jurors paint a picture less sanguine. Realism proves to be **epistemologically naïve**. Jurors make up their minds almost instantly, even before evidence arrives. From the trial that straggles far behind juror intuitions, panel members seek points supporting their freshly-minted certainties. Demeanor of lawyers presenting a case counts as

---

342 Manne, *Down Girl*, 290. And yet, Manne's book induced just such reflection and consideration in me.

343 The common sense realism of which I speak is the notion of untrained people that what they perceive is what exists. This perspective came under criticism from thinkers who doubted the reliability of human perception, and had much to say about its flaws. Generally, these critics relied more heavily on ideas as the backbone of understanding. Common sense realism, or naïve realism, was defended by Scottish philosophers, as part of the Scottish Enlightenment in the 18th century. Responding to the skeptical and paradoxical in the work of Locke, Berkeley, and Hume, Scots such as Thomas Reid and Dugald Stewart resisted. Reid said: "If there are certain principles, as I think there are, which the constitution of our nature leads us to believe, and which we are under a necessity to take for granted in the common concerns of life, without being able to give a reason for them — these are what we call the principles of common sense; and what is manifestly contrary to them, is what we call absurd." Scottish common sense realism is often criticized as a philosophy committed to opposing intellectual change of any sort. Common sense realism has not well-weathered the onslaught of scientific studies of cognition, perception, and fundamental physics.

much as evidence.[344] In the end jury trials are contests of perception, besmirched by copious bullying behind the sealed jury room door.[345]

Carrie Menkel-Meadow[346] finds the American approach to jurisprudential fact-finding problematical. She says:

> Binary, oppositional presentation of facts in dispute are not the best way for us to learn the truth; polarized debate distorts the truth, leaves out important information, simplifies complexity, and obfuscates rather than clarifies. More significantly, some matters—mostly civil, but occasionally even criminal, cases—are not susceptible to a binary (i.e., right/wrong, win/lose) conclusion or solution. . . . Modern life presents us with complex problems often requiring complex and multifaceted solutions. Courts, with what I have called their 'limited remedial imaginations,' may not be the best institutional settings for resolving some of the disputes that we continue to put before them.[347]

One hears in Menkel-Meadow's critique echoes of the many critics of common law previously described. Ultimately, Menkel-Meadow's critique of the common law is epistemological.

> If late-twentieth century learning has taught us anything, it is that truth is illusive, partial, interpretable, dependent on the characteristics of the knowers as well as the known, and, most importantly, complex. In short, there may be more than just two sides to every story. The binary nature of the adversary system and its particular methods and tactics often may thwart some of the essential goals of any legal system. [I] argue that our epistemology has changed sufficiently in this era of poststructural, postmodern knowledge so that we need to reexamine the attributes of the adversary system as the 'ideal type' of a legal system, and also reexamine the practice based on the premises of that system.[348]

---

[344] Montaigne (16th century philosopher) said: "We must shun lawsuits . . . . I . . . will never, if I can help it, place myself in the power of a man who can dispose of my head, when my honor and life depend on the skill of a lawyer more than my innocence." Cited in Frank, *Courts on Trial*, 40.

[345] Learned Hand said: "Let us at the outset disabuse ourselves of the notion that we are engaged in an impartial and disinterested inquiry into objective truth. We have no right to the fine detachment of spirit of the scientist." Hand, "The Deficiencies of Trials to Reach the Heart of the Matter," 310.

[346] Carrie Menkel-Meadow is a Distinguished Professor of Law at University of California, Irvine School of Law. She previously taught at UCLA and Georgetown. Menkel-Meadow received the Outstanding Scholar Award from the American Bar Foundation in 2018. She primarily teaches out-of-court processes for dispute resolution.

[347] Menkel-Meadow, "Trouble with Adversary System in a Post-Modern, Multicultural World," 6-7.

[348] Menkel-Meadow, "Trouble with Adversary System in a Post-Modern, Multicultural World," 5.

To summarize Menkel-Meadow, the common law's approach to truth fails because truth is not the sort of beast our jurisprudence imagines. Truth is not simple, not transparent, not unitary, not dimorphic, not universal, not free-standing, and (very possibly) not accessible to trials—jury or bench.[349] Generally, what we have learned about Truth is that one should rid the term of the capital "T" and don a sackcloth of humility when assessing juridical fact-finding.[350] What gets presented in courtrooms is a kaleidoscope of fact fragments, themselves contested.[351] Juries do not get to truth. On a good day, a jury may arrive at conclusions that are not wholly counter-factual.

Knowledge evades humans readily. Truth is yet more slippery. The uncertainties of Truth have troubled thoughtful people from the early Greeks to yesterday's newsroom. How can one segregate random prejudice from reliable insights? Rene Descartes (17th century French polymath), in his *Discourse on Method*, retreated to an isolate mind frame, and sought to exclude all causes of uncertainty. He said that one should never rely on "truths" that may be corrupted by prejudice or by leaping to conclusions, but rather rely only on that which is so clear and distinct as to exclude all possibility of doubt. Using this blade, Descartes pared away all knowledge, except for one thought which he could not doubt. *Cogito ergo sum.* I think, therefore I exist.[352] Descartes's parsimonious sentiment pervades modernity. Human knowledge deserves critique; truth may be generally inaccessible. People are mostly deluded. Finding "truth" lies with careful explorations of deeply-thoughtful persons

---

[349] David Luban likens courtroom adversarial contests of truth to a scientific experiment: "A beam of invisible electrically charged particles—charge and origin unknown—travels through a distorting magnetic field of unknown strength, then through an opposite field of unknown, but probably different, strength. The beam strikes a detector of undeterminable reliability, from which we are supposed to infer the nature and location of the beam's source. That is the adversary system at its worst." Luban, "The Adversary System Excuse," 95.

[350] There would never again be a death sentence if juries understood the infirmities of their shared perceptions. Law has presumed much. Some of its worst excesses occur when it self-elevates, finding in the dictates of law concordance with the universe itself. Consider Cicero, who has drunk natural law to the dregs: "True law is right reason in agreement with nature, diffused among all men; constant and unchanging, it should call men to their duties by its precepts, and deter them from wrong doing by is prohibitions; and it never commands or forbids upright men in vain, while its rules and restraints are lost upon the wicked. To curtail this law is unholy, to amend it illicit, to repeal it impossible." Cicero, *de Re Publica*, Volume III, page 211.

[351] Frank, *Courts on Trial*, 86.

[352] From this bare nugget, Descartes proceeds to reconstruct all of his society, including its Christian tenets and prejudices. So much for a reliable epistemological blade. [One might equivocate for Descartes, noting that if the philosopher intended to retain his head and occupation, his theory may have been required to fudge in favor of the religious convictions of the powers that governed his society.]

investigating small slices of human experience. More expansive claims to Truth are bombast.[353]

But our common law and its sentiments emerge from an earlier, less analytic, more self-congratulatory philosophical era. Truth was abundant. You could get some right off the shelf for the asking. Courts sniffed stink in the epistemology of commoners. Evidentiary rules and exclusions ensued, by which judges sought to corral unbridled juror speculation and surmise. But common law clung to its core conviction: naïve realism. Things are as they seem. Even if they are not.

So, I conclude chapter two with a step back from immolations of critique. The many detractors of common law groan their complaints. Their chorus chants a dirge of lament, lingering upon deficiencies of common law theory and practice. Yet American courts slog along, not doing what needs to be done, but also not doing nothing. Judge's calendars are full. Court dockets are jammed. Many constructive aromas waft from their stew of strife. A high point in my monthly entertainment calendar is the arrival of the little green paperback which contains the newest batch of appellate court advance sheets.[354] In those booklets, redemptive talk, both legal and social, graces many pages.[355]

My appreciation for the efforts of appellate judges does not gainsay the critiques of common law I have surveyed. America's common law *needs* criticism. Karl Llewellyn said: "Criticize such a decision, attack it—yes; attack it with all vigor that is in us, as we attack the others that we doubt. *The courts need such attacks*. The court

---

353 Though I note that my preferred local television news team "Stands for Truth." And I tend to opine that there is something generally true about this tome's critique of common law.

354 Advance sheets are the final decisions of the three divisions of lower appeals courts in Washington, arriving approximately every other week,. These cases are presented in their final form, but in paperback. The decisions are not yet bound into the green hardback volumes one surveys in the backdrop of personal injury lawyer's television advertising.

355 I have less affection for the advance sheets of SCOWA (little yellow paperbacks). The nine Olympians often labor in the quicksand of our money vortex, and politics lie very near the surface of deliberations. Perhaps the Courts of Appeal have the easier job. Theirs task lies in stating and applying Washington's law. The really hard questions land before SCOTUS. To read the little green paperbacks is to loll at the feet of gifted educators, getting virtually-free tutelage. To plow through the SCOWA advance sheets troubles me, though I have appreciation for that court's recent interest in confronting racial prejudice in Washington's common law criminal system, and the tentative exploration that is the "informal family law trial." SCOWA has also proposed rules that allow legal participants to choose their personal pronouns, in an attempt to counter gender bias and discrimination against persons who do not identify in a gender-binary manner. Proposed Rule of Court, GR 44. Still, at least with me, SCOWA has a difficult climb to surmount my disdain for its irregular and precipitous termination of the limited license legal technician program. My snit being noted, I thank the judges of the WACA and SCOWA for their diligent and thoughtful efforts in sorting the gusher of disputes which our aggression-addled culture spouts. My reservations about our common law system do not throttle my measured appreciation for those who march into its muddy trenches.

If only these officials wielded more adequate jurisprudential theory. Someone should write a book.

requires attack upon its *decisions*, because the *court* is strong. The law requires detailed surgery, the law can stand the shock. Four-square it stands, upon its whole performance. He who helps cut out error gives it strength."[356]

Perhaps Llewellyn bloviates. Our legal system needs painful redirection. But it appears disinclined to embrace rudimentary change. Such revision would entail plunging deep into antiquity—past Rome, past Greece, even past Egypt and Mesopotamia—to construe afresh our life together. We could embrace the insights of anthropology, sociology, philosophical ethics. We could set aside our grim labor to tame enmity, which in the end promotes what those endeavors oppose.

As the title of this tome indicates, most practitioners of common law brook no criticism. They jam fingers in ears. They study distraction. They hum laudatory ditties to themselves. They dance limping jigs to adversarial drumbeats. They salve critique's wincing wounds with spasms of nugatory juridical tinkering. These morally-maimed hobbyists are "meticulous in perversity," luxuriating in an ugly garden of ill-deeds, wherein they "irrigate iniquity."[357] If critique leaks past feigned deafness, they lash out. Vengeance smites. For incomes are at risk. Change induces fetid corporate collywobbles.[358] And, after all, the dissident few can be disposed. Like a surfeit of rats or termites. Or so the deaf suppose. So they hope.

To these reticent colleagues, I repeat. Fess up, my friends. Almost every dispute in which you become involved resolves outside a courtroom. You, like me, evade courtrooms vigorously, and cherish scant admiration for the outcomes which the common law mandates. Unless you cannot hear (as I suspect may be the case), you too recognize inanity in our legal culture and sentiments.

The common law stages a battlefield on which coercive class competitors indulge their melees. Enmity drives common law. Our common law jurisprudence staggers; it is confused, scattered, elitist, metastatic, coercive, adversarial, vapid, pessimistic, ill-judged, juried, partisan, corrupt, under-funded, inaccessible, oligarchic, duplicative, an agent of wealth, deeming, jurispathic, delayed, misdirected, unresponsive, hidebound, untailored, anti-communal, pathogenic, monetized, racist, misogynistic, and epistemologically naïve. To ignore such critique invites moral self-mutilation, the inmost self fatally-flagellated. Humans ignore what they suspect may be right at

---

[356] Llewellyn, *The Bramble Bush*, 149. I suppose my proposals in this little book exceed cutting out errors, since I advocate wholesale revision and, as a philosophical proposition, starting over with a fresh theory for addressing disputes.

[357] Snippets from the Egyptian Middle Kingdom (~2000 B.C.), in "Tale of the Eloquent Peasant," in *The Literature of Ancient Egypt*, 25-44, at pages 32 and 39.

[358] Jayne Mansbridge frames cognitive dissonance more charitably: "Most of us will go to some lengths to avoid living in states of emotional or philosophic tension. If our ideals conflict with the ways we feel we must act, or if one of our ideals clashes with another, we unconsciously modify the ideals or find ways to put the conflict out of our minds. Our compromised lives thus ensure cloudy understandings of the ideals we profess." Mansbridge, *Beyond Adversary Democracy*, 233.

their peril. We lawyers need not cling to five thousand years of mistakes and inadequacies, as though we suffer congenitally-impaired imagination. We might take a deep breath and peer at possibilities. We could attempt something better, in little increments, without overturning the judicial applecart all in a bustle.[359] Warren Burger, then Chief Justice of SCOTUS, asked the American Bar Association of the common law approach, "Isn't there a better way?"[360] We might seek collaborative consensual companionships. We might forsake common law pugilism and, instead, fashion and then embrace a legal regime that fosters friendship and community—a jurisprudence of amity.

If we will.

---

[359] I am concerned that such a concession might result in degeneration toward yet another round of judicial tinkering. Going slowly does not exonerate our current legal regime and does not admit its adequacy. Rather, a structured march toward an amicable regime acknowledges that there are mistakes to be made, fruitless ideas to be explored, and people to be convinced, on a path to a legal regime that fosters friendship and celebrates collaboration.

[360] Burger cited (with approval) Dean Charles Halpern: "The idea of training a lawyer as a vigorous adversary to function in the courtroom is anachronistic. With court congestion and excessive litigiousness drawing increasing criticism, it is clear that lawyers of the future will have to be trained to explore nonjudicial routes to resolving disputes." Burger, "*Isn't There a Better Way?,*" 275. Burger identified these non-judicial dispute resolution approaches: arbitration (on which he focused), negotiation, administrative adjudications, and mediation. I propose to superimpose Klatching upon Burger's list, with the hope the Klatch will ultimately supplant court-orbiting ADR and the common law system generally.

## CHAPTER 3

## COMMON LAW SUPERSEDED

How might one reframe law, once one accepts that our common law jurisprudence is irreparably misdirected? Assuming you are convinced by the critique of the eminent many,[361] and assuming you, as you have read, silently augmented those broadsides from your own purse of legal suffering, then where might one find purchase to lever aside the common law in favor of an alternative approach? Bluntly, how might amity displace enmity as the jurisprudential lodestar? [362] And what might such a supersession look like?

If you imagine that the structure of law, while interesting, consists mostly in philosophical mumbo-jumbo for heady people lacking real jobs, then hear Ronald Dworkin: "We live in and by the law. It makes us what we are. . . . It is sword, shield, and menace. . . . We are subjects of law's empire, liegemen to its methods and ideals, bound in spirit while we debate what we must therefore do."[363] To

---

[361] If you, my reader, are not convinced by this juncture that we require a conscientious (and probably somewhat onerous) alternative, you should preserve your valuable time by closing this book and sending it off to Goodwill or the trash bin.

[362] Lawrence Friedman, who has thought deeply about law, thinks no such path exists. He said: "If law means an organized system of social control, any society of any size and complexity has such a system, and lots of it. As long as the country endures, so will its system of law, coextensive with society itself, reflecting its wishes and needs, in all their irrationality, ambiguity, and inconsistency. It will follow every twist and turn of development. It will reflect the yearnings for justice—and also the thirst for power, the deep inequality built into the structure of society. The law, after all, is a mirror held up against life. It is order: it is justice; it is also fear, insecurity and emptiness; it is whatever results from the scheming, plotting, and striving of people and groups, with and against each other. None of this is going to change." Friedman, *A History of American Law*, 694-695. I ask Friedman why law should differ from all other things, which constantly mutate. Is Friedman not mired in that all-too-common conservatism, which deems human peccadillos immutable, and things-as-they-are a granitic certainty?

I propose no revolution. I do not want our common law courts to crash to a halt, leaving society in the lurch. I propose that, as amicable processes invade conflict resolution, common law courts should retreat appropriately, leaving a growing portion of matters to other, healthier processes for resolving disputes. When amicable process collapses, or when disputants refuse reconciliation, the adversary regime of courts should linger in the background as a second-best and lamentable fallback. If there comes a time when no adversarial courts are needed, then the common law could take its place among moribund systems, like the steam locomotive or the theory of the humours or flat earth speculations. We dwell in a churn of ideas and values. Some age and pass, while successors emerge and rush across the collective human psyche. If we choose well, what comes may exceed what vanishes. It may startle imagination and leave the world's Friedmans agog.

[363] Dworkin, *Law's Empire*, vii.

understand ourselves, we inspect law. Law is us speaking to ourselves, mostly unrecognized. Ideas infect humans. Law boasts a cornucopia of concepts, critically, concepts about humans and our moral status among companions and neighbors. We suffer the pandemic, law. Since we have been afflicted, we might dare to examine the infectious memes. But, where to begin? Where might one find purchase to examine pernicious, mind-cramping law?

As is the habit of philosophers, we might begin at first principles. What sort of animal is a human? What drives the species? If, as Karl Llewellyn asserted, our society is "honeycombed with conflicts," why is that so? What is the nature of adversarial jousting? Have human societies always been riven by disputes? Must they be? Or is our society oddly pathological in its welter of conflict? Diagnosis may well suggest a remedy.[364] Further, one wonders just what sort of thing "law" is. Legal philosophers wonder, despite their long deliberations on the subject. Grant Lamond said that conceptual analysis of law "is extremely vague and open-ended, and any folk theory we might extract is correspondingly thin and indeterminate. It is not even clear that the variety of things we believe about the law are internally coherent."[365] If Lamond is correct, we should not demand too much from any analysis we attempt. Nevertheless, we must try.

All systems of thought spring from compelling narratives. Their motive force leaps from analogy buried in metaphor. Think of manifest destiny, or evil empires, or the sacrificed divine, or the Buddha beneath his bodhi tree, or Descartes winnowing knowledge while shuttered in his oven.[366] Perhaps a few politically-salient stories might help clarify my meaning. None offers historical recollection. Rather, each is a myth intended to guide thought and provide deep rationale for a political system. Recall with me the Ur-story, Aristotle's town polity, and Hobbes's dystopia of alienation.

---

[364] Jared Diamond argues we might improve our lot in modern cultures by mining traditional small societies for solutions that elude us. "Traditional societies in effect represent thousands of natural experiments in how to construct a human society. . . . We shall see that some of those solutions—for instance, some of the ways in which traditional societies raise their children, treat their elderly, remain healthy, talk, spend their leisure time, and settle disputes—may strike you, as they do me, as superior to normal practices in the First World. Perhaps we could benefit by selectively adopting some of those traditional practices." Diamond, *The World Until Yesterday*, 9. I have elsewhere proposed that we restructure our societies to enhance just this sort of small group experimental adaptation, which I call quad sociality. See Lancaster, *Cull: Choosing Well*. An abridgement of selected segments of *Cull: Choosing Well,* concerning the political theory, kithdom, begins below at page 138.

[365] Lamond, Grant, "Methodology," 20.

[366] Descartes did not perform his quasi-mathematical reductions in a literal oven, but probably in a *zpoele*, a small room heated by a cocklestove (a form of masonry heater), to which he retreated to escape the cold during military service.

## UR-STORY[367]

Humans lacked the State for ninety-seven percent of our existence.[368] Archeological evidence suggests that during this long prehistory (195,000 years) humans lived in small bands or tribes, groups which foraged widely and were, in some seasons, peripatetic.[369] Lives were lived among a relatively stable small collection of persons, many related by blood ties, who shared much and supported one another. These groups suffered frequent raids from competing groups, and so lost members to opportunistic human-on-human predation. Such bands acquired few possessions, since one had to carry everything during moves. If surviving hunter-gatherer societies are any indication,[370] human ancestors lived **face-to-face** with one another in **small bands**, viewed one another as **functional equals**, and practiced **consensual decision-making**. Within their context, these prehistorical groups[371] churned out widely-diverse solutions to their problems. Prominence among persons might emerge from utilities some members offered (skilled hunting, religious insight, an

---

[367] "Ur" means primitive, original, or earliest.

[368] The first written records (probably the Kish Tablet for the Uruk Period in Mesopotamia) were created around 3200-3500 B.C. Humanity, in its modern form (*homo sapiens sapiens*) emerged 200,000 years ago, and began spreading across the planet in earnest around 50,000 years ago. "Most of human history is irreparably lost to us. Our species, Homo sapiens, has existed for at least 200,000 years for most of that time we have next to no idea what was happening." Graeber and Wengrow, *The Dawn of Everything*, 1.

[369] As a thought experiment (and not as a pre-historical history), Rousseau proposed that pre-modern people dwelt in an innocent State of Nature of simplicity, from which they were rudely expelled by the arrival of agriculture. After agriculture made it possible for larger aggregations of people, the miseries of modern existence were sown. See Rousseau, *Discourse on the Origin and the Foundation of Inequality Among Mankind* (1754). Note the consonance of Rousseau's tale with that hyper-familiar myth recounted at *Genesis* 2-3.

[370] These hunter-gatherer societies may, in fact, tell us nothing about our pre-historical past. Robert Kelly argues that ethnography of present hunter-gatherer societies offers no insight into the past. Such tribes are not living fossils of pre-historic society. Ancestral groups expressed diverse lifeways to which we have very limited (or no) access. Kelly asserts: "It appears that *analogies* from living foragers cannot be extended back any time at all. . . . If humans lived in various environments in the past, then we can expect them to have lived in various kinds of foraging societies. . . . Foragers, past and present, live and lived under specific environmental and social conditions and within particular historical trajectories, as do all peoples. The variability present among living and ancient foragers demonstrates that as a group, foragers are no more representative of human nature than any other kind of people. They can be used to support whatever image you wish: generosity or greed, violence or peace, monogamy or polygamy, attentive or aloof to children, and so on." Kelly, *The Lifeways of Hunter-Gatherers*, 271-272.

[371] These relic tribes are exemplified by the New Guinea Highland Dani, Australian aborigine, Luzon Island Agta, Andaman Islanders, Tanzania's Hadza, Kalahari !Kung, Sudanese Nuer, Central African Aka, Alaskan Inuit, Paraguayan Ache, Amazonian Piraha, and Venezuelan Yanomamo. Whether these tribes reflect the lifeways of their (and our) ancestors is disputed.

ability to soothe social disturbances, ribald story-telling). But such inequalities were personal and temporary, not structural and enduring.[372]

Study of the few such tribes that have endured to the present paints a picture of these ancestral lives that feels distant in time, but familiar. We live lives embedded in mass culture and technological webs. Ours is a culture drowning in conflicts, and cherishing few, if any, common values. So, we devolve into impersonal, majoritarian, deeply-classed and contested existence. Yet, in our privacies, many engender egalitarian friendships, question the worth of our many possessions, and seek to care for our companions. And all find some others on whom to lean, with whom to share. Recall where I began, asking you to observe gregarious yammer at a local pub, or hilarious, probing, sometimes difficult exchanges around a family dinner table. Despite our urbanity, we dwell, in a deplorably-attenuated fashion, in bands as intimate and supportive as the Yanomamo or !Kung.[373] But only for a fraction of our existence. The Ur-Story beckons us to nurture intimate connections, and to distance one's deep inwardness from urban individualistic isolation, and to step away from our class

---

[372] To alleviate concern that these generalities might be the spawn of fecund imagination by armchair anthropologists, I offer some of Margaret Shostak's 1971 conclusions related to her twenty month's stay (with her spouse) among the !Kung, who inhabit the Dobe area of northwestern Botswana on the fringe of the Kalahari Desert, near the Namibian border. Shostak's informant was Nisa (a pseudonym), a fifty-four year old, gregarious female story-teller of the !Kung. Shostak limited her work to !Kung women. Shostak said: "I observed their sharing of vegetable foods, meat, and material goods so that no one had substantially more than anyone else. I saw how disputes were defused by discussions that went on for hours, long into the night, in which all points of view were expressed until a consensus was reached. . . . I noticed in each presentation a modesty akin almost to bashfulness, and I learned that it was considered bad manners to brag or to act in an arrogant way. I sat at their medicine ceremonies and saw the community bound together in a powerful, moving ritual. . . . Adaptability is the key to their success. People live in semi-permanent villages, or camps, numbering from about ten to thirty individuals. Personal property must be minimal (the total weight of an average person's belongings is less than twenty-five pounds), because everything has to be carried when the band moves. . . . All [hut] doors face inward toward a large communal space. The intensity of social life that this fosters seems deliberate, as space is abundant and privacy could easily be arranged. . . . Companionship is cherished and sought at most times. [T]he !Kung do not have status hierarchies or legitimized authorities, such as chiefs or headmen. Group decisions are reached through consensus. . . . !Kung women contribute the majority (from 60 to 80 percent by weight) of the total food consumed. [The women] average close to four hours a day in maintaining their subsistence tools and in housework. . . . Men average three hours a day. . . . Women's status in the community is high and their influence considerable. [The women] are often prominent in major family and band decisions. . . . [T]he !Kung kill only what they need and use every part of the animal. . . . Food is rarely stored for any length of time. . . . Dietary quality is excellent. . . . This does not mean that !Kung health is, in general, good. It is not; nearly 50 percent of children die before the age of fifteen. 20 percent die in their first year, mostly from gastrointestinal infections. . . . Their life is rich in human warmth and aesthetic experience and offers an enviable balance of work and love, ritual and play." Shostak, *Nisa: The Life and Words of a !Kung Woman*, 6-14.

[373] The post-War, East London community depicted in *Call The Midwife* (a British ensemble drama presently to be found on NetFlix) exemplifies the sense of what I mean when I say we live in an alienated urban context, but create for ourselves an intense amicable milieu that shelters in cracks in the edifice of the anonymous horde.

fixations. The Ur-Story suggests that other, more primordial, forms of association are possible.[374]

## ARISTOTLE'S STORY

Aristotle told a story about States, an account far afield from our own. Aristotle's tale is a bridge story, straddling the Ur-story's idyll of small community and Hobbes's nightmare of self-interested solipsism.

Aristotle argued that good people are those who share life with other good people. These become friends. They augment one another for deep-seated improvement, to live their shared life in *eudaemonia*.[375] Aristotle's term can be rendered "flourishing life in the company of friends," or, less adequately, "happiness." Aristotle said:

> It is clear then that a state is not a mere society, having a common place, established for the prevention of mutual crime and for the sake of exchange. These are conditions without which a state cannot exist; but all of them together do not constitute a state, which is a community of families and aggregations of families in well-being, for the sake of a perfect

---

[374] Though I doubt any one among us longs for life at the edge of a desert without an air conditioner. Intentional communities around the planet, of which there are thousands, best exhibit the possibility of socially-smaller living. Perhaps best known is the kibbutzim movement of Israel.

A kibbutz is an egalitarian Israeli residential community, of which more than two hundred exist in Palestine and Israel. The fundamental values of kibbutzim are: 1) physical labor has a moral and redeeming character, 2) all property produced by a community belongs to the community, 3) all members are socially and economically equal, 4) members give according to their abilities, and receive according to their needs, 5) the community may not inhibit individual choices in opinion or influences, 6) the group and its processes are ends in themselves, 7) all member relations should be characterized by mutual concern and intimacy, and 8) such living will redeem Jews of the diaspora from the injurious effects of hundreds of years absent from the land. This description derives from Melford Spiro's analysis of an unnamed Israeli kibbutz in 1951, which Spiro names *Kiryat Yedidim*. Spiro, *Kibbutz*, 10-37. This kibbutz was socialist, even communist, in its economics. There existed no private property and individual ownership was, at least at the beginning, discouraged. The community had an ascetic tendency that well-fitted the shortages that plagued Israel of that time. All decisions were made in town meetings by consensus. Law had little force, but public opinion was potent. Spiro, *Kibbutz*, 98. Formal proceedings were reserved for misdeeds that might result in expulsion. Spiro, *Kibbutz*, 101-102. Members expressed interpersonal aggression as gossip, pettiness, quarrels, and complaining. Problematical persons and behaviors were lampooned in public skits. Spiro, *Kibbutz*, 105. Outsiders were viewed with great suspicion, especially non-Jewish foreigners. Spiro, *Kibbutz*, 107-109. Prestige in work replaced money as social currency. Spiro, *Kibbutz*, 85-89. Universal provision of all needs by the community alleviated much insecurity among members. Spiro, *Kibbutz*, 86-88. Israel's kibbutz movement has moved toward private ownership, commercial sophistication, and some permitted individualism in the last half-century, which events are much lamented by some anarchist commentators. See Horrox, *Living Revolution: Anarchism in the Kibbutz Movement*.

McKnight and Block offer a rationale for urban community and concrete suggestions about how to turn an anonymous American neighborhood into an urban non-residential fellowship, including a description of how one neighborhood accomplished the transition. McKnight and Block, *The Abundant Community*, 145-148.

[375] Aristotle, *Nichomachean Ethics*, 193-199 (1175b-1179a).

> and self-sufficing life. Such a community can only be established among those who live in the same place and intermarry. Hence there arise in cities family connexions, brotherhoods, common sacrifices, amusements which draw men together. But these are created by friendship, for to choose to live together is friendship. The end of the state is the good life, and these are the means towards it. And the state is the union of families and villages, in a perfect and self-sufficing life, by which we mean a happy and honourable life."[376]

For Aristotle, "that form of government is best in which every man, whoever he is, can act best and live happily."[377] Its size is small—by contemporary standards, tiny. "[T]he best limit of the population of a state is the largest number which suffices for the purpose of life, and can be taken in at a single view."[378]

Aristotle's State grounds itself in friendship. It embraces smallness. It relies on the principled involvement of its members. Aristotle's State sorts among the many good things humans imagine, and brings some of them to fruition.[379]

Aristotle's story teeters at the edge of a precipice. Behind Aristotle's story lies the long course of human pre-State existence, the Ur-story. At the cliff's edge lies the long sweep into a populous and impersonal world, a yawning ravine in human sociality, into which we all might tumble (Hobbes's story). Aristotle calls people to cling to friendship and smallness, and to lurch back from the canyon lip. Large and impersonal States pare convivial sociality. States render humans mere nubs of themselves.

## HOBBES'S STORY

Two thousand years after Aristotle, the bloated aggregate society of which Aristotle warned had come to pass.[380] Thomas Hobbes told England a famous story, which is now American "common sense ."[381] Hobbes reports that humans hunker in

---

[376] Aristotle, *Politics*, 74 (1280, lines 30-40).

[377] Aristotle, *Politics*, 168 (1324, line 25).

[378] Aristotle, *Politics* 173 (1326, line 24).

[379] Sounds utopian, and it was. Every State in which Aristotle lived suffered political murder, wars, slavery, misogyny, rampant ignorance, and levels of disease and poverty we can scarcely comprehend. Alexander the Great, who indulged unprecedented wars of conquest, was, as a child, Aristotle's student. With Alexander, Aristotelian political philosophy failed to take root, and Aristotle's compromises with regal court of Philip II of Macedon came home to roost.

[380] The global population of 1650 is estimated to be 500 million persons.

[381] Note how neatly the hand of the Genesis story of Adam's fall fits the glove of Hobbes's tale. Hence, the appeal of Hobbes's polity to conservative Christians and autocrats. Those who espouse total depravity find comfort in Hobbes's nasty embrace.

fear. Hobbes's humans are nasty, contentious little primates, self-fixated and given to violent outrages. Apart from government restraints, the interactions of people spiral toward an ugly free for all.[382]

Humanity leans upon the chastening hand of coercive government to separate combatants, to supplant battle axes with contests of words.[383] Hobbes is not wrong, even if he is also not right. In recorded history, death by violent encounter was rampant. In the archaeological record, the same was true, as far back into the frozen or peat or fossil record as evidence extends. Hobbes's story chides us that, without

---

[382] Dacher Keltner, a professor of psychology at University of California Berkeley, argues otherwise. I have summarized Chapter 4 of his book as follows: "**Chapter 4: Survival of the Kindest**. Darwin believed that social instincts are part of humanity's evolutionary heritage. What were characteristics of the environment in which humanity evolved (which Keltner calls the "environment of evolutionary adaptedness" or EEA)? Early humans lived closely with thirty to seventy-five troop members. Females gathered and cared for children. Males hunted and made tools. Unlike other higher primates, human collectives provided care to one another. They raised offspring collaboratively. Humans operated face-to-face, in deep coordination. Facial expression and vocal sounds were critical to group cooperation. Culture resulted, with artificial memory transmission across time and space. Human troops were hierarchical (but relatively flat), and higher status individuals kept peace for others, from which derived their power. Conflict pervaded troop life, from sibling to members to outsiders to natural threats. And extensive repertoire of reconciliation behaviors evolved to keep the cooperative ship afloat. Relatively chaste sexual patterns (as compared to other higher primates) promoted peace. Strategically, cooperation is a winning strategy. Emotions that promote cooperation promote the interests of others, which could be evolutionary suicide. Emotion removes this threat. Human emotions create a cost-benefit reversal by providing reliable means of identifying pretenders. Also, humans reciprocate cooperation when cooperation is exhibited. This means that 'meaningful life' is contagious." See Epitome 4: Keltner, *Born to be Good,* toward the end of this book.

[383] Thomas Hobbes styled human life thus: "[D]uring the time men live without a common Power to keep them all in awe, they are in that condition which is called Warre; and such a warre, as is of every man, against every man. . . . and which is worst of all, continuall feare, and danger of violent death; And the life of man, solitary, poore, nasty, brutish, and short." Hobbes, *Leviathan*, 89. Hobbes contemplates that, to avoid the evils of ungoverned life, all men consent to an absolute sovereign. "And in him consisteth the Essence of the Commonwealth; which (to define it,) is *One Person, of whose Acts a great Multitude, by mutuall Covenants one with another, have made themselves every one the Author, to the end he may use the strength and means of them all, as he shall think expedient, for their Peace and Common Defense*. And he that carryeth this Person, is call SOVERAIGNE, and said to have *Soveraigne Power*; and every one besides, his SUBJECT." Hobbes, *Leviathan*, 121.

There is certainly some truth to Hobbes's view. Nicholas Wade describes our distant human ancestors: "The ancestral people had a major limitation to overcome: they were too aggressive to live in settled communities. Early human societies lived as small bands of hunter-gatherers, their existence dominated by incessant warfare. For 35,000 years after leaving the ancestral homeland, these nomads were unable to settle down. Only gradually did humans evolve to become less aggressive. The tempo of warfare eased and a more gracile, or delicately boned, human form evolved in populations throughout the world. In the Near East, around 15,000 years ago, people at last accomplished a decisive social transition, the founding of the first settled communities. In place of hunter-gatherers' egalitarianism and limited possessions, people in settled societies developed a new social structure with elites, specialization of roles, and ownership of property." Wade, *Before the Dawn*, 9.

I would counter Wade is some respects. For 35,000 years after leaving Africa, humans did not settle because, when confronted with aggressive neighbors, it was always prudent for highly-mobile groups to decamp to unpopulated regions. Only 15,000 years ago was the bulk of prime real estate occupied, or unoccupied precincts were too far to reach. This picture helps explain the rapid spread of humans across the planet, to the far reaches of Pacific archipelagos and distant climes of near-Antarctic Chile.

intervention of an absolute monarch, we miscreant humans will make of ourselves a harried, flea-bitten mob, bent on blood-fest. So Hobbes calls us to hunker down and thank God for the king. Our law, the common law, gulped Hobbes's tale to the dregs, and has now grown drunk on his ale.

Hobbes's anthropology is a bug in amber—dead and unchanging. It fails to embrace the facts of growth—cultural growth, to be sure, but also moral growth. Humans are not violent children; rather, we evolve in our deeply-held convictions. Our species mutates, both physiologically (slowly) and ethically (rapidly). To a degree that would have startled Thomas Hobbes, humankind grows peaceful.[384] Nicholas Wade argues:

> And who, exactly, was domesticating them [these violent humans]? The answer is obvious: people were domesticating themselves. In each society the violent and aggressive males somehow ended up with a lesser chance of breeding. This process started some 50,000 years ago, and in Wrangham's view, it is still in full spate. "I think that current evidence is that we're in the middle of an evolutionary event in which tooth size is falling, jaw size is falling, and it's quite reasonable to imagine that we're continuing to tame ourselves. . . . This puts humans in a picture of now undergoing a process of becoming increasingly a peaceful form of a more aggressive ancestor." . . . [D]espite many setbacks and reversions, human societies have made vast gains in peacefulness, complexity and cohesion in the last 15,000 years[385]

Michael Taylor turns the tables on Hobbes. Rather than tamping down conflict, States and their conflict interventions are a substantial *cause* of declines in civility, cooperation, and altruism. Unfettered, calm humans are sociable and generally trusting. Taylor says:

> I suggest that the more the state intervenes in such situations [conflicts over distribution of important public goods], the more 'necessary' (on this view) it becomes, because positive altruism and voluntary cooperative behaviour *atrophy* in the presence of the state and *grow* in its absence. Thus, again, the state exacerbates the conditions which are supposed to make it necessary. We might say that the state is like an

---

[384] Though Middle East conflagrations and Russian aggressions in central Europe and pogroms in West China and India's Hindu oppressions lead one to question the peace statistics.

[385] Wade, *Before the Dawn*, 177-178, citing Richard Wrangham's interview in *Edge* on February 2, 2002. Steven Pinker, in his *Better Angels of Our Nature: Why Violence Has Declined*, sides with Hobbes. We are less violent because the State has tamped or redirected our aggressions. Pinker's work mobilizes a great deal of research in support of the proposition that human societies grow more peaceful. Graeber and Wengrow dissent. Pinker's view is not guided by evidence (though Pinker undeniably loves evidence). Graeber and Wengrow say that Pinker's *Better Angels* "is, to put it bluntly, a modern psychologist making it up as he goes along." Graeber and Wengrow, *The Dawn of Everything*, 13.

> addictive drug: The more of it we have, the more we 'need' it and the more we come to 'depend' on it.
>
> Men who live for long under government and its bureaucracy, courts and police, come to rely upon them. They find it easier (and in some cases are legally bound) to use the state for the settlement of their disputes and for the provision of public goods, instead of arranging these things for themselves, even where the disputes, and the publics for which the goods are to be provided, are quite local. . . . In the presence of a strong state, the individual may cease to care for, or even think about, those in his community who need help; he may cease to have any desire to make a direct contribution to the resolution of local problems . . . The state releases the individual from the responsibility or need to cooperate with others directly; it guarantees him a secure environment in which he may safely pursue his private goals, unhampered by all those collective concerns which it is supposed to take care of itself. . . .
>
> [A]ltruism and cooperative behaviour gradually decay.[386]

So, individualism runs amok, etching, then corrupting, *homo socialis*. Citizens find the needs of others an intrusion and distraction and annoyance, rather than a chance to care for neighbors.[387] To be humane is adjudged a foible, altruism a weakness, and cooperation a fool's errand. Many say, "I paid my taxes. You are the government's problem, not mine." And so, governments, fashioned (in Hobbes's rendition) to attenuate the war of all against all, fuel that very war. Government control instills in citizens just the sort of learned sociopathy that militaries teach soldiers.[388]

If Taylor is right, such problems (which I call egotistical solipsism) will not be resolved until governments behave differently. Richard Sennett[389] writes:

> Really decentralized power, so that the individual has to deal with those around him, in a milieu of diversity, involves a change in the essence of communal control, that is, in **the refusal to regulate conflict**. For example, police control of much civil disorder ought to be sharply curbed; **the responsibility for making peace in neighbourhood affairs ought to fall to the people involved**. Because men are now so innocent and unskilled in the expression of conflict, they can only view these disorders as spiralling into violence.[390]

---

386 Taylor, *The Possibility of Cooperation*, 168-169.

387 Martin Luther King Jr. offered penchant pushback: "Injustice anywhere is a threat to justice everywhere. We are caught in an inescapable network of mutuality, tied in a single garment of destiny. Whatever affects one directly affects all indirectly." King, *Letter from Birmingham Jail*, 2-3.

388 See Epitome 1: Glover, *Humanity*, at Chapter 13.

389 Richard Sennett is a professor of Sociology at London School of Economics and a former Professor of Humanities at New York University.

390 Sennett, *The Uses of Disorder*, 164 (emphasis added).

Sennett argues that our culture needs less, not more, order. We should seek to loosen the joints of our relating; we should strive for "nonroutine life."[391] Top-down has merits. But hierarchical stiffness also stifles innovation and closets oddness and stunts psychological maturation.[392]

These stories (Ur, Aristotle, and Hobbes) describe points on a spectrum. At one end stands face-to-face, egalitarian collaboration in small groups. When conflicts emerge, the small group affected works out solutions to which all agree, or, at a minimum, from which none dissents (consensus). Its tools are morality, chiding, shaming, social esteem, and concern for the well-being of the community. Social ostracism is a final, seldom-employed, tactic. At the other end lies populous classist enmity, sometimes suppressed by a potent centralized government. Self-interested conflict with anonymous others, with whom one shares few core values (or none), defines Hobbes's public space. To cope with widespread conflict, despots use threats of physical force, incarceration, legal codes, enforcement personnel, and seldom-employed executions. Aristotle hopes to split the baby, retaining universal friendship and collaboration, while expanding the population involved from scores to a few thousand. The tools of an Aristotelian polis use strategies from both the other alternatives: formal procedures and codes, but deployed among people one knows or recognizes. Socrates suffered the final solution of the Greek polis: death by mandated self-poisoning. His fate conjoined the moral sting of Ur-like social censure with the heavy hand of nascent political oligarchy.

## UNITARY VERSUS ADVERSARY DEMOCRACIES

What are we to make of this spectrum of stories? We experience, if we are not sorely isolated, the warmth of family and friends with whom we collaborate and live. This intimate womb is a truncated facsimile of Ur-life. We also suffer the intrusions and dysfunctions of anonymous aggregates in their Hobbesian imposed-moralities and ubiquitous half-baked statutes. We may even taste Aristotle's small town polity if one resides in a tiny hamlet with a town meeting tradition, or works closely with esteemed colleagues on common questions, or participates in a small labor union.

Yet, seldom-discussed counter-currents swirl. As to Hobbes, one notes pockets of amicable intimacy (say, among some United States senators or, less frequently,

---

[391] Sennett, *The Uses of Disorder*, xix.

[392] Sennett says: "I think certain kinds of disorder need to be increased in city life, so that men can pass into full adulthood and so that, as I hope to show, men will lose their current taste for innocent violence." Sennett, *The Uses of Disorder*, xxi.

between opposing counsels in litigation hell, or among neighbors sorting matters of local concern), despite the State vortex of coercion and violence. As to the Ur-story, one recognizes that, even in the closest collaborative setting (say, in communes or political action committees), disputes arise that cannot be settled by consensus, no matter how patient the dialogue. Clearly, one must grant that time has passed Aristotle by. There are no States comprising the number of people one can take in at a glance, and no States that can readily identify the common good of citizens. We could restructure ourselves to gain the Aristotelian prize. But no modern State intentionally fragments itself.[393] For values determinations, States vote on issues simplified to yes-or-no alternatives, or for (or against) candidates of which one lacks personal knowledge. Manipulated rules and voter disinterest rut the plebiscite road, but this process passes muster for determining the common good. It is not the common good, but to keep a State functioning among hordes of strangers, we call such election results close enough.[394] The "common good" in the parlance of States consists in those policies a majority imposes upon the disinterested and dissenters. Election results are not the common good. But States deem them the best substitute possible, given the limited intrusions citizens will tolerate. For majoritarian democracy consists in fitting dissenters with muzzles. All growl, no bite.

So, what shall one make of these generative stories, and the mixed states of play within any one story? Jane Mansbridge[395] analyzed these complex issues. She used as her vehicle-of-insight two small societies: town meeting culture embedded in (pseudonymous) Selby, Vermont, and aggressively-egalitarian labors of a small service organization she (again, pseudonymously) calls Helpline Crisis Center. Mansbridge theorizes that democracies come in flavors: unitary and adversarial.

**Unitary democracy** "makes formal and extends to the level of a polity the social relations of friendship."[396] The core features are common interests, social equality, consensual decision-making, and face-to-face interaction. Unitary democracies are necessarily small, because friendship cannot extend to a host of barely-known acquaintances. Unitary democracies do not scale up from their associational roots.

---

393 We would seem to be too busy maintaining nuclear arsenals, indulging proxy wars, whipping up frenzies of purchasing goods, and working ourselves to death.

394 "In current adversary theory, there is no common good or public interest. Voters pursue their individual interests by making demands on the political system in proportion to the intensity of their feelings. . . . [M]any modern political scientists also believe either that equally weighted votes, majority rule, and electoral competition can in principle aggregate millions of selfish political desires into one common good, or that, because no one can know the common good, the aggregation of selfish political desires is the best substitute." Mansbridge, *Beyond Adversary Democracy*, 17.

395 Mansbridge is a professor of political science at Harvard.

396 Mansbridge, *Beyond Adversary Democracy*, 8.

Mansbridge puts it simply: "[U]nitary democracy has had no large-scale form."[397] Mansbridge points out flies in the unitary ointment. The unity of unitary democratic polity does not emerge solely from shared values, common interests, and altruism. Fear of humiliation, public embarrassment, fear of conflict, exhaustion with long meetings, the repetitive exchange of views when a member exercises his consensus veto can motivate a mere appearance of equity. Participants worry that expressing opinions may lead to social disruption. Mansbridge says: "Informal arrangements for the suppression of conflict . . tyrannize as well as protect. To preserve an atmosphere of agreement, the more powerful participants are likely to withhold information and to exert subtle pressures that often work ultimately to the disadvantage of the least powerful."[398]

At the opposite pole, Mansbridge identifies the core components of **adversary democracy** as conflicting interests, equal protection of individual interests, majority rule, and voting by secret ballot (an extension of anonymity). So, adversary democracy describes the American approach, as well as that of many western polities. Strangers, represented by other strangers who are chosen by anonymous majoritarian plebiscite, determine policy. Most Americans find this arrangement familiar, but unsatisfactory. Mansbridge explains: "As a people, we in America are starved for unitary democracy. . . . Unitary appeals [however] fall into an institutional void. Most Americans experience democracy only in the voting booth."[399] One might add that we seem to be disappointed by our voting booths, missing that heartfelt engagement of working out difficult problems with people with whom we share common goals, with people whom we know and with whom we live.

Mansbridge argues that both unitary and adversary regimes are needed. "[W]e must distinguish ideals appropriate to situations where we all have common interests from ideals appropriate to situations where we have conflicting interests. In the real world, we always have both." Mansbridge contemplates that communities must shift back and forth from unitary (face-to-face consensual common-interest dialogue) to adversary approaches (anonymous majoritarian conflicting-interest voting), as circumstances dictate. Such oscillations may prove dislocating, or more complex than some people can navigate. Mansbridge warns of whiplash: "We find it hard to dip in and out of adversary mode without being tainted by it, hard to be selfish now and selfless ten minutes later."[400]

---

397 Mansbridge, *Beyond Adversary Democracy*, 13.

398 Mansbridge, *Beyond Adversary Democracy*, 71.

399 Mansbridge, *Beyond Adversary Democracy*, 301.

400 Mansbridge, *Beyond Adversary Democracy*, 298.

Mansbridge concludes that large polities foster conflicting interests, and so necessitate adversary approaches. This is, for her, a "bitter conclusion."[401] Yet, Mansbridge has hope for unitary processes: "Local assemblies always tend to apply unitary procedures even when interests conflict. But if they could learn to guard against the tendency and to shift from unitary to adversary procedures and back again, depending on the goals they wish to pursue and the extent to which their members actually have interests in common, they would serve their members' interests better . . .."[402]

On a hopeful concluding note, Mansbridge imagines workable oscillation between unitary and adversarial approaches: "In short, by fostering decentralized and highly participative units, by maintaining a few crucial remnants of consensus, by instituting primarily cooperative economic relations, and by treating adversary methods not as an all-encompassing ideal but as an unavoidable and equitable recourse, a nation can maintain some of the conditions for community, comradeship, selflessness, and idealism without insisting that on most matters all its citizens have a common interest."[403]

## DOWNSHIFT

Similarities between Mansbridge's unitary and adversary regimes mirror the amity-enmity distinction I describe in this book. Mansbridge's scope exceeds my own, since she addresses the structure of democracy generally, while I limit my task to supplanting the common law regime. But Mansbridge's core insight, that democratic decision-making must bring to bear those values well-suited to the common or conflicted interests of members, may well apply also to the amity-enmity regimes. Where participants cling to the possibility of ongoing friendship, a jurisprudence of amity must prevail. One never knows where amity might flower. Patience recommends itself.[404] Yet, if those involved in a disputed matter spiral toward vendetta, then an

---

[401] Mansbridge, *Beyond Adversary Democracy*, 293. Mansfield wishes unitary approaches would predominate.

[402] Mansbridge, *Beyond Adversary Democracy*, 292.

[403] Mansbridge, *Beyond Adversary Democracy*, 298.

[404] Mohandas Gandhi, before he became India's peaceful revolutionary, worked as a South African barrister. Gandhi reports events, early in his career, that changed his assessment of the law. Dada Abdullah's business contract dispute involved substantial sums, tortured accountings, and allegedly coerced promissory notes. The opponents, who were relatives and neighbors, engaged excellent barristers, who, at each client's urging, argued each precedent. They battled, at absurd expense, to stalemate. In 1893, Gandhi entered the case midstream, fresh from English law training, a very junior associate. Gandhi observed that animus hardened, and rising litigation costs threatened to obliterate recovery by either side. Gandhi felt disgust with the legal system. Even litigation's winners lose; the disputation culture gobbles any award. Gandhi got the case promptly arbitrated. He fought for terms of settlement payment workable for both parties. The case was resolved. Gandhi concluded that a lawyer's true work lies in appealing to the obscured goodness in disputants. An attorney inches into the troubled hearts of people in conflict. Lawyers mend sundered relationships, nurturing durable peace. Gandhi, *Autobiography: The Story of My Experiments with Truth*, 131ff.

amicable regime may become incommensurate with circumstances.[405] Society knows no alternative but to crash in upon warring parties with coercive rigor.

The task in a jurisprudence of amity is to ascertain just when friendship slips beyond reach, at what exact moment a switch to coercive measures grows unavoidable. I call this recognition of needed transition the "**downshift**." Participants recognize that the conflict ethos they deliberate cannot preserve friendship and must downshift to adversarial pugilism.[406] These downshifted battlers ignore the fact that sticking with amicable approaches may well secure non-zero-sum resolutions and succor social structures they value, such as friendship, equity, unity, community. Warring factions brook none of that. Adversaries believe features of their particular conflict preclude amicable outcomes; the zero-sum game hammerlocks[407] them. Miseries avalanche upon adamant litigants. Suffering waxes. But pugilists spit out amity. Since they insist on coercing others, even forthcoming pacifists admit it may become necessary, in rare instances, to counter-coerce adversaries.

One recognizes the need for downshifting when a participant remains adamant after patient irenic engagement. Irenists make friends of enemies. For friends heed friends. Only the adversaries themselves can change their course. None can coerce cooperation. One might compel conforming behavior; but that is faux reconciliation.[408] Such outcomes birth a resentful rebel, sowing contention, breathless to retaliate. These antagonists plummet toward litigation hell, poised to become fresh fodder in its rotten maw.

One must sort why rabid conflicts riddle American culture. Conflicts pervade human history, so one cannot lay blame at the feet of America's individual solipsism,

---

Robert Yazzie, Chief Justice of the Navajo Supreme Court (1992) introduced traditional peacemaking back into the tribe's westernized jurisprudence. He declined to call Navajo peacemaking "mediation," and rejected the term "alternative dispute resolution" in favor of "original dispute resolution" (in the sense of primordial dispute resolution). In effect, Yazzie and subsequent developers created an opt-in parallel system of conflict resolution operating side-by-side with western hierarchical courts. Zion and Yazzie, "Navajo peacemaking," 159. For further descriptions of indigenous judicial concepts and their struggles to resist jurispathic demolition, see McCaslin, ed., *Justice as Healing: Indigenous Ways*.

[405] "Only when there is congruence between individuals and their community, with shared commitment to common values, is there a possibility for justice without law." Auerbach, *Justice Without Law?*, 16.

[406] Warren Burger, then Chief Justice of SCOTUS, said: "I do not suggest in any sense that arbitration can displace the courts. Rather arbitration should be an alternative that will complement the judicial systems. There will always be conflicts which cannot be settled except by the judicial process." Burger, "*Isn't There a Better Way?*," 277.

[407] Hammerlock of the wrestling, not the ballroom dancing, sort.

[408] "For never can true reconcilement grow Where words of deadly hate have pierced so deep." John Milton, *Paradise Lost*, Book IV.

at least not solely upon that misconstruction of humankind. Steven Pinker argues (persuasively) that human life is more peaceful at present than in any past era.[409] If Pinker is right, perhaps all one needs to do to achieve a more peaceful society is wait. Pinker lays the credit for accelerating peace on women and institutional governments.

Pinker is at odds with Michael Taylor's assessment of the cause of our culture of conflict.[410] Taylor argues that the State, by inserting itself strongly into conflicts, debilitates the population's capacity for self-resolution of disputes, by inducing (or mandating) reliance on institutional channels that address conflicts. The more State, the less community. The more courts, the less private resolution. The more mandates, the less initiative. So, in Taylor's view, our culture grows less and less able to resolve conflicts locally because, in part, courts insist on their worldview and procedures as the paradigm upon which all conflict resolution should be modeled. That model cherishes procedure over content, individuality over communality, compliance over serendipity, and money over equity. The State paradigm is jurispathic; poisonous attitudes leach into the bloodstream of amicable conflicts. For none can befriend another and simultaneously anticipate self-interested savagery from him at every turn.

Thus framed, questions press one seeking amity-at-law. How might one minimize the need for conflict downshifting in our culture? What steps might we take to insure that disputes are settled in amicable groups of involved neighbors? How might one divert disputes spiraling toward enmity-processes?

## SHAPING OURSELVES

Amity-at-law sounds preposterous, possibly oxymoronic. Our conflict expectations emerge, at least in part, from the conflictual culture of common law. That censorious canker has spread throughout the western ethos. Our minds are beholden to law's pretense of rationality, enamored of its many procedures, inspired by its medieval regalia, and prohibited from considering alternatives by its humblebrag self-assurance. Which is to say (as I have said before): common law is jurispathic. It infects and kills alternatives. Those it fails to exterminate, the common law adopts, baptizes, and banishes to legal slackwaters. So, the common law is entrenched. Its sovereignty

[409] If you have not taken time to read Pinker's *Better Angels of Our Nature*, you should make time. Pinker's evidence for growing global peacefulness overwhelms contrary perspectives. His analysis of why peace sweeps the planet, however, proves less convincing. Pinker's appreciation of western social institutions whitewashes the inherent coercive impetus of those structures. Is it "peace" when one is coerced into non-violence. Is human existence improved when killing decreases, at the cost of burgeoning neurosis and anxiety and petty criminality? Perhaps. Perhaps not.

[410] See some thoughts on Michael Taylor above in this chapter, in the section on Hobbes's Story.

is compounded by the fact that its practitioners feed at its litigation trough. Momentum seems inexorable.[411]

I certainly do not want the common law to vanish, for it is my livelihood and I am loathe to abandon the sunk costs of law school and many years learning the intricacies of my practice areas. I also do not want the common law to vanish, because I do not want America to suffer the abrupt dislocation and loss of life that would inevitably follow upon so shocking a change. So, we dither. We suffer common law meandering incrementalism erected on a foundation of sand. **Apparently, we are mired in the legal regime we deserve and want**.[412] In reciprocal isomorphism, the common law has made us what we are, and we have made it what it is. We imbibe its structure; it lives in the way we then think. Back and forth, forth and back: we grow mutually misshapen. Intruders, such as an upstart jurisprudence like amity-at-law, or tinkerings like drug diversion court or even mediation, meet sullen glowering. Their intrusions are tolerated, provided these alternatives pose no threat to the economy of enmity. Conflict-resolution oddities are granted their own chapter of the Revised Code of Washington, thereby being tamed or corralled within acceptable bounds. So, common law trundles on. The common law system is a cockroach in ancient amber. We ourselves are fossilized in yellow rock with that seldom-loved bug.

Despite our extensive indoctrination, many (most?) of us have substantial reservations about our common law worlds. Lawyers write papers and propose improvements (which I believe to be pointless tinkering). When we read critique of the common law, we nod in understanding. We would do better, if only we knew how to fabricate such an invention. But how?

Robin Kimmerer, a Potowatomi botanist, says: "Imagination is one of our most powerful tools. What we imagine, we can become."[413] Kimmerer hopes she will

---

[411] Jerome Auerbach said: "The rhetoric of 'community' and 'justice' should not be permitted to conceal the deterioration of community life and the unraveling of substantive notions that has accompanied its demise. There is every reason why the values that historically are associated with informal justice should remain compelling: especially the preference of trust, harmony, and reciprocity within a communal setting. These are not, however, the values that American society encourages or sustains; in their absence there is no effective alternative to legal institutions. . . . Our legal culture too accurately expresses the individualistic and materialistic values that most American deeply cherish to inspire optimism about the imminent restoration of communitarian purpose. For law to be less conspicuous Americans would have to moderate their expansive freedom to compete, to acquire, and to possess, while simultaneously elevating shared responsibilities above individual rights. That is an unlikely prospect unless Americans become, in effect, un-American. Until then the pursuit of justice without law does incalculable harm to the prospect of equal justice." Auerbach, *Justice Without Law?,* 145-146.

[412] In comprehending our current enthusiasm for common law adjudications, which he styles as "legal pollution," consequent to "hyper-lexis," Jerold Auerbach says: "[L]aw is our national religion; lawyers constitute our priesthood; the courtroom is our cathedral, where contemporary passional plays are enacted." Auerbach, *Justice Without Law?,* 9.

[413] Kimmerer, *Braiding Sweetgrass*, 184.

induce some (mostly some of her own people) to adopt her indigenous alternative worldview. Her preferred world comprises persons: sky-persons, river-persons, sea-persons, alligator-persons, sweetgrass-persons, insect-persons, pecan-tree-persons. For Kimmerer, the world is replete with persons, each deserving respect, each making their contribution to the common weal: a pan-personal communion of reciprocal beings, only a few of which are mammals. She hopes for fragmentation of the unitary worldview of science, leading it to embrace, in addition to its own methods and assumptions, the old knowledge of places and persons, the indigenous ways. In that knowledge, one surveys communions, not collections. One harvests from plant and animal communal friends, and nurtures those diverse communities in return, taking only what those mostly-silent friends can give and still prosper. A polyculture is a patch of earth on which many different plants and animals dwell beside one another. Kimmerer imagines an intellectual polyculture of complementary knowledges.[414]

Kimmerer's quest mirrors the plight of amity-at-law. All knowledge arrives embedded in a worldview. Indigenous ways do not nestle comfortably alongside capitalism and scientific objectivity. Science is indigeno-pathic. It actively disparages native insights, since these are "non-scientific." Amity-at-law's insights are non-legal. Amity is a worldview without law, relying instead on community tools for settling disputes. Can we imagine a world in which common law lingers in dim recesses, while amicable approaches predominate? Can we imagine the sort of people we would have to be for amity to proliferate? Can we be more involved and connected with neighbors and the world? More skilled in conversation? More savvy in redirecting others? More caring about ourselves and our friends? Less willing to burn bridges? More convinced that wealth is relational, not material? More steadfast in confronting spasms of reactionary retroversion, in which grieved groups seek to enact miscomprehensions of historical norms? **Can we imagine ourselves becoming people who deserve and choose amity?**

My request here is not for lip-service or facile nodding, but for personal change. Amity requires quiet conviction. Amity dwells in earnest, simple acts. Amity asks for inner fealty, which we used to call faith.[415] If Kimmerer is right, the mere act of imagining ourselves as amicable folk launches us on a path toward amity-at-law.

For involved neighbors to resolve conflicts, one requires, first, involved neighbors. In many cities, these are, to all appearances, scarce. In other towns, they are endangered. In many boroughs, the "involved neighbor" seems either abhorrent or apocryphal. The involved neighbor emerges not from ethical heroism, but rather from recognition. All "I"s are fragments of "We"s. We guide one another, and share

[414] Kimmerer, *Braiding Sweetgrass*, 139.

[415] Here I use the term "faith" not in a religious sense, but rather in the sense of "keeping faith," which means to persevere loyally. I do not use the term "faith" in the sense of "having or finding faith," which means to believe propositions for which evidence is scant, or to relate to a person whom none sees.

zucchinis and jam. We raise one another's children, both formally at schools, but more importantly, in sports leagues and backyard imaginariums. We share money and laughter and abundant mythologies.[416] More critically, we leak into one another's psychologies. We share much of which we seldom think: gut biomes and menstrual cycles and off-color humor and whiskey preferences. Behavioral and intellectual habits crowd our giggling, shaping us invisibly beneath mirth. Styles make us look like one another, or, more probably, like a model whom we jointly aspire to resemble.[417] We interpenetrate; fragments of you take up residence in me, and memes of me migrate to you.[418] Aristotle said of dear friends that they become one person, so mutually-involved are they. Interpenetration, however, extends to all humans. To the extent we relate, we grow linked. This does not mean we necessarily enjoy one another. The fact of interpenetration creates jubilance, but also frequent frustration. The more dissimilar our companions, the less felicitous is our linkage.

Critically, our psychological bonds point to a different way of conceiving ourselves. This novelty is not novel at all, but rather the human norm, now lost to much of modernity, as are the writings of Diogenes and most of Egypt's pharaonic bling. Commonplace ideas concerning individuals and societies misconstruct humankind. People exist only as members and dwell only in small communities which members comprise (or in withered caricatures of such togetherness; consider the nuclear family[419] or bowling alone). It is a pathology to imagine oneself an individual. Of bees, what does one learn inspecting a hiveless worker?[420] What is a crow absent its murder. At the far end of distortion, societies incomprehensibly agglomerate communities, smashing together what is discrete (and wreaking inestimable damage in doing so). Adequate human relating occurs on a fabulously-smaller scale. To inspect human relating, one requires a magnifying glass, not a telescope. Kenneth Cloke avers: "[O]ur true opponent and adversary in every conflict is always ourselves, and . the real purpose of conflict is, has always been, and can only be to reveal what stands in the way of our learning and growth, our development of character, and our capacity

---

[416] Mythologies spread willy-nilly now, a new pregnant tale on widely-viewed streaming sources nightly.

[417] Hence, the nouning of the verb "model."

[418] A person, herself conceived as a group of interacting systems, then interacts with other persons in her social circle in a manner that spawns personality. Personhood is a social construction.

[419] Many conceive family relations as the essence of community. I dissent. The nuclear family, shorn of its penumbra of aunts, uncles, cousins, and friends, is a boat that barely floats. This human fragment devolves toward abject isolation as relocations sever relations and divorces scuttle household ships abruptly.

[420] Not nothing, but not much.

for empathy and honesty, integrity and intimacy, caring and compassion."[421] To deserve and want amity, we must, bluntly put, change.

So, to have involved neighbors to enact amity-at-law, we must rearrange priorities. We need imagine ourselves to be involved neighbors. We need to become what we have imagined. We must scan ceaselessly for other involved persons and groups. Once a cadre of such persons has connected, they are jointly-positioned to meet community needs in Klatches.[422] The Klatch[423] can solve problems, but it also gives birth to the fabric of communities where Klatching has grown habitual. So, Klatches are a process, a habit, and a womb from which human community issues.

I will describe Klatch conclaves below, after a brief pause.

## AN ASIDE

These juridical ideas have political and economic implications, to which I am sure many of you are sensitive. *If you are not one such, just skip what follows, and resume reading, ten pages hence, in the sections that follow this triple-lined aside. There I will describe some practical thoughts on the structure of community Klatch and argue for its adoption.*

I indulge this midstream interpolation for these purposes:

1. To describe what I have previously written on the political implications and structures implicit in these psycho-sociological ideas. I call this complex of ideas, taken together, a "quad sociality," and the resulting polity, "Kithdom."

---

[421] Cloke, *The Crossroads of Conflict*, 3.

[422] This book is not autobiographical. I have, however, been encouraged to speak of my personal experience with Klatching. In the 1970s, long before I recognized the pattern of Klatching, I encountered the Numinous in a group of singing Presbyterian teens (of which I was one). Always in circles, we intoned and shared. In a 1980s house-church (Cornerstone), my companions and I met for worship and communal living. In circles, we debated our course, and uttered what thanks we could muster to the Unseen. I left the church, but not circles. In the 2000s, I taught elementary school students advanced reading in a circle around tiny tables with chairs substantially under-sized for my prodigious hindquarters. For twenty-three years (that ended in 2023), I met about a large somewhat-circular table at Third Place Books with members of the Witless Protection Program. We shared our lives, puzzled our ethical dilemmas, and read mostly philosophy. Throughout my law practice, I have used Klatches in mediations, many as small as three, others larger. It is a challenge to induce Americans to listen. Silent attention is not a value we teach in our culture. Last, I have for several decades (with many others) built a community that emerged from sharing stories and troubles and joys in a weekly roundtable. We have grown too large for a single table, but we still prefer an architecture approximating roundness for our talking. We share and listen; community emerges, like tulips in a warm April morning.

I call all these permutations Klatches. I am ever grateful to have stumbled into the habit of Klatch. (I call this circle-talking "Klatch," though no one else does, to divert criticism from other similar movements and nomenclatures, and to reserve blowback from my atonal colleagues for myself alone.)

[423] I use the term Klatch in a technical way. I sought a low-frequency term to invest with novel connotations. The word "Klatch" derives from a German word for meeting to talk over the affairs of other people, with a connotation that such conversation may not always be truthful. Hence, the German term can mean "gossip," the subject of which may be a community scandal.

Of this, I have written extensively, which text I have epitomized in *Cull: Choosing Well*, at pages 431 to 455. Portions of that synopsis follow.

2. To flesh out a different form of political life, so you can see that amity-at-law could find natural refuge among large numbers of affiliated small communities. Klatching might prove to be stepping-stones to those foundational communities.
3. To answer Jerome Frank's assertion that society-wide court-less, litigation-less conflict resolution is impossible, and so does not deserve our attention or devotion (see the second epigraph in Second Epigraphs, just before this book's *Introduction*). Frank is wrong. In kithdom, I imagine and describe in some detail what Frank dismisses.

## THE POLITY OF KITHDOM

**I. Cull.**

The author addresses his young friend, Kate, asking her to think about human conduct. He invites Kate to disagree, and seeks her patience in the sometimes difficult conversation.

1. *Choosing.* [1]

Consider decision-making. Have you, have we, chosen well? Most would confess not. Our characters disappoint. Our communities suffer. Might we do better? Might you make of yourself a moral wonder? Together, how might we flourish?

When we make a decision to act, we sort better from worse alternatives. That is, we cull. When we choose, our acts make us better, or worse, people. Our communities prosper or suffer. Our lives become meaningful or empty. We flourish or we suffer or we die. Choosing well amounts to a finely-elaborated cull of conduct. In culling, one rehearses for oneself the likely outcomes of an act, and chooses the best among the apparent alternatives. Recognizing the best acts from among the welter of alternatives is what we call wisdom. We have no choice but to act. Even doing nothing is an act. We flourish when we choose and act well.

Choosing happens together as well as alone. In the author's view, we should substantially alter the human social pattern. He proposes revised language for human togetherness. A "cadre" is a group of eight to fifteen intimate friends. A "circle" associates ten or so cadres. A "community" creates a context for ten or so circles. A community is the basic building block of global humanity. The "Commons" gathers the global community of communities for deliberation and reporting and recollection. The Commons is the global fire pit around which the human tribe gathers to share, to talk, to remember, and to choose. The author calls this nested social structure "Quad sociality" (the four "c"s of cadre-circle-community-commons). Quad society is kithdom, that is, a community comprising all of earth's communities of friends.

Choosing well proves difficult. One suffers confusion and ignorance that she needs to dispel. Culling well has a structure: urges are modified by emotions, and both are deflected by thought. To assist in talking about choosing wisely, the author suggests some words to help clear brittle brain brush and tangled confusions. He lists the quagmires. The author describes the parts of this book and suggests reading strategies. Seeking to benefit oneself by making good decisions may seem selfish at first glance. But one lives with others; each of us leaks into others, and they into us. Choosing well enhances the lives of all. That is virtue.

*Objection 1: Good and Evil.* [12] *An objector criticizes the author's use of the terms "good" and "evil," preferring less loaded language.* The author answers that he rejects the theological baggage of these terms, but finds no adequate alternatives.

*Objection 2: Urban Trajectory.* [15] *Another objector criticizes the author's rejection of urban existence; surely, mankind cannot lunge backwards into villages.* The author answers that, though density is helpful, overpopulation crushes mankind. We must reduce human numbers dramatically. The author is, however, unwilling to coerce people into producing fewer babies. The author would nurture every child born, and trust people, well-informed, to voluntarily curb their procreation, except when called to bear the next generation.

*Objection 3: Putrescence of Communism.* [19] *Yet another objector dislikes using words employed in communist ideology, such as circle and cadre.* The author asks to steal a few terms back from misguided, violent communist thinkers, since we need words to think adequately about choosing and living together.

*Objection 4: Identifiable Evil.* [21] *Still another objector complains that none can reliably identify evil as it happens. Evil hides and cannot be exposed, until it is too late.* The author responds that evil can be identified if one grasps its structure. Evil erodes meaningful community. None evades what he cannot identify. Every morality specifies what, in its scheme, constitutes evil.

Good acts build meaningful community; evil acts erode it. [23] We constantly employ feedback from our actions to guide future acts. When we do this well, we make better choices. We and our communities prosper. When we cull poorly, all suffer. Humans are predisposed to optimism, which may make us blind to what is not working. Each of us must doubt our rosy optimism. When we discover acts that work well, we make them habits. Our habits, personal and communal, constitute our character. To some habits we are predisposed by our evolution on African plains; we alter these with difficulty. Other habits we invent. These can be changed more readily, but not without effort. Crucially, habits can improve or demolish our lives. So, as we get wiser, we grow cautious about our choices. We deliberate. We have to face the possibility every day that we have chosen poorly and simply missed our errors. Ill-considered habits can savage life, leaving one feeling empty, grumbling that life is meaningless. Evils are habits chosen because they seemed good, but proved otherwise. When this happens, we need to stop and examine how we made that bad decision. Humility helps. Some diseases (sociopathy, for example) and personality problems (narcissism, for example) lead regularly to choosing evils.

Members and communities shape one another. The errors of either become the problems of both. With wonders, it is the same; they spread. Despite the influence communities have on their members, every person hides a kernel that remains unaffected. We are, in deep recesses, unique and resilient.

Humans manufacture meaning for themselves. [35] We do so in the same way we erect buildings or undertake journeys: one brick at a time, one step at a time. We choose habits individually and collectively. These habits become routines. Routines become social structures. We tell supportive stories about our way of doing things, and invent shared tales that put life's difficult moments in perspective. If we forget that we invented our structures and imagined our stories, we may believe gods made them. That can make a community unable to adapt. These are stifling places to live. Some people eventually get fed up with being stuck in the mud. They rebel and establish revised habits. People get hurt and suffer unwanted change. This "invention, ossification, revolution" pattern injures us deeply. We tear up habits that should be retained, and fail to amend other habits that are killing us. We need to get clear on what helps us and what hurts us.

[38] Meaningful human communities: 1) provide shelter and food and care, 2) keep life safe, 3) resist fighting, 4) choose openly how to live together, 5) persevere when problems arise, 6) fit members to jobs that suit them, 7) encourage intimate friendship, 8) tolerate weird and difficult people, 9) make a living by producing something others need, 10) adapt to changes as they occur, 11) revere life and the depth that lies beneath all living things, and 12) seek to cooperate with all human communities.

> *Objection 5: Trivializing Evil.* [47] *An objector argues that evil exists more substantially than mere poor decision-making. Humans are utterly sinful, and Satan induces that horror.* The author rejects personalized evil spirits, arguing that these do not help us make better decisions.
>
> *Objection 6: Diversity of Purposes.* [48] *Another objector rejects the author's values. Other values exist and may be preferable. We need values diversity.* The author counters that meaningful community encompasses all values. Diverse values, even evil values, may find expression in some communities. Those failures will teach as much as successes.
>
> *Objection 7: Existential Death.* [49] *Yet another objector asserts that meaning lacks meaning. All ends in death, so meaning is vacuous.* The author answers that none knows what follows life. Humans know life. One can make of life a meaningless hell. Or one can make something substantially better than that. Death is no horror to those who have lived well in the company of friends. Meaning is the final word in ethics.
>
> *Objection 8: Authorial Hubris.* [50] *Still another objector complains that the author's assertions claim to apply to all humans. No man knows so much. None knows what creates meaning. The author is full of himself.* The author agrees he is arrogant, as are all authors. He hopes speaking his mind helps people make better decisions.

[51] Eroded human communities: a) overpopulate, producing scarcity, then raiding, b) fail to attach to their babies, c) neglect nurture and mentoring, d) imagine life is aimless, e) persecute odd people, f) tolerate selfishness and violence and war, g) coerce members, h) treat animals badly, i) fail to support members, j) tolerate substitutes for meaningful community, such as drug abuse, free-riding isolation, hysterias about global disaster, and rabid pessimism, k) let members feel utterly alone, m) encourage members to doubt the possibility of meaningful community, n) let members get addicted to owning more and more stuff, and o) permit despair that ends in suicide.

> *Objection 9: Dominating Species.* [62] *An objector asserts that overpopulation is not mankind's big problem. Sufficient funds exist, if wars and luxuries were abandoned, to nurture all seven billion humans. Species extinction occurs because humans dominate. That is the natural course of things. Species come; species go. Humans are, frankly, coming.* The author agrees that we could feed all. Mere sustenance will not solve the problem of overpopulation. Without a choice to procreate differently, scarcity will soon return to meet twelve or fifteen billions. Conscientious childlessness and contraception can remedy overpopulation, and leave room on the planet for animals other than man.

> *Objection 10: Immoral Morality.* [64] *Another objector complains that morality is immoral. Morality makes people compliant with States and religions. Humans are unique, resistant to rules.* The author responds that none stands alone. Every human is social, built for life together. Those who imagine themselves imperious and alone self-delude.

In making decisions, a member sees a problem, checks how she feels about it, thinks it over, asks others, guesses what might happen if she does this or that, takes another hard look, then acts, evaluates the results, makes needed changes, adjusts her habits, then starts again. In making decisions, a community sees a problem, waits, communicates among members and gathers facts, hears and reconciles disputing groups. If the disputing parties cannot be reconciled, they segregate themselves, and eventually fission (split apart) to form new communities. Decision-making seldom follows these lists in any linear fashion, nor should it. Member and community decision-making often occur simultaneously, and cross-influence one another.

Every community, every individual culls. We deliberate, well or poorly. All weigh self-interest against group well-being. Communities and members help one another, expressing very ancient life imperatives. Some decisions prove to be errors, which blossom into evils. None can know for certain when she chooses whether the outcome will be good or evil. One must watch and learn. Where evils take root, neighbors should converse. Where diseased people or communities undertake evil intentionally (the author calls these "wanton" acts), communities must intervene peacefully (which interventions express "irenism," a term the author prefers over "pacifism") to divert the errant member and work reconciliation.

[72] In the history of ethics, schemes at odds with irenic Quad kithdom are plentiful. Some are: virtue ethics (desirable character traits listed), hedonism (raw pleasure), Epicureanism (deferred pleasure), acquiescence ethics (expect less to avoid disappointment), consequence ethics (choose what benefits most), Thou ethics (relationships matter), divine justice ethics (god speaks), legal ethics (human rules), ego ethics (gifted people usurp), duty ethics (reason guides duties). Quad sociality borrows from several of these traditions. No ethical system can be proved. They either help create meaningful life or they do not.

## IV. **Communal Culling.** [305]

*8. Communities Choosing: Thanatoid Transgenerational Deliberation.* [309]

Members and communities affect one another, but members take the moral lead. Thinking about how to shape communities requires free thinking. The way we presently structure life together needs extensive revision. We drown in ill-wisdom.

Thanatoid transgenerational deliberation envisions life thousands of years into the future. We cannot see; we squint. We see better when we take the perspective of people near life's end (thanatoid perspective). We see better when we recognize that though we die after a few decades, the human community may persevere for hundreds of thousands, even millions, of years (transgenerational perspective). All those involved in such deliberation may not be old; all will, however, be mature. We deliberate, when we cull, promising community experiments from failures and extrapolate (deliberative perspective). We look for thanatoid savants, people with special gifts for imagining our future. We grant such people no power, since we prefer that no person exercise power to coerce. When one peers forward in time, one sees that we can deliver meaningful community to our descendants, that we must cast off useless structures and ideas for fresh ones, that we must go slowly and choose with care, and that we need to be able to see how meaningful community can persevere at least 30,000 years from now.

> *Objection 34: Predictive Astigmatism. [316] An objector complains that the distant future is invisible. We can neither see nor predict so far. Humans plan tomorrow, not next week. Talk of 30,000 years hence lets nut-cases project hallucinations on a blank screen.* The author counters that man is changing, maturing. We are positioned to choose how to flourish. We see our impacts and deficiencies. We are African primates with attendant wonders and flaws. Where the future blurs, alternative visions arise. We can experiment with those. Peering, we will see further. Critically, we must stop crushing our seers, and start mining them. Optimism is warranted.
>
> *Objection 35: Dissembling Revolution. [317] Another objector spits out the author for preaching revolution, then denying he does so. When one changes marriage, education, economics, family life, nation-states, the military, and death wholesale, that is revolution. The author is dangerous; he is utopian. He shares views of the worst of recent mass murderers. Ignore him.* The author apologizes for scaring the objector. Much should change. Change will be painful. But the author seeks no revolution. Nor do we need revolution. Society trends toward kithdom, unawares. The author asks the objector to avoid wild hyperbole in criticisms. Such is the bane of our day, truncating every conversation. The author declines revolution; it betrays poverty of patience.

Society suffers misdirections. These we should correct. We should link people together in friendship. We should depopulate. We should consume only sustainable products, and direct inventive energy toward needful technologies. We should fashion dense communities of limited footprint, to make room for other species. We should shift values from money to relationships, from financial to social capital. We should stop warring and build a wealth of conflict-resolution resources. We should limit coercive activities to emergencies, and then to designated martials only (the author promises explanation below). We should open virtual connectivity to all and freely offer every form of knowledge, which the Commons holds in trust. We should amend human identification from nations and land and football teams to communities and the Commons. These topics might serve as kindling for the Commons thanatoid transgenerational deliberation.

Humanity will transition to kithdom slowly. It may take centuries or millennia. Our self-inflicted injuries have cumulated for millennia. None need wait for the dawdling many to adopt kithdom. Deepen intimacies. Form a cadre, then a circle. If others nearby have done likewise, commence a community, an economy, an alternative to anonymous conformity within States. Put the technology wizard among you to the task of building an infrastructure for the Commons dialogue. Do it whatever way works for you. There is no template. Tell your grandchildren to keep encouraging chatterers to get serious about flourishing. But most, flourish yourself. Do it for you and those you love, Kate.

*9. Quad Community Life.* [326]

Quad communities shape themselves: cadre, circle, community, commons. They also reshape politics itself. Perhaps, Quad communities practice anti-politics. For in kithdom, no States exist.

Quad communities differ from States by virtually eliminating coercion, abandoning law as a theory of human relations, putting discussion of human structures and futures on the table every day, shifting decision-making from distant experts to small communities, encouraging communities to adopt social experiments and report results to the Commons, and suggesting periodic reshaping of each community to adopt the best recent ideas. Kithdom also differs from States in demanding the discipline of consensus, refusing majoritarian coercion, discouraging mobility and changes of residence, addressing fundamental moral and ethical questions, making choices in these debates community by community, cherishing diversity, tasting a bit of asceticism, relying on local action, and relishing the global community of communities in Quad sociality.

States have rationales, which the author reviews. Some argue gods authorize States; god chooses a king or noble class (kingdom, aristocracy, plutocracy, timocracy). Others support social contract theories; ancestors agreed, so we must as well (Rousseau, Hobbes, Hume, Locke, Kant). Many have argued that might makes right; those who can compel have a right to do so (Nietzsche, Han Fei Tsu, Hitler, most majoritarian democracies). Some believe that enlightened bureaucracies should rule, imposing a system of compassionate order (Confucius, Mencius, Rawls). A few believe that governments should be as small as possible (Nozick, Thoreau). Some dispute the validity of any government whatsoever (Gandhi, Bakunin, Godwin).

Strong reasons exist for adopting kithdom. Kithdom admits no coercion, except in emergency circumstances, and, so, respects persons. Consent rules; consensus is the norm. Coercion is immoral; it engenders bad faith, fear, and retaliation. Coercion is ineffective; coerced people comply until their first opportunity to resist or rebel. Coercion corrupts; the moral sense of those charged with coercing erodes, leading to power-mongering. Consensus works; all are valued and heard. Gods endorse consensus (the author makes a tongue-in-cheek natural law argument for kithdom). Kithdom effectively addresses wanton deviancy by supervised reintegration of offenders into their communities. Communities retain a truncated, but effective, degree of coercive capability in their martials. Kithdom supports the cooperative impulses in humans. And kithdom unleashes creativity that is presently suppressed.

> *Objection 36: Informal Oppressions.* [354] *An objector fears Quad sociality will open the door to oppressions eradicated with great effort over the last 500 years. Hosts of half-baked ideas may dominate communities. If we seek wisdom, the collective insight to date has been that anonymous bureaucratic States are much preferred over wacky oppressive hamlets.* The author responds that some communities will undoubtedly err. One learns by error. Centuries of slow, deliberate change may pass before kithdom predominates. Communities of remarkable wonder may also emerge. Our "rights and freedoms" culture of coercion serves us poorly. We can live in a more deeply humane manner.
>
> *Objection 37: Big Brother Commons.* [357] *Another objector complains that the Commons is global government. Will not some communities prosper while others languish? We need coercion; it smacks those that need smacking.* The author clarifies that the Commons is governed by consensus among human communities. The Commons helps keep mankind working toward good purposes. Only martials coerce, and they do so seldom and with grave limitations. Information and dialogue are tasks of the Commons. The Commons exists so that some communities can influence others. It might prove necessary to restrain a community. If that happens, the Commons should determine how it missed that glaring problem.
>
> *Objection 38: Quagmire of Consensus.* [358] *Yet another objector asserts consensus will not work. Consensus grants dissenters a veto, which will hobble communities. No alternatives to majoritarian coercion exist.* The author answers that consensus is not unanimity. Consensus includes acquiescing dissenters. Communities act, awaiting outcomes.

Majorities need their dissenters to clarify decisions. Never ignore them. Convince them to acquiesce, or revise proposals, or wait. Consensus cannot work in bloated institutions of strangers accustomed to coercing. Consensus requires interpersonal relationships, and their attendant preference for accommodation. Coercion alienates. We presently cook in the cauldron of coercion's incivilities. Can we agree to respect one another and try something new?

*Objection 39: Bridling Corruption.* [361] *Still another objector complains that the author understates the human inclination to ill-behaviors. Without coercion, society turns ugly. We need potent oversight, with penalties in tow.* The author agrees that many presently suffer moral collapse. Matters improve as nurture improves. When global nurture prevails, we may still find that some remain rapacious. We might have to coerce them. But, generally, humans are as inclined to good as evil.

*Objection 40: Abandoning States.* [363] *Yet still another objector asserts that States solve problems, not create them. Look. Life spans have doubled, relative peace prevails, crimes decline, technologies proliferate, wealth grows, and science marches. Who can gainsay that track record?* The author replies that the objector whitewashes States. State solutions are as bad as the problems they address. Several factors have improved the world, not just the State. Kithdom is not tribalism resuscitated. Kithdom's members stand deeply educated, thoroughly nurtured global participants in a high technical culture. We can dispense with coercions, for the most part.

*10. Nurturing Members.* [365]

Communities nurture members by insuring members find physical sustenance (shelter, clothing, food, water), meaningful activity, well-fitted productive activity, constructive leisure, and deep socialization by means of mentoring and technical training. Communities nurture members by supporting well-structured cooperative contracts for forming, sustaining, and living within cadres, circles, and communities.

*Objection 41: Absent Intimacies.* [372] *An objector notes that intimacy is not nearly so intense as the author represents. Friends can be replaced. Even spouses and children neglect one. Quad sociality will not work, because friendship is not all that intimate.* The author recognizes that intimacy is an endangered species in America. Many cultural demands wither intimacy. To find intimacy, one must shelter portions of life from that inimical heat. One works at intimacy. It cannot be purchased off the shelf.

We tend to overcoerce. Dissenters, the odd person, people of flighty talk, bad breath, or infrequent bathing: all get coerced. Coercion and nurture work poorly together. People who are different deserve a place at our common table. They bring value. Neurodiverse people innovate, exhibit admirable courage, are not captured by normalcy, and gainsay committees. Among the ranks of the neurodiverse stand savants, upon whom our weal and future lean. Neurodiverse savants inoculate members against crippling arthritis of mind; they rattle chains of conformity; they birth tomorrow. Not only individuals, but also communities under the influence of neurodiverse savants, may become savant. These open vistas neurotypical communities never consider. We injure ourselves when we persecute neurodiverse savants.

Even outliers, who spit out their communities in favor of isolation, deserve nurture. We should relate to and support them, to the extent they permit. For, despite their prickly personas, they remain members.

Communities nurture members by keeping them secure. Where all irenic interventions have failed to prevent community injury, communities may coerce wanton members. These maximally-minimal coercions aim to use the least force possible on the smallest number of persons for the minimum time necessary. Every intervention, even where potent, is not coercive. Coercion occurs where someone making a choice is effectively deflected from that preference by another, where the other is not a trusted friend acting in good faith, or where an emergency exists threatening the chooser's well-being or prospects. Choosers bear some responsibility for the coercions they suffer.

[386] When coercion of a member proves necessary, the militance of irenism reveals itself. A priority in meaningful community is creating a safe environment within which to live and experiment. Wanton actors fail to care about outcomes for others. Coercion within kithdom commences with a wanton actor's friends. They do the irenic work of caring for and convincing a member to desist. When they fail, community coercion steps up. Coercion aims to address the problem behaviors and reintegrate the wanton actor into his community. In coercions, communities should seek Commons input. Others may have faced similar difficulties. Coercions occur in an ascending order of severity: mandatory evaluation and counseling, mandatory reconciliation efforts, travel and association limitations, prohibitions on dangerous substances, random monitoring, uninterrupted monitoring, transfer to preferable community, and transfer to an encapsulated therapeutic community. Because of coerced transfers, every community may need to welcome wanton transferees.

> *Objection 42: Coercive Paternalism.* [389] *An objector argues that people make such poor decisions that wiser heads must intervene to protect them from themselves. We must legislate people's personal choices if we are ever to have a semblance of sanity in our societies.* The author answers that no one knows what errors should be quashed or who should choose. Communities must experiment with meaning and observe results. Humanity does not presently know what forms of life may prove best. So, we guess and hope. Many look to the past, to geniuses long dead, and call their rote formulae good enough. Coercion does not create compliance, but rather recalcitrance. To make members wise, we must mentor them to be such.

*11. Nurturing Communities.* [391]

Communities exceed their members and require nurture. One nurtures her community by content-full talking, demonstrative affection, frank assessments, linking one's identity to her community, enduring with a community, keeping one's life simple, forging necessary contracts with other communities, expressing oneself into the community's life, dissenting from a community's erroneous decisions, and discovering useful exemplars and advice from the Commons.

Communities should consider, but need not adopt, the following policies. First, a martial designee may be needed. Such a person is a peacemaker, and controls the instruments designed to kill humans in a community. Communities may need to pool their martial designees to form temporary militias. The author endorses an exponential consent rule, in which the number of consenting communities endorsing formation of a militia is the integer two to the power of the number of martials to be joined. Second, the concept of property should be amended, since economic inequality poisons communities. Property held at the time of death passes to one's community. Regular transfers of excess to struggling communities should be expected. The origins of wealth are suspect. Wealth should be an embarrassment, not cause for praise. Excess should support less-productive members. That said, communities should not forbid wealth to its maker. People differ. Some lives generate excess. Wealth may derive from a person's essence. Third, communities need to discuss and care for human genetic fitness. Given our control of our environment, we no longer can rely on hostile circumstances to keep the human genome adaptive. We must prune ourselves. Fourth, our culture consumes resources that cannot be regenerated. Communities should consider setting aside a generational reserve to help descendants address the depletions our current consumption and overpopulation creates. Communities, when structuring themselves, weigh dualities of competing interests: communal versus private ownership, indifference versus involvement, old versus young, female versus male, and aspiration versus disillusion.

[404] Communities may adopt evils. One hopes sister communities will intervene early, preventing the eruption of ill-deliberate communal acts. Regardless, war must be avoided. If war occurs, the Commons should stop to re-evaluate its function. Weapons of war should not be manufactured, except to provision martials. If an erring community proves recalcitrant, neighboring communities should address the difficulty with militant non-violent activism in an approach of increasingly invasive intervention. Neighbors should inquire and listen, seek to persuade, immigrate into the community to create a dissenting voice, protest visibly and persistently, station observers with recording devices, meta-protest (which consists in alleviating the root causes of a community's evil acts), boycott and decline to collaborate, and, finally, discorporate the wanton community. If such occurs, the Commons should deliberate causes, and remediate as needed. For the Commons has, under such coercive circumstances, plainly gone astray.

> *Objection 43: Irenic Coercion.* [410] *An objector asserts that pacifists lack gumption. The sociopath is serious; he does damage for its entertainment value. To address the wanton community, one brings overwhelming responsive coercion, or nothing at all.* The author agrees that sociopaths present dangers. So too our own prejudices and blindnesses. All must intervene with others as needed. Sociopaths were once children, not leaders of wanton communities. A host of errors over decades promoted the sociopath to leadership and power. We must coerce under such circumstances. We should do so with restraint, in a manner that expresses our values.
>
> *Objection 44: Utopian Blather.* [412] *Another objector finds irenic kithdom silly. Violence demands perpetual armed vigilance.* The author insists his is no utopia, but rather a decisional scheme for improving matters. Practicality describes the usual. *Cull* contemplates a degree of change that departs the usual. The author could be wrong. Experiment. Report. Prove your point. Will the objector confess if experiments prove him wrong?

*12. Nurturing the Commons.* [415]

The Commons conducts a global conversation about human life. The Commons serves as a global fire pit around which the human tribe gathers to sort itself.

The Commons has tasks. At a minimum they include the following: maintaining an accessible repository of global knowledge, facilitating innovation exchanges between communities, structuring the global dialogue about human weal and the far-sight horizon, recording contracts, presenting alternative community structures for consideration, and creating an agenda and format for Commons participation.

The Commons is not a global State. Though deeply influential, the Commons lacks power to coerce. States exist because overpopulation creates scarcity that leads to pillaging. States sunder human relationships. States privilege some by depriving many. The State withers, as a theory. Persistent war, plagues, starvation, obscenities of wealth maldistribution, and so forth: the list goes on and on. Vital communities find States a threat. One need not revolt. Build a community. Create the Commons. Let States atrophy. Lavish indifference upon them.

To prevail, communities must remain small. Humans have limited abilities. Do not overwhelm members socially by letting numbers bloat. That leads to threat and States. Keep everyone known and valued. Permit no anonymity. Small grows meaningful. States pare member life, slashing the intimacy members require, subverting their communities. Resist. Nurture your community and yourself. Deny the State your loyalty or attention.

> *Objection 45: Technical Regression.* [422] *An objector fears that reducing human population to one billion might cause technical regression in which humanity loses core technologies on which we depend. We might plummet back into the stone age.* The author counters that population will plummet one way or another. We stress the planet and ourselves. We decide not whether to reduce population, but only *how* it will be reduced. Technical innovations might slow; that might allow our moral deliberations to keep pace.
>
> *Objection 46: Hopeless Optimism.* [423] *Another objector complains that Quad sociality is hysterical in its optimism.* The author declines to apologize for being hopeful, and hopes he is not hysterical.

## V. Culling Futures. [425]

### *13. A Thousand Generations.* [425]

We choose together. We choose in the ongoing stream of humanity, launched from a deep African past, hurtling toward we know not what. So we guess and hope. Despite our fragility and evanescence, our thoughts and choices ring forward millennia. We boom transgenerationally. Let us take care with our legacy.

A desirable future commences today. Militate, but be patient. Act potently, knowing we do not well envision the distant impacts our choices generate. Leave big talk to chatterers. Devote yourself to irenic change. Love your community, your friends. See as far as you are able.

Communities persist long after their members. The human community of communities, if it proves wise, has a lifespan limited only by that of the universe itself. You are yourself, nothing more. Give what you can. Build what you are able. Humanity is more than you and me. We crew a species-spanning ship, sails filled with gusts of life. We do our part, then die, confident in others to chart a constructive course. As have we.

### *14. Answering Kate.* [428]

One makes good decisions by culling conduct well. Good decisions build meaningful community. Bad decisions erode meaningful community. Recognize your nature. See where it leads and the weaknesses it entails. Choose rules for yourself that promise well-being for you and your friends and community. Make peace, nurture children, learn how to agree with others, work meaningfully, and die well. Keep unborn generations near the front of your mind. Be devoted to flourishing. With such attitudes deeply-rooted in yourself, you will make good decisions, Kate.

*15. Conclusion: Meaningful Community.* [429]
Humanity can make better decisions. Books are thin, while humans are thick. Still, a good book is not nothing, if one lets it in. We can create meaning-laden lives in a meaning-laden Commons. Finely-elaborate your culling, Kate. Peer forward. Cull. Act. Flourish.

Buried deeply in this political structure lies a nascent economic theory that diverges from American capitalism. Robin Wall Kimmerer, a botanist whom I have previously mentioned, describes gift economies. In these arrangements, members share abundances, rather than hoard them. "A gift economy nurtures the community bonds that enhance mutual well-being; the economic unit is 'we' rather than 'I,' as **all flourishing is mutual**."[424] Kimmerer describes the guidance offered by the indigenous principles of Honorable Harvest, which direct one to take only what is available without harm to the resource being harvested or to other plant, animal, or human persons. Honorable Harvest emphasizes caring for others and for the plants and animals harvested by giving back to them. Share what abundance you find. Kimmerer notes: "Anthropologists who study gift economies note that they function well in small, tightly knit communities. You might rightly observe that we no longer live in small, close-knit societies, where generosity and mutual esteem structure our relations. But we could. It is within our power to create such webs of interdependence, quite outside the market economy."[425]

## KLATCHES AND KLATCHING

Now, after that wee sip of divergent political and economic spirits, I return to the Klatch. [426] Klatching restates an old habit (that may seem novel, given the withered state of our social connections). Klatching may have originated pre-historically in gathering around campfires, where heat and food and company waited. Today's neighbors, if accustomed to Klatching, meet to build their community and enjoy its fruits. The most common uses of the Klatch are 1) to talk in an organized fashion

[424] Kimmerer, *The Serviceberry*, 33. Emphasis added.

[425] Kimmerer, *The Serviceberry*, 91. Alexsandr Solzhenitsyn argues similarly. He said: "Society must cease to look upon 'progress' as something desirable. 'Eternal progress' is a nonsensical myth. What must be implemented is not a 'steadily expanding economy,' but a *zero-growth economy*, a stable economy. *Economic growth is not only unnecessary but ruinous*." Solzhenitsyn, *Letter to the Soviet Leaders*, 21-22. Solzhenitsyn also contemplates social revisions not unlike those I advocate in *Cull: Choosing Well*: "An economy of *non*gigantism with small-scale though highly developed technology will not only allow for but necessitate the building of *new* towns of the *old* type." Solzhenitsyn waxes nostalgic about old Russian villages as locales for moral development and the sort of quiet that fosters health. "The present-day centralization of all forms of life of the mind is a monstrosity amounting to spiritual murder." Solzhenitsyn, *Letter to the Soviet Leaders*, 37-38.

[426] The Klatch, as described in this book, draws substantially on the circle tradition and restorative justice and indigenous practices, but gives the Klatch a primary role in community structure, to which circle practitioners may be unaccustomed.

about a topic or share accounts of events, or 2) to welcome new faces to a community, or 3) to address needful healing, or 4) to express or strategize support for someone in difficulty, or 5) to celebrate a joy or success. Where a group is well-versed in Klatching, neighbors may extend a Klatch 6) to formulate responses to local matters of import, or 7) to resolve conflicts (which makes Klatching a core habit of amity-at-law). If necessary, a Klatch might 8) address anti-social activity and propose remedies (and so encroach upon the realm of the justice system). Also, Klatches might be employed 9) to address solutions to societal difficulties, for the purpose of sending reports to courts and legislatures charged with those tasks. Ultimately, Klatches are neighbors caring together for their circumstance and one another.[427]

Klatches have a structure. Neighbors gather at a convenient local site. They sit in a circle. The keeper has stated the purpose of the Klatch. Neighbors affirm the values that draw them together, and those which guide Klatching generally. They pass a talking piece[428] around the circle. Only the person who holds the talking piece speaks. Others listen and ponder. The keeper (who can speak without the talking stick, but seldom does so) participates in the conversation and keeps the Klatch on track (with the help of all other participants). Wisdom flows from the stories participants recount. Ideas are tested. A Klatch lasts one to two hours. Not every Klatch results in a decision. When consensus does emerge, the scribe writes the Klatch report and forwards it to any person the Klatch deems appropriate. This said, Klatches have no formal structure. This paragraph contains only recommendations. Neighbors will structure circles in a manner that makes sense to them. The best approaches drink deep from the history of circles. Every circle is unique, for the persons involved and the issue at hand are unique.

Permit me to back up a bit, to set Klatches in their context. Further, in what follows I set aside many uses of the Klatch (which are as diverse as the concerns of a community) to focus exclusively on those relevant to amity-at-law. I call such law-adjacent Klatches "extra-legal."

## FIRST PRINCIPLES OF KLATCH

What sort of decisional regime might amity jurisprudence issue? What would conflict resolution look like in American society, if common law litigation was relegated to a deeply diminished domain, for which its capacities are better suited? How

---

[427] "We need [dispute resolution] systems that empower people to manage conflict in ways that enable them to tackle challenges together. . . . creating processes and structures that enable people to have access to voice and justice." Amsler, Martinez, and Smith, *Dispute System Design*, 1. Cruikshank and Susskind advocate that adequate dispute resolution systems are fair, efficient, stable, and lean upon shared wisdom. Amsler, Martinez, and Smith, *Dispute System Design*, 13.

[428] A small object passed from participant to participant. When one possesses the talking piece, one can speak. All others listen.

might one heed Roscoe Pound's admonition to stop tinkering with the common law system and promulgate "**a new set of premises, a new order of ideas**" by which to address community conflicts?[429]

I have previously suggested that one must recur to first principles in framing a jurisprudence of amity. What perceptions might guide a reframing of issues that give birth to a legal system? I briefly attempt such a foray.[430]

- **Origins.** Humans share an evolutionary history marred by violence, competition, intolerance, and ignorance. Our origins also hold cooperation, friendship, patience, and learning. As a species, we have been trending away from the former and toward the latter for tens of thousands of years. Our development is slow, but persistent.[431]
- **Belonging.** People join communities, when their participation is something other than historical habit, because they want to *belong and collaborate* with a group with whom they have emotional connections on projects they find meaningful and useful.[432] By belonging, people add communal concerns to to individual awareness. In so doing, they become members. Membership, not individuality, enshrines the human norm. Klatches assume "a universal human wish to be connected to others in a good way."[433]

---

[429] Christine Zozula, in a "new order of ideas" frame of mind says: "In my view, the criminal justice system is a glass shattered across the kitchen floor. Debating whether to first glue together the largest pieces or the smallest shards is fruitless—the glass is broken. Community courts are a shard amid this mess. I hope that instead of trying to cobble together something usable from the jagged pieces, thirsty readers close this book and demand a new glass." Christine Zozula. *Courting the Community: Legitimacy and Punishment in a Community Court*, xi.

[430] I have elaborated this line of thought in greater detail in my book *Cull: Choosing Well*, especially pages 245ff.

[431] Though one would never guess that from reading the newspaper or watching the evening news. Consider the arguments convincingly deployed in Pinker, *Better Angels of Our Nature*.

[432] Contrary to the Hobbesian anti-social assumptions of the common law. Humans cooperate. E.O. Wilson argues that the human capacity for cooperating deeply on the basis of intimate mutual knowledge creates human eusociality, just as pheromones and instinct created ant eusociality. "Eusocial" species rear their young cooperatively across generations, and divide labor with some members sacrificing personal reproductive success in favor of the breeding success of other group members. Natural selection operates to preserve genes in human groups that tend to create cooperative communication and labor, with competition among groups. [♪] Wilson, *The Meaning of Human Existence*, 19, 75.

[433] Pranis, *The Little Book of Circle Processes*, 24. Pranis is quoting language from Judge Barry Stuart of Yukon, Canada.

- **Human-sized.** Members hope their communities remain *small*,[434] because limited numbers make joint efforts comprehensible and emotionally-salient.[435]
- **Tolerating Foibles.** Members are creatures of purposes and dreams. All sometimes find themselves at odds with members of different intentions and aspirations. Interpersonal stresses can lead to relational dissonance, which may grow to pose a threat to collective well-being. Most such frictions among members resolve naturally by: waiting, hoping, letting bad ideas play out and chasten their perpetrators, insulating oneself from the annoying behavior, growing calluses at social rubs, fact-finding, education, and generosity. The relevant habit of character in such resolutions is patient tolerance.
- **Antagonisms.** One addresses more troubling *antagonisms* interpersonally, by irenic interventions: listening, talking, reaffirming friendship, compromising, seeking wise counsel, resolving factual indeterminacy, learning things, being patient, recognizing that either or both members may be wrong, considering the needs of one's own community and of other communities, and imagining better outcomes.[436]
- **Community Intervention.** When interpersonal antagonisms cannot be resolved by members and their intimates, the community may need to become involved, to restore amity and protect the group from divisive rhetoric or

---

[434] That is, at or below the Dunbar number of 150 persons, which number when surpassed renders the community less comprehensible in direct correlation to the excess members. The slippery slope toward anonymity commences. See Robin Dunbar, *How Many Friends Does One Person Need?: Dunbar's Number and Other Evolutionary Quirks*.

[435] Contrary to the alienating one-size-fits-all commitment of common law procedural rules, purporting to govern the disputes of hundreds of millions of similarly-situated citizens.

[436] Friends heed friends, but tend to ignore adversaries. Morphing from adversary to friend is possible. There is a pattern to adversary interpersonal transformations:

- Initiative: One offers friendship,
- Conversation: One reasons,
- Caring: One demonstrates compassion,
- Listening: One learns the participant's view of the matter and the life experiences pertinent to that view,
- Frankness: One notes the participant's shortcomings and role in the distressed relationship, as well as one's own shortcomings and role in the distressed relationship,
- Forgiveness: One embraces the person despite their flaw(s),
- Perspective: One details the role of all players in the underlying problem(s),
- Imagination: One suggests a view of the dispute that exceeds the complexity of a we/them tale,
- Wisdom: One specifies downsides of adversarial tilting under the given circumstance,
- Intimacy: One diverts the participant's broadsides toward "long conversation," which brims with detail and genuine dialogue. Such is the talk of friends working on a common problem,
- Recursion: One again solicits the participant's friendship,
- Community: Then one involves others in resolving the dissonance.

acts. Decision-making may improve with input from additional members, especially when those members are involved in some way in the matter or possess pertinent expertise. Disputes often reach loggerheads because no good alternatives lie open to the members. Community involvement increases the likelihood that all available resources are being deployed and all promising avenues are being explored.[437]

- **Downshifting**. Some matters may not bend to amicable interventions.[438] Likely candidates for downshifting include violent crime and the depredations of ill-restrained sociopaths. If, after the minutes, hours, days, (or weeks, months, or years) of patient irenic effort, if after community Klatch, the participants remain oppositional, then one must downshift. Courts and quasi-judicial adversarial proceedings beckon. Battle is joined, much to the dismay of all.

## COUSINS OF KLATCH

Non-legal dispute resolution stretches deep into the past and widely across the globe. Almost all conflicts are settled without juridic interventions. When one peers at a social context, inquiring how members resolve conflicts, one discovers a host of methods: friends advising, cups of coffee, circles, the wisdom of elders, non-litigating attorneys, religious companionship, helpful books, family interventions, diversion to shared tasks, and the healing balm of time.

More broadly, when one peers into global precedents, a welter of communal conflict resolution peeks from behind judicial obscuration. "The relentless force of law in modern American society can be measured by its domination, and virtual annihilation, of alternative forms of dispute resolution."[439] So, shovel in hand, let us exhume some deceased or ailing alternatives, American and otherwise, to the common

[437] Resources that may help resolve a dispute might include the following:

1. Employment opportunities,
2. Mediators,
3. Housing services,
4. Therapists,
5. Mutual friends,
6. Non-profit services,
7. Psychiatrists,
8. Addiction programs,
9. Books and articles addressing the relevant problems,
10. Respected elders,
11. Trusted professionals.

[438] Conflict recalcitrance may lie in the adamance of perpetrators, or in the poor resourcing of affected communities. A group cannot intervene effectively if it lacks psychiatric care for persons suffering mental illness or rehabilitation programs for those dealing with drug addiction.

[439] Auerbach, *Justice Without Law?*, 15.

law, some which have not yet wholly expired. And let us recognize that, except for mostly urban settings in the last three thousand years[440], non-judicial dispute resolution was the only game in town.

1. **Pre-historical Solutions.** Humans have existed for around 200,000 years. Before *homo sapiens sapiens*, others of our hominid bush existed for a few million years. Throughout, conflicts existed, but no courts. Of their solutions, we know little or nothing. But we are well assured that they had approaches (perhaps utterly deficient approaches) by which they resolved disputes. Courts are a relative innovation, guiding disputes for less than three percent of homo sapiens's existence. Common law courts and their progenitors are yet more fresh than their Egyptian or Roman ancestors.

2. **Early Church.** The early Christian church cast its member dispute resolution format into the mouth of Jesus: "If your brother sins against you, go and tell him his fault, between you and him alone. If he listens to you, you have gained your brother. But if he does not listen, take one or two others along with you, that every word may be confirmed by the evidence of two or three witnesses. If he refuses to listen to them, tell it to the church; and if he refuses to listen even to the church, let him be to you as a Gentile and a tax collector." The nascent church sought interpersonal reconciliation, followed by small group intervention, followed by church shaming, followed by excommunication. (*Matthew 18:15-17*: Revised Standard Version.) This view was to have much salience for Christian utopians in early America.

3. **Kpelle Moot.** The moot of the African Kpelle people in Liberia sorts disputes informally, avoiding the more modern courts of that country. Kpelle tribal organization is acephalous, lacking one head in favor of multiple heads and associations, each having its say in group matters. The moot is preferred when complex family or multi-party issues emerge, since the formal courts of Liberia tend toward coercion and arbitrary decisions, which, in family matters, tend to further alienate, rather than reconcile, disputants. Kpelle moots occur promptly after an offense occurs, and so reduce hardening of positions among the distressed participants. Procedurally, the complainant calls the moot. He chooses a kinsman to mediate, usually one of the several elders of his

---

[440] That is, for all but 1.5 percent of human existence, the cousins of Klatch were the only game in town.

clan. A large group attends the moot, all those who have knowledge or concern. Participants are packed tightly in a room. An elder offers blessing, a rhythmic responsive prayer to yala, their deity. All respond "so be it" to the elder's supplications, which continues in chanted antiphonal give and take. Participants wear their better clothes. They sit in no particular order. The complainant speaks first, and may be questioned at any time by any participant. Then the accused speaks, and answers questions. Then both question one another and question other participants. Those who are out of line are fined, being then obligated to provide rum for the group to imbibe. The mediator and others state how each participant contributed to the problem under consideration. The person mainly at fault formally apologizes by offering token gifts to his opponent. The prevailing party also offers gifts, though lesser ones, to the guilty person. The losing party is fined, incurring an obligation to provide rum to the mediator and other participants. All drink. The elder again blesses the group and asks all to be kind and cooperative with one another.

The Kpelle moot tends to create consensus, since no participant exercises coercive powers. The result apportions blame, and usually attributes fault to both principals and sometimes others as well. The process, unlike adversarial courts, is expressly conciliatory, and its procedures therapeutic. Further, moot procedures encourage input from anyone who participates. The moot outcome addresses broader concerns than those that convened the moot. The goal is to reach a point where participants say that they agree with all that has been said in the moot and have nothing further on their minds. A party who rejects the view of the moot may face disapproval from his tribal group, and he may suffer social censure. The costs of accepting the moot's judgment are nominal, and the rewards lie in informal social benefits, such as reconciliation, repair of ruptured relationships, and restored respect.[441]

4. **North American Colonial Conciliation.** Colonists in North America resisted common law approaches to disputes. Communitarian principles and religious convictions led to rejection of law as a theory, and to censure for individual assertiveness. Not only values, but also much land, were held in common. Law was, in their vision of human togetherness, "an alien value system, antithetical to Christianity itself."[442] The

---

[441] Gibbs, "The *Kpelle* Moot," 33 *Africa*, No. 1 (1963), as contained in Podolefsky, Aaron and Peter J. Brown, *Applying Anthropology*, Third Edition, 1994.

[442] Auerbach, *Justice Without Law?*, 22.

goal of these immigrating groups (Puritans, Quakers) was to establish the Kingdom of God in their new land. So, disputes required a holy solution. Disputes were settled by congregational pastors, elders, or membership. To the extent that this resulted in suppression of conflicts, rather than their resolution, anti-legal approaches to disputes contributed to community schism. As their numbers grew and religious fervor dissipated over time, law courts crept into the governance scheme. In the end, only courts offered a forum for residents who no longer shared a common faith or similar values.

Anti-legalism again surged during the Great Awakening of the American 1740s. George Whitefield said: "As for the *Business* of an *Attorney*, I think it *unlawful* for a Christian, or at least *exceeding dangerous*: *Avoid it therefore*, and glorify God in some *other Station*."[443]

Utopian communities of the nineteenth century, such as Oneida community or the Mormons or Swedenborgians recurred to establishing communities of believers where anti-legal sentiments might safely harbor. John Noyes, who founded Oneida, asserted it was better to suffer than to litigate, and he intended to make litigation impossible within Oneida.[444]

5. **Commercial Arbitration.** Merchants, from the mid-eighteenth century, preferred arbitration for its speed, privacy, and reduced expense. In 1768, the New York Chamber of Commerce created private tribunals for settling merchant disputes, asserting that "All controversies are antagonistic to commerce."[445] Lawyers, perceiving danger to their prestige and monopoly, tried to quash the development. Lawyers were, after all, excluded from these early arbitrations. In the end, the Bar was unsuccessful, for businesses preferred non-governmental negotiations in which trade practice, not legal precedent, guided resolutions. Businessmen styled themselves a community of honorable men, in which legal rules and procedural straight-jackets were unnecessary. Attorneys did, however, succeed in co-opting the arbitration associations, bringing the process under judicial oversight and involving lawyers in its administration. And this development commenced the jurispathic emasculation of arbitration theory. Opponents argued that lay arbitration was private

---

443 Auerbach, *Justice Without Law?*, 41. The italicizations are original.

444 Auerbach, *Justice Without Law?*, 51.

445 Auerbach, *Justice Without Law?*, 33.

government, and so, inimical to the constitutional order. Law corralled arbitration, and lawyers monopolized its more lucrative cases and roles. So, arbitration became another wan adjunct of law, but with slightly different rules. Nevertheless, arbitration remains, to this day, the preferred dispute resolution procedure for most businesses, so much so that many refuse to deal at all unless arbitration is agreed in advance, should some dispute arise.[446] Auerbach concludes: "If the impulse toward justice without law is periodically irresistible, the legalization of dispute settlement seems inexorable in our modern culture."[447]

6. **Conciliation Districts.** Scandinavian communities (mostly in North Dakota and Minnesota) stitched homeland practices to their adoptive American fabric. Communities consisting in twenty or more families were a "conciliation district." In private meetings convened by a conciliator, disputes were discussed and settled. Lawyers were excluded entirely, for they made "acquiescent participants adversarial," and every case into a tiny war.[448] Local courts refused to process any case in which no effort at conciliation had been attempted.

7. **Chinese Headman Adjustments.** Nineteenth century immigrant Chinese communities, responding to their cultural heritage and American racial discrimination, transplanted their tradition of benevolent despots. Wealthy merchants addressed disputes, and a combination of ostracism and shame buffeted those who declined their interventions. Two proverbs captured the impetus behind acquiescence. "It is better to be vexed to death than to bring a lawsuit," and "Once go to law and there is nothing but trouble."[449]

8. **Early-Twentieth Century Conciliation Movement**. In Cleveland, Ohio, in 1913, a municipal court offered lawyer-free resolutions to low-value disputes without arcane legal procedure or lawyers or legal rules (judges relied on common sense). These courts promoted compromise and reconciliation. Conciliation spread to Chicago and New York, and

---

[446] I am one such. A binding arbitration clause lies in each of my attorney-client contracts. I have never, to date, suffered arbitration with a client, since I prefer more irenic processes of dispute resolution.

[447] Auerbach, *Justice Without Law?*, 114.

[448] Auerbach, *Justice Without Law?*, 72.

[449] Auerbach, *Justice Without Law?*, 73-75.

its emphasis on peace and friendship grew. A newspaper editor called conciliation "a movement toward justice in spite of lawyers." Conciliation died the death one would expect. Lawyers criticized it for not being "legal" enough; they alleged it would devolve into two-tier justice. Conciliation's patrons lacked funds, and so the process starved. Patrons also failed to understand the process. Courts they discussed at bars; conciliation, not so much. Finally, conciliation's subject matter failed to inspire: causes under thirty-five dollars.[450] Conciliation's comrade, arbitration, however, appealed to commercial interests. Businessmen adopted extra-judicial proceedings and paid staffs. Arbitration ascended. Conciliation slunk to its grave.

9. **Therapeutic Courts**. Washington courts, with the support and approval of the Washington State legislature, have created special purpose courts that operate parallel to the criminal and civil trial court system. These institutions operate within (but somewhat outside) the common law judiciary. They lie within the common law system in that a judicial act creates these outlier courts, pursuant to the powers inherent in the language of Washington Constitution, Article IV, Section 1.[451] Their existence is further specified by statute at RCW 2.30.[452] Therapeutic courts lie outside the common law system in that their goals and procedures differ, though they are part of the common law courts administratively. Common law courts aim to provide well-wrought recompense for criminal or civil violations. Therapeutic courts aim to provide treatment for an individual's specific needs, thereby improving the life of the identified individual and their community, while reducing recidivism and costs of court process and incarcerations. These are promising developments. Yet, therapeutic courts remain part of the court system,

---

[450] Today, that inflation-adjusted value would be $1,123. For further descriptions of conciliation, especially in industrial and union contexts, see Lowell, *Industrial Arbitration and Conciliation: Some Chapters from the Industrial History of the Past Thirty Years*.

[451] *Washington Constitution*. "The Judiciary. Article IV Section 1, JUDICIAL POWER, WHERE VESTED. The judicial power of the state shall be vested in supreme court, superior courts, justices of the peace, and such inferior courts as the legislature may provide."

[452] This statute specifically refers to, but does not limit the possibilities of, therapeutic courts to the following: adult drug court, juvenile drug court, family dependency treatment court or family drug court, mental health court, which may include participants with developmental disabilities, DUI court, veterans treatment court, truancy court, domestic violence court, gambling court, community court, homeless court, and treatment, responsibility, and accountability on campus (Back on TRAC court). The statute excludes some individuals from therapeutic courts: previous serious violent or sexual felons, those who employed firearms in criminal offenses, those charged with vehicular homicide, those charged or previously charged with substantial bodily harm or death of another.

subject to its vagaries of funding and tempted by its preference for coercion. And, as do other courts, they still frighten and mystify participants.

Some characterize therapeutic courts as "problem-solving courts." These courts address underlying social dysfunctions that rise to public attention in the misdeeds of some. Their goal, being therapeutic, is to care for offending individuals more than control them.[453]

10. **Ubuntu in Post-Apartheid South African Truth Commission.** South Africa sought to mend its ugly history of apartheid violence, following collapse of its racist government, by a truth and reconciliation commission (TRC). Such commissions are temporary governmental bodies that detail an historical pattern of (usually governmental) misbehavior by means of direct interviews with those who have been injured, resulting in a final report of findings and recommendations. South African Constitutional Court Justice, Albie Sachs, wrote of the creation of their nation's TRC, which addressed apartheid violence of the regime and its ANC opponents. Its proceedings were public. Those who truthfully confessed their behavior, and whose acts were proportional to their political objectives, received amnesty. The TRC sought acknowledgement of events and reparations and reconstitution of a workable polity. Revenge and retaliation were not goals.

    The *South African Interim Constitution of 1993* contained a postscript that indicated the purpose of the new constitution was to correct past crimes by means of reconciliation and ubuntu. "Ubuntu" stands for the "sense of belonging to a community. I am a person, because we are all persons. We become human through living with other human beings, respecting and acknowledging each other. It is a very embracing, affirmative and warm concept, which finds its place in the post-script to our constitution."[454]

---

[453] Snedker calls the therapeutic work of mental health courts "social work criminal justice." Such courts move away from social control of offenders, and toward care for perpetrators. With these sentiments, mental health courts are neither courts in the traditional sense nor ordinary social service agencies, but something of a hybrid organization. Snedker, *Therapeutic Justice*, 265. Berman and Feinblatt chronicle the growth of problem-solving courts across the nation, especially in criminal justice. Berman and Feinblatt, *Good Courts: The Case for Problem-Solving Justice*, 2005. For information on such alternative approaches to justice outside the United States, see Abel, *The Politics of Informal Justice: Comparative Studies*, Volume 2 (1982). For a lightly critical view of alternative courts, see Harrington, *Shadow Justice: The Ideology and Institutionalization of Alternatives to Court* (1985). For an appreciative survey of the various sorts of problem-solving courts, see Higgins and Mackinem, *Problem-Solving Courts: Justice for the Twenty-First Century?* (2009). For case studies in community justice centers, see Murray, *Community Justice Centres: New Trajectories in Law* (2022).

[454] Sachs, "Truth and Reconciliation," 52 *SMU Law Review*, 1999, 1567. Oddly, the *ubuntu* postscript was omitted from the ultimate South African constitution.

Of ubuntu, Archbishop Desmond Tutu, who participated in the TRC as a judge, repeated an African proverb: "A person is a person through other persons."[455] Elsewhere, Tutu described the thrust of ubuntu so: "My humanity is caught up, is inextricably bound up, in yours."[456] These and other similar thoughts lead to community restoration and forgiveness in conflict interventions. And ubuntu frontally contradicts American individualism and its entrenchment in common law courts.

11. **People's Assemblies.** People's assemblies welcome all to a meeting to discuss relevant topics; they are a form of direct democracy.[457] People's assemblies claim historical antecedents in the *ekklasia* conclaves of ancient Athens, the recent democratic upsurge of Kurdistan, the Spanish municipal movement (Indignados), in Senegal's Y'en a Marre movement, and other groups. Relying on unfettered inclusivity, active listening, and mutual trust, people's assemblies can be adapted to many purposes. This approach has been used in Petaluma, California, to consider future uses of an abandoned fairgrounds.[458]

12. **Adaptations of Indigenous Circles**. Circle practice has been adapted from Amerind cultures to address common social and criminal matters.[459] A circle convenes all parties to an untoward event and other interested or helpful persons to address the facts of a matter, and seek resolution of injuries suffered.[460] The restorative justice movement

---

[455] Tutu, Desmond. Foreword to Ngomane, *Everyday Ubuntu: Living Better Together, the African Way*. London: Bantam Press, 2019. At page 8.

[456] Ngomane, *Everyday Ubuntu*, 13. The author, Mungi Ngomane, is Tutu's granddaughter.

[457] People's assemblies differ from citizen assemblies. Citizen assemblies are selected from the population at large to be representative. The topic is specified, and the group provided with experts and stakeholders in that topic. *Community Assembly Manual*, published by ExtinctionRebellion.UK. (This document is a nuts-and-bolts user's guide for outside-the-box organizers.)

[458] Fryer, "Seattle, here's something we haven't tried: A people's assembly," *Seattle Times*, February 26, 2023.

[459] William Isaacs said: "As far as I know, no indigenous culture has yet been found that does not have the practice of sitting in a circle and talking." Pranis, Stewart, and Wedge, *Peacemaking Circles*, xiii.

[460] Circles have many other incarnations. They are used for talking, addressing issues, seeking understanding, providing support and fostering healing, community building, cooling conflicts, addressing crime and civil injuries, sentencing parties who have injured others, reintegrating challenging persons into their community, and celebrating events important to participants. The structure works well in neighborhoods, schools, book clubs, social organizations, businesses, and families.

employs circle practice to divert adjudication from blaming-and-punishing to addressing the many causes of an anti-social event and restoring relationships. The best-known such effort lies with the Navajo Peacemaker Courts, established in 1982.[461]

One finds in the American cousins of Klatch a unifying fact, which Auerbach admirably captures: "[L]itigiousness was intolerable as long as a community of common interest transcended individual self-interest. Once that (usually foreign) community dissolved amid the promise of individual opportunity, the immigrants (or their children) were just normal Americans."[462] Which is to say that these acculturating people abandoned communal values for the crass scrum of business wrangling and pugilistic courtroom spectacles.

Pound asserted that common law courts have inherent limitations as to the number and type of social problems that can be loaded on their back. Pound recognized "intrinsic limitations upon effective legal action; not every social problem had a legal solution."[463] The landscape harbors a push-and-shove between justice-according-to-law and justice-without-law. One learns that the many deficiencies of our common law cannot be cured by another round of legal reforms or tinkered adjustments. To open space for "**a new set of premises, a new order of ideas,**" one must shrink the territorial boundaries of common law to hew adequate space for a different genus of governance, for *non-law communal solutions to everyday conflicts*. Where communities fail to evict the common law, that regime will linger and meddle, forever a recalcitrant squatter. So intrusive has common law's theory become, that many can conceive no other, better approach to resolving the problems troubling local communities. We need sparks for kindling imaginative fires.

---

Circles share structure and values and an assumption. **Structurally**, a circle's keeper invites participants to circle, if appropriate. Circle participants divide their time in equal shares between 1) *community building* (introducing themselves, setting values for the circle, trust-building by sharing stories from their lives) and 2) *addressing the issue* that caused the circle to form. Participants open and close ceremonially, pass a talking piece around the circle (possession of which gives permission to speak and asks all others to listen), rely on a keeper (who guides, but does not control, the circle), make all decisions by consensus (not always by agreeing, but some may decline to dissent), communicating by story-telling from the heart (not lecturing or demonstrating expertise), and emphasizing building high quality relationships. **Of values**, circles determine those for themselves, but these priorities usually include committing to interact with participants with respect, honesty, humility, sharing, courage, inclusivity, empathy, trust, and forgiveness. (See Pranis, *Circle Processes*, 25.) Further, participants **assume** that all people share a desire to connect to other people in a good way.

461 McCold, "The recent history of restorative justice," in *Handbook of Restorative Justice.* Edited by Dennis Sullivan and Larry Tifft. New York: Routledge, 2008, at page 28. The United Nations has published instructions: *Handbook on Restorative Justice Programmes*, Office on Drugs and Crime, November 2006. See also Noll, *Peacemaking*, 284.

462 Auerbach, *Justice Without Law?*, 94.

463 Auerbach, *Justice Without Law?*, 96.

I turn now to further describe a new set of premises, a new order of ideas: the Klatch.[464]

A FRAMEWORK FOR KLATCHES

1. **Klatch Described.** A neighborhood Klatch is a meeting-for-discussion of persons involved in an issue. Those Klatches intersecting with the legal system (extra-legal Klatches) would aim to vest decisions about needs or conflicts in the hands of the people coping with those problems. An extra-legal Klatch[465] would convene ten or so persons, with respect to an event: a **convener**, the person **injured** (injuree), the person causing **injury** (injurer), a **friend** of the injurer, a **friend** of the injured, a **police** officer (if a crime was involved), a **person trusted** by both injuree and injurer, **authority figures** in the community in question, **eye witness**(es), and any other **persons of relevance** to the injurious event or dispute. For a period not to exceed two hours, Klatch members introduce themselves, describe their values for the Klatch, discuss the event in question and possible resolutions of the conflict, reach a consensus (if possible), and offer evaluation of the Klatch. A **scribe** briefly reports the course of Klatch and its consensus, and a **Klatch keeper** monitors and adjusts the tone and progress of dialogue.[466]

---

[464] Perhaps I over-promise here. The Klatch is one among many cousins that have origins both ancient and recent. Nevertheless, considering the entrenchment of common law jurisprudence, the old can smell surprisingly fresh. And the role in everyday life for Klatching and jurisprudence may exceed that contemplated by cousin approaches.

[465] Here, one imagines a predicate of tort, or criminal misdemeanor, or landlord-tenant dispute, or real property encroachment.

[466] Carrie Menkel-Meadow would probably characterize the Klatch as a specimen of informal justice. She says: "Thus, core claims of value for 'informal' justice included:

- Direct party empowerment and participation in case 'presentation' and resolution
- Self-determination
- Consent
- Tailored solutions, based on party needs and interests, not necessarily 'rights' and claims of law (utilising tailored individual, religious, ethical or communitarian principles for resolution, eg 'joint custody' in divorce and children's custody)
- Non-monetised outcomes and solutions (apologies, trades, in-kind, other forms of 'relief')
- Future, not just past, oriented problem solving, without need necessarily of fact finding or assessment of blame
- Confidentiality, producing the opportunity for changed 'positions', trades and non-precedential accommodations or solutions, as well as privacy protection for disputants of all kinds, individuals and organisations
- Inclusion of more than two litigant 'parties in interest' (multi-party dispute resolution)
- Reduction of elite and professional decision makers in parties' lives and disputes, utilisation of party 'consent', not command, as legitimating value
- Flexible, situation specific, rules and practices of proceedings
- Contingent solutions (capable of being revisited with changing conditions) without precedential force or rigidity

The Klatch is not a less-formal addition to the long list of non-judicial dispute resolution approaches (for example, mediation, collaborative law, arbitration, therapeutic courts), all of which function in the shadow of the common law, and most of which (all?) are beholden to courts and the laws governing courts. Nor is the Klatch a surrogate or replacement for circles and conciliations and Kpelle moots, which are Klatch's cousins.

**The Klatch asserts a non-constitutional, but constitutionally-permitted, prerogative—to address and resolve one's own problems without intervention of strangers. As such, Klatches constitute a non-enumerated liberty interest. Klatches resolve conflicts locally and personally. Courts are jurisdictional. Klatches are neighborly. Well-practiced, the Klatch would supplant most functions now dominated by (or neglected by) courts and court-subservient processes. Every conflict (even international and corporate and constitutional disputes) could be subject to Klatch interventions. They would do so outside law.[467] The Klatch, when addressing matters of constitutional import, is not illegal, but *extra-legal* in its theory.** The Klatch lodestar is interpersonal harmony and gentle admonition. Klatches abandon rule-mongering and finger-pointing by which courts foster enmity and exacerbate adversarial hostilities. Klatches, where they are able, restore amity.

Klatches invert common law.[468] Courts begin with a demand for presence (summons) and threats for non-compliance, requiring one to hear what unknown persons

---

- 'Reorientation' of the parties to each other—promoting healing relationships, not rupture and continued conflict and resentment of formal litigation or punitive results in criminal matters
- Potentially faster and cheaper dispute resolution ('efficiency')
- Greater legitimacy of and compliance with party-chosen outcomes."

Carrie Menkel-Meadows, "Regulation of Dispute Resolution in the United States of America: From the Formal to the Informal to the 'Semi-formal'," at pages 433-434.

[467] Though a law specifying that no law shall govern Klatches would be welcomed.

[468] Matt Halling argues for a systemic inversion of the courts, which he styles as "participatory law," or "par-law": Halling asserts that authority in America derives from the consent of the governed. Yet judges come to power with scant public involvement. When it comes to judges, the public has no meaningful say in who sits upon their benches. When we vote, we know little of candidates because they are forbidden to speak of their values. When we enter courtrooms, we, who have not consented to the authority of this judge, have no alternative but to knuckle under to her coercive potential. Participatory society (parsociety) aims to invert our hierarchies. In parsociety, the local council (30-50 persons) has the greatest power, and so every member can, and is required to, make decisions with local others about their lives. Councils relate to one another by contract and regional agreements. Participatory law would share parsociety's bottom-up organization. Commencing from a society governed by local concern, parlaw would emphasize voluntary compliance, customary practices, and federal cooperation (with the local community wielding the greatest authority). **So, parlaw is an attempt to reconceive law from the needs of commoners.** "Parlaw is hostile to the notion of a centralized judiciary and rather resembles a huge network of agreed upon dispute resolutions."[468] Parlaw judges are selected randomly from citizen rolls and for limited periods. See Halling, "A Law of No Gods, No Masters—Developing and Defending a Participatory Legal System," 248.

have to say in language most cannot comprehend. Klatches begin with invitations and promises of cookies and coffee, and proceed in your neighbor's vernacular on matters of community import.

- *Where.* Courts own single-purpose premises for their proceedings, purchased at public expense. Klatch participants own no such buildings, but use community facilities or invitations to private premises.
- *Who.* Courts rely on deeply-trained judges and attorneys. Such persons hold no special role in Klatches; no formal training is required for participants. Rather, Klatch participants are players in the event under consideration, or are socially connected to those who are players. No participant is paid. None are experts. All become part of the Klatch consensus, or decline to do so.
- *How.* Courts seek to exclude prejudicial evidence in order to arrive, to the extent possible, at pristine, impartial decisions, in a painfully slow deliberative examination, often spanning several months and sometimes years. Klatches deride such thinking, arguing that those involved in a circumstance, knowledgeable about the facts of the matter, together with their prejudices and doubts, are best positioned to conceive and adopt workable solutions. The facts of a matter are either known to participants or derived from knowledgeable sources, with their evidentiary prickliness intact, for sorting by those present. Klatches end in two hours.
- *What.* Courts recognize causes of action deriving from the history of common law, and ignore others. Extra-legal Klatches address what troubles neighborhoods, from dam placements to errant parking to airport regulations to crime to vendettas to vehicular collisions. Klatches intervene when conflicts are nascent and, therefore, pliant. Courts reach disputes only after dust-ups have hardened into hatreds. Where Klatches have matured, no court should deign to hear any matter than has not been taken to Klatch. No legislature should deliberate any issue that has not been the subject of at least one Klatch.
- *When.* Courts work generally from nine to noon and one-thirty to four-thirty, Monday through Friday, and never on holidays. In other words, courts make themselves available at those times least accessible and most costly to working people. Klatches convene at times chosen to accommodate participants (most probably, weekends and evenings and holidays).
- *Why.* The rationale for court decisions lies in a long trail of prior court decisions, constitutions, and legislative statutes. Courts shoehorn the facts of a matter into the mold of a vaguely-similar historical case (*precedent*). They adhere to the idea that a court must apply the rule established in that historical matter to the current dilemma (*stare decisis*). Klatches acknowledge no precedents, since persons knowledgeable about a circumstance know this

particular event has never before occurred and will never again be repeated. Since every person is unique and every person's relations to others are likewise unique, all matters brought to Klatch are wholly without precedent. No precedent should be sought. None should be accepted.[469]

2. **Klatch Roles**. While individual Klatches may differ, many extra-legal Klatches will invite a predictable cast:
   - Klatch **keeper**, who sets a time and place and issues invitations, and keeps proceedings civil and timely and short.
   - **Injurer**, who harmed someone or something.
   - **Injuree**, who was harmed or damaged financially.
   - **Support person of injurer**, who is a friend present to provide emotional support.
   - **Support person of injuree**, who is a friend present to provide emotional support.
   - **Representative of law enforcement** (if a crime may have been committed, and the other participants consent to an enforcement presence).
   - **Persons trusted** by both injurer and injuree, who may offer guidance.
   - **Authority figure**, recognized by injurer and injuree as a person who may contribute useful perspective on a matter and has connections to government agencies.
   - **Witness(es),** who have first-hand knowledge of events.
   - **Other persons of relevance**, who have other sorts of knowledge or important relation to the matter considered.
   - **Scribe**, who writes a brief report of the Klatch.

3. **Klatch Values**. In Klatches, character and expertise matter. Wealth, class, power, and beauty do not. Klatches share values and commitments and purposes:
   - supportive toward neighbors,
   - prompt,
   - brief,
   - egalitarian,
   - non-hierarchical,
   - solution-oriented,

[469] Some argue that, absent precedent and the practice of *stare decisis*, societal stability would suffer, and the predictability of court guidance would be fractured for businesses. These persons dramatically overstate the predictability of court outcomes, and have failed to notice that our law-ridden culture grows less, not more, stable.

- humble,
- honest,
- heartfelt,
- spiritual,
- therapeutic,
- non-adversarial,
- agreement seeking (that is, working toward deliberative consensus),
- listening deeply (a talking piece may be used to designate who is authorized to speak),
- non-professional (but not anti-professional),
- inexpensive/free,
- fosters community,
- builds social-competence.

4. **Klatch Education:**

    - Brief training for Klatch keepers and scribes.

    - Introductory booklet provided to those who have never before participated in Klatch.

    - Elementary education should include Klatching to help students address problems they are having. Klatch process should be taught every year in every school, and employed in every school every year.

5. **Expense**. Klatches meet in free locations. There is no cost to participate. Participants who can pay bear any costs incurred, if they wish. Klatches should never seek or accept public funding.

6. **Consent**. Only those remedies to which all participants consent bind the participants. Consent consists in approval of a Klatch proposal, or acquiescence in an outcome one cannot endorse, but will not oppose.

    - Keeper should issue monthly reports on compliance to all Klatch members for a period determined in Klatch. If non-compliant, the keeper re-convenes the Klatch to address that non-compliance.

- If a Klatch fails to reach consensus, that Klatch has failed, and its report should reflect such failure.

7. **Courts and Legislatures.** All disputes or communal decisions, large and small, may commence in Klatch. Courts and legislatures should decline cases and issues that have not engaged in Klatch. The court or legislative rule might be: only after failing to reach consensus in Klatch may a cause be downshifted to courts or legislatures. All issues of public governance may be considered by Klatches. Constitutional organizations, such as councils, courts, law enforcement, and legislatures, should seek Klatch reports, and should show due deference to them. Klatch reports are not jurisdictional documents. Rather, Klatch reports represent the considered opinion of those persons most familiar with an event or matter. For widespread issues, many Klatch reports may exist. Since these are non-precedential, such reports may not reach similar conclusions, nor should they be expected to do so.

8. **Remedies.** A Klatch may reach any consensus it can, and agree to any penalty or remediation participants endorse. The injurer must consent to any impositions.

9. **Confidential Proceedings.** Participant opinions, when expressed in Klatch, are confidential, unless the Klatch endorses a participant's perspective in the matter at hand. Who participated, the subject of the Klatch, the Klatch report, and subsequent compliance reports are not confidential.

10. **Non-Judicial.** Klatch stands outside the constitutional framework of government, residing in rights reserved to the people, but constitutionally unspecified.[470]

11. **Non-Precedential.** How one Klatch resolves a matter guides no other Klatch. Participants of one Klatch should not expect a different Klatch addressing a similar matter to agree to remedies preferred by any previous Klatch.

12. **Klatch Report.**

    - Klatch reports should be expressed in language easily comprehended by middle school students.

[470] Specifically, those rights preserved but unspecified in the United States Constitution at the Tenth Amendment: "The powers not delegated to the United States by the Constitution, nor prohibited by it to the States, are reserved to the State respectively, or to the people." And those rights preserved but unspecified in the Washington State Constitution at Article One, Declaration of Rights, at Section 30: "The enumeration in this Constitution of certain rights shall not be construed to deny others retained by the people."

- Klatch proceedings may be recorded for scribal use. Any such recording shall be deleted when the scribe completes his or her Klatch report.

- The scribe should issue a brief report (one to three pages) of issues and outcomes, reported in English, Spanish, and any other language the Klatch deems relevant.

- If downshifted, Klatch reports of a dispute should become evidence in litigated proceedings, and Klatch-prescribed remedies should be due a presumption of deference from judges.[471]

## DANGERS FACING KLATCH

The preeminent danger facing any Klatch system is **judicial assimilation**. Were extra-legal Klatches to prove both viable and effective, there would follow attempts by the judicial system or legislature or the alternative dispute resolution (ADR) practitioners to draw Klatches into the judicial orbit or its satellite ADR regimes.[472] Promises of financial support, and legitimacy, and regularity may entice. There exist significant threats in such assimilations. Though adoption by the courts might lend legitimacy and funding, courts are jurispathic. (See Chapter 2, in the section that commences "Some argue the common law is deeming and jurispathic.") Law warps

[471] Warren Burger said: "[I]f a system of voluntary arbitration is to be truly effective, it should be final and binding, without a provision for *de novo* trial or review." Burger, "*Isn't There a Better Way?*," 277.

[472] In a discussion of informal justice systems that stand outside of their formal counterparts, Tilmann Röder said: "[M]ore recent efforts focus on *strengthening and reforming existing traditional institutions* and *linking them to state institutions* rather than trying to marginalise them. A purely state centered concept of the rule of law finds less and less support while informal justice institutions are more and more acknowledged as functional equivalents of state courts. In the latter sense Brian Tamanaha has stated that 'although non-state justice systems do not meet the requirements of the rule of law, they can and do satisfy rule of law functions', at least insofar as they can 'play an important role in connection with establishing and maintaining rule governed behaviour between citizens'. They complement – and often even substitute – the state infrastructure for conflict resolution, may enable the restoration of the social peace, and even provide better legal certainty." Röder, Tilmann. (2013). "Informal Justice Systems: Challenges and Perspectives." Pages 58-61. Note the presumption that dispute resolution systems outside formal justice structures need linkage to the formal system. This, I confute.

associated systems to its own curvature.[473] Organizations that decline to conform are exterminated.[474]

A more subtle, but no less fatal, tendency creeps in. Associated organizations grow to mirror one another, even when once they were deeply distinguishable. Some call this organizational **isomorphism**.[475] Timothy Hedeen describes isomorphism struggles of community mediation programs.

> The consequences of institutionalizing are not restricted to coerced participation, an emphasis on cost and time efficiency, or the pressure to mediate inappropriate cases. Institutionalization leads not only *toward* the goals of the justice system, but *away* from other goals, including the community focus and community ownership envisioned by many practitioners. . . .
>
> Some hoped that community mediation would provide a "**first-resort conflict-settlement service for local residents outside the perimeters of the formal legal system**. Despite these hopes, the typical program remains neither a first resort nor very far (if at all) outside the legal system. . . . Another article in this volume recommends that the field of dispute resolution should "yearn for paradise, live in limbo." Coincidentally, sociolegal scholars tracing a regional history of restorative justice—an umbrella term for community dispute resolution

[473] Courts have long tolerated alternatives to their own processes, and even situated some within their system. The Washington Court of Appeals has written: "We recognize that "[a]dult drug courts are philosophically, functionally, and intentionally different from ordinary criminal courts. . . . Drug court is designed to be collaborative rather than adversarial, and that collaboration differentiates drug court from ordinary criminal proceedings. . . . In fact, it is because drug courts operate outside of the traditional adversarial process that they have been more successful at treating addiction and related criminal behavior than conventional justice system interventions for some offenders." *State v. Harrison*, 24 Wn. App. 2d 40, 50 (2022) (citations omitted). Consider also juvenile court, mental health court, and the innovation of "parenting coordinator" (in which an unelected professional makes substantial decisions about the structure of litigants' care for their children). ADR (mediation, arbitration, and settlement negotiations) amount to litigation-lite, at least where attorneys conduct those efforts in the shadow of the threat of litigation. "To some extent it makes little sense to examine these [ADR] means of dispute resolution in terms of the elements of adversarial adjudication because they are not elements of an adjudicatory procedure, but rather are alternatives to that procedure." Sward, "Values, Ideology, and the Evolution of the Adversary System," 345. Would that it were so. Menkel-Meadow identifies non-adversarial approaches: mediation, inquisitorial-bureaucratic investigation, public fora or conversations, "intermediate sites of discourse," private problem-solving (negotiation) or group negotiation, and coalition and consensus building. Menkel-Meadow, "The Trouble with the Adversary System in a Postmodern, Multicultural World," 12. Some dispute resolution approaches adopt structures that absent themselves from the judicial system (collaborative law, for example, or fastidious facilitative mediators). But collaborators and mediators are still making documents and agreements they believe a court will endorse. Hence, isomorphic pressures endure.

[474] Exterminated, not by malice, but by poo-pooing, withdrawal of funding, benign neglect, negative press, and lack of enthusiasm. Is jurispathic termination not the fate suffered by Washington's limited license legal technician program? For a silly poem on this event, see Appendix C: "Nine Olympic Lords."

[475] Isomorphism is a concept borrowed from evolutionary biology. It identifies the convergence of form by highly differentiated organisms due to the evolutionary effect of environmental pressures. Where all food is shelled, all mouths become nutcrackers.

> processes employed as a response to crime, and a close relative of community mediation—have described a phenomenon similar to "limbo." They observe that local restorative justice efforts began as a non-governmental, "communitarian" enterprise, one that has now been adopted by the formal criminal justice system. Many communitarian restorative justice practitioners have long operated outside the perimeters of the formal system and express dismay about the appropriation of their processes by government. They cannot fail to recognize, however, that through the criminal justice system comes broader acceptance, awareness, and use of restorative justice. The simultaneous attraction toward government-sanctioned legitimacy and repulsion from governmental cooptation leads to an "oscillating space." . . . Community mediation resides in a similar space, as the field has maintained an ambivalent relationship with the courts."[476]

So, Klatching faces serious threats from jurispathic courts and creeping isomorphism. Klatches are well-advised to distance themselves from courts (and most lawyers as well).[477]

Further peril lies in **public apathy**. All Americans are enculturated to leave problems to experts and officials. Troubling acquiescence ensues, and the belief burgeons that the problems of neighbors belong to them alone, not to all of us. Apathy emerges from social isolation. Alone, one finds no reason to act to protect any but oneself, which is the core mantra of septic individualism. So, the answer to apathy lies not in programs or booklets or mandates, but rather in welcome and affection and relational bonding. One can do more to reduce public apathy with sports pubs and bowling leagues and neighborhood barbeques (and Klatching) than with a thousand exhortations and slick videos.

Any substantial societal change induces **antipathy**. Many Americans think that change should be countered with fisticuffs and spasms of protest. Klatch will change things, and so will encounter antipathy. For this threat, the attitudes that enliven amity will serve well. Amicable processes make friends of enemies. Friends do not always agree, but they do offer support and seek understanding.

To conclude, Klatch, if widely practiced, would supplant all but that fraction of the judicial system dedicated to blunting sociopaths. Imbibed, Klatch is a habit of character. People sort their own problems with friends. Most feel good about themselves for the effort. Klatches teach one to savor smallness, to cherish intimate conversation with friends and neighbors, to desire self-management of life's

---

[476] Hedeen, "Institutionalizing Community Mediation: Can Dispute Resolution 'of, by, and for the People' Long Endure?," 274-275 (emphasis added).

[477] Except, as one would expect, me and my ilk.

complexities. A world that savors Klatch would still value experts, but they would be fewer in number and in control of nothing. Every person needs the counsel of persons who curate ideas in difficult topics, but wishes to manage the tiller of life's catamaran personally. Truth be told, many of us already Klatch regularly, sharing recipes and stories, difficult discussions and joyous outcomes. Dilemmas receive circle insight, though the circles are often much un-round. Courts even teeter near the edge of considering cousins of Klatch as other legitimate ways to cope with disputes. But the Klatch has a life of its own, sucking constitutional milk from reserved-but-unspecified teats of the commonwealth. Klatch may shrink the common law and, fat on hardy lactation, constitutionally re-constitute our peoples.

This "tone poem for the deaf" calls Justicia, our venerable myth-symbol, to pull off her blindfold, lay down her sword, and take a hard look at the balance of her scales.[478] If the legal system would smile upon Klatchers, Klatches, in their autonomy, would make some bad decisions, but more often good ones. People would feel connected again to their neighbors and solicitous of their good opinion. Klatches would spill into barbeques and nights in the park together. We might make fewer children, and better care for those we have made. Relating well to others, we might love ourselves more deeply. In the end, we might waken from our solipsistic nightmare.

We are members together, like it or not.

Prick up your ears.
Strain to hear this tone poem.
Perhaps you are less deaf than I imagine.
Would it were so.
One can but hope.

[478] Some contemporary clothing would also be an improvement.

CHAPTER 4

## AMITY AT LAW DEFENDED

> He said to his heart: . . . I am thinking about what has taken place. Misery is ushered in / today, By the morning the strangers have (still) not passed away. Everyone is silent about it. The entire land is in a serious plight, and here is nobody free from wrong: all people alike do it. Hearts are dejected. . . . There is no man wise enough to know it, / and there is no man angry enough to speak out. Every day one wakes to suffering. . . . Silence about what is heard is painful. It is miserable to have to give an answer / to the ignorant. To oppose a speech makes for disaffection. The heart cannot accept truth. A reply to a speech is insufferable. All a man wants is his own talk. Everyone is based in crookedness. Precision in speech is abandoned.
>
> "Lamentations of Khakheperre-Sonbe"
> *Literature of Ancient Egypt, 211*
> Reign of Senusret II, Middle Kingdom
> ~1,880 B.C.

Since I propose much change to everyday life for most people, as well as to our culture at large, much can be said in opposition. Not all such protests are slap-happy aspersions. Well-considered and prescient objections arise, though I find none fatal to what I propose. In what follows, I address some of those thoughtful demurrers, at least those that have pressed my mind or those of sympathetic editors. Like most authors, I find my rebuttals sterling and unimpeachable. Yet, being old, I know hubris and critical myopia plague us all. I can only hope that our mutual remonstrances will loft a song both measured and temperate, and a pleasure to read and deliberate. We shall see.

If you, my reader, are dead set against amity-at-law, make your alternative known to all. Further tinkering with our common law regime lacks warrant. It wastes time and resources better spent on societal change and legal humility. People need workable habits to address conflicts. Ours have failed. And law, whatever form it may take, seeps into our psyches, governing expectations, inciting coercive retribution. Law sparks a logic that comes to seem incontrovertible to adherents. So, our choices about amity may birth a nascent culture much at odds with that which we presently suffer. Our choices may also abort such cultural change.

Now, on to objections.

## OBJECTION 1: RULE OF LAW AND SOAPY BATHWATER

*The common law specifies the American (and in its origin, the British) approach to settling disputes, which we call "the rule of law." Supplanting the common law guts the rule of law itself. This proposition ought to inspire fear. Let me explain.*

*United States jurisprudence welcomes no emasculate tradition such as amity-at-law. Ours is, instead, a beefy, even virile, take on human relations. Its tools are forge and hammer, rationally deployed, to incapacitate (for a time), to deter, to punish, and (on good days) to rehabilitate those whom the common law has crimped or scorched. The common law enshrines assertions which are, to our culture, commonplaces. Some individuals behave badly. Those whom they injure complain, or the State complains on victims' behalf. Citizen panels, subject to rational procedures, assess blame. Common law censures wrongdoers and benefits those injured (at least obliquely). The common law system falters, even limps, but hardly deserves the dustbin. Lancaster proposes, proverbially, dumping the common law baby with its be-soaped bathwater.*

*To take a medieval excursion, Thomas Aquinas argues that, in the calculus of any contemplated change, one must weigh the disruption caused by change of any sort, even changes that are wise and well-intentioned.*[479] *Humans are creatures of habit and custom. Change disrupts both, and erodes our collective sense of normalcy.*

*Lancaster would shove society toward a foolish lunge into wholesale judicial mutation. He seeks to purge judging from matters judicial. He argues that we should, in resolving disputes, rely on human cooperative instincts and the unregulated wisdom of commoners. Humankind struggled for five thousand years (and probably very much longer) scratching a path that cast aside personality in public decision-making. Where enacted, the author's prescription for tailored dispute resolution will issue spates of political witch hunts and illiberal pogroms. Anonymity is the price of equity. Tailored justice, cut and sewn by personality for personality, is inimical to the rule of law. Raw equity matters. Beware Lancaster's addled imagination. Governance without precedents renders life rudderless. Were amity to usurp law's impersonal rudiment, much that we all value would collapse.*

---

[479] Thomas Aquinas (1225-1274 A.D.), author of *Summa Theologica*, addresses law in Questions 90-108. At Reply 4 to Question 92, Aquinas asserts that tyrannical laws are not laws at all, but perversions of law. The Angelic Doctor therefore opens the door to all manner of criticism of laws. He further argues, at the second article of Question 97, that human laws should be changed but only when "conducive to the common weal." Aquinas warns: "But, to a certain extent, the mere change of law is of itself prejudicial to the common good: because custom avails much for the observance of laws, seeing that what is done contrary to general custom, even in slight matters, is looked upon as grave. Consequently, when a law is changed, the binding power of the law is diminished, in so far as custom is abolished. Wherefore human law should never be changed, unless, in some way or other, the common weal be compensated according to the extent of the harm done is this respect. . . . Wherefore the jurist says that in establishing new laws, there should be evidence of the benefit to be derived, before departing from a law which has long been considered just." Aquinas, *Summa Theologica*, Question 97.

**RESPONSE**: Dangers lurk in amity-at-law. Intentional change expects benefit, but inflicts unwelcomed damage as well. Aquinas's moral scales are warranted. Will change, weighed against its inherent damage, augment human weal? Haste, especially, beckons ugly outcomes; urgent lunges summon misery. Were amity-at-law a revolution, sweaty with impetuous imminence, the objector's warning would chasten me. Amity, however, is nothing new. All savor friendship and cherish its allure.[480] Friendship predates law by at least two hundred millennia, and nestles primordially in the human psyche, as do bones in legs. Law emerged when we forsook low-investment migrations (hunting and gathering) for capital in fields and abodes (landholder agriculture). Our common law evolved over a mere thousand years in response to fundamental change in the human landscape. Its impersonality well suits a planet trembling at the verge of over-population (as it was even a thousand years ago—then, 300 million souls). By dint of sheer volume, none can know the details of strangers, so we chose a system of law that seeks ignorance of pertinent matters (which we call impartiality or even fairness). Such is common law's rationale. Where its nescient premise pertains, where we cannot know a citizen's details because there are just too many citizens, then common law's depersonalized approach tempts one.

The objector dramatically overstates the objectivity and regularity of law. Juries, and the secrecy that surrounds their deliberations, mask the reality that most often the twelve neither "determine the facts" nor "apply the law." As Judge Jerome Frank said: "The [jury's] general verdict serves as the great procedural opiate, . . . [it] draws the curtain upon human errors, and soothes us with the assurance that we have attained the unattainable."[481]

One might fear that absent law, and, particularly, without *precedent*, community decision-making may wander and stutter, searching for consistency but finding none. In its worst incarnations, Klatches might tumble into religious zealotries or pompous pontifications, endorsing half-baked resolutions where circumstances demand greater deliberative effort. I acknowledge these possibilities.[482] One must, however, admit that in our bitter adversarial hotbed, cults and blowhards and lame solutions abound. One cannot, in truth, lay blame upon amity for such confusions. These excesses are

---

[480] If there are any who do not, for them I grieve.

[481] Frank, *Courts on Trial*, 114. This is to say nothing of the facts of criminal matters. In 1998, ninety-four percent of all felony convictions were obtained by plea bargaining. Hence, these many sidestepped the imagined rigors of fact-finding by judge or jury in favor of a summary disposal by nods and winks between prosecution and defense counsels. Berman, *Good Courts: The Case for Problem-Solving Justice*, 18

[482] Jan Oppermann, who has reviewed this *Tone Poem* in a late draft, shares these concerns. He worries that, absent "universal abstract and abstractly administered law," decisions may fall to those who are rich or powerful or intelligent or educated or sociopathic, which defaults, in America, can have distinct "racial overtones." His additional concerns include domination of neighborhood Klatches by religious pedantries characteristic of the many "weird groups" which call America home. Oppermann thinks Americans should divert their energies from earnest moral excursions to "the possibilities of informality and casualness" (for example, resolving disputes in pubs or during rounds of golf). Dr. Oppermann also urges that Klatching should start small to avoid widely propagating deficiencies in the theory that experimental efforts might expose. Once confidence in the approach waxes, then one can attempt to broach subjects in Klatch that presently devolve upon adversarial law. My heartfelt thanks to Jan Oppermann for his ever-penetrating analysis on my nascent books. Email from Jan Oppermann to author, dated July 29, 2025.

human foibles to be met with kindness of the steely variety. Apart from law, as are we all in our privacies, we do not scutter in a muddle. We sense where lie desirable outcomes. These sentiments are not precedents. Nor are they wholly reliable. They have been called "common sense," though they are often neither universal nor reasonable. My point is this: humans are not rudderless. We have a sense of what makes for meaningful life. That intuition nestles beneath consciousness; its pressures are gentle, its directions more impressionistic than intelligible. Klatches emerge from this inner compass, which issues in compassion.

The rule of law lies, not in any given political or juridical arrangement, but rather in a societal conviction that whatever rules exist must be applied similarly to all entities and persons. The objector conflates the common law with law itself. Amity-at-law, if adopted, would be a "rule of law," just a different rule. The objector also misconstrues equity in a familiar manner. She errs when she asserts that equity requires anonymity. The anonymous equity proffered by common law truncates fundamental fairness. Equity, as an historical proposition, emerged to offset the excess harshness of royal legal adjudications.

Contrary to common law practice, one receives justice and savors equity when one, individually and consensually, deserves a compensatory outcome. In unneutered equity, participants—**knowledgeable** in a matter, and mature enough to grasp **the uncertainties of human comprehension**, and convinced that **shared responsibility** for ugly events lies with most (or all) of the actors involved—deliberate changes that remediate circumstances at issue. Tailored outcomes define equity. Such genuine equity emerges only among involved persons. The common law dispenses such justice as persons without knowledge, convinced they are finding Truth, and focused on one person, can muster. The product of common law decision-making tends toward procedural conundra and cookie-cutter impositions, ending at sad silliness. Injustice marauds as justice, inspiring dissent and disparagement and fearful political instability.

Law must be the handmaiden of morality, not its master. When law and morality contest in a mind, morality should prevail. One may break with law—thoughtfully, but decisively, where law strays. One should then acquiesce at censure for disobeying those misbegotten laws. But immoral laws have no warrant whatsoever.[483]

At best, humans live about one hundred years. So, no person remembers a world unencumbered by anonymous law. There persist, however, islands of amity law, atolls of respite amidst a tumultuous common law sea. These isles float mostly in rural communities or under-developed countries, but they hide also in our urban lives, across family dinner tables or in gatherings among neighbors and friends.

I assert that amity-at-law improves law's rudiment fundamentally, abandoning hateful revenge for friendly deliberations and accommodations among knowledgeable participants. Those who savor American society's judicial ambience should cling to the common law. Bad habits are tough to break. For the rest of us, amity-at-law proposes a revised jurisprudence to explore, to embrace, to practice, to live. Amity-at-law warrants careful consideration. Regardless, I am assured that many will reject

---

[483] See the remarkable discussion in Peters, *A Matter of Dispute*, 349-352, dissecting Lincoln's suspension of *habeas corpus*.

amity's allure because they imagine they have more important things to do. These colleagues are wrong.

## OBJECTION 2: GUTTING THE GLOBAL ECONOMY

*Lancaster's law-scheme rests on the premise that most people will consent to divert their energies from money-making to other endeavors, among which are his homespun conflict resolution process. The economy will shrink. If large populations of American workers make less income suffice, then their reduced labor, conjoined with the overall labor shortage in America, will kill the United States economy. As goes America, so goes the world. The moral of this story is that you should not get your economic advice from lawyers.*

**RESPONSE**: First, I respond by noting that, whatever regime we dwell in, the global economy will slow, as it must. This outcome has nothing to do with amity-at-law. Though the human population continues to increase, "[s]ince procreating is a more popular activity than dying,"[484] raw materials are delimited and sustainable industrial energy lags (physical scarcity), and the human psyche suffers deficits induced by economic growth frenzy: alienation, anxiety, crime, disinterest, loneliness (psychological scarcity), and the like. Draw the chart. Read the trend lines. Recognize the implication. Herman Daly asserts that economic change slavishly follows changes in human values. Little would be left to do in reaching a steady-state economy, if only people generally abandoned the idea that *more-is-better*, and adopted the concept that *enough-is-best*.[485] Daly notes that all economic theories (but his own) appear to have adopted an unlimited growth lodestar. Kohei Saito, an environmentalist and attenuated Marxist, advises us to shrink (or abandon) the market economy, both for self-preservation, but also for psychological health.[486] Saito calls for degrowth communism. He argues that fragmenting individualism and insatiable lust for possessions are intrinsic flaws in capitalism, and we shall not prosper absent a smaller and sustainable economy such as ecological Marxism.[487]

---

[484] Daly, *Steady-State Economics*, 8.

[485] Daly, *Steady-State Economics*, 2. Daly cites Aleksandr Solzhenitsyn in the Russian's *Letter to Soviet Leaders*: "What must be implemented is not a steadily expanding economy, but a *zero growth economy*, a stable economy. *Economic growth is not only unnecessary but ruinous*."

[486] Saito quotes Kenneth Boulding as follows: "Anyone who believes that exponential growth can go on forever in a finite world is either a madman or an economist." Saito, *Slow Down*, 16. Saito himself puts the situation thus: "We are living in an era where mutual aid and trust in others has been thoroughly dismantled by the forces of neoliberalism. The only way to rebuild these trust relationships is through face-to-face community building and local municipal politics, at least at the start. . . . Where will this great leap take us? To a future founded on mutual aid and self-governance—to a future of degrowth capitalism." Saito, *Slow Down*, 228-229.

[487] Saito's admirable book is marred by an apparent conversion or mathematical error in stating the United Nations' target global temperature rise. Saito's error evidences a failure of scientific comprehension. Which is not to derogate Saito's book as a whole. His is a readable and useful Marxist rant, with an ecological twist. See Saito, *Slow Down*, 3, 52, 171.

Second, the market economy expends tremendous sums convincing us to purchase things we never knew we needed. We fill empty souls with stuff, thinking therein lies some remedy. The empty cavern within needs not things, but persons, to fill it. The federal Surgeon General (in 2024) has warned that social isolation is epidemic among Americans, and threatens their health. Suicide rates continue to climb (most years). He reports that federal resources should be expended improving social connection both structurally (parks, common areas) and programmatically (efforts to foster connection between people).

Third, this objector endorses a fantasy. Economies cannot expand perpetually. At some point, the global economy will find a sustainable and stable point. We passed that sustainable point some centuries ago, and have since that doubtful day lived in metastatic economies. Our concern should be that the inevitable degrowth stable point is not so abysmally low that only a few million people can survive as modern civilization collapses. We are already warming and polluting and breeding and warring ourselves to death. Our animal companions perish in droves, never to be seen again. Others we nurture, then slaughter, in their billions. We will plan degrowth of the economy or suffer its many recessions and truncations and miseries. We tempt extinction.

Fourth, putting community peace-making on everyone's agenda will not leave us without employment. Americans will still work, still spend, still dream. They will just be taking better care of themselves and their neighbors. Which, yes, takes a bit of time.

Finally, I agree that lawyers should not take the lead in degrowth efforts. They should play their usual role, advising people in difficult circumstances and helping them through their travails. Lawyers can also write books, point out our economic problems, and note for all that most economists appear to be possessed by the fevered mythology of perpetual economic expansion. In other words, economists fantasize. So, to augment my objector's view, perhaps a wise man takes no economic counsel from economists either.

## OBJECTION 3: ADDRESSING DEVIANCE

*Amity-at-law downplays the incorrigible pest that lingers in most human hearts. For most of us, the inner imp merely tempts and annoys; we resist it. But in more than a few, inner demons burst the cages we and others build for them; some grow cruel or even wicked. These sociopathic deviants demand a cultural response all out of proportion to their relative number. Though few, as a percentage of the American population, their absolute number is millions. Lancaster's optimism about a non-coercive regime gabbles naïve gladtalk. Sociopaths do not stop wanton depredations because you ask nicely. They manipulate situations, despite grave reasoning with them. Sociopaths are incorrigible. They will do as they wish, unless we constrain them. Though only four percent of the population, a much larger percentage of the*

---

I would jettison the label "communism," in Saito's degrowth communism, since his proposal bears none of the hallmarks of the political system with which we associate the term. The word, with respect to Saito's argument, misleads.

*miseries we suffer as a culture can be laid at their feet. Lancaster's amity regime has no answer for sociopaths.*

**RESPONSE**: Is humanity congenitally prone to coercion? Is humankind a bent twig, fatally abrading its issuing branch in every inclement gust? Or is humanity bootstrapping itself from gory African predation toward global hyper-cooperation? Is violence essentially human, like language and complex ideation and upright ambulation? Or is the human legacy of bloodshed a jarring rapids to be painfully negotiated in our long seaward tumble toward a mutually respectful future?

Thomas Hobbes (English, 18th century) styled human life lonely, nasty, impoverished, carnage-ridden, and, hence, brief. The cause of human misery is mankind. Left to his own devices, a man wars with every other. Ultimately, for self-preservation, survivors appoint a Leviathan to aggregate their lethal powers, relinquishing to a monarch their several privileges of homicide. Might the ego-maniacal excesses of the British Empire be one result of Hobbes's popularity? Friedrich Nietzsche (German, 19th century) painted mankind as sheep waiting for slaughter at will by supermen exempted from social norms, as eagles soar far above the slavish morality of bleating lambs. These are sociopaths. Hitler embraced Nietzsche. Might one fount of the Nazi horrors be the belief systems of the many whom Nietzsche convinced? Grim views of human potential abound. Augustine's original sin, Calvin's total depravity, Darwin's survival of the fittest, and Ardrey's violent African ape shape the expectations of many.

Not all close the human book at its damp crimson pages. Mohandas Gandhi (Indian, 20th century) argued that every man harbors a good heart. Evil is appearance, not reality. When confused or threatened, some persons behave badly. Those who err must be opposed, but gently, nonviolently, without disparagement. One ends war only by making the enemy a friend. Influenced by Gandhi, India drove Britain from its hegemony over the subcontinent, mostly nonviolently. **See Epitome 5: Gandhi, *Satyagraha*.** Martin Luther King Jr. (American, 20th century) confronted racial prejudices bluntly, but nonviolently. He and civil rights activists suffered, some fatally. But, influenced by King, millions self-criticized, finding within themselves that of which King complained. Many moderated their prejudices, and the United States made room at its social table for the descendants of slaves. **See Epitome 7: King, *Autobiography*.** Peter Block (American, 21st century) builds restorative communities. He urges members to stop recriminating about systemic injustice, and remediate the present ethos of one's own particular small group. Healthy small groups make this meeting right now the sort of place they dream of inhabiting years from now. Such communities, Block argues, are the natural home of healthy humans. **See Epitome 2: Block, *Community*.** Dacher Keltner (American, 21st century) argues, based on recent neuroscience, that humans are built for relating, for compassion, for doing good. Human-effected horrors evidence natural human systems gone terribly awry. **See Epitome 4: Keltner, *Born To Be Good*.** My point here is this: One can, without fatuous glibness, contemplate in humanity a core of goodness that warrants predicting good outcomes. The bloody facts about mankind remain equivocal, an emphatic counterpoint which requires moral reckoning.

Yet, I offer a confessional anecdote, one that discomfits a pacifist, in the vein of giving my objector her due:

My waitress had taken my dirty breakfast plate and refilled my decaf. I paged through the New York Times, slurping. Murmurs arose. Jen, the morning-shift waitress, whispered to regulars what the kitchen Sony blurted. Hijacked planes had slammed into New York's World Trade Center towers. Online, I saw the south tower fall, then the north tower. Thousands died. The nation grieved. Al-Qaeda's Arab street-cred skyrocketed.

The bookend moment arrived years later. United States stealth helicopters flew low and fast into Pakistani airspace. Navy Seals landed in an Abbottabad residential compound, where they conducted a brief firefight. The soldiers killed, among others, Osama bin Mohammed bin Awad bin Laden, founder of al-Qaeda's terror network. Some Americans rejoiced, even cavorted in streets. I could not join them; inside, I shuddered that we (with our taxes and votes and acquiescence) had murdered another human being. Yet neither could I deplore President Obama's decision to assassinate the Saudi-born terrorist.

The concept of "evil" is a problem among peacemakers. Sentiments about evil also have bookends. At one end, some peacemakers deny that evil exists. Here is how their argument goes. Accusations of evil, according to evil-skeptics, emerge when intemperate people fail to invest the energy necessary to understand and show compassion to opponents. All humans have constructive impulses, as well as demented ones. One must appeal to the good in others, without triggering ugly motivations in them or us. What appears as evil is nothing more than mis-comprehended good. The evil-doer is confused enough that he has failed to recognize the injurious outcomes of his good intentions. "Evil" disappears, so the evil-skeptics argue, where lovers of amity interject sufficient education, listening, compassion, and patience. The evil-skeptic often finds in the concept of "evil" a theological distortion of reality. Carefully-crafted, compassionate conversation unmasks evil. Behind that veil wilts a confused human in sore need. When that person feels understood and valued, he will see the harm he creates and desist.

Mohandas Gandhi stood with the evil-skeptics. In Gandhi's view, no matter how monstrous a man's evil acts, beneath that horrid crust lay a soft heart ready to be touched by innocent suffering. Gandhi survived World War II. He advised Germany's Jews to resist non-violently, ending Hitler's national manhunt. Jews could offer themselves publicly and peacefully for imprisonment or slaughter. That spectacle would lionize human dignity. Gandhi believed that annihilation of innocents saps armies. If India were invaded, Gandhi said he would erect a human wall of willing unarmed victims, perhaps millions, as cannon fodder. (*Satyagraha*, §§ 165, 169, 178).

As an advocate of amity, I travel only so far with Gandhi and evil-skeptics. One must begin in all circumstances assuming that those who injure do so uncomprehending. One educates. One listens. One shows perseverance in compassion. One corrects oneself, where necessary. These steps remedy most conflicts, and chasten most erring actors. But some prove recalcitrant. These persons intentionally erode meaningful community in familial, societal, or international relations. They persist despite compassionate listening and generous education and longsuffering patience. Adamantine pathologies drive such people. A cacophonous host of defects and mishaps (for example, substance abuse or sociopathy or sadistic psychoses or habitual violence) hurtle them beyond the pale of normal human relations. Responsive measures must meet the challenge of pathological evil. Coercion may, in the ugliest circumstances, prove necessary. Gandhi's pacifist vision fails in these dark fastnesses. Ideological non-violence would require one to spectate preventable horrors, rendering peacemakers a hapless audience to abuse or genocide. Aspiration to unattainable personal sanctity would hobble us. That I do not condone. Gandhi would call mine a deficient spirituality. At some level, I agree. But still . . .

Many peacemakers are conflicted. The non-coercive bookend of peacemaking beckons, but seems to require that, in extremity, a coercive response remains possible. We long for utopian remedies in which the coercive bookend atrophies from long disuse. Sadly, at least for now, without both bookends, the upright books of life tumble.[488]

So, amicable persons may have to tolerate a modicum of coercive responses to unfettered wrongs. The goal is to employ such extremities as infrequently as possible. To answer sociopathic deviancy demands moral mettle. Often, with some justice, advocates of peace are imagined to be sad mumblers, much given to whining and handwringing. William James argues that advocates of peace must adopt a martial stance, find effective tools of change, and wield them potently. James asserts that, to prevail against warmongers, one must wage peace as viciously as those maulers swing their axes and hammers. **See Epitome 10: James, *The Moral Equivalent of War*.**

Lawyers, long-inured to litigation, criticize peacemaking. They say that the weapons of peacemakers are, well, puny. What is empathy when compared to contempt proceedings? What is deflecting a dispute toward joint problem-solving when measured by the criminal indictment? How does confidence in the possibility of peace stack up to a summons and complaint? What might curiosity unearth that a hundred pages of interrogatories fail to expose? War lawyers munch coercion for breakfast. They salt their raw meats with assertion and pepper with threats. Worst for the litigator, peacemakers whine. Litigators spit them out. They are a stench in the nostrils. Peacemakers harp, like ill-parented children: the wasteful expense of litigation, the emotional carnage, the futility. The inured litigator knows martial values: discipline, equanimity, and the mettle of humans under stress. Mamby-pamby well-wishing serves none. Take up the sword, so litigators counsel. Litigators nod at Athens's negotiation with Melos.

During the Peloponnesian War (431-404 B.C.), Thucydides reports that Athens opened a dialogue with the people of the small Aegean island of Melos. (See **Epitome 9: Thucydides, "The Melian Debate" in *Peloponnesian War*.**) Melos had been settled by Athens's mainland opponent, Sparta. The Melians retained loose ties to their mother city. Melos chose neutrality in the Greek civil war, as is wise for tiny persons ill-situated between sparring giants. Thirty ships from Athens dropped anchor at Melos, brimming with troops. The Athenian delegation flatly demanded immediate surrender. The Melians argued that Athens abandons justice, which should concern all peoples. Melos neither sides with Sparta nor presents any threat to Athens. The Athenians countered that the strong do as they wish and the weak as they must. Melos replied that history is long; today's victors become tomorrow's

---

[488] I have written at some length on appropriate boundaries for member and community coercion. See Lancaster, *Cull: Choosing Well*, at Section 10.9 (member coercion, page 378ff), and at Section 11.12.4 (community coercion, page 408ff).

vanquished. Athens will one day wish people valued justice. Athens thanked Melos for its concern, but enjoined Melos to look to its own well-being. Athens noted that its empire comprises many small principalities; failure to compel one today invites all to rebellion tomorrow. Melos suggested that Sparta might defend Melos. The Athenians laughed; Sparta is corrupt. Whatever Spartans enjoy, they deem just. Athens restated its offer to Melos: surrender, pay tribute, and live. Melos, after due deliberation, declined, reiterating its neutrality. Athens besieged Melos, killed all fighting men, and enslaved the women and children. Athenian immigrants repopulated Melos. Athens ultimately lost the Peloponnesian War. Sparta installed a puppet government over proud Athens, which paranoid sycophants eventually executed Socrates (399 B.C.) for his seditious corruption of youths. (For some serious thought about ending the human habit of war, see **Epitome 11: Kant, To Eternal Peace**. For equally potent thoughts about the critical role that small human communities play in promoting less-violent existence, see **Epitome 15: Taylor, Community, Anarchy, and Liberty**.)

I listen to litigators. I see litigators wince at amity happy-talk. The litigators are right; peacemakers should spit out their Kool-Aid. Peacemakers need to let the unbridled ugliness that some disputants sow seep into consciousness. All parties are not misunderstood, unheard puppies. Some are wolves, best tranquilized then muzzled. Remember the Melians. I hear litigators tout the martial values of courtroom conflict. Courtrooms burst the thin-walled ego of puffers. Litigation inculcates sterner stuff: hardiness, vigor, discipline, honor, calm in the face of extremity, occasional dignity, dramatic action in response to dire predicaments. I agree with my litigator friends. Most amity-lovers are wedded to a culture of indulgence that has spawned hippie anarchists and incomprehensible religions and mumbo-jumbo optimism. Peacemakers must set aside the heady hope of peace long enough to smell the latrines.

To my litigator friends, I say: Amity brings swords; these are "weapons of mass construction." Ears are one such weapon. Ears can be militant. A peacemaker who listens is a soldier on patrol, armed, action-ready. The martial listener demolishes the definition of battle that fixates the parties. The listener asks and seizes answers, exploring responses with incisive curiosity. The listener presses stories without accusing. The listener paraphrases to confirm comprehension, mirrors to build rapport, and takes a guess when parties seem stuck. The martial listener moves beyond receiving communication accurately. Amicable listeners drive talk toward workable consensus. Listeners agree where they agree, emphasize missed commonalities, and disagree without disrespect. Peacemakers know disputants quietly long for restored community. Like soldiers at arms, peacemakers seize and hold that prized turf for clients.

Perhaps in peacemaking there hides values even a litigator might adopt, were she listening with martial intensity. For a legal amity-builder accomplishes what no litigator imagines. Amity makes friends of enemies, ending bitterness without a dollar spent or drop of blood. Does that possibility not deserve our attention?

To recur to this objector's challenge about sociopathy, what is to be done with the unshackled sociopath? These often sparkle and amuse. Many psychopaths revel to entertainment, sucking their victims into amusements and fascinations, before inflicting injury. One thinks of social media gurus and cult leaders and certain prominent politicians of recent vintage. Sociopaths were, in a less charitable and scientific age, designated *moral morons*. They, quite literally, lack the neural architecture that graces moral self-restraint. I propose that we should treat sociopaths not as criminals (unless they have committed crimes), but rather as people with untreatable mental defects. Our cultural response to people in dire need is to provide care and assistance. Since sociopaths cannot regret the injuries they inflict, each needs to be tended and watched, as might we do with persons bent on self-injury. This poses a serious burden on our togetherness. But then, sociopaths pose substantial dangers.

Amity is no less capable in coping with sociopathy than is our coercive regime of common law. The problem of sociopathic deviance is greater than we imagine most days. Robed in guns, these folks dominate our airwaves and newsfeeds. They haunt our twilight insecurities. None is safe from sociopathic predation, despite draconian punishments. Perhaps amity deserves a try.

## OBJECTION 4: DELUSIONS ABOUT CHANGE

*To divert law's fundament from coercion to amity imagines that many Americans long for such change, and are willing to tolerate attendant discomforts. I detect no such longing, and no such tolerance in my social circles. Many compatriots avoid public involvements. We are wary of disruptions to our private endeavors. No one casts about for one (or several) additional meetings to attend. None thirsts for the frustrating false starts that trail the wake of substantial undertakings. Case in point: Voting takes a few minutes every other year. Yet less than half of the electorate casts a ballot in most elections. Lancaster imagines that many, like him, hunger for social connection. He imagines many Americans would solve problems, if offered the opportunity. He is wrong. Our vast majority wants nothing more than some privacy. We pray for our neighbors to constrain their children, turn down their music, and drive soberly. We do not want to solve their problems, but rather to shed them. Is that not what our Constitution contemplates? Do we not have a right to isolate? Is it not our birthright to shun irritating people? We want to be free, and, largely, that means to be at liberty to escape, or at least ignore, the chaotic, tasteless lives of others.*

**RESPONSE**: We Americans are indeed worn out; we seek respite. Will we find such, however, by hunkering? We have lived all of human history under the aegis of bloody coercion. Will a time ever arrive when we are self-confident enough to attempt a different theory?[489] We are all going to get up tomorrow and work all day anyway. The question is, At what shall we labor? I ask that we work toward amity. I ask that we structure our society expressly to attain that purpose. Let's hope that deep strata in human psychology await us, big rich veins of compassion and cooperation and creativity. If we end our regime of coercion, which drives most into perpetual fear, perhaps veins of goodness will reveal themselves and enrich us with startling rapidity.

Paradigm shifts startle. One goes along, laboring under some decrepit regime. Then, boom. Something we barely recognized becomes a new norm. Women run

---

[489] Wendy Tremayne credits Jiddu Krishnamurti for the following: "It is no sign of wellness to be well adjusted to a sick society." Tremayne, *The Good Life Lab*, 39. Elsewhere, one finds the citation as, "It is no measure of health to be well adjusted to a profoundly sick society."

the Washington Supreme Court. Gays marry. Gadgets replace Gidgets. Cars growl less and purr more. Pay phones disappear. Not many generations ago none drove or flew or telephoned or watched television; most owned a horse. None owned a computer. Now, most do. Soon, some friends will be silicon-based, and we are likely to have embedded uplinks to the net in our skulls. Usually, critical change waits the funerals of a passing generation. Those well-meaning elders glued their "old ways" in place. Younger minds, with different affections, take their vacated seats at culture's table. Jaak Panksepp ruminates, "Science progresses, funeral by funeral."[490] Thomas Kuhn noted the structure of change (for him, in scientific revolutions). Paradigm shift begins with outliers.

> Any new interpretation of nature, whether a discovery or a theory, emerges first in the mind of one or a few individuals. It is they who first learn to see science and the world differently, and their ability to make the transition is facilitated by two circumstances that are not common to most other members of their profession. Invariably their attention has been intensely concentrated upon the crisis-provoking problems; usually, in addition, they are men so young or so new to the crisis-ridden field that practice has committed them less deeply than most of their contemporaries to the world view and rules determined by the old paradigm.[491]

Kuhn taught that an entrenched (usually aged) elite can forestall paradigm revision, but the grave defeats them. Contrary to this objector's wishes, change is coming. It is always coming. Evade as you wish, isolate extravagantly if you will. Nevertheless, change will sweep over you, as do illness and aging and grief and, eventually, death. None dams change. The question is not whether to change, but what change to seek. Since our common law structures have failed us so badly, we should move on to a fresh idea. I propose a revised rudiment: amity.

## OBJECTION 5: SCUTTLING INDIVIDUALITY

*The Enlightenment elevated the individual. That has saved us. For 200 millennia, humans wandered in tribes governed by headmen, wandering afoot to the ripening fruits and animal migrations, fighting with neighbors, living in beclouded ignorance under mostly-African skies. There had always been individuals. But these were conceived as members of their local group, and never as stand-alone exemplars of humanity. For these last fifteen thousand years, humankind has lingered in larger groups, in towns and cities and religions and orders. We stopped wandering; we tilled and planted and husbanded. But still, man lingered as a member. Communality tarnished the wonder of extraordinary individuals, dimming their contributions. With*

---

[490]Panksepp, *Affective Neuroscience*, at a page I can no longer identify. Max Planck may be the origin of the saw.

[491]Kuhn, *The Structure of Scientific Revolutions*, 144.

*wondrous invention and intellectual feats, individuals have elevated the species. Give thanks.*

*Lancaster would unwind individuality. He would cast us back into the Gehenna of small towns and Crusades, of witch burnings and obligatory worship. He would welcome barn raisings and even contemplates individuals declining to aggregate wealth in favor of general short-term weal. Lancaster errs. We are, one and all, individuals. Our collectivities are transient agglomerations, gathered for one purpose, then another. Like the collectivities, our human connections are fragile or imagined. For many, our parents are gone and siblings distant. Our beloved spouse has departed to death or to another. Our children, also being individuals, have departed for parts unknown, only, in a good year, to return for Christmas or July Fourth. Individuality is the deep truth of humans. Communality impairs us; we are not fitted to it. Our sordid deep history notwithstanding.*

**RESPONSE**: It is not so. We are not given to solitude. "In the web of life, nothing living lives alone."[492] Our relational excisions inflict incalculable pains and these endure because they injure us in our collective essence. Our enduring achievements are communal, not individual. Behind every eminent person stands a host that made her so. Beside her stand communities of like-minded, or critically-inclined companions, who share interest or living quarters or bonding affection. To deny communality dishonors friends and denies dependence and support. I shall not be able to convince my objector by argument, for his thoughts betray attachment dysfunctions. So, I answer with a story.

How does human conflict emerge? Some suggest economic analysis: conflict emerges when many seek scarce resources. Others prefer a social systems perspective: conflict emerges when some oppose change that others advocate. A theological tale tempts many: conflict emerges when evil persons oppress God's chosen. I suggest a fourth alternative, which I call the cob corn theory of conflict genesis.

I volunteered with some thirty-five others, most of them strangers, at Food Lifeline some years ago. Food Lifeline collects bulk foods from agricultural producers and repackages the foodstuffs for distribution at local food banks. On this particular August day, the agricultural donor was Kroger. The donation was cob corn, those little three-inch frozen cobs one finds in the frozen food section at any big grocery. These cobs, however, arrived in palletized bulk cartons, thousands of cobs per container. The task for our daunted thirty-five was to don blue hair nets (I, bald as a cue ball, was required to wear a blue "hair" net) and disposable gloves, then divide the contents of these huge containers into family-sized bags of twenty or so mini-cobs each. Food Lifeline staff, vastly experienced with volunteers, merely showed us the pallet jack, freezer bags, labels, pallets, corn, and abandoned us to our own lights.

Tentatively, we probed the task. Muscled workers slowly organized boxes and pallets. Kids distributed bags. Small groups plopped twenty cobs into ziplocks, then filled boxes with them. Boxes stacked on pallets. Pallet-loaders applied labels. The burly among us moved our product away on rolling pallet jacks. Within twenty minutes, without an authoritative word or leader, the group coalesced into a corn cob

---

492 Pranis, Stuart, Wedge, *Peacemaking Circles*, 95, citing Wheatley, *Turning to One Another*.

bagging machine. All labored for three hours without conflict, amidst much laughter, despite sundry mishaps. When our shift ended, thousands of pounds of cob corn were reconfigured, and back in the freezer awaiting Monday delivery to area food banks.

The Food Lifeline cob corn project tapped a pre-programmed script buried deep in human brains. In small groups, we work to common ends hand in hand with friends or strangers, suppressing conflict by accommodating others generously in good humor. This is a normal human state. We evolved these collaborative tendencies in Pleistocene Africa on fluctuating savannahs that were home to our distant ancestors. Humans lack fangs and claws. What saved nascent humanity was task cooperation and social smoothing.

If one erodes the premises of the cob corn phenomenon, another pre-programmed response emerges. If one excises from the cob corn regime its face-to-face component, its common goal, its physical activity, or its accommodating sense of humor, then at each hiccup, humans bare teeth and raise fists. Even when prepared to fight unnamed opponents of inimical purposes, persons whom we have never met, groups with whom we have never cooperated, humans prefer to rattle sabers, withdraw, and emigrate from the problem. This human tendency to avoid violent conflict when possible has been a huge challenge for military organizations. In World War II, eighty to eighty-five percent of American soldiers could not pull the trigger when face-to-face with enemy soldiers (Report of S.L.A. Marshall, Brigadier General. Subsequent Army training changes resulted in a ninety percent firing rate in Vietnam). Humans, despite our ignominious history of slaughter, brutality, and genocide, turn homicidal only under limited and quite specific conditions. Violence demands that victims be depersonalized. One must kill enemies without taking personal responsibility, say, upon command by a superior, or in "saving" one's comrades. The opponent must be stigmatized, rendering him a detestable cipher. A mere whiff of shared humanity can trigger the cob corn phenomenon and derail homicidal intent.

Our litigation system, unfortunately, fails to promote cob corn collaboration. Litigation opponents, though named, seldom meet. Antagonists are discouraged from speaking directly. Their disputes are framed not as common problems to be solved, but as polar opposites, only one of which has merit. Litigation rhetoric often dehumanizes opposing parties. In courtrooms, attorney proxies wage battle, sometimes with gladiatorial glee. Judges adopt attire, position, and tenor designed to mimic the divine seat of judgment. Legalese, incomprehensible to clients, makes them itinerants in a foreign precinct. Courtrooms quash cob corn impulses.

Conflicts aggregate when the collaborative cob corn predicates suffer.

In finding amity, we pack cob corn.

I trust my objector, after reading this bit, phones Food Lifeline. One call could change his life.

## OBJECTION 6: UTOPIAN BLATHER

*I have heard Lancaster's story before. From Marxist revolutionaries with their bristling guns. From Christian ascetics, hoary in deserts. From Keil's orchards at Aurora Colony. From the desert climes of Rajneeshpuram, near the mighty Columbia. From the eschatological frenzies that periodically savage these United States. Where are these? Whence these perverse energies, purporting to stride history and render of man a fresh version? All are gone. Of no enduring import. Just utopian blather. Blah. Blah. Blah.*

*Now comes this Seattle yammerer, whose "music" I cannot hear, with his dangerous dreamy-eyed chant of monotone mumbling. Lancaster would have the Bar substitute his nothingness for the estimable rough and tumble of life at American law. Lawyers should chew the tough nuts, not wish them away. Lancaster's sentiments indicate nothing more than that he is a bad lawyer. Lawyers are not seduced by utopias. The Bar has harder noggins than that. Lawyers take the world as it is and gnaw—often with frowns and scowling. We spit out rocks and pebbles and ingest what remains, grimly. Lancaster would seem to lack the mettle for law. Ignore him.*

**RESPONSE**: I agree that heaven shall never take up residence upon the earth. I do not advocate a utopia, but rather a revised theory of law. Let us call utopian pacifism "PEACE." Let us call labor to re-orient errant jurisprudence "peace" (or amity).

PEACE is heaven on earth. Unfortunately, PEACE is a putty that mashes into any shape one prefers. The same is true of PEACE's cousins, LOVE, FREEDOM, BEAUTY, HONOR, and JUSTICE. These capital-letter aspirations trumpet cherished human values. Yet, none has concrete referents. We cannot point and say, *PEACE resides in Marysville. Did you catch that glimpse of FREEDOM on the evening news? Whoa! I just saw JUSTICE on that bus.* The world is just too muddy for Big Ideas to root themselves. Big Ideas guide us, like maps. Yet, they detail terrain that exists only in our hearts. We worry (or should worry) that PEACE suffers such intellectual plasticity that it lacks meaning altogether.

Much amity-talk is utopian. Lions and lambs snuggle together. Swords disappear; plows abound. Evildoers are reconfigured as misunderstood children suffering attachment disorder. The libertinism of militant crowds is deemed to express only repressed, well-justified political rage. God frequently sneaks into our PEACE talk. Human and urban perfection awaits, according to Augustine, at the *City of God.* Jesus and his disciples marched toward a shining Yahwist city on a hill. Utopias seem forever distant. Thomas More's *Utopia* lay on an imaginary Atlantic island off the shores of the New World, a frolicking pastoral vision of Christian communism. "Utopia" means "no place," which renders more candor than utopians prefer. Plato's *Republic* was inaccessible, not by virtue of distance, but because of the mire of ordinary minds. We muckers are chained in dark caves; none but philosophical elites glimpse utopian suns. Seyyid Qutb, a militant Islamic theorist, urged Peace by Islamic war against all non-Islamic authorities (*Milestones*). Only when Divine Law (Shariah) is every land's rule will people be truly "free" to choose Allah. Then Qutb's version of PEACE will blossom. Hitler's Germanic utopia was Jew-free. Violence and utopia seem intellectual cousins, chummy at family dinners. I have little interest in PEACE, because I cannot really get hold of it. I doubt courts and lawyers have much to do with PEACE. Utopias seem the bastions of mystics and prophets and dreamers. An outcome that lawyers and courts might make is peace, lower-case peace. Peace without theological pretensions or eschatological hoopla.

Peace is not necessarily insignificant. Martin Luther King Jr. and his activists employed non-violent means to push back American racial segregation. They marched in Birmingham and Washington and Detroit to the beat of King's sonorous speeches. They avoided retaliation (mostly) when attacked. They forged unlikely alliances. Mohandas Gandhi drove the British Empire from India by *Satyagraha* (non-violent resistance). He taught countrymen to weave native thread and boycott British textiles, to harvest their own salt from the sea, and to resist injustice first within, then without. It is important to recognize that the peace of King and Gandhi was earthly and flawed. Each leader suffered foibles. Gandhi was an ascetic anorexic; King suffered an ill-restrained appetite for sexual escapades. Occasional violence erupted from followers, usually in response to outrageous mistreatment by opponents. Both King and Gandhi died by assassination. These sad blemishes teach that peace is a human artifact. Real people with feet of clay make peace. The upside is this. We can make peace, despite our shortcomings, if we wish. But there will be obstacles.

Our courts have peacemaking quite backwards. We lawyers, in our various capacities, comprise the courts. The habit of many is to file suit, then negotiate.[493] This required procedure is utterly backwards. When we file lawsuits, we lead with coercion. Savor a summons. It bursts with compulsion. When we acquiesce in the rules of civil procedure as a guide to conflict resolution, we affirm predicates of violence. Unwilling participants may be compelled to accept unchosen outcomes. The results dismay. Legal peacemakers invert the civil rules. They do not begin with the summons, but end there, only with reluctance, on those rare occasions when listening, negotiation, patience, mediation, and collaboration have, after long perseverance, failed. Peacemakers recognize their skill deficits as part of the problem. They train themselves to hear, to care, to succor creativity, to find common ground, and to narrate a broader, more constructive, more humane story about opponents.

Lawyers seeking amity help people cope with conflicts constructively. Lovers of amity settle divorces when they lead negotiating clients toward hard-won agreements and compromises in a threat-free, information-laden environment. One can drag warring siblings to probate mediations, put doctors and their unwittingly injured patients at the same table, and give bitter neighbors cups of coffee from a common pot. Or one can rush off to the court, brandishing swords. Peacemakers teach disputants narratives that weave and transcend divergent perspectives, and harbor previously unimagined solutions. Peace is real people in gritty conflict unearthing workable solutions without coercion. Lawyers of amity midwife recalibrated social equilibrium.

Peace does not aggregate to PEACE. Peace never beckons the kingdom of heaven. Peace is penultimate. We all imagine better, more utopian, outcomes. But, unlike PEACE, I can get hold of peace. On good days, I can even make some. So too can you. (Though perhaps this objector might not manage such.) It is critical that we make what peace is within reach. Our moral fabric has coarsened in the last century. We risk communal disintegration. (See **Epitome 1: Glover, *Humanity***, which is a moral history of the twentieth century).

---

[493] Some counsels negotiate first as a matter of principle. Others negotiate first as a cheap sort of discovery, probing for the strength of their client's position or the weakness of opponents. Yet others, negotiate first as a fee-maximization strategy. But most lawyers just file.

## OBJECTION 7: SUB-RATIONAL DISTRACTION

*Lancaster's paraplegic proposals lean on moral and affective crutches. All lawyers do not share his feelings or dubious grasp of right and wrong. What lawyers do share is commitment to rational procedures and argument. Such is the stuff of civil procedure and case analysis. Shelving feelings and personal relationships—that is the stuff of law. Humankind lifted itself over millennia from a world of impetuous subjectivity into a spot from which a deeply-educated few might grasp the world more objectively. Lancaster wishes to cast Americans back into a purgatory of moral spasms and half-baked insights, a realm tyrannized by emotional whims. That's the catch with Klatch. We ought not to entertain his ramblings. Rationality is our game. Law is rationality in a complex context. If Lancaster wants to do feelings, let him become a therapist.*

**RESPONSE**: Words transmit ideas. Hearts[494] communicate values. Most lawyers share words more readily than hearts. To share one's heart requires listening more than talking, hugging more than clarifying, crying more than strategizing. Heart "talk" is the older, and more compelling, rubric. We inherit emotive exchange from deeper DNA than language. Affective communication predates humans, emerging long before the hominid lines troubled Africa's Rift Valley. Watch cows in herds, bitchy queues of wrens at birdbaths, and dogs at play. Their exchanges are ancient stuff. But nary a word. All is prelinguistic jabber. Americans, especially American lawyers, are not so comfortable in the mute zone of the heart. We retreat to terminology and analysis and the surface scum of ideation that floats upon our deep, nutrient-laden social waters of existence.[495]

Heartful encounters exhaust. What resources would a lawyer tap to engage clients heartfully? Practicing American law consumes somewhere between forty and one hundred hours each week. Little zest remains, after family and hobbies and sports

---

[494]Critics ask, helpfully, what I mean by the human "heart." I mean that we are not our jobs or marriages or ideas or educations or properties or locations or skills or infirmities. Each of those personal features informs identity, but the insistence of change betrays that personal features do not lie at one's core. The rich become poor, young become old, some knowledgeable become demented, many married become partnerless, employed become idle, some sick recover, some will decompensate. Yet, we persevere. Further, our core identities are not all that unified. We change, and our parts fit together only loosely. Still, we remain ourselves despite maelstrom metamorphoses. I do not wish to claim too much for the human heart, which is, after all, not a human organ, but a metaphor. It too changes, for better or worse, but hesitantly, as sparrows greet tomcats. The heart is a human essence, the deep, infant-attachment core of self that endures. The heart is born in relationship, at maternal breast and paternal bicep. One's heart finds nurture in adult friendship, wherein hides its engine of adaptation. Hearts sink deep beneath life's flotsam fancies, for they are heavy and dark. The heart embraces meaning. It guides life, though lightly. Hearts suffer progressive putrefaction or purification. Time, and the timbre of decision-making, right or rot the heart. I worry about mine.

[495] Lawyers like to style our social distance as "professional objectivity." Our insularity is neither professional nor objective. We may distance ourselves to regulate the pain we feel at the troubles of others. Professional objectivity self-medicates secondary PTSD. From the client's perspective, our objectivity is just indifference to their agony. Struggling clients need the benefit of objectivity, but seldom relish it at time of delivery.

and religious exertions nibble the scant remainder. What passion perseveres for re-plumbing pipes of personality? If the lawyer has young children, the project of self may suffer a decades-long hiatus. Any rare, snatched moment sinks in a well-snored pillow. Exhaustion prevails. Caring is energy profligate. One's empathizer sputters. Sympathy gutters at the travail of empty tankitude.

To what effect? Many lawyers[496] lead lonely lives. The jackhammer of individualism has pummeled communal life, rendering the hard brick of humanity mere dust and powder.[497] Many lawyers languish for lack of meaningful community. They drown in crowded urban isolation. Though immersed in a sea of people, few friends warm their hearts. They suffer secondary post-traumatic stress from emoting with the contortions of their conflict-demented clients. Life in community has crumbled. Many lawyers' cupboards are bare of social food. How might one nourish a depleted client when one perishes of relational hunger herself?

Peter Block writes of restoring communities. (See **Epitome 2: Block, *Community*.**) He urges that our language, our rooms, our faces, and our openness build community. He asks us to focus on now. Is this meeting peaceful? Are my thoughts the sort that build resilience in this room now? Block believes that our lives stutter from want of communal belonging. He urges people to bind up their wounded sociality and make it meaningful for all involved. He suggests skills and methodologies. But most, Block urges us to be deeply connected to one another.[498]

Amity lingers in meaningful communities. Peace stays in a community not because members sing songs or pray to beneficent gods. Amity exists because a community's members know how to build amity and how to make peace. They do so. Lawyers cannot make peace if they have no context for doing so. The lawyer needs support. Her clients need support. Amity fabricates community where none previously existed. The peacemaker heals communities torn asunder by improvident acts. Amity beckons collaboration, and vetoes zero-sum competition. Amity imagines an improved status quo, and inspires seeking it. The lawyer seeking amity makes of his clients peacemakers.

To do so, amicable attorneys must themselves belong to peaceful communities. Otherwise, they hawk that of which they know little, and cry "Peace, Peace" where there is none. Many lawyers endorse a doubtful measure of job completion. These

---

[496] Indeed, many Americans. "[T]he number of Americans who said they had no close confidants tripled from 1985 to 2004." Russo, "Toxic Well of Loneliness," 66.

[497] The "dust and powder" image derives from Edmund Burke, *Reflections on the Revolution in France*, page 96 (of 250).

[498] Restorative justice, which is one irenic approach, seeks to heal (mostly) criminal injuries. It puts victims, offenders (when appropriate), the families of both, and community stakeholders together in a room to talk, usually with professional assistance. It aims to restore and reintegrate those harmed, those causing harm, and the community at large. It assesses responsibility to the individual and his community, which is often the community of the victim as well, seeking to balance the concerns of the parties. Howard Zehr, an early advocate of restorative justice, identifies five core principles: 1) focus on the needs of victims, but also the needs of offenders; 2) address obligations that emerge from the offender's harms, as well the failings of the community and general society; 3) create a collaborative process of resolution; 4) involve anyone who has a legitimate stake; and 5) repair harm and right wrongs to the extent possible. Zehr, *The Little Book of Restorative Justice*, 43.

say, "Glad the trial is over. We settled in the hallway during lunch recess." Then comes their bill. Next case.

Can amity be law's goal? Or is law merely conflict, process, and profit, followed by another dispute, more civil procedure, and another paycheck? I—and I am not alone—want more. I want my colleagues to make amity, real down and dirty reconciliation and restoration of human communities to revised, but stable, equilibrium.

My objector vaunts rationality. I value rationality; no author can do otherwise. Yet, there appears to be more story to tell about the rational mind than the tale my objector spits. It would appear that ratiocination, if it makes an appearance at all, is a latecomer to the human conversation. Let me explain. I beg your indulgence for some anecdotal intrusions.

Kim (my spouse and work-mate and a fine human being) and I watched *The Tudors*, an HBO series depicting the homicidal self-indulgence of King Henry VIII of England. Nightly, the Lancasters slip into a semi-comatose state in ritual preparation for sleep, melting into massive mauve La-Z-Boys like lumps of sun-struck butter. Our min-pin's dream-barks muffle beneath a lap throw. *Dexter*, *Six Feet Under*, *Sopranos*, Jack Bauer's *24* hour days, *West* Wing's improbably fine federal administration, *Band of Brothers* celebrating what little there was to celebrate about World War Two, Tara's multiple personality gyrations, *Breaking Bad*'s perfection of the winning anti-hero, *Broadchurch*, *Hinterland*, *The Last Kingdom* (with Uhtred von Uhtred, the beautiful barbarian), Walt *Longmire* of Absaroka County, Wyoming, *Battlestar Galactica*, *The Queen*, all of the *Walking Dead* mayhem, infant-obsessed *Call the Midwife*, a host of British and Australian and Finnish and Danish and Swedish and German murder mysteries and police procedurals, the imagination and antics of locally-filmed *Northern Exposure*, and a long trail of Netflixed and Apple Plussed others murmur from our absurdly-large Samsung television. Henry Rex's tale mimicked all the others. A hero (or anti-hero) confronts a villain (or anti-villain), stumbling over ethical hurdles while saving (adventures) or failing to save (tragedies) mankind (or its surrogate—a country, town, family, or friend). Right prevails (as justice demands) or doesn't (as infamy mandates). The storylines are fustily trite, yet quietly fulfilling. The stories touch me deeply, even when inane. Perhaps this betrays the shallowness of my pond. Or perhaps these tales recapitulate myths, abyssal narratives that loop ceaselessly just below the thin skin of consciousness.

Much conflict, and therefore much peacemaking, concerns the stories people tell themselves. Most people prefer to play the hero in their dramas. Conflict resolution often consists in getting everybody to set their white hats aside and consider a different tale, especially a less virulent narrative about their perceived opponent. People find this task difficult. So do their mediators. Surely, we are ignorant about much concerning people with whom we have conflict. We could inquire. Certainly, we are prejudiced about some facet of the habits, body, illness, sex, creeds, deviancies, race, dialects, friends, inflections, or clothing of an enemy. We could confess. Most, we fear creating anything better with "nasty" people, because we do not know with certainty the outcome of stories that have never before been told. We could get a grip. The same old story is not *that* safe or interesting. What, then, makes the Hero-Villain story so compelling?

Jaak Panksepp, once a professor at Washington State University and author of *Affective Neuroscience: The Foundations of Human and Animal Emotions*, studied the neuroanatomical structures from which emerges mammalian emotion. Dr. Panksepp argues that "affects," which include both emotions and the rudimentary drives we share with all mammals, undergird all consciousness. Unawares, we feel or desire. After the fact (if at all), we rationalize our urges. The brain structures that move us or make us feel what we feel are more primitive than the newer, bigger parts of the human brain. Consciousness blossoms (if it blooms at all) atop a stew of unconscious drives and affects. Our affects are not rational. Nor do they necessarily nestle well with one another. Affects are what they are: sleep cycles, urges toward chemical homeostasis, fear, seeking, anger, lust, social bonding, play. All cavort upon our basal sense of existence in the world, which Panksepp identifies as a function of a deep brain fraction called the mesencephalic periaqueductal gray (MPAG). Such consciousness is the way of mammals. It is our way. If the human brain were a tree (a coppice, to be exact), its roots would plunge deep in the soil of the MPAG. Its several trunks erupt lightward through a dark subconscious forest, lofting the emotions that our hypothalmic structures generate. Its leafy canopy undulates with higher neocortical processing. At the canopy apex, consciousness skips fitfully across a field of arboreal green, scarcely aware that the giant organism laboring below determines its topography.[499] Consciousness can see the heavens deep, but barely notices its roots and trunk.

To return to Hero-Villain epics, we choose dualistic stories because, when affects rage, no other tales come to mind. That emotive duplex rouses us to flee faster than we thought possible, or fight with fury we never imagined lay within us. So the Story is good for survival on the rolling savannahs of east Africa, where predators aplenty prowl. The problem is this: we no longer inhabit African veldt.

For the peacemaker, the coppice of consciousness, this metaphor for neuroanatomical subtleties, prescribes a path. People's brains tell that story their affects demand. Fearful, agitated persons shoehorn players into one of the Hero-Villain myth's hackneyed roles. Peacemakers evade this casting by distraction. We calm participants. We talk of banalities. We avoid coercion. We offer respect and a beverage. We preserve dignity. We sometimes joke. We balance power. On good days, we settle storm-whipped affects. The calm mediator midwifes calm. She offers stable relationship, which, in the end, is the only thing that heals, and, ultimately, the only thing humans want. Then, occasionally, when hearts slow and respiration normalizes, a wiser narrative sounds marginally plausible to combatants, a different story peopled by fewer ogres and princesses. Amity, occasionally, happens.

So, if Panksepp's research is a true beacon in our storied night, rationality will help, but not all that much. Ours is a wind-whipped emotive sea, and that of our clients more so. When we attempt reasonable talk, say about civil procedure or a case decided eighty years ago, clients nod off. They are right to do so. We tell a tale they do not understand, a view for which they have little patience.[500] This objector's

---

[499] This "coppice of consciousness" metaphor is more deeply elaborated in my earlier work, *Cull: Choosing Well*, 132-134. The image rests upon Jaak Panksepp's description of human consciousness and affect as a tree. Panksepp, *Affective Neuroscience*, 302. Gottman and DeClaire have popularized Panksepp's neuro-affective research in their book on improving relationships. **See Epitome 13: Gottman and DeClaire, The Relationship Cure.**

[500] Which calls to mind *Silas Marner*: "[A] settler, if he came from distant parts, hardly ever ceased to be viewed with a remnant of distrust, which would have prevented any surprise if a long course of

perspective is one which clients do not want to know, and are unlikely to invest any energy learning. Lawyers should speak intelligibly.

## OBJECTION 8: THE CLUTCHES OF KLATCH

*Lancaster hatches the Klatch from his none-too-supple imagination with dire warnings of jurispathic murder or bad faith isomorphic assimilation of the Klatch into constitutional governance. Attorneys, in Lancaster's parlance, are voracious little predators, habituated to ignoble processes and disposed to drown the fires of communal warmth to service their cash-driven frenzies. Lancaster would upend a thousand years of jurisprudence in favor of an untested scheme of neighborhood wrangling, which scheme would inevitably reek of ignorance and prejudice and pettiness. Lancaster's proposal throttles professionalism and makes of disputes a desert scorched by irrational excess.*

*Lancaster is a hypocrite. I do not mean that he is not a perfectly pleasant human being, most days. Let me explain. Lancaster is an attorney, one of our "corrupt" brethren. He has made his living by the common law, and enjoyed its fruits. Lancaster would interject an alien approach to conflict into the lives of millions, for which he lacks consent of the many. Most particularly, Lancaster would thrust the Klatch onto others who have not sought his assistance in any regard. Is that not the essence of Lancaster's complaint about the common law, that it imposes an alien and unwelcome regime upon an uncomprehending populace. Is that not exactly what Lancaster seeks in his amity proposal, to deflect the many into the clutches of Klatch?*

**RESPONSE**: As to this objector's aspersions upon lawyers, I do not assess my colleagues (or myself) so uncharitably. I would, however, change the rudiment of the common law from inimical adversity to amicable collaboration, from reasoned revenge to community restoration. We should devote our deepest thoughts and grueling efforts to outcomes that ennoble and elevate us. We might depart hoary carnage for finer endeavors. We might grasp that of which humankind has long dreamt, life absent homicides, both figurative and literal.

As to the remainder of this objector's complaint, I agree. I have not been commissioned expressly to repurpose the halls of jurisprudence. Yet, I experience law. I mull those encounters. I have formed an opinion. I have stated my sentiment. That effort now lies in the reader's hands.

This objector speaks uncharitably. His fears, I understand. To hypocrisy, I confess. The objector's rant seethes *ad hominem* venom. Perhaps warranted. Perhaps not. You, my reader, have the final say.

---

inoffensive conduct on his part had ended in the commission of a crime; especially if he had any reputation for knowledge, or showed any skill in handicraft. All cleverness, whether in the rapid use of that difficult instrument the tongue, or in some other art unfamiliar to villagers, was in itself suspicious: honest folk, born and bred in a visible manner, were mostly not overwise or clever—at least, not beyond such a matter as knowing the signs of the weather; and the process by which rapidity and dexterity of any kind were acquired was so wholly hidden, that they partook of the nature of conjuring." Eliot, *Silas Marner*, Chapter One.

## OBJECTION 9: DUE RESPECT IN BOILING WATER

*Lancaster's aspersions aside, the common law deserves respect. Justice Oliver Wendell Holmes urged that the heart of common law is experience. Judicial governance merely rationalizes the experiential evolution of society's rules. By those rules, we manage to live together civilly in a frequent approximation of fairness. Certainly, the common law is enmeshed in the miseries of adversarial dispute resolution. Yet, as I look back on my legal education, I find that appellate cases reflect the best efforts of careful thinkers to establish rules of fair interaction in a society where crowds of strangers are constantly colliding with one another, like molecules in a pot of boiling water. Statutes and common law are the rules of engagement in society and, as such, I find them valuable. With Lancaster's critique, I find myself agreeing, but I remain plagued by frequent whispers: "Yes, but...". Perhaps Lancaster respects the common law less than it deserves.*[501]

**RESPONSE**: Of the common law system, I aim to speak frankly. More sandpaper, no varnish. Applause will in no way improve the common law's outcomes or remediate its inherent defects. Yet, it is not my purpose to vent disrespect. Like this objector, I find many colleagues at law admirable and their thinking stellar. A few I hold dear. My arguments are not *ad hominem*. I do not intend to belittle individuals. Many of them I like. Some I wish I could better emulate. Many are shell-shocked into nastiness, which injury I lament (in them and me). We share a plight. We, one and all, find ourselves bugs in the ancient amber of the common law. We should wriggle free before we become strange rock, encased and very dead.

My broadside is systemic. We people-at-law (me and you, my reader) are enmeshed in a system that produces outcomes abominable: racist, sexist, classist, competitive, coercive, confused, naïve, and so forth, as I have trumpeted as some length (much greater length than, I suspect, many readers prefer). It remains the task of law-people to address this dystopia, to imagine changes that improve our societal lot. It is true that the common law takes the stuff of life and aims to smooth its torn edges. That I admire. That I attempt in my own practice, and I am sure you do as well. The common law, however, undertakes this sorting in a coercive and competitive manner, ever mindful of class and prejudice. We wish it were not so, but it is. The tools we are given more resemble hammer-and-tongs than kindness-and-cooperation. We call our fellows to heel, not to character. We err. To be sure, this is not our intention. It is, however, our result.

## OBJECTION 10: EXTRA-CONSTITUTIONAL RUBBISH

*Lancaster woos you readers to Klatch, dripping sweet talk about unspecified precincts in our constitutional regimes. This rubbish about vacant constitutional turf*

---

[501] This objection substantially reflects thoughts proffered by Joseph Shaub, to whom this little book is dedicated, in an email sent to the author on August 14, 2025. To Joe, I am, as always, grateful.

*annoys. Our federal constitution enumerates the republic's powers and defines a government of three branches. The canopy of this foundational tree stretches from morning's glimmer to nightfall's sputter, through all the sleepy, inky parts, and from an ocean to the east to that ocean of the west and parts beyond, to lunar space and to interplanetary voids beyond. Wan tendrils of power even limp to the interstellar abyss. State constitutions gap-fill federal enumeration with their plenary (that is, unenumerated and all-encompassing) powers wherever a bit of daylight peeks through the federal canopy. We dwell in pervasive constitutional shade, there sheltered from scorching blasts of human distempers. There simply is no room for Lancaster's extra-constitutional nonsense. These constitutions, federal and state, either expressly or through field preemption, preclude innovations that are not agreed through the process of amendment to constitutions. No stream remains for individuals to freelance or innovate, except where floating in the constitutional river and its tributaries.*[502] *Were Klatching to become prevalent, it would be (and should be) subsumed into law by legislatures, enforced by various executives, and, to the extent it addresses disputes and crimes, swallowed by the judiciary. This inevitability Lancaster laments. But this constitutional plenum is our fundamental law. As it should be. Hear no more. Put Lancaster's extra-constitutional hallucinations out with the trash.*

**RESPONSE**: The United States Constitution provides, at the Ninth Amendment: "The enumeration in the Constitution, of certain rights, shall not be construed to deny or disparage others retained by the people." The United States Constitution provides, at the Tenth Amendment: "The powers not delegated to the United States by the Constitution, nor prohibited by it to the States, are reserved to the State respectively, or to the people." And unspecified rights are preserved in the Washington State Constitution at Article One, Declaration of Rights, at Section 30: "The enumeration in this Constitution of certain rights shall not be construed to deny others retained by the people." Facially, then, both the federal and state (at least in Washington) regimes contemplate fields of endeavor and powers to be exercised by people, outside constitutional structures. I have called such powers "extra-constitutional," for such acts are neither allowed nor prohibited by constitutions. Extra-constitutional powers are commonplace. Constitutional conventions are extra-constitutional, since they convene to create constitutions. The state and federal constitutions suffer lobbyists, families, administrative agencies, non-profit organizations, business entities, a welter of clubs, neighborhoods, and religious institutions. All are extra-constitutional, though for

[502] Antonin Scalia (1936-2016) approximated this sort of constitutional absolutism, and the Roberts court seems to be of similar dismissive sentiment as to extra-constitutional liberties (consider the rationale of the *Dobbs* anti-abortion case). Scalia opposed recognition or enforcement of "unenumerated" rights, especially those contemplated by the Ninth Amendment or judges interpreting the due process clause. His view was that all enforceable federal rights are explicitly stated in the federal constitution. (Scalia was less draconian about state constitutions.) See *Troxel v. Granville*, 530 U.S. 57, 91 (2000) (concerning the unenumerated right of parents to direct the upbringing of, and to control who visits, their offspring) (Scalia, J. dissenting) where Justice Scalia argues that refusal to deny or disparage other rights not enumerated in the U.S. Constitution (per the Ninth Amendment) is far removed from affirming any such rights, and even further removed from authorizing judges to identify what these non-descript rights might be, and to enforce those judges' lists of concocted "rights" against laws enacted by Congress. In his famous dictum, Scalia asserted the U. S. Constitution is not a living instrument, but rather "dead, dead, dead." This manner of conservative jousting renders the last two Amendments of the Bill of Rights toothless, and my assertion of "extra-constitutional" powers a figment.

some of these power-centers, constitutions acknowledge their actual or potential existence. Governments have regulated their peripheries, or attempted to do so.

So, this Objector is factually wrong. Extra-constitutional powers exist. One might call them abundant. If people Klatch and opine loudly, so be it. We have a right to assemble (even Klatch), a right to voice opinions (even obnoxious political screeds), and a right to attempt to convince our neighbors concerning matters we deem relevant. Klatching, widely-practiced, would be an extra-constitutional power-center. I advocate Klatchers should resist absorption by the judiciary, and maintain strict separation from all branches of government. Klatchers should influence our various regimes, without being themselves usurped. Most Klatches should address matters of neighborhood concern, since all politics is local. One finds scant amity in structures built to govern the urgencies of strangers. These enmity-structures tamp perversity and regulate feuds, but are a Klatch mismatch. One Klatches with friends, existing or those becoming. Klatch is a vehicle and portent, a path to tread, a habit that transforms, a spigot that fills our guttering bucket of friendship. If you have never Klatched, try it. You might be surprised.

## EPILOGUE

# AMITY AT LAW

Is amity, conceived as the revised rudiment at law, mere wishful thinking? Is there anything more to amity-at-law than frustration with American jurisprudence prettified by this book-length tumbling word confetti? Might amity-at-law, instead, be "thinkful wishing"?[503] Could amity-at-law, when one of our culture's increasingly-frequent dislocations derails normalcy, quietly slide into legal dominance? Might hope be more potent than we imagine? Might jurisprudential longing, buttressed by potent rhetorical defense, ease aside our common law enmity jurisprudence, giving the adversary proceeding the mandatory retirement it so richly deserves? As you have probably gathered from the title of this book, I deem such change necessary, but improbable.

A people share a character. Despite the innumerable oddities of our individual existences, we all participate, often with no small measure of disgust, in a collective character. Some people call this aspect of common life a "culture." But the matter seems to me something deeper than that. Culture is an accoutrement, jewelry for a mask, baubles to be worn or shorn, whereas collective personhood drapes the depths of human hearts, like a winter's fleece in a bitter spell. Perhaps culture insinuates bands and food fads and coiffures, while our collective person spurs courage and conscience and resilience.

The collective person that is America deeply resists change, and clutches its petty prejudices close to the heart. Can we, as a people, engage principled change? Do we have the moral resources to muster self-correction? Evidence of the capacity for both possibilities pelts us from newspapers and televisions. We cannot part with our guns, the cursed results be damned. But we treat black Americans more like people than was long the case. We invite women to be CEOs and soldiers, but still want to control their uteri. We are generous with our assets, but only toward those we already approve. Pertinent to the topics of this book, will we ever, as a people, look within and find that we value peace and friendship more than dominance and wealth? Maybe. Maybe not.

If we are able to change our personal aspect, then our collective personality, to shift toward kithdom with its celebration of the small and intimate, to adopt a tractable polity, then amity-at-law peeks onto our horizon. Instead of unknown neighbors, we might recognize strangers as people who are part of us. We might embrace them, and be embraced by them, after kegs of beer, summer picnics, and winter bowling. We

503 Jerome Frank alleges that he lifted this turn of phrase off a fellow named Neurath, whom I have been unable to further identify (could be Otto, the Austrian, or Konstantin, the German Nazi). Frank, *Courts on Trial*, 79.

might solve problems together, keep our children safe, and earn less money and share more. We might, when circumstances warrant, convene as a Klatch, together with disputing friends and their cherished others, to fashion resolution. That would be a beginning. That would be amity-obviating-law, which is just an inch or two from amity-at-law. When legal scholars parse amity, when the political power of friendship tilts the ballot box, when judges make careers of sending litigants to hallways of rooms dedicated to amicable processes and processors, knowing that those outcomes surpass any that a judge might command, then amity-at-law finds breath. When courthouses are retired, and community centers host Klatches and other amity sessions, then amity-at-law matures. When courtrooms are reserved for sociopaths and rapists, and no others, amity-at-law will have prevailed. We will then have new problems. But not the old ones.

I began this tone poem with a dirge lamenting the alienating vicissitudes of courthouses. I end with a paean extolling a jurisprudence aimed at preserving and restoring friendship. Evidence of schizophrenia, perhaps.[504] Or, perhaps, I hum my primal song of longing, a tune performed by an odd orchestra most decline to hear. The voluntary deaf suffer a dire impediment: intentional inattention.

My silent, unheard symphony convenes sub-harmonic collaborators: ambiguous measures, odd notation, empty staffs—bass and treble, clarinets without reeds, trombones lacking slides, stringless cellos, lost-bow violins, and an armless conductor. These blare an inaudible concert of impenetrable subtlety, a revelatory concerto for headstrong lawyers—my tone poem for the deaf.

Listen closely, my colleague.
Do you hear music?
I trust you can.
If you will.
Try.

---

[504] Around four thousand years ago, Egypt's well-spoken commoner, in his eighth petition to a judicial officer, said: "Now my body was full, my heart was burdened, and it has poured from my body of its own accord; There was a break in the dam, its water gushed out, And my mouth opened to speak. Then I plied my sounding pole and drained off the flood (within me). I have unburdened what was in my body, I have washed my soiled linen. My harangue is (now) completed; my misery is fully in your sight. What (now) do you lack?" "The Tale of the Eloquent Peasant," lines 276-280, in *The Literature of Ancient Egypt*, 40.

## EPITOME 1

**Glover, Jonathan. *Humanity: A Moral History of the Twentieth Century.* New Haven, Connecticut: Yale University Press: 2000.**

*Jonathan Glover (born 1941) directs the Centre of Medical Law and Ethics at King's College, London.*

**Preface.** What lessons in ethics ought one to derive from the violence of the twentieth century?

**Chapter 1: *Never Such Innocence Again.*** At the end of the twentieth century, one cannot be certain of the existence of a moral law or of moral progress. Intellectual repudiation of moral law and last century's history argue against them. News tends to anesthetize viewers to events. Everything gets forgotten in the endless news cycle. Glover has not experienced the events of which he writes. He is attempting to get perspective on them. In philosophical ethics, there has been a move from theoretical ethics to applied ethics, putting human concerns squarely in philosophy's crosshairs. Ethics generally should be more empirical. Enlightenment confidence that rationality would banish war and cruelty proved shallow. Glover looks at human spiritual darkness, in the hope of restraining it in the service of a better future. [505]

---

[505] A word about epitomes. In my view, the best books are colloquia. Those excellent tomes bring together the thought of diverse others, often the best minds history offers, to hone some topic. An "epitome" summarizes a written work. Such a brief version of a book could also be called an abstract or abridgement. I epitomize the works of others because, first, those works are excellent, and, second, because you need to read them (but probably never will).

As I epitomize other people's work, I attempt to focus on the author's core argument, to the neglect of digressions, examples, illustrations, tables, worksheets, and other useful, but voluminous, explanatory tools. Generally, my epitomes capture twenty to forty pages of original material per epitomized page. Habitually, Greeks and Roman authors epitomized the works of colleagues, often for the purpose of arguing intelligently against their core points. Epicurus epitomized his own work. He argues that, for those unable to examine his longer works, capturing an outline of thoughts is better than nothing. Epicurus, *Letter to Herodotus* in *The Essential Epicurus*, 19. Kant also self-epitomized. See *Prolegomena to any Future Metaphysics*, 9 (Introduction). More recently, Peter Block self-epitomizes his work, *Community*. I have epitomized my most expansive work, *Cull: Choosing Well,* at page 431 of the first volume of that two-volume effort.

One may ask, *Why condense pivotal books to a few pages? Should one not just read the originals?* Summaries distort what they condense; these epitomes are no exception. Still, epitomizing forces one to decide an author's meaning. Given the time constraints of life at law, few legal professionals read broadly. These time-starved denizens of courtrooms and legal departments, nevertheless, suffer an unrecognized need for the counsel and offense these unread texts impart. The wisdom closeted in these texts informs the global deliberation of human weal, as well as the direction of law itself. Epitomes provide a texture, if not the entire fabric, of core books and essays. Some ethical classics are, frankly, opaque and ponderous (though worth the effort to digest). Epitomes offer guidance in comprehension. As opportunity emerges, read originals, at least those which pique interest. Until then, read epitomes.

I attempt, when epitomizing, to state an author's argument plainly. I do not interpret or apologize, except to the extent required for understanding itself. I attempt to approach each author's work with diligence, sympathy, and openness. I am certain I have failed in this effort regularly. Where an author's

## PART ONE: ETHICS WITHOUT THE MORAL LAW

**Chapter 2:** ***Nietzsche's Challenge.*** Friedrich Nietzsche foresaw the collapse of religious morality in the twentieth century. Nietzsche valued self-creation, and castigated all authorities that might claim to govern or restrain that project. In Nietzsche's view, god is dead. Religion is poison and must be swept away. Governments rely on confusions of the masses. A self-created man is noble in the sense that his superior completeness frees him to do whatever he may need in order to self-create. Life lacks intrinsic meaning. The human beast makes of it what he will, if he has the strength. The self-created man grasps life with a clenched fist, choking any weakness he finds in himself and strangling the masses, who are uniformly weak. Women are, by definition, flaccid. Altruism disguises pallid souls. The brilliant souls of self-created aristocrats may exterminate lesser men at will. The weak are born to perish, lambs in the talons of eagles. Glover accepts Nietzsche's view of religion, gods, and human self-creation. Glover rejects Nietzsche's particular recipe for self-creation. Values other than cruel domination exist, and may become one's self-program. But what does one say to the Nietzschean amoral superman when he runs amok?

**Chapter 3:** ***Self-Interest as a Restraint.*** Amoralists reject ought-ness. Still, even they have strong motivations to behave well. Some are naturally generous. And self-interest often dictates fitting in and behaving well. Reciprocal altruism inclines others to assist you. To the extent life resembles the simple dual prisoner's dilemma, the best strategy is tit-for-tat: I defect after you defect, I cooperate after you cooperate. In more complex versions of the prisoner's dilemma, other strategies prevail. Social approval depends not upon moral conviction, but upon the appearance of moral conviction. Gyges's ring (Plato, *Republic*) rendered him invisible and unleashed his inner pestilence. Perhaps being good is the best way to appear good. But a mixed strategy may prevail, in which one is good in many aspects, but hides a sanctum of dissent from others. Social pressure fails as a moralizing force when a culture goes awry, pressuring others to immorality (Nazis, Chinese cultural revolution). Social pressure has no effect as between nations.

**Chapter 4:** ***The Moral Resources: Humanity.*** Moral restraint has roots in human respect and sympathy. People who aver Nietzschean amoralism nevertheless frequently have self-creation projects quite different from Nietzsche's *Ubermensch* ideal. Respect acknowledges the essential dignity of another. Sympathy grows from human drives to belong, and extends to strangers. Personal suffering may expand

---

terminology hides his argument, I abandon or simplify that terminology. Words, phrases, or sentences in quotation marks are the terminology or language of the epitomized author (except when added to indicate a term is being used oddly). I seldom quote the epitomized authors. Rather, I put each author's thoughts in my own words, without (hopefully) departing from the author's intent in any dramatic manner. All title, chapter, and section names are those of the epitomized author. I have written diminutive biographical introductions for each author without any undue hand-wringing about the historicity of anecdotes I report. If you seek deeply-vetted historical information about epitomized authors, it might be wise to inspect scholarly biographies.

one's capacity for sympathy. "Humanity" means to respond to others with respect and sympathy. Not all humans exhibit humanity.

**Chapter 5:** ***The Moral Resources: Moral Identity***. Part of self-restraint derives from the task of becoming the person you imagine yourself to be. Socrates argued that happiness springs from internal integration. Other theorists chose other ethical bases: self-interest for contractarianism, sympathy for utilitarianism, respect for Kantian ethics. No single basis suffices, especially when ethics moves outside a single community. The moral gap between what we will do for insiders and for outsiders explains much cruelty. Glover recounts the Athenian conquest of their small neighbor, Melos, in Thucydides's history. Athens argued that might makes right, Melos offered neutrality and warned about Athens's own future need for fair play were they to be defeated. Athens destroyed Melos. Human internal resources are insufficient to restrain us in dealing with outsiders.

**Chapter 6:** ***The Festival of Cruelty***. Humans are artistically cruel. Humans 1) can love cruelty, 2) are driven to cruelty by emotional deficiencies, and 3) restraints on cruelty can be overcome. Some deep motivation in mankind seeks cruelty under certain circumstances. Some individuals yield more readily to the impulse to cruelty than others. Moral identity itself can erode, growing weaker in the presence of emphasis on the differentness of the non-member. The dehumanization includes "cold jokes," which bring black humor to cruelty. Still, our best sentiments can break through the intention to be cruel, when the object is restored unexpectedly to common humanity (Glover tells the tale of a South African Afrikaner policeman, intent upon beating a woman; she loses her shoe, he picks it up and returns it to her. The officer can no longer chase his intended victim.) Glover speculates that it may be possible to overcome the impulse to cruelty in humans.

**Chapter 7:** ***Answering Nietzsche***. To answer Nietzsche, Glover seeks a post-theological morality, an ethic recognized as a human artifact, and designed to address human needs and weakness. Most morality is local. Part of our task is to widen our moral scope to all of humanity. We need institutions opposing cruelty (like UN Peacekeepers and mediation of disputes). We also need cultural change aimed to more deeply restrain cruelty. The task is to refashion ethics with a collective bent. The new ethics must be empirical, investigating human moral fragility and answering it systematically.

## PART TWO: THE MORAL PSYCHOLOGY OF WAGING WAR

**Chapter 8:** ***Close Combat.*** Glover estimates that in ninety years of the twentieth century, on average 100 people were killed every hour in war. Killing directly with guns or blades puts soldiers to the task of behaving differently than they would in normal life. This possibility emerges from depersonalization of the soldier, from dehumanization of the enemy, from inuring the soldier to wartime cruelty, and from giving young men a defined path to recognition as adult soldiers (through killing). Despite these forces, moral revulsion occasionally breaks through. Humiliation may lead to bursts of violence. So too, an intense sense of camaraderie can lead to violent outbreaks often citing revenge or release of frustration. Some soldiers report experiencing the killing as fun "in strange and troubling ways."

**Chapter 9:** ***The Case of My Lai.*** Glover recounts the American massacre of villagers at My Lai in Vietnam. The commanders encouraged the carnage. The soldiers followed orders, then lost control. Some few resisted, but did so bravely. My Lai is noteworthy because it is so well documented, but its psychological features are common to "normal" combat responses.

**Chapter 10:** ***The Shift to Killing at a Distance.*** The twentieth century innovation in war lies in the cold violence of killing at a distance by technical means. The first instance lies in Britain's blockade of Germany during World War I, from which around 500,000 Germans died of starvation and associated diseases. War at a distance needs fewer erosions of individual morality than does the hot violence of hand to hand combat. Still, moral identity must be suppressed. Moral identity proves less inhibiting when the killings seem justified; when, at least at first, no civilian deaths are caused intentionally; when the transition to civilian deaths comes incrementally; when the deaths are caused by inaction, rather than action; and when the policy is implemented by many people in many places. Eventually the instrument of civilian killing becomes a bureaucracy, with its own institutional inertia.

**Chapter 11:** ***Bombing.*** The intentional mass starvation of German civilians broke through the taboo on killing noncombatants, and serves to justify bombing of civilian centers in all subsequent war. British carpet bombing of German targets had three phases: 1) bombing of military targets, 2) the recognition that targeting was too inaccurate to assure only military targets were being destroyed, and so inadvertent destruction of civilian targets, and 3) intentional destruction of civilian targets to demoralize the population and inhibit industrial workforce participation in the German war effort. Bomber crew mortality was very high (only 16% survived two tours of duty). On the ground below the bombers, more than a half million civilians died. Glover reports from Dresden. Physical distance makes civilian retaliatory death more acceptable. Glover recounts the moral insensitivity of the commanders of the British bomber attacks. There were few breakthroughs of sympathy for the German victims. Retaliation breeds legitimacy. Glover reports that the officers in charge of ordering the bombing of cities did not believe themselves to be making those decisions, but merely responding to orders from above. With options open, bombing civilians is war atrocity. Just War Theory contemplates civilian deaths as unintentional results of permitted killing. No innocents can be intentionally targeted. The emphasis on intention slides easily to dissembling. Strict pacifism offers an alternative, but few are willing to accept the control of evil actors in consequence. How does one adjudicate the killing of civilians, say by carpet bombing, if one rejects a divine mandate and rational quibbling about outcomes? Glover recounts the opposition to bombing of civilians by Bishop Bell, who emphasized the moral degradation wrought on the bombers and their civilization by the acts. Each act of civilian killing justifies the next yet-greater insult. The British blockade leads to area bombing, which leads to Tokyo firebombing, which leads to Hiroshima.

**Chapter 12:** ***Hiroshima***. Willingness to use an atomic bomb against Axis powers in WWII grew from callousness deriving from massive conventional civilian bombings, fear of Axis nuclear programs, and the mere fact of the existence of the American bomb. The American bomb program began as a deterrent to a possible German weapon. Among the Germans, the nuclear scientists were ambivalent, both wanting Germany to win the war, but not wanting a Nazi nuclear hegemony. The Japanese theater of WWII took a tremendous toll on civilians and soldiers alike. The case for a rapid end to the war was compelling. Eisenhower argued against using the atomic weapon on cities. Truman overruled him. Other considerations intervened, like the enthusiasm of the military for demonstrating the weapon militarily, and the need to intimidate the Soviets in Europe. The Japanese feared that, if they surrendered unconditionally, the Emperor would be forced to step down. The Hiroshima bomb killed 200,000 persons within five years. The Nagasaki bomb killed 140,000 within five years. American moral identity, which might have restrained the Japanese atomic bombs was eroded by physical distance from the killings, evasions about the effects of the bombings, and by the relatively small contribution made to the events by any one individual (fragmentation of responsibility). Among Truman, Churchill, Oppenheimer, and the Stimson committee (which considered the likely outcomes of various uses of the atomic weapons), no one took final responsibility. A moral vacuum ensued. Glover suggests that Truman could have suggested another test of the weapons on American soil in which Japanese observers participated, and a negotiated peace without the demand to depose the Emperor.

Glover recounts Elizabeth Anscombe's impassioned argument at Oxford University against giving Harry Truman an honorary degree. She was a minority of one, when the vote was taken. Anscombe's argument was based on just war theory. In its double effect doctrine, innocent deaths, when limited, are permitted to achieve military results of protecting oneself or others. Glover examines the double effect doctrine, noting two different rules: 1) were innocent deaths wanted? and 2) were innocent deaths so integral to the act that we cannot call them accidental? Both rules are premised on an absolute prohibition on taking innocent life, part of Catholic orthodoxy. As an appeal to authority, many will find her argument unappealing.

Glover argues for an open world in which an international authority controls all weapons of mass destruction.

**Chapter 13:** ***War and the Moral Resources***. In close combat, soldiers' moral identity may be eroded by dehumanizing the enemy, emotional defensiveness, training, the alien unfamiliarity of the battlefield, contempt for moral dialogue, emotional outbursts in vengeance or humiliation, or battle ecstasy. In long distance war, moral identity suffers from distance and passivity, fragmentation of responsibility, and the effect of ill-precedents in mass killings.

## PART THREE: TRIBALISM

**Chapter 14:** ***Rwanda.*** "Tribal" conflicts flare between neighbors so frequently that they form part of the human condition. In the Rwandan genocide, around one million people died. The tribal hostility was aggravated by a political campaign inciting the populace and international non-action, particularly on the part of the United States.

**Chapter 15:** ***The Tribal Trap***. Tribal conflict usually requires political propaganda to emerge into killing. One group's nationalism spurs that of another, then both descend in a spiral of growing distrust and antipathy. Glover recounts the brutal disintegration of Yugoslavia into its component nationalities and religious identities, along with the propaganda that engendered public fears. Glover reports rape camps and intentional killing of young children. Fear of attack operates as well as actual attack as a motivator for war. The "Hobbesian trap" consists in motivation to strike first to prevent a devastating first strike from an opponent. Pluralist states make diverse persons citizens. Tribal states conceive themselves as consisting of one race, nationality, or religion; those who differ are outsiders.

**Chapter 16:** ***The Political Containment of Tribalism***. Tribal wars flag when diverse societies are created and fear is doused. One may concede that tribes may become nations. But usually within tribal states are minorities wanting their own independence (the Russian doll problem). Blurring the concept of sovereignty may help, or sharing territory or allowing dual citizenship of disputed regions might ease tensions. Disturbed areas need a Hobbesian Leviathan, an international force with sufficient power to quell intertribal violence. Glover recounts the disdain with which the Serbian forces treated the UN peacekeeping force in Bosnia, which had no authority to use force. The "international community" was no more effective. The Serbs dismembered a recognized state, committed genocide, and profited from the acts. To control tribal conflicts, from the first world to the third world, a credible and permanent international police force is needed, one with clear rules of engagement and an international court to authorize its engagement. If the international community will not enforce its sense of appropriate boundaries, then the violent will prevail.

**Chapter 17:** ***The Roots of Tribal Conflict***. Tribal conflict emerges from the human propensities for simmering historical hatreds, political propagandizing, being captured by beliefs, fear of unrestrained others, and a weakness for group conflicts. A genetic basis for the human disposition to group conflict may lie in the evolutionary pressure of inclusive fitness (individual fitness combined with survival of similar genes in kindred others). Psychologically, nations are the us-of-imagination, which is tribal consciousness. Having a sovereign territory is not essential. Tribal identity comprises charged elements, such as common appearance, customs, religion. Possibly, tribal identity is deeply linked to our individual sense of meaning. The narrative we tell ourselves gets fundamentally bonded to the places where it takes place. With its further links to common language, religion, and customs, slights to these places or habits injure individual self-concept. Slights may kindle wars. Tribal-national entities create narratives that justify violent acts; these tales unbend the bent twig. Violent acts justify further narratives supporting vengeance. The tribal vendetta results.

**Chapter 18:** ***The Capacity to Unchain Ourselves***. To bridle tribal war in the short term, we need a global police. In the longer term, we may be able to erode tribalism itself, as a psychological proposition. Tribal mentality is a fact of human psychology. But can a global humanism replace it for most people? Tribal enmities are inhibited when other tribes respect equality among tribes. Individual acts of empathy and sympathy contradict the narrative of violence, and weaken it. An expanded sense of moral identity also weakens tribal hatreds: we are not merely Serbs and Croats, but also parents, humans, religionists, music lovers, walkers, and readers.

## PART FOUR: WAR AS A TRAP

**Chapter 19:** ***The Trap of the Trenches.*** War entraps its participants. Aggression explains little of war. Glover recounts events of World War I: the mutual slaughter at Somme, the general sense of futility among the troops, fraternization between enemy lines, informal troop-led cease fires, and cooperation among the troops to reduce casualties. Superiors fought back. Soldiers who declined to fight were executed. The war trap extended to propagandized civilians, who seemed pathologically incapable of receiving information that contradicted the war narrative.

**Chapter 20:** ***The Home Front.*** Civilian populations think what they learn from their media. Civilian war moods are divided; people feel fear and interest in peace, but also exhilaration. The media of both warring nations tell stories supporting war. Governments censor news to maintain morale at home and avoid encouraging enemies. Soldiers self-censor to avoid distressing homefront non-combatants. Public feedback (not wanting to hear stories contradicting their war narrative) discourages media from telling the truth. Mutual racism in the Pacific theater of World War II was rampant. Ten percent of Americans supported extermination of the Japanese.

**Chapter 21:** ***The Stone Has Started to Roll: 1914.*** In deliberating war, most people participate passively. Even leaders taking the decision to fight feel trapped into war. Such was World War I. The war started with the assassination of Franz Ferdinand by a group of young Serbian men redressing a battle lost in AD1389. Austria warred on Serbia, then Russia on Austria and Germany, then France on Germany, then Britain on Germany. Glover recounts the events of the growing conflagration. What accounts for this slide into a war it seems none of the nations involved wanted? 1) *Confusion and Ambiguity*. Ambivalence and confusion in the policies of one country impair the ability of others to respond rationally, when considering the question of war. Misunderstanding and mis-assessment are inevitable. 2) *Military Preparations*. The parties' military preparations for defense of their homelands forced all to become more war-ready. Mobilizing one army caused all to mobilize, leading to arms races. Defensive alliances among countries primed the conflict, rapidly leading all the European powers into a war none wanted over a non-governmental provocation (assassination of Archduke Ferdinand). 3) *Public Mind-Set*. Willingness to war was considered the essence of national identity. Social Darwinism predicted a global fight for survival, with the nation-state as the selection units. Nations were conceived as individuals, suffering dishonor or enjoying glory. To break the trust of an ally was thought to be worse than war. In the end, the public mind was distracted from the effects of war on people to its effects on abstractions.

**Chapter 22:** ***Sliding out of the Trap: 1962.*** Glover describes the Cuban missile crisis, which drove the United States and Soviet Union to the brink of nuclear war. The motivating factors were, for the Soviets, fear of American intervention in Cuba, changing the balance of nuclear power, and answering American missiles sited in Turkey. For the Americans, concern about no-warning nuclear strikes, possible Castro control of the weapons, and loss of prestige predominated. Other factors influenced the standoff: slow communication by telegram, unclear intentions, growing military independence and influence, American public hostility toward Cuba, and emotional pressure for quick action. The crisis was avoided when both civilian leaders checked their militaries, when both recognized that their situation was a trap, when both spoke with conciliation, left one another ways out of the trap. Hawks emphasized the irrationality of Soviet responses to American attack. Doves emphasized human fallibility under great emotional pressures. To resolve the crisis, Khrushchev backed down and Kennedy deceived the American public (about the tradeoff for Turkish missiles). But they avoided nuclear war.

**Chapter 23: *Ways Out*.** Comparing 1914 with 1962 leads to some conclusions about avoiding war: 1) make policy clear to opponents, 2) assert strong control of the military, 3) respond slowly and with caution, 4) stay aware of human fallibility, 5) speak without provocation to avoid generating fear or anger, 6) join the opponent in acknowledging the war trap and set a joint plan to work out of the trap. Politically, a Hobbesian Leviathan (control by superior coercion) may impose peace, but that peace will be only as enduring as the Leviathan. We should rig the international game for peace, learning lessons from game theories (dollar auction, tit-for-tat). The world needs a Kantian cooperative arrangement. Immanuel Kant, in his *Eternal Peace* essay, recognizes the Hobbesian state of nature, but offers a cooperative solution. Nations join a republic, relinquishing sovereignty to the republic as to the right to war. The federated nations are otherwise independent. Kant argues that the effects of war drive nations toward this solution, but so does morality. Democratic states are more likely to agree to federation, and less likely to war, because the government's policies have to be approved by those who bear the human costs of war. Psychologically, public opinion influences governments. To steel public opinion against war, one requires public skepticism about partisan political ranting, willingness to endure humiliation or disrespect in the name of avoiding war, sensitivity to the human moral resources of compassion and sympathy. National self-interest is a sometimes self-defeating rational enterprise, like the dollar auction. Skepticism about coercive approaches is critical to creating a different, less war-prone global culture.

## PART FIVE: BELIEF AND TERROR: STALIN AND HIS HEIRS

**Chapter 24: *In Those Years*.** Stalinist purges murdered tens of millions of Russians. The methods were execution pits, slave labor camps, deliberate starvation, forced relocation, and political persecution. Stalin encouraged torture. Yet it was normal people who murdered and tortured. How shall one understand this fact?

**Chapter 25: *The Trap of Terror*.** Aristotle said that a tyrant retains power by keeping his people strangers to one another. Fear without companionship leads to submission. Lenin gave instructions: Have tough people hang opponents publicly, broadcast their names, and take all their property. Stalin universalized Lenin's approach. Leaders as well as normal people suffered. Of the original eight members of the Politburo of 1917, six died violently. Only Lenin and Stalin survived. They murdered the others. They orchestrated show trials of thousands, even their own closest colleagues. In the end, Stalin had a stroke, and his closest allies would not call a doctor. Stalin was desperately lonely, and died that way.

**Chapter 26:** ***Belief: Ends and Means***. Ideological faith in Marxism loosed Stalin's cruelty to its exorbitant excesses. Faith in Stalin himself reached religious proportions. The great task of remaking capitalist humans into perfect communists justified any excess. Society is either a factory producing communists or defective products to be rejected. Indifference to suffering became the Soviet rule. Eggs were broken for the Russian omelette. Morality was the hogwash of ruling capitalist elites. The perfect state was justified in exterminating its enemies.

**Chapter 27:** ***Stalinism and the Moral Resources***. In the face of Stalin's terror, kindness came to be ridiculed, and fear drove people to ignore the cruelty paraded before them. In those executing the policies, hardness and black humor replaced sympathy. Glover tells the story of Nikolai Bukharin, a Soviet Party leader whom Stalin executed.

**Chapter 28:** ***The Working of a Belief System***. Beliefs form systems that function as mental maps. When experience contradicts one of our beliefs, we may revise the belief or doubt the evidence or criticize the purveyor of that evidence or abandon the belief system or claim ignorance. Our options in the face of inadequacy of a belief are many. Any belief can be conserved if one is willing to employ dramatic strategies to retain it. If core beliefs remain static, the belief system flexes to accommodate that fixity. Not all beliefs are equal. Structural beliefs dictate how one adjudicates among various belief options. Glover cites the ideological gyrations of the British Communist Party in response to Stalin's political machinations to invade Poland and sidle up to Hitler, during the run up to World War II. The British Party believed in Soviet infallibility. All doubts were doubted. Where beliefs grow from authority, rationales subside. The Soviet International was Communist authority. No individual opinions stood against it unpunished. The Party affirmed patent falsehoods to make Stalin's positions more palatable. It is a picture of the effect of ideological belief without fear.

**Chapter 29:** ***Stalinism, Truth and Moral Identity***. Ideological belief with fear of reprisal characterized Stalin's Russia. Pressure to inform and terror of being denounced drove most to abandon their values. Survival was at stake. Most compromised. Stalinism supported skepticism about objective truth, as has been fashionable since the late-1800s. Stalin put truth in the service of political strategies. Communist political ideology commandeered law and even biology (forsaking Mendelian for Lamarckian genetic theory). Even the philosophical community cowered silently. Stalin recommended that philosophers focus on berating or assaulting his opponents. Abandoning moral objectivity (truth) begins with speaking without truth to oneself. That spills over into talking with others. Eventually, misrepresentations need to be defended, and one begins to lie to oneself. Our penchant for partial knowledge, inaccuracy, and bias can be exaggerated into justification for moral relativism. The liar rigs evidence to support his views, and the breach between the world and one's views widens. Self-deception self-perpetuates. Self-talk generates moral identity. When self-talk consists in lies, any act can be justified morally. Moral identity collapses into delusion.

**Chapter 30:** ***Mao's Utopian Project***. Mao and Pol Pot followed Stalin's lead. Mao's agricultural policies (the Great Leap Forward) were built on baseless ideas. Millions starved. Yet Mao failed to heed warnings and reports of famine because these contradicted his opinions. In the end, no one told him of his errors. He had jailed or killed all those who might. The Cultural Revolution afforded Mao opportunity to kill his political opponents and regain control of China. He encouraged young uneducated people to up-end society, purging Confucian ideas and institutions. Millions died. Systematic humiliation drove thousands to suicide. Mao demanded, and got, conformity. Our beliefs rely heavily on the views of others. We conform provisionally, subject to further investigation and skepticism. Such conformity forms the background to all innovation. Where usual doubts are squelched, groups become vulnerable to sociopaths like Mao. The Cultural Revolution left no private space for personal moral identity. All was sacrificed to the Revolution. People came to mistrust and hate one another. Mao thought himself a philosopher. He lacked moral restraints. He took the Chinese people as a canvas on which he believed he could paint what he wished. All of human life was, to Mao, plastic. It could be remolded in the fire of class conflicts.

**Chapter 31:** ***Overturning the Basket: Cambodia***. The Khmer Rouge, upon taking power, drove the population into the countryside, emptying the towns and villages. Many died. Only six years earlier, the Khmer Rouge was small. They grew large when the Nixon administration commenced Cambodian bombing, killing up to 600,000 people. Their nominal American target was North Vietnamese bases inside Cambodia. The Khmer Rouge were quite consciously following a Maoist program. The Khmer's calculation of future human bliss entailed current human death and misery. The Khmer were given to torture and the cold joke. The Khmer Rouge killed two million of Cambodia's eight million people. The Khmer's total redesign of society without regard to morality, which it shared with Mao and Stalin, collapsed in the destruction of its people.

**Chapter 32:** ***Utopia and Belief***. Some social redesign may be worthwhile. Communism, however, was disaster. Communist redesign, as practiced by Mao, Stalin, and Pol Pot, was self-enamored, inflexible, oppressive, immoral, and ultimately ill-fitted to its task. The communist program ignored people's need for self-respect and choice of their own goods. To achieve its utopian ends it employed terror and an oppressive mandatory belief system. Stalinism teaches mankind to disdain utopian social transformations. The ideology that accompanies such efforts is at least as dangerous as barbarism.

## PART SIX: THE WILL TO CREATE MANKIND ANEW: THE NAZI EXPERIMENT

**Chapter 33:** ***The Core of Nazism.*** Hitler exceeded Stalin, Mao, and Pol Pot, not in the number killed, but in the darkness of his vision. Nazi belief employed social Darwinism in support of a Nietzschean exaltation of will and rejection of biblical morality. Nazi belief was tribal and racial, including Germanic types outside Germany, but excluding non-Germanic types (Jews and other groups) within Germany. Historically, Nazism was driven by the 1918 Armistice, which Hitler theatrically reversed by receiving France's surrender at the same spot and rail car as the Germans had surrendered in 1918. Hitler suffered a British gas attack in 1918. It hardened him. He advocated gas for gas, and thought the poison should be used on the corrupting Jews within Germany. Nazism supported racial hygiene. "Defective" citizens should be euthanized, sterilized, or otherwise prevented from breeding. Preferred citizens should be encouraged to have large families and protected. Desirable children of others should be stolen to protect their genetic legacy. The national genetic heritage was, according to Hitler, at risk from interbreeding with inferior tribes. Hitler adopted some of Nazi doctrine from Nietzsche, especially his rejection of Judeo-Christian values related to assisting the weak. Morality was a poison. Nazism substituted hardness and conflict for peace and support as the best of human values.

**Chapter 34:** ***Obedience and Conformity***. Nazism sought uncritical obedience from Germans. Hitler cultivated a religious legend about himself. His subordinates were exalted by their association with Hitler. Glover speculates about the role of strict paternal authoritarianism in German families and the subsequent willingness to obey in the Nazi regime. Hitler's own father was distant and demanding and brutal. Hitler became rigid in his own personal habits. In the Milgram psychological studies, volunteers administered shocks to "learners," from slight to extremely painful. Unknown to the volunteers, the shocks were false, and the learners' responses acted. Twenty-six of forty volunteers administered the full spectrum of shock upon command, despite their belief that they were inflicting significant pain. In subsequent variations, when the disobedience of some volunteers was disclosed, only four of forty participated. In addition to pressure to obey, Nazis created peer pressures to conform. The social ties of the obeying groups created genuine friendship among them. As social animals, our autonomy is necessarily limited. We rely on authorities as shortcuts to good decision-making. When that presumption goes awry, we must abandon obedience, despite the costs. Bertrand Russell's family bible's leaf contains a handwritten sentence: "Thou shalt not follow a multitude to do evil." Nazi beliefs strained normal human moral resources. Added to the pressures of obedience and conformity, most Germans acquiesced or joined.

**Chapter 35:** ***The Attack on Humanity***. Nazism stripped Jews and other unwanted peoples of their dignity, characterizing them as animals or diseases. They were intentionally humiliated. Cold jokes abounded with respect to the executions. Dehumanization of victims made their murder easier for the soldiers. Nazism urged people to replace sympathy with hardness, to participate in the cold machinery of the State. Sympathy sometimes broke through the discipline of hardness, usually in the presence of individual women and children victims. Such breakthroughs were not uncommon, but seldom worked to prevent executions. The Nazis had a strict rule against exceptions, so no individual considerations were valid excuses for leniency.

**Chapter 36:** ***The Erosion of Moral Identity***. After accounting for obedience and a penchant for conformity, it is still difficult to comprehend how normal Germans participated in the Nazi mass murders. Other psychological features assisted: bureaucratic wrangling, technical problems, denial, euphemisms, and a sense of unreality. Still, normal human compassion erupted occasionally. Even Nazi leaders felt embarrassment, hid the genocide camps, and forbade speaking of the Final Solution. Nevertheless, the policy endured.

**Chapter 37:** ***The Nazi Moral Identity***. Nazism promulgated a post-Christian morality. It did not reject God, but railed against Christianity. Conscience was, per Nietzsche, a Jewish conspiracy. Revaluation of all values (again Nietzsche) was a Nazi goal and slogan. Nazi morality emphasized duty and opposed filth. The Nazis took themselves to be presenting a high moral exemplar to their victims. In Nazi parlance, the SS was a moral elite.

**Chapter 38:** ***The Willingness to Believe***. Hitler understood that propaganda aimed at human emotion. Only critical thinking inoculates from propaganda. Himmler lacked such abilities; he cherished a potpourri of nonsensical ideas. Nazism offered the German people a vision of the glory of Germany, the Thousand-Year Reich. Nazism addressed the need people feel for transcendence. Glover recounts the case of neo-Nazi Jim Keegstra, Alberta high school teacher, who, in the 1970s, convinced numerous students and teachers of outrageous falsehoods about the Nazi regime. After his removal from teaching, many students and teachers persevered in believing Keegstra's assertions, long after contrary evidence had been offered. Where critical thinking flags, propaganda predominates.

**Chapter 39:** ***Philosophers***. Intellectuals keep a culture's thought independent and critically examine beliefs. Hitler had little use for them, and contemplated a purge. Many important thinkers in Hitler's Germany were driven out or killed. The remainder of inferior minds served Nazism, parroting its views and burning books of its opponents. Glover analyzes the life and philosophy of Martin Heidegger, who became a Nazi and thought himself a Nazi philosopher. Heidegger's philosophy is discredited because its obscurity discouraged critical thought, just at a time when clarity was needed. Glover also considers Gottlob Frege, who was a thorough nationalist and anti-Semite. Frege's philosophical work, on non-political topics, was seminal. Brilliance in one philosophical enterprise is no assurance that the same intelligence will be brought to bear on political questions.

**Chapter 40:** ***Bystanders***. Many Germans knew of events in the death camps. They comforted themselves that their roles in the killing were insignificant. Others feared to speak or simply relied on denial. The Germans relied on splitting opponents, offering deals that saved one's own while sacrificing unknown others. Some opposed the German genocide. Studies have shown that those persons grew up in homes that emphasized rationality but were not too strict, a contrast to the families of Nazi members, who tended to authoritarianism and automatic obedience in children. The minority who opposed Nazi purges did so for many reasons: professional standards, commitment to truth, religious conviction, or raw compassion. But they were few. Most began with small collaborations and found themselves thereby committed to increasingly large accommodations of the Nazis. The French village of La Chambon resisted, citing their Christian duty to feed the hungry and shelter the innocent. They hid 5,000 Jews in their midst. The Danes rescued most Danish Jews from Nazi roundup by transporting them to Sweden. Many Italians also resisted German orders regarding Jews. Opportunities to help were also declined. Eichmann offered one million Jews condemned to death in exchange for 10,000 trucks. The British declined. Those who helped avoided erosion of their moral identities. It is a difficult question to answer, how much risk people should undertake on behalf of the plight of strangers. Still, one thinks there is some standing obligation to assist persecuted minorities.

**Chapter 41:** ***Interpreting the Nazi Episode.*** Nazism grew from a collapsed German economy and the humiliations and hardships imposed by the World War I victors. The intentions of Nazi leaders matter, but are not the whole story. Nazi atrocities fit within a pattern of 20th century genocides, but have a darker aspect than most, because of the clear intent to bring all the machinery of a state to bear on extermination of one group of citizens based solely upon hatred. Nazism teaches that one must nurture skepticism about government action and maintain a sense of moral identity resistant to public propaganda.

## PART SEVEN: ON THE RECENT MORAL HISTORY OF HUMANITY

**Chapter 42:** ***Some People and Not Others.*** Within every person lies the capacity for cruelty. Yet not all become murderers. Choice matters. Culture matters. Upbringing matters. One may bolster, or erode, moral identity. Moral identity may be overwhelmed by fear or conformity. Moral identity may be neglected incrementally or dulled by failure to appreciate one's role in a larger structure of evil. Upbringing that emphasizes respect and reasons over obedience and compliance nurtures human empathy. Through all the influences, there is individual choice. People can bootstrap their moral tenacity. Even robust moral identity can be hobbled. If redirected to narrow channels (tribalism, racism), moral identity may not speak to atrocities. Moral identity needs to be wedded to human responses like compassion, empathy, understanding.

**Chapter 43:** ***Ethics Humanized.*** The conviction that there exists moral law has faded as institutional religion has weakened. All should be concerned that without God, every man's morality is just the opinions of his neighbors. Non-theological morality is provisional, setting hypotheses and assessing outcomes. We are much given to averting our eyes from atrocities. Looking away bolsters our denial, making it possible for us to go on convincing ourselves that the world is acceptably constituted. Our moral identities falter when propaganda denigrates intended victims, robs them of dignity, or makes them the butt of cold jokes. Sympathy fails when fear grips, when ideology overwhelms, when the sense of normalcy is assaulted, when we fail to see that our little part is a component of the larger crushing machine. We bolster moral identity in everyday actions. If we know how moral identity fails, we will be stronger in resisting its descent into atrocities. Theological ethics is senescent. We must step forward with moral imagination sufficient to promulgate man-made ethics, more tentative, but also perhaps less pretentious.

## EPILOGUE: THE PAST ALIVE IN THE PRESENT

The past shapes the present. Past acts are thought to justify present undertakings. Humans show inclination to think armed conflict unavoidable and cruelty necessary. Advanced technologies dovetail with these propensities in mankind in a manner that promotes barbarism, now often at a distance. The technical genie is out of the bottle. Our only recourse is to address the psychology of moral identity and restraint.

## EPITOME 2

**Block, Peter. *Community: The Structure of Belonging.* San Francisco, California: Berrett-Koehler Publishers, Inc., 2008.**

*Peter Block writes about structural change to human relationships and communities, the workplace, and society at large. Mr. Block lives in Cincinnati, Ohio. His office is in Mystic, Connecticut.*

**Welcome.** Block writes to encourage people who build well-being in their communities. Community is belonging, where membership entails a sense of ownership and accountability. Communities have structures. Structures that facilitate connectedness among members have the possibility of creating a future different from what we now have.

**Introduction: The Fragmented Community and Its Transformation**. Our lives are hobbled by structural isolation and self-interest. Healthy communities focus on member interdependence and belonging. Such communities emphasize optimism and members' gifts. These communities build social capital, which is the quality of their members' relationships. Such communities recognize that our social fabric is immensely valuable and fragile. This book will use the word "community" to designate this latter sort or community, not its distorted competitor.

### I. The Fabric of Community.

Community expands belonging in a series of very small steps. It forsakes ten year plans in favor of making this meeting, now, the sort of meeting of which we want our futures to be full.

**Chapter 1: Insights into Transformation**. Communal social fabric grows by creating a new language and structure. Its focus is associational life, members' gifts, our worldview (which may need to change), the future, the quality of "aliveness," and evolution (not revolution). Most groups focus on what is wrong or missing; community seizes on member gifts and how they may be employed. Association is people coming together to do good. Language has much to do with how we come to see the world. When we put words to our hopes, they become more real, and more likely to be enacted. Communities create themselves by addressing the form of life they want in small groups, which groups then reassemble to share with the larger community. Communities begin small and emerge slowly.

**Chapter 2: Shifting the Context for Community.** A human community is an interdependent interpersonal system structured by its internal conversation. Communities build themselves by creating social fabric, emphasizing associational life, working toward a future they value, employing small groups, and changing their conversation. Our current worldview emphasizes deficiencies, interests, and entitlement, which leads to the conclusion that suffering is a set of problems to be solved. A better future lies, so most believe, in better definition, analysis, and study of problems. It attempts to fix the current approach to community, not change it. Because the worldview encourages people to feel victimized by "others," to feel disenfranchised, and to feel alone in the social mass, the current worldview erodes community. These stories limit the future to permutations of the past. These stories deny that our future can hold fresh and as-yet-unimagined possibilities. Most present the old worldview as "fact," but they fail to recognize that all our worldviews are fiction in the sense that we make them up. We must name and abandon the old worldview, the view of matters that precludes community.

**Chapter 3: The Stuck Community.** The predominant paradigm at present emphasizes fear, fault, and self-interest. Its prescription for better life is more law, oversight, and centralized leadership. It emphasizes the reasons we have to be afraid. Its intention is retribution. This paradigm urges us to do more of what already does not work. It encourages us to romanticize leadership and to defer to leadership. It relishes cynicism and marginalizes hopeful outcomes. It ignores associational life in favor of local murders. It glorifies money and treats compassion as mere sentimentality.

**Chapter 4: The Restorative Community.** Restoration happens when a community chooses to look hopefully to the future and emphasize relatedness. Restoration happens as communities abandon their old worldview and ask "What can we create together?" The community shifts from retribution to restoration, from fragmentation to belonging, from incivility to listening. To put words on it, the shift is from centrist self-interested individualism to pluralist interdependent communalism.

**Chapter 5: Taking Back our Projections.** The old worldview preaches that someone else, somewhere else causes our suffering. Someone else should do something about that. Fundamentally, the old worldview projects our pain. We must take back this projection. The suffering is ours; we are the ones who can do something about it. We can transform our circumstance by reaching across boundaries to create relationships and by encouraging focus on gifts and capacities, rather than deficiencies.

**Chapter 6: What It Means to Be a Citizen.** Citizens, in an interdependent communalism, are responsible and committed to communal well-being. Citizens choose activism and care. They hold themselves accountable, exercise power rather than defer or delegate, welcome those at the margin, acknowledge that community grows from the hearts of citizens (not from great expert leadership), and find ways to use the gifts of others. Citizens are sure "we" create our world. Peter Kostenbaum said, "The chicken is the egg's way of reproducing itself." It sounds inverted, but maybe not. Perhaps eggs create chickens, youths create adults, audiences create performers, and prisoners create wardens. This is an idea to play with. Citizens are accountable (take care of the whole) and committed (promise action for its own sake, with no expectation of return or bargaining).

**Chapter 7: The Transforming Community.** Community transforms members. For a community to be transformational, it must choose connective structure, provide a worldview that reinforces community values, ask the right questions, and choose deep relating over swift global change. Leaders must be held to three tasks (and no more): help shift worldview, name the debate, and listen. Structurally, transformative community is a network of social networks. It meets in small groups with others meeting in small groups. Transformational community focuses on transforming questions: How do we choose to meet when we meet together?" and "What do we want to create together?" The old worldview tells us to 1) identify a need, 2) study and analyze, 3) search for solutions, 4) establish goals, 5) get others on board, 6) implement the solution program , and 7) loop back to look for new problems to solve. The problem with this view is that it prevents anything fundamental from changing. It asserts that things are great except for this one little problem, so let's fix that. Things are not great. We need a different approach. The transforming community starts small, seeks engagement and commitment, stays small, and builds a structure of belonging for every member. This is more important than a vision and well-stepped plan. *We must recognize that one of the critical goals of our meeting together is to do so well. It is an end in itself. It is the better future we seek.* As we begin to meet transformationally, we can identify a task and set a plan.

## II. The Alchemy of Belonging.

Transformative communities have leadership that convenes, meets in small groups, focuses on transformative questions, emphasizes six conversations (invitation, possibility, ownership, dissent, commitment, and gifts), exaggerates hospitality, and creates physical and social spaces that facilitate belonging.

**Chapter 8: Leadership is Convening.** We must de-glamorize leadership and know that all humans have the capacity to lead. We must spread leadership around as much as possible. Leaders are social architects; they create social experiences for others. Leaders convene gatherings. A leader tends the social fabric. Leaders are responsible to nurture an alternative worldview, to start and sustain critical conversations that help people shift their worldviews, and to listen to the ensuing conversations with attention.

**Chapter 9: The Small Group is the Unit of Transformation.** "Each gathering needs to become an example of the future we want to create." We seek to build "intimate and authentic relatedness." "We change the world one room at a time." Whatever creates energy is more important than the content we want presented. Small group structures (gatherings of three to twelve) make every voice heard. Being heard, we believe we belong. Every group moment combines methodology and metaphor. We should ask people speaking to physically stand (since they stand for what they say). We should make sure everyone is amplified if anyone is (since all voices matter). We should ask important contributions to be restated (since what they said is important enough to hear twice). We should acknowledge anyone who speaks (since it takes courage to speak at all).

**Chapter 10: Questions Are More Transforming Than Answers.** Well-framed questions are ambiguous, personal, and produce anxiety. Such questions help people transform themselves and their communities. Questions about explanation, study, analysis, definition, and wishful thinking do not assist transformation. These are questions about the past; they project the past into the future. These old questions tell us the lie that by answering them, we take uncertainty out of the future. The old questions tell us the future will be the "present projected forward." The future is unknown, clothed in unpredictability and mystery. Good questions evoke accountability and commitment, and lead us to requests, offers, declarations, forgiveness, confession, gratitude, and welcome. To have good conversations based on transformative questions, we must set up the conversations well. If we fail to do so, people will repeat the default conversation. Good setup requires that one: 1) distinguish the question from the old worldview default question, 2) give permission for dissenting answers, 3) avoid advice in favor of curiosity, and 4) name the question precisely.

**Chapter 11: Invitation.** Invitations must be unadulterated. Do not promise incentives or rewards other than authentic community. Invitation is more than creating open communities. It is a way of life, a commitment to collaborate with others. We invite people to show up, but also to engage. They must do so. Block says that critical change is a self-injury. We must reach out to include all who belong in the conversation. Invitation also means that those who show up are the right people. To invite, we declare what we hope, frame the choice we ask, name the hurdle to overcome, restate and reinforce the request, speak in the most personal form possible. Those who decline an invitation should be told they will be "missed but not forgotten." Refusal carries no cost for the refuser of the invitation.

**Chapter 12: The Possibility, Ownership, Dissent, Commitment, and Gifts Conversations.** The sequence of the six conversations (invitation, possibility, ownership, dissent, commitment, and gifts) is not important, because each leads to the others.

- "Possibility" is a declaration of the world that we want to inhabit. To address this question, we speak of crossroads, inspiration, and what we can create together.
- "Ownership" believes that our affairs are ours to create. This community is ours to shape and make our own. Innocence or indifference are denials of ownership. People are accountable only for that which they own. Ownership confronts us with our freedom, and our failure to use it. Owners are authors of their own experiences. This gathering, and our world, are "ours to construct together." Ownership asks about value, risk, participation, investment, and ultimately about our contribution to that about which we complain. It asks us what story we tell ourselves that makes it okay for us to do nothing. It asks what that story is costing us. Usually, the cost of the do-nothing story is the death of our sense of aliveness.
- "Dissent" recognizes that thoughtful people see downsides. Reservations and doubts are normal and desirable. Group response to doubts and dissent must be curiosity and thankfulness. Making room for dissent is what validates our decision to commit. It affirms freedom. Dissent refuses to live a life someone else planned. We must make sure that dissenters retain their place in community. Inauthentic forms of dissent are denial (the status quo is good enough), rebellion (others, not we, control

the situation), and resignation (passive control deadening others). Dissent raises questions about doubts, saying no, yeses we have said but no longer mean, forgiveness, resentment. "Dissent is a form of caring, not one of resistance."

• "Commitment" promises without expecting return, without barter for consequences. My promise is not contingent upon others' actions. Contingent promises are contracts, not commitments. The deadly enemy of transformation is lip service. It says "I will try" when it means "I will not commit." Commitment is "promise to peers about our contribution to the success of the whole." Commitment raises questions about promises, meaning, costs, failure, risks, postponements, and refusal. When a person declines to commit, honoring that refusal validates the choice of all who chose to commit.

• "Gifts" conversation emphasizes what we have to contribute and how that capacity might be employed. We do not focus on deficiencies or weaknesses. Transformative communities bring the gifts of those on the margin to the center. We say: "I am not what I am not able to do. I am what I am able to do—my gifts and capacities." Gifts conversations raise questions about what we have received, strengths, uniquenesses, needs, and making a difference. We talk of unutilized gifts, what people do not know of us, gratefulness, gifts we deny. We must discuss in our gatherings what gifts have been exchanged. Talking about a thing strengthens it. We must avoid discussing weaknesses and what's missing. Gifts are not gifts until offered to others.

**Chapter 13: Bringing Hospitality into the World.** Hospitality matters in transformational community. Greet people at the door, and seat them. They enter isolated; relieve that. Restate for all the invitation, why we are gathered. Make sure people connect with one another before any content is discussed. Connection happens best in small groups of three to six. Late arrivers must be welcomed, and a place made. Stop what you are doing, greet them without humiliating them, and connect them somewhere in the group. Early leavers leave a hole behind in the meeting. Ask people who plan to leave early to give notice of their plan, stop the meeting and acknowledge their leaving, ask them to tell the group they are leaving and where they are going, have the group tell the leaver what they contributed to the meeting, ask what the leaver got from the gathering, thank the leaver for coming, remove the leaver's chair, do it all (though it takes time) because we must choose depth over speed. Share food (healthy food, not snack food).

**Chapter 14**: **Designing Physical Space That Supports Community.** Physical spaces support (or hinder) transformational community. Every room is a metaphor for the community we want to create. Spend time and energy designing the space for human interaction. Prefer circles and rooms with views. Bring in plants. Amplify everyone if anyone needs amplification. Choose chairs that swivel and roll. Avoid stages and raised platforms. Include art; mark meeting transitions with a song, poem, story. Art magnifies the sacred in our gatherings. Fill walls with meaning. Consider a talking stick if some members tend to dominate conversations.

**Chapter 15**: **The End of Unnecessary Suffering.** Block hopes to end unnecessary suffering. Some suffering, such as loneliness, illness, loss of meaning, sadness, death, is unavoidable. Other suffering, mostly political, we inflict on ourselves. We can end political suffering. Lack of belonging is a political pain. It can be fixed. Block applies his framework to youth, public safety, economic development, families, and health care. We need to see youth more positively, even the upside possibilities in some very dubious activities. We need to believe neighbors can keep their neighborhoods safe; police cannot keep us safe. Economically, developers and social activists must build relationships between their groups. Families need to be seen as people with gifts in a system, not as dysfunctions needing intervention. Health care needs to focus on health, not disease. Collaborative consultation, not professional expertise, should make health care decisions, considering all impacts on patient well-being.

***Book at a Glance:*** Block offers his own epitome of his book.

***Role Models and Resources:*** Block lists individuals and organizations doing their community work in the transformative manner he appreciates.

## EPITOME 3

**Seneca. "On Tranquillity of Mind," in *Dialogues and Letters*. Translated and edited by C. D. N. Costa. London: Penguin Books, 1997.**

*Lucius Annaeus Seneca (4 B.C. – 65 A.D.) wrote Stoic philosophy and plays, and served as occasional statesman in first century Rome. Seneca taught Nero as a child, and later served as advisor to the Emperor. Seneca was accused of plotting to assassinate Nero, of which allegations he may have been innocent. Seneca was compelled to suicide. His elder brother, Gallio, dismissed charges brought by Jewish opponents against Paul of Tarsus, writer of New Testament epistles (Acts 18:12-17). Gallio also was asked to commit suicide. He complied.*

*[Seneca counsels Serenus, a close friend who commands a police and fire brigade in Rome.]*

*Serenus:* Some of my vices are plain. Others are hidden. Some, which prove most troublesome, are intermittent. These last make me bad company. I find that perseverance in virtues makes them more accustomed, but the same is true of vices. I learn to love both. I seem incapable of seizing the good, but rather waver weakly. I love simplicity in furniture, clothing, food, and servants. Yet, I am dazzled by fancy frills and ostentation. I wonder if I should not pursue a pretentious superiority. I am shaken and disquieted. I follow Stoic teachings. I live simply. I serve. I refuse distractions. I eschew fame. I do not imagine glory. I restrain myself. Yet, my good intentions remain feeble. I can barely tell the truth about me. I flatter myself ceaselessly. Can you help me find tranquility? My trouble is no storm, but perhaps only a gusty breeze.

*Seneca:* Stop chiding yourself, Serenus. You do not need to block or chide yourself. Have confidence. You are on the right track. Do not notice the swerving paths of the lost. Tranquility has a steady course; it deviates neither right nor left. Most people lack quietude. They hate themselves for their pretenses. They are fickle, ever swapping this for that. Others are steady, but merely stuck in ruts. Inertia drives them onward. To fail of tranquility, one needs nothing more than dissatisfaction with oneself. Such people live tentatively, hoping more than acting. Some are simply frozen in place and bored to death. The tranquil do public service, act purposively, and persevere, despite their likely shortcomings. The tranquil do nothing that encourages malice toward others. One can come to want others to suffer. Minds are made to move and act. Some miss tranquility by travels. It is as though men flee themselves, but find no escape. The fault lies not in circumstances, but within us. Avoid all this seeking. Get involved politically; do civic service. Tend your community; care for individuals.

> *Athenodorus's Objection*: People seek glory and bend right into wrong. It is safer to withdraw to pursue private scholarship and counsel. Private service—teaching, criticizing the excesses of wealth, and encouraging virtue—

is worthy, though not public. I do not recommend mere hiding, which robs one of useful activity. Such people die with nothing to recommend them but their age.

*Seneca:* Athenodorus retreats too soon, Serenus. If one must retreat a bit, give ground grudgingly. If life denies you a leading role, cheer on those who undertake those tasks. Some path of useful and virtuous activity will lie open to you. Seize it. Socrates taunted the tyrannical Thirty, even as they condemned him to death. Socrates went to the grave teaching. Vices often reign: worship of money and jealousy of others. Do not be afraid. Step up. One wants to live while living, not endure death while living.

We tend to flatter ourselves ceaselessly. Take your frank measure. Do not love any one thing too much. Stay within your means. Work reasonably. Do not stress yourself by taking jobs to which you are ill-suited. Tame your tongue. Match endeavors to your abilities. Finish what you begin. Choose friends carefully. Are they worth your time? Do they appreciate it? Know yourself, and follow your inclinations. Your predispositions are stronger than you. Work with them, not against them.

Find loyal friends. They keep your secrets, comfort you, advise when necessary, and make jokes. Choose good people as friends. Vice spreads like contagion, hand to hand. Friends need not be perfect. Choose those who are least bad. Avoid complainers, whose gloomy outlook smudges life. They steal tranquility.

Possessions create misery. Money shatters lives. It is best never to acquire excess funds. You will not then suffer at lost wealth. Live near poverty. Be thrifty. Value things for their utility, not their show. One can restrain himself and find riches within, rather than waiting for fortune to beam upon one. Keep your library small. Devote yourself to the best authors. Generally, avoid excess in all things. When troubles find you, make light of them. Get in the habit of bearing them silently. Every person suffers. Find the advantages in every circumstance and take consolation in them. Think of ways to make things better for yourself. A wise man confronts misfortune. He lives life as though it were on loan from the universe. One lives badly if he cannot die with equanimity. Fear of death kills us. We self-deceive. Whatever happens to others can happen to us.

Avoid pointless activities. They waste life. Rush nowhere. Slow down and make your actions count. Choose an end; pursue it. Busy idleness springs from misperceptions, and leads to madness. If you have nothing important to do, do nothing. Leave your plans flexible, so you can adapt as changes occur. The tranquil mind welcomes change and endures with confidence. Such a mind has a safe harbor within to which it retreats to trust, rejoice, admire, and salve itself. Seneca recounts the equanimity with which Canus embraced execution at the command of Gaius.

Sometimes, the vices of men breed hatred in one's quietude: simplicity and innocence and loyalty are rare, but not crimes and lust and ambition. View vices with ridicule. Laugh, do not cry, when life is vicious. If you let the misfortunes of others derail you, you will be perpetually derailed. Grieve to the extent you feel grief. Never sorrow for show. Some good men die badly at the hands of wanton actors. Imitate bravery; eschew cowardice.

Do not worry about the opinions of others. For some, knowing means hating. Avoid them. Pretending causes much more suffering than simplicity or poverty. Live simply, not stupidly. Mix solitude with groups. The one mends damage done by the other.

Keep your life diverse. Relax, work, relax, work. Overwork makes one dull. Sleep enough, take a holiday. Rest midday, and do less demanding work in afternoons. Leisure nourishes. Let yourself get a little drunk sometimes. Being a bit off center once in a while boosts creativity.

So, Serenus, tend your mind, heed my advice, and you will find tranquility.

## EPITOME 4

**Keltner, Dacher. *Born to Be Good: The Science of a Meaningful Life.* New York: W. W. Norton & Company: 2009.**

*Dacher Keltner teaches psychology at University of California, Berkeley, and directs the Greater Good Science Center.*

**Preface.** "[E]motion is the source of the meaningful life." The key to happiness is seeing and experiencing positive emotion in oneself and others. This emotional structure is built into us by evolution. The kind, not the brutal, survive. One is good by acting to complete the good of others. Meaning can be measured by the "jen" ratio: the abundance of positive emotions, divided by the sum of negative emotions. One should strive for jen ratios above one.

**Chapter 1: *Jen* Science**. A core concept in Confucius's *Analects* is "jen." "Jen" is variously translated, but represents the "kindness, humanity, and respect" between people. One achieves meaningful life by cultivating jen. America's jen ratio is falling. Humankind is not a collective of self-serving economic animals driven to compete by choosing bad over good means. Money provides little motivation to the middle class (though more to the under class). Another understanding of mankind exists, the jen concept. High jen ratios make us happy.

**Chapter 2: Darwin's Joys.** Darwin described at length the physical manifestations of emotion in humans. Three principles guided Darwin's thought about expressive behavior: 1) expressive behaviors are remnants of full-blown actions that enhanced survivability in evolutionary history, 2) opposing expressive states are associated with opposing expressions (antithesis), and 3) undirected expressive energy is released in random behaviors. Paul Ekman's New Guinea research proved that much emotional facial expression is universal, transcending any particular culture. Ekman and Friesen developed the Facial Action Coding System (FACS) by which all facial muscle movement can be systematized. Emotion: a) expresses our deepest commitments, b) is hard-wired into our nervous system, and c) guides our moral judgments.

**Chapter 3: Rational Irrationality**. Emotions are involuntary commitment markers. Commitment may be feigned, but emotion betrays false promises. Commitment demands willingness to set aside short-term, self-interested behavior. Emotions identify who has that willingness. William James proposed that emotions reflect visceral responses. Emotions follow the gut. Moral judgments arise from emotional intuitions, which are sometimes modified by subsequent deliberation. Virtue and our sense for right and wrong are hard-wired into our brains. "Reason and passion are collaborators in the meaningful life." Emotions point toward moral action, and deserve equal footing with rational review.

**Chapter 4: Survival of the Kindest**. Darwin believed that social instincts are part of humanity's evolutionary heritage. What were characteristics of the environment in which humanity evolved (which Keltner calls the "environment of evolutionary adaptedness" or EEA)? Early humans lived closely with thirty to seventy-five troop members. Females gathered and cared for children. Males hunted and made tools. Unlike other higher primates, human collectives provided care to one another. They raised offspring collaboratively. Humans operated face-to-face, in deep coordination. Facial expression and vocal sounds were critical to group cooperation. Culture resulted, with artificial memory transmission across time and space. Human troops were hierarchical (but relatively flat), and higher status individuals kept peace for others, from which derived their power. Conflict pervaded troop life, from sibling to members to outsiders to natural threats. And extensive repertoire of reconciliation behaviors evolved to keep the cooperative ship afloat. Relatively chaste sexual patterns (as compared to other higher primates) promoted peace. Strategically, cooperation is a winning strategy. Emotions that promote cooperation promote the interests of others, which could be evolutionary suicide. Emotion removes this threat. Human emotions create a cost-benefit reversal by providing reliable means of identifying pretenders. Also, humans reciprocate cooperation when cooperation is exhibited. This means that "meaningful life" is contagious.

**Chapter 5: Embarrassment**. Brain trauma patients demonstrate that jen emotions are elements of brain structure. Eadweard Muybridge, J.S. and Phineas Gage are core examples. Embarrassment, evidencing respect for others and their opinions as well as submission to the moral order, is a "porthole onto the ethical brain." Keltner recounts his studies with Ekman in FACS: startle response, then embarrassment. Evolutionarily hard-wired emotional displays typically last two-three seconds, and exhibit stereotypical patterns of condensed behavioral clues. Embarrassment defuses conflict situations: gaze aversion, an appeasement smile, a face touch. Damage to the orbitofrontal cortex (near the eyes) creates sociopathy by erasing the capacity for embarrassment. Embarrassment undergirds modesty.

**Chapter 6: Smile**. Smiling promotes cooperation, perhaps more powerfully than any other gesture. Smiling reduces stress in giver and receiver. Contra Darwin, smiling does not derive from laughing. A smile is deferential submission in possible conflict situations. Laughter accompanies play. They have different evolutionary origins. Typology of smiles: Duchenne smile (orbicularis oculi active, evidencing high spirits and good will), non-Duchenne smile (obicularis oculi inactive, evidencing masked negative emotion). The D-smile is the dessert of social life. The Mills Longitudinal Study (110 Mills College grads from 1959-1960 followed for fifty years at ages 27, 42, and 52) shows that D-smiles in college graduation photos correlate to high jen ratios and successful lives. Judeo-Christian view of human sinfulness supports a view that smiling evidences relief from anxiety, threat, anger. In primates with social structures similar to humans (some macaques), smiling expresses friendliness or affection. Human "ultrasociality" required a universal signal of cooperative intent: the smile.

**Chapter 7: Laughter**. Laughter is social and contagious. It induces relaxation (limpness) during exhalation. Voiced laughter exhibits pleasure; unvoiced laughter does not. Antiphonal laughter (laughing in the same space) expresses/creates affection. Laughter differs from language in its sound output, a third register of voice: vowel, consonant, laughter. Laughter evolutionarily predates language, arising from the pons, a limbic/brain stem structure. Less than twenty percent of laughter is preceded by humorous events or language. Laughter expresses cooperation by inducing contagion and signaling shared success. Laughter stimulates the supplementary motor area (SMA), which links to the amygdala and insula, regions deep in the limbic system. Together, these have been called "mirror neurons." Mirror neurons activate brain regions that imitate the laugher's laugh. "Laughter is the great switch of cooperation." Laughter accompanies imagination, in which people take a little vacation from reality's rules. Keltner studied forty-five individuals whose spouses had died six months ago. Freudian analysis predicts that adjustment occurs as individuals express their negative emotions, and expressing positive emotions is denial. Keltner's study showed that laughter reduced grief, even when adjusted for basal individual temperament and the nature of the spouse's death. And those who laughed when speaking of their deceased spouse related better to others and created new intimacies sooner. Keltner recounts the story of Siddartha Gautama and the Buddhist view of suffering appreciatively.

**Chapter 8: Tease**. A tease is "an intentional provocation accompanied by playful off-record markers" intended to expose the teasee's social commitments. Off-record markers are the non-verbal acts associated with the tease that signal its non-hostility and playful intent. Sincere communication, which the speaker hopes will be interpreted literally, should be truthful, informative, relevant, and direct. We violate these rules to express politeness or to soften potential conflict situations. Teasing uses exaggeration, repetition, exposure of idiomatic expression and winking to reduce the social stress of negotiation rank and power distribution. The more a high rank teaser receives submission gestures, the more the teaser likes the teasee. The more laughter they share, the more they like one another. Teasing preserves intimate bonds, when done artfully. Artful teasing hurts little physically, uses non-verbal markers to communicate fun, permits the teasee to respond in kind, and is more likely to occur with persons over age ten. Sufferers of Aspberger's Syndrome lack the ability to tease.

**Chapter 9: Touch**. The "contagious goodness" hypothesis proposes that self-interest is subsumed in groups when individuals effectively signal their intent to cooperate. Touch is central to such goodness transmission; touch is "the primary language of compassion, love, and gratitude—emotions at the heart of trust and cooperation. Human skin and hands developed evolutionarily to cool us and produce tools, but they were concurrently used to communicate. Touching creates a surge of pleasure reward for both toucher and touchee. Touched babies thrive, while untouched ones do not. Most people identify love, sympathy, and gratitude poorly from verbal sounds and facial expressions. They identify these emotions much more readily from touching, even apart from sound and faces. There are gender differences: men communicate sympathy poorly to women by touch; women communicate anger to men without using touch. Our society is "touch-deprived," hampered by Puritan moralities and sexual harassment fears. Our need for touch takes refuge in massages, pedicures, cuddle clubs, sports, medical visits.

**Chapter 10: Love**. Sexually, humans tend to serial monogamy, with the males actively involved in child-rearing (unlike 90% of mammals). Four loves describe human loving: 1) parent-child, 2) sexual desire, 3) pair-bonding, and 4) love for non-kin (friends and fellows). The thirty-five documented cases of feral children show that lack in parental relations impairs language, morals, manners, cooperation, sexual interest, and self-awareness. Early attachments create the capacity for interpersonal connections. Impaired attachments create pessimistic, depression-prone, suspicious, insecure persons. Human monogamous pair bonding differs from gorillas (alpha harems), chimpanzees (indiscriminate mating during estrus), and bonobos (multi-purpose sexual encounters). Attention-getting behaviors lead to more intimacy, with keeping-time synchronicity and then pair-bonding frenzy. This last turns off the sense of self, clearing the way for a new pair-bonded identity. The risks are high. Evolution's answer to the risk is romantic love, which derives from increased oxytocin production. Oxytocin shuts down threat detection and creates partner idealization. For pair bonding affection to persevere, the ratio of positive feelings to negative feelings must be five to one, per Gottman. Sexual desire is not pair bonding. Pair bonding (love) and sexual desire displays differ. Pair bonding displays lead to talk of commitment. Sexual desire displays lead to copulation. Women have on average seven times the oxytocin blood levels compared to men. Non-kin love, also enhanced by oxytocin levels, increases conviction of the goodness of others and urges to trust and sacrifice. The signals of community affection are: feelings of devotion and sacrifice, perception of the goodness and beauty of others, warm touching, oxytocin increasing brain reward circuitry, shutting down threat circuitry, mutual smiles and head tilts, open hands, and soft, affectionate vocal tones.

**Chapter 11: Compassion**. History may be a "contest between cruelty and compassion." Human nature may be stretched between tendencies to self-interest and pressures to care. Evolutionarily, sympathetic communities increase the likelihood their children will mature and reproduce. Historically, compassion has been dismissed as a religious imposition. Those who so contend are wrong. Compassion is "a biologically based emotion rooted deep in the mammalian brain, and shaped by perhaps the most potent of selection pressures humans evolved to adapt to—the need to care for the vulnerable." The vagus nerve bundle may be the biological root of compassion. It originates at the hindbrain and winds through the body involving brain, larynx, heart, lungs, stomach, and other organs. The vagus nerve causes a systematic brief sigh at other's plights, slows the heart rate, (may) release oxytocin, and is unique to mammals. Some scientists dissent on the role of the vagus nerve and the autonomic system's involvement in emotion. Keltner's own research indicates that humans respond to harm to others from infancy. We are "attuned to those in need." Some researchers attribute altruism to selfish behaviors or kin-selection behavior. Keltner cites studies that he believes show that compassion is not a blind emotional surge, but is directed toward individuals suffering harm. Shy people have elevated stress response that can be observed as early as four months old. It takes shy individuals two extra years to marry and longer to settle into stable careers. Heightened vagus nerve tone correlates to extroversion, mood elevation, and physical health. It also correlates to "transformative experiences of the sacred." Depressed individuals suffer low resting vagal tone. Evolutionarily, big-brained progeny necessitated two parent care and the involvement of kin and tribal caregivers as well. The nurturance period is more than a decade for human children. Selection pressures affected the appearance of babies to elicit caregiving responses from adults around them. Sexual selection pressures created a kinder population, because the most important criterion in mate selection is kindness. Social selection pressures favored kind individuals, because groups with larger numbers of kind persons cohere better and better support members. We need to identify and augment compassion-developing environments.

**Chapter 12: Awe**. The experience of awe has been, in modern times, extracted from its solely religious context to experience generally. Features of awe: 1) vastness, 2) accommodation, flavored by a) threat, b) beauty, c) ability, d) virtue, and/or e) the supernatural. Paul Woodruff analyzed Greek and Chinese conceptions of awe. Awe leads to modesty which incites a sense of commonality with other humans, which induces respect and reverence. Evolutionarily, David Sloan Wilson argues that awe serves to subjugate the sense of self in the communal identity. Awe is difficult to study because it is intermittent and depends upon experiences unlikely to happen in a laboratory. People experiencing awe report goose-bumps and feelings of social connection. Several different brain structures relate to "good feelings."

Keltner concludes: "We are wired for good."

## EPITOME 5

**Gandhi, Mohandas K. *Non-Violent Resistance (Satyagraha).* Edited by Bharatan Kumarappa. New York: Dover Publications, Inc., 2001.**

*Mohandas K. Gandhi (1869-1948 A.D.), a political activist and attorney, worked first in South Africa, addressing the needs of Indian expatriates in that then racially segregated nation, and later in India. While in India, Gandhi served for a time as the head of the Indian National Congress, and confronted British rule with a public campaign of non-violent non-cooperation. Gandhi urged Indians to dry their own salt (to bypass the British salt tax) and to spin yarn and weave their own cloth (to bypass British and Chinese mills and create Indian employment). The Hindi non-violent movement, and the less pacifistic activity of the Muslim community, resulted in independence from British rule in 1947, but with partition between Hindu and Islamic populations. A Hindu extremist assassinated Gandhi in 1948.*

**Section First: What Satyagraha Is.**

1. *Satyagraha, Civil Disobedience, Passive Resistance, Non-Co-Operation.* The word "Satyagraha" means to cling to Truth. Truth is life of the spirit, and so Satyagraha is spirit-force. Non-violent resistance requires strength of character. It entails more than passive resistance. Civil disobedience, which calls one to violate immoral laws, and non-cooperation, which calls the people to decline to participate in corrupt government, are branches of non-violent resistance.

2. *Domestic Satyagraha.* Gandhi's wife was ill, and Gandhi believed, after trying everything else, that she should forsake salt and pulses (a leguminous crop, similar to lentils) to cure herself. She refused. Gandhi then vowed to forsake salt and pulses for a year; she relented and begged Gandhi to eat as he wished. Gandhi refused, asserting that self-denial improves a person. A self-restrained person's diet differs from that of pleasure-seekers, just as do their lives.

3. *Satyagraha.* Non-violent resistance entails seeking truth without violence, and turning opponents from error by patience and sympathy. When an opponent perseveres in error, the non-violent resister takes the punishment and suffering on oneself, without bitterness. Non-violent resistance includes breaking unjust laws and submitting to the penalties for those actions. It may entail refusing to cooperate with the government. For example, Gandhi encouraged all India to decline to work on the sixth of April. They did so. He was arrested shortly thereafter.

4. *Means and Ends.* A reader asked Gandhi why, since the people have sufficient power, they should not exercise it to be rid of the British. Surely, that end justifies any means. If a thief enters a house, we expel him. If a child thrusts its foot in a fire, we forcibly pull him back. Gandhi responds that means are seeds and ends are the resulting trees. One can never plant violence and reap peace. Opposing thieves can become outright war, robbing all of peace. Ignored petitions to the government may nevertheless educate people. An unanswered petition may cause people to refuse to cooperate with the government. Pulling a child from fire ill-describes the English role in India. When one pulls a child from fire, one acts solely in the child's interest. England has its own interests.

5. *Satyagraha or Passive Resistance.* A reader asks about soul-force, whether history records that any nation arose by spirit. Gandhi responds that history records disturbances of the normal course of things. Soul-force is normal; it keeps mankind alive by making peace among men. History records tales of cataclysmic outbreaks of violence. A reader asks about "passive resistance." Gandhi responds that the non-violent resister wins political battles by personal suffering. Soul-force requires a person to act in accord with his best lights, right or wrong. A reader asks why, when laws are bad, the people cannot drive out the corrupt lawgivers by force. Gandhi responds the rules majorities lay does do not necessarily bind minorities. No one should comply with unjust laws. They should decline to obey, and happily suffer whatever the government does in response.

6. *Evidence Before the Hunter Committee (Extracts). 1. Examination by Lord Hunter.* Hunter questions Gandhi about his movement. Gandhi characterizes it as an attempt to create alternatives to violence. Non-violent resisters disobey unjust laws to influence the government. Gandhi states that he objects to laws of good purpose when their means are objectionable. Hunter asks about the April 6th strike and some violence that attended it. Gandhi condemned the violence but declined to provide the names of offenders. He also notes that the government had some hand in the violence that day. Non-violent resisters are not mere Indians. They are humans. Gandhi cannot decide if he would give evidence to police of a criminal he observed in the act. *2. Examination by Sir Chimandlal Setgalwad.* Setgalwad asks who decides truth, when men differ in their views. Gandhi answers that each individual decides, where there is a vow of non-violence. Setgalwad asks if good moral character and high intelligence are not required for determining truth. Gandhi answers that they are not. Most people can determine truths for themselves. Setgalwad inquires about the violence in connection with strikes. Gandhi notes that the violence is rare, and self-restraint is the vast rule, considering all the people involved. Gandhi believes the violence came from people who lost self-control. These persons have experienced violence for decades, and could not abstain. Setgalwad asks if Gandhi intends to embarrass the government, bringing disorder. Gandhi answers that people breaking laws without violence will not disrupt government. *3. Examination by Pandit Jagatnarain.* Jagatnarain reasserts that non-violent resistance intends to embarrass the government. Gandhi says that non-violence does not depend upon numbers or embarrassment, but on truth and willingness to suffer for it. Ordinary people grow moral; that is what non-violent resistance may accomplish. Even if Home Rule comes and the British depart, non-violent resistance may continue. Indian leaders can be wrong-headed as well. Jagatnarain asks if unrest will follow non-violent resistance. Gandhi answers that there will be no violence, but the non-violent resisters will form a line to go to jail together.

7. *The Theory and Practice of Satyagraha.* Gandhi writes on the eighth anniversary of his non-violent resistance movement in South Africa. Spiritual power can only be exercised by people who eschew violence. Non-violence can transform homes, towns, cities, nations, and the world. Within each person lies the potential of non-violence. Governments cannot govern unjustly over non-violent resisters. Governments require consent of the governed, and non-violent resisters resist injustice. The South African movement took years because their non-violent resistance was imperfect; some pretended non-violence, few were willing to make necessary

sacrifices. The non-violent resister must be indifferent to his physical well-being. Where non-violence is perfected, results are immediate. But this perfection requires extensive self-training. If the values of non-violence pervade the world, militarism would vanish. We should train our children in non-violence first, so they know what humans can become, that love defeats hate and self-suffering banishes violence. Only then should we teach them to read and write.

**Section Second: Discipline for Satyagraha.**

8. *Satyagraha Ashram Vows. Importance of Vows.* When one vows, one must follow through. Do not say, To the extent possible. That is no vow. Vows purify a man. *Truth.* Nothing exists but Truth. Truth is God, from which we derive life. Our entire lives must be devoted to Truth. In it, we find inward peace, which guides us in selecting what we should do and not do. Men may differ about the truth. That matters not at all. Where one pursues Truth, one finds it. All errors are resolved in the course of suffering. *Ahimsa or Love.* (Non-violence) In our bodies we cannot know perfect Truth. But non-violence can guide us. Instead of responding in kind with the violent, we can suffer with them and possibly bring them out of their confusions. When we fight external enemies, we are missing the real battle within. Endure thieves, and find a way to win them over. The body prevents us from non-violence in its broadest sense. So long as we are attached, we remain in the body in the ceaseless cycle of death and rebirth. *Brahmacharya or Chastity* (Celibacy). Sex makes a man divided, pursuing family and household as well as Truth. All can forsake sex. Married partners can see one another as siblings. Sexual lust sullies a man. Celibacy relates not only to sex, but to all sense organs. All need control and restraint. *Non-possession.* Lovers of Truth abandon all possessions. They retain nothing for tomorrow. The rich should give away their wealth to create global contentment. Few can endure non-possession. We are weak. Such should examine their possessions and reduce them to a bare minimum. Non-possession means to freely reduce one's desires. Then one is free to serve. Life is service alone. This brings real happiness.

9. *Yajna or Sacrifice.* Sacrifice is action aimed to benefit others, without return. The "others" are not only humans, but all life. Animal sacrifice, even if found in the Vedas, is inconsistent with Truth. When we serve deliberately, our desire to serve grows, as well as our happiness. All our goods should serve mankind. We should give all away and keep none. But do not do so if you feel oppressed by the giving. When freely undertaken, a sacrificial life is a work of art. When Truth brings you possessions, take only what you strictly need. Leave the balance for others. Give your best efforts to deliberate service; save second-best for your own needs.

10. *Protecting Hinduism.* Islamists present a threat to Hindus. Hindus must protect themselves by self-purification. Gandhi would gather a group of young Hindus, go to the Muslims, and be killed. Some object that in scriptures, God sent soldiers. Gandhi responds that Hindus are not pure enough now. Have they abandoned untouchability? Have they addressed their own souls? Focus on Hindu purity, not Islamic misconduct.

11. *Moral Requirements for Satyagraha.* A reader asks if passive resistance is the weapon of the weak. Gandhi replies that soul-force is superior to weapons in every way, and requires of the passive resister immense courage. What soldier can

stand at peace before a cannon to be blown to bits? Kings are trained to violence. Their subjects, whom they command to use weapons, desire no guns. The non-violent resister ignores unjust orders. They refuse to cooperate. Regardless who rules India, non-violent resisters will decline to follow injustice. That is true Home Rule. The passive resister must train his body, for strong minds dwell in strong bodies. India must rid itself of child brides and luxury. Non-violent resisters: abandon sex, even if married, avoid becoming parents, avoid wealth and, if they have wealth, treat it with indifference, cultivate fearlessness especially as to death. The fearless man finds strength in himself to suffer pains; he drops his sword.

12. *Conditions for Successful Satyagraha.* To prevail in a just cause, endure endless suffering, avoid all violence of any form (mental, verbal, or physical), and persevere to the victory.

13. *Non-Retaliation.* Successful non-violent resistance requires that great crowds learn to hold their tempers. Every Englishman must not only be told he is safe, but also actually feel safe, as Indian protests occur.

14. *Courage and Discipline Necessary.* Non-violent resisters do not comply with rulers' humiliating demands. They stand and are shot instead. The power of rulers is frustrated by persistent non-retaliation. The tyrant's lunges injure himself. Our movement is still weak, ill-prepared for general civil disobedience. Our leaders should look to their own shortcomings.

15. *The Need for Humility.* Non-violent resisters rely upon Truth; he can only be approached humbly. The non-violence movement does what it says. Still, how many parents have removed their children from British schools? How many are spinning their cloth and refusing English textiles? We have cause for humility. Humility convinces many of the rightness of our cause. If we are humble, Home Rule may be attained within the year.

16. *Work in Jails.* Shall imprisoned non-violent resisters comply with jailers' demands? Yes, Gandhi replies, unless prisoners are treated inhumanely. Civil disobedience requires willingness to suffer the penalty for noncompliance. To resist laws and their sanctions is anarchy. What bothers Gandhi most is not blood, but blood spilled by non-violent resisters.

17. *A Model Prisoner.* A friend telegrammed Gandhi, asking him to address non-violent resisters' duties as inmates, since so many were going to jail. Gandhi replied that model prisoners comply with all jail restrictions. The willing compliance melts the hearts of fellow prisoners and wardens. Non-violent resisters may resist jailers, but only for inhumane treatment, unfit food, or refusal to permit religious observances.

18. *Satyagrahi Prisoner's Conduct.* Prison agitation has no place in non-violent resistance. The non-violent resister treats a prison as a neutral institution with which he cooperates. Non-violent resister prisoners act honestly, cooperate, set an example, ask no favors, seek what they truly need but avoid irritation if refused, and do their assigned work. Quiet suffering of humble men is the weapon of the non-violent resister. One may resist prison officials when those administrators fail their duties, but not when they perform their duties.

19. *Pre-Requisites for Satyagraha.* When a son disapproves a father's decision for moral reasons, he asks his father to change his mind. Being denied, he leaves his father's home, with respectful firmness. The father may resist, but most will finally

turn from their decision. Non-violent resistance demands, first, willing reasonable obedience to laws. Second, it demands tolerance of inconvenient laws because only people who have proved active loyalty to the state have a right to civil disobedience. Third, non-violent resisters must suffer, for that is the result and point of civil disobedience. Few are prepared for the spiritual rigors of civil disobedience. To disobey when ill-prepared leaves people injured. Much reform could be accomplished by people willing to serve others silently.

20. *My Political Programme*. Gandhi's political program is simple: spinning wheels, welcoming untouchables, and finding common ground between Hindus and Muslims. The primary obstacle to Gandhi's political agenda is failure of self-discipline in truth and non-violence. When motivated by love, civil disobedience is every person's right.

21. *Limitations of Satyagraha*. Non-violent resistance is more than civil disobedience. If people will spin their own cloth and eschew British textiles and make peace between Hindus and Muslims, they will go far in establishing non-violent resistance. Gandhi prays for one worthy non-violent resister to walk to Calcutta to the seat of government, ask them to release wrongfully detained persons, and endure what follows. Then the government will change its approach. Gandhi is not pure enough to undertake this task. The pure non-violent resister has no anger, yet hates wrong. Gandhi tends the lighthouse of non-violent resistance, but has no patent on it.

22. *A Great Satyagrahi*. Gandhi praises Nanda, who shamed persecutors into better actions. Gandhi wonders whether non-violent resistance can spread to millions across time and continents.

23. *Neill Statue Satyagraha*. Protest of an offensive statue of a British officer led thirty volunteers to be imprisoned. Gandhi advises patience, since patient suffering is the essence of non-violent resistance. Gandhi critiques their petition to the government for its anger.

24. *A Himalayan Miscalculation*. Gandhi called for civil disobedience in the Kheda district. The result dismayed him. He called the Kheda results his "Himalayan miscalculation," meaning gargantuan error. He defends his self-criticism. One must see one's own errors with a convex lens, and those of others with a concave lens, in order to re-balance the human propensity for self-adulation and other-criticism. Civil disobedience by non-violent resisters is ripe only where the resisters have long obeyed the law from their hearts, enabling them to see the injustice of some laws. Gandhi noted that, with emphasis on peace and inner work, the number of teaching volunteers was falling, as was the number of new recruits.

25. *Qualification for Satyagraha*. The non-violent resister believes that every person, no matter what evil he may have done, can be redeemed by love. One purges evil by love. The non-violent resister inspects herself, rooting out her own anger and ill-will. The non-violent resister prefers quiet action to speeches. In acting against an evil, first, rally public opinion. The person who, against public opinion, nevertheless, persists in the evil confronted should be ostracized. The purpose of ostracism is not injury to the evil-doer, but to deny cooperation to him. A man purposely injuring society has no claim to society's service.

26. *Some Rules of Satyagraha*. Non-violent resistance insists on truth. Its spiritual force, which is never physical or violent, addresses evils in families, friends, leaders, governments, or the whole world. The force is suffering without complaint,

even death. Non-violent individuals avoid anger, practice forbearance, never retaliate, submit to legal authorities for their resistance, resist encroachment upon trust funds, avoid foul language and insults, and protect evil-doers from the wrongs of errant non-violent resisters. Imprisoned non-violent resisters show civility to guards, consider themselves no better than the other criminals nor seek privileges not accorded all prisoners, and avoid fasting over issues other than those showing personal disrespect. As a group, non-violent resisters obey their superiors' orders. One may quit a group he believes wrong-headed, but not disobey. No non-violent resister should ask for financial support for his family; trust them to God. In conflicts, the non-violent resister avoids quarrels and helps those in the right, protects those not of his own religion from attacks by the non-violent resister's people, and avoids any action that injures the religious scruples of any group.

27. *Full Surrender.* Non-violent resistance requires surrender of possessions, but not honor. One loses when clinging to things and positions.

28. *To Weaken Communalism.* One weakens communalists by yielding to them. Non-violent resisters oppose only those whose obstruction portends violence.

29. *Political Power v. Satyagraha.* Political power emerges from constructive action, not from controlling the mechanisms of governments. Laws without the support of public opinion avail nothing.

30. *For "Followers."* Answering queries about conduct of Gandhi's followers, Gandhi replies that he claims no followers. Non-violent resisters should never demean opponents; they are likely to be honorable people. When an opponent is not a good person, resistance must undo the effect of ill-action. Meet lies with truth, incivility with civility, violence with suffering, evil with good. Non-violent resisters avoid public office, except in serving the greater good.

31. *Maintenance Allowance.* Workers must take their wages. Organizations need strong rules of conduct; without them, they are rudderless ships. Our needs are modest if we have not allowed our desires to be artificially increased by plenty. Non-violent resisters cut their coats to their available cloth.

32. *A Non-Violent Army.* Gandhi envisions an army of non-violent resisters doing police work. They quell riots by dying at the hands of rioters. They spend their time between outbreaks doing constructive activities that make riots less likely, seeking chances to reconcile disputants, knowing every person in their precincts.

33. *To Volunteers.* Gandhi redirects volunteers ready to immolate themselves in response to distant riots to devote themselves to constructive activity in their local and personal lives.

34. *Requisite Qualifications.* Quality, not quantity, of non-violent resisters is what matters. Never embarrass opponents, appeal to their hearts, seeking to convert, not coerce, them. Act from conviction and inwardness. Non-violent resisters must have faith in God, believe in the efficacy of truth and the innate goodness of humans, live with chastity and sacrifice his goods and even life if called, must wear local cloth and weave constantly, avoid alcohol, follow rules of discipline as they emerge, and when incarcerated follow jail rules.

35. *Qualifications of a Peace Brigade.* Peace brigades are non-violent police. Members must have living faith in non-violence, which can only come from God, hold equal regard for all the great religions, know their localities and work there, find like-minded individuals and form brigades, get to know all the people in his precinct,

have spotless character and a reputation for impartiality, seek to intervene preemptively in volatile situations, seek other good people to serve with him, and wear a distinctive form of dress. Gandhi notes that he cannot be directly involved in formation of brigades because his other duties already overwhelm him.

36. *The Necessity of Training*. Gandhi accepts responsibility for civil disobedience by non-violent resisters in which violence occurred. His thoughts move away (1939) from mass non-violent resistance, because the masses are not adequately trained or disciplined. He recommends the spinning wheel as the best form of training.

37. *Physical Training for the Satyagrahi*. Non-violent resisters train by doing good for the community, not by wielding weapons. The weapon of non-violent resisters is faith in God. The resister has no external enemies, since he believes that all men are good within, if only they were wooed to right behavior by the sacrifice of others. Some forms of Yoga provide the right sort of physical training; the goal is to secure control of one's mind by disciplining the body. Sexual abstinence preserves a person's vital energy, but to lust in one's mind is worse than living sexually in a household. Lust makes men craven and a burden on others.

38. *Brahmacharya for Satyagraha*. Chastity (*brahmacharya*) means more than sexual abstinence. Chaste persons marshal and sublimate their vital energy by controlling their thoughts and senses. Creativity emerges. Chaotic thinking and evil acts dissipate vital energy. Sex, except for procreation, squanders this energy. Those who wish to be non-violent resisters must avoid sex altogether. The drive is quenched by the presence of God.

39. *Discipline—Satyagrahi and Military*. Military soldiers know only what they are told to do; generals plan and soldiers execute. So too among Satyagrahi. The leaders obey their inner voice, and the individual non-violent resisters do as they are told. Gandhi says he always tries to provide his reasoning, but in the end, soldiers must have faith and follow orders.

40. *Scorched Earth*. Non-violent resisters do not poison wells or destroy foodstuffs, for fear their enemies will eat, drink, and pursue. Non-violent resisters ennoble themselves by feeding and watering enemies. It is a sacrifice.

41. *Training for a Non-Violent Army*. The essential training for non-violent resisters is solid faith in God, obedience to their non-violent generals, and cooperation with other non-violent resisters.

42. *Constructive Preparation*. The non-violent resister movement is not for everyone. Their motto is maximize work, minimize words. Non-violent resistance works constructively to promote textile independence, literacy, abstinence from alcohol and drugs, good hygiene, and good relations with all local persons. The task of change may take 1,000 years. If one cannot accept this approach, one should leave the non-violent resisters, and do as one wishes.

**Section Third: Non-Co-Operation and Civil Disobedience.**

43. *The National Week*. In response to the British massacre of Hindus and Moslems peacefully protesting at Jalianwala, Gandhi urged the week leading up to the event be annually celebrated by fasting on the first day, service to the community throughout the week, and fasting and prayer on the day of the massacre, April 13$^{th}$.

44. *The Satyagraha Week.* Gandhi urges prayer and fasting on Satyagraha Week, to make the nation ready to be a nation. This week is not for civil disobedience.

45. *Jalianwala Bagh.* Gandhi defends Indian purchase of the Bagh, where 500 died in peaceful protest. The death of such is a necessary adjunct to becoming a nation, and honoring them a duty. He urges that General Dyer, who ordered the massacre, be removed as a lunatic, but that he should not be hated. Given his unfortunate circumstance, we all would do as he did.

46. *Neither a Saint Nor a Politician.* A friend sent an article that accuses Gandhi of creating and fanning political factionalism in his strike leadership. Gandhi responds that he responds to criticism only when he can admit mistakes or affirm the principle behind the criticism. Gandhi praises the character of his critic. Gandhi searches for truth, like a scientist, but his methods are so poor that he cannot claim any tangible results. Gandhi seeks no political gain. He is caught and surrounded by politics as by a boa constrictor. He cannot escape, so he wrestles. Gandhi has consciously thrust religion into politics, the religion superseding religions that all men venerate. Such religion drives men to direct action, which is the fount of all change. Gandhi hopes to revere the memory of the innocent dead at Jalianwala Bagh, so their sacrifice can remind people it is better to die victims than tyrants. To teach people direct action, imbued with affection for their opponents, is to follow Buddha and Jesus. If we will stop preying upon our neighbors, the world will come to unity. As the atom, so the universe.

47. *The Law Of Suffering.* All life emerges from death. India will become a nation through suffering. We cannot follow the Europeans. Their history is one of powerful men chasing right heedless of the innocent suffering wrought. We make suffering more potent by avoiding all violence on our side. Progress is measured by the amount of suffering endured. World War I was pointless; the Allies were just as rapacious as Germany. Nothing was gained. Infinite patience is not warranted. Direct action works, when conjoined with the nonviolent resisters' willingness to suffer. We refuse to cooperate with wrong-doers, and quietly suffer their consequences. Depart the roof of an unjust father. Withdraw from an immoral teacher's classes. Quit your job at an unjust corporation. Decline to cooperate with wicked governments. Direct action instructs actors doing evil. Yes, you will suffer for direct action. Suffering leads to freedom.

48. *How To Work Non-Cooperation.* Non-cooperation has four stages: a) surrender of titles and honorary jobs, b) strikes by civil servants, c) strikes by military and police, and d) refusal to pay taxes. Gandhi thinks only the first two steps will be necessary. There are risks in non-cooperation. But there are risks in taking no action as well. Those who oppose non-cooperation should speak with the people, who are incensed. Every citizen has the right to refuse to help a government that ignores him.

49. *How and When to Act.* Non-cooperation, which commences on August 1, will be universal. Those unable to act will provide labor and money. If non-cooperation proves necessary, despite ongoing negotiations, the people will surrender titles and honors, stop borrowing from the government, lawyers will stop practicing before the courts, parents will boycott government schools, reformed councils will be avoided, as will participation in government parties, people will decline military or

civil posts in foreign actions, and people will continue using only Indian-made products. There must be calm, coordination of efforts, and absolutely no violence.

50. *At the Call of the Country*. Dr. Sapru convinced the Muslims to avoid non-cooperation, thinking it will lead to worse circumstances than those it is intended to remedy. Sapru wants high office holders to resign too, not just doorkeepers. Gandhi agrees. High civil servants, like officials and judges, should join non-cooperation. If they wish to serve, the people speak with one voice. The government offends them and ignores their wishes. Successful non-cooperation will compel the British to change course. The alternative would be martial law, and the world community will not stand by for that. Non-cooperation will be the most peaceful revolution in history. If employed globally, bloodshed would cease.

51. *The First of August*. On July 28, 1920, Gandhi wrote of the commencement of non-cooperation on August 1st. The great threat is mob violence. Government violence is much easier to cure. The non-cooperation requires complete coordination, discipline, and organization. People fail to understand how much government relies on their acquiescence in its acts. To make non-cooperation a success, all violence must be avoided. Every non-cooperator must keep his own neighborhood in order.

52. *Who is Disloyal*? A British official alleges that non-cooperators are disloyal to the crown if they boycott the visit of the Prince of Wales to India. Gandhi counters that the Prince's visit is a political ploy to prop up the discredited British bureaucracy. The Indian people mourn deeply over the wrongs committed against them by British agents, and cannot at this time welcome the Prince. All Indians have a duty to avoid the Prince.

53. *Non-Violence and Swadeshi*. On July 29, 1920, Gandhi said the time for action had arrived. Two conditions must characterize non-cooperation: absence of violence and self-sacrifice. If violence erupts, Gandhi vows to help the government put it down. Non-cooperation must proceed by denying support to the government to the extent possible without chaos. The first stage of non-cooperation is intended to ask little and risk little: giving up titles, attorneys ceasing to use the courts, and people withdrawing their children from schools. A second act would be Swadeshi, which as a spiritual discipline means giving up fineries. Particularly, Indians would wear locally woven cloth, rough but beautiful, and give up imported cloths from Britain and China.

54. *Programme for Satyagraha*. Gandhi writes from jail to a Muslim leader. Gandhi urges Muslim-Hindu unity. Though they have made great strides, there still exists distrust and fear. Gandhi recommends the spinning wheel as a spiritual discipline, a sacrament. Spinning and weaving will unite Muslims and Hindus. Intolerance in words and acts is a form of violence. The non-cooperators must take pains to insure that British people and Indians who cooperate with the government feel safe and are safe. The power of non-cooperation lies not in generating fear, but in the pressure a government feels when it persecutes patent innocents. No further persons need to go to jail. They have imprisoned Gandhi; that is sufficient. In the non-cooperation program, untouchability has to go. Every good Hindu believes that.

55. *The Doctrine of the Sword*. People write Gandhi asking when he will authorize violence. These persons think that Gandhi does not really believe in non-violence to the end, but harbors secret violent intentions. Gandhi thinks for those with no alternative, violence may be employed. A man may violently prevent

violence. The British may put down the Zulu rebellion in South Africa. It is better than cowering. But in non-violence lies an utterly superior alternative. Strength comes not from physical coercion, but from unyielding wills. India has a right to feel injured. But, if India will forgive and act spiritually, it may deliver the world from violence. Gandhi denied being a visionary. His religion aims not at spiritual athletes, but at every man. Non-violence is natural to man, as is violence to animals. They have no alternative. Man has spiritual strengths and possibilities. A single person, possessed of the power of non-violence, might bring down an empire or reform it. India could prevail by violence. That would be an impossible day for Gandhi. India has a duty to the world to show others the power of non-violence. This religion, which is the root of Hinduism, lacks boundaries. It will prevail.

56. *Renunciation of Medals*. Gandhi returns medals awarded him by the British government for his humanitarian work and complains to the Viceroy of India about his government's abuses in the Khilifat and Punjab matters. Gandhi briefly explains the non-cooperation movement and its aim to cause the Viceroy's government to remedy its wrongs.

57. *Non-Payment of Fines*. The British government levied fines against non-cooperators, which some refused to pay. The government issued attachment writs and seized goods to pay for the fines. Some scoffed at this. Gandhi congratulates the resisters. Multiplied by thousands, such resistance would inconvenience the government and bring attention to the matter the non-cooperators protested initially. Gandhi cites Thoreau on resistance to slavery by even one man.

58. *Non-Payment of Taxes [1]*. Gandhi cautions followers about failing to pay taxes in non-cooperation. Though the path would be rapid, it is dangerous for people not thoroughly ensconced in non-violence, and might lead to violent uprising.

59. *Non-Payment of Taxes [2]*. Gandhi reiterates his concerns about violence in relation to non-payment of taxes. To withhold taxes wrongly is criminal. Further, even if non-violence is firmly entrenched in the peasants, they may still be spiritually wanting. They may avoid untouchables, or treat other religionists as outsiders, or fail to make and wear local cloth. Throwing off British rule without these disciplines will be meaningless.

60. *Boycott of Courts and Schools*. Lawyers must suspend their legal practices and induce their clients to follow suit. They can set up arbitration courts to address ongoing legal needs. Lawyers legitimate the government, cooperating by the nature of their employment. Parents must remove their children from government schools, and each village should manage the education of its children locally. If no schooling can be provided, the children should participate in their parents' political agitation.

61. *Empire Goods Boycott*. The Indian Congress's ineffective retaliatory boycott of British goods, where adequate alternatives exist only, wastes the movement's energy. Gandhi opposes this boycott. He boycotts all mill cloth (including Indian) because it makes paupers of the villagers.

62. *Social Boycott [1]*. Non-cooperation seeks by propaganda to convert its opponents, not coerce them into compliance. Slavery to non-violent protesters would be no better than slavery to British bureaucrats. We must grant the same freedom to disagree to our opponents that we claim for ourselves. It seems possible that social ostracism might be needed at some point in the future when a minority might refuse the majority from raw rebellious spirit. But that time is not now.

63. *Social Boycott [2].* Social boycott, used improperly, injures and may kill the movement. There have been reports of an opponent being denied medical treatment or use of the only well in a village. One cannot compel another to agree or respect an opponent's position. Impatience of this sort will kill the spiritual aspects of Gandhi's non-cooperation revolution. Social ostracism may exist in the form of refusing gifts or declining to attend celebrations with the person being sanctioned. Nothing more.

64. *Sympathetic Strikes.* Premature sympathy strikes injure the movement. Self-interest is so liable to creep in. Strikes must not embarrass the government. Strike leaders must insure that a real offense underlies the strike, that strikers support themselves and do not seek government assistance, and that a demand upon which they will not compromise is made before the strike commences. The goal is to cause others to sympathize with the strikers because of the suffering of the strikers. The goal is not to coerce others into compliance.

65. *More Objections Answered.* Some think Gandhi has abandoned tax revolt and military strikes as strategies. Gandhi denies these allegations. When people acquire sufficient maturity in dignified non-violence that they are not tempted to violence when wrongs are done to them, then these steps may be possible. The tax resister must remain non-violent as his goods and land are sold. The police or army men must do what they did for pay now for nothing, as national servants.

66. *Answers to Questions.* There have been outbreaks of deplorable violence in some of the non-violent protests. Gandhi goes forward regardless. Success will come to the Indians when British people in India know they are safe not because of superior weaponry but because no Indian will harm them. Then attitudes will change. English lives are as sacred as Indian. Gandhi admits that his Muslim colleagues tolerate non-violence only because they have no alternative. They would do violence if they could. Gandhi believes, as a religious proposition, that no man is his enemy.

67. *Non-Cooperation Explained.* Gandhi is interviewed by a Madras Mail reporter, long after a non-cooperation event was marred by violence. Gandhi asserts that people better understand now than then. Governments depend upon the cooperation of the populace for their functioning. Where cooperation is withdrawn, governments will heed. Among Muslims, more advocate non-violence than violence. In boycotting the visit of the Prince of Wales to India, Gandhi hopes to register the people's discontent. This unjust government must become just. Non-cooperation is not obstruction; bad governments thrive on obstruction. Non-cooperation will be engaged only as India is ready to take care of itself. Not many lawyers have taken up Gandhi's call to cease practice. But his ultimate hopes lie with the masses, not with lawyers.

68. *Love.* Love does good to men who do evil. This does not mean that no harm comes to evildoers. The non-violent resister resists a man's evil by dissociating, even though that may injure or even kill the evildoer. When an evil man repents, non-violent people welcome him back. We refuse to help men killing innocents, but nurse their injuries. We take nothing from hands stained with blood of innocents. We go to jail rather than endure the praise of those who insult the Muslims.

69. *The Poet's Anxiety.* Dr. Tagore, India's poet, disapproves non-cooperation. It is, according to him, beneath Indian dignity. Gandhi answers that non-cooperation resists British evil, as delivered by India's forced entry into market capitalism. The

British education system, which Gandhi encourages children and parents to abandon, teaches discontent with no remedy. The poet laments the negative in non-cooperation. Gandhi answers that rejecting untruth is an ideal, as well as adopting truth. India has adopted non-violent non-cooperation, as is natural for Hindus. Only this path will lead to national independence.

70. *What It Is Not.* A British writer criticized the non-cooperation movement as one of veiled violence. Non-cooperation injures some, as would milk-deliverers' refusal to deliver injure and kill babies in Lancashire. Gandhi answers that non-cooperation makes life difficult for unjust and evil actors. Lancashire will be injured by Indian independence, because Indian trade with Lancashire was bought at sword point. Those who suffer from non-cooperation have been done no violence. India is merely defending itself.

71. *The Non-Cooperation of a Satyagrahi.* A critic accused Gandhi of cooperating with the British by going to see the governor. Gandhi responds that he meets his opponents whenever possible, for the purpose of converting them to his cause. Gandhi has no enemies. Satyagrahi suffer to win people over.

72. *Civil Disobedience [1].* Civil disobedience has become popular. Gandhi sees a time ahead when he may be called to refuse to obey all British laws, even though bloodshed will result. Such non-cooperation is vicarious and selfless. Mass civil disobedience is otherwise. The protesters think to gain benefit. Arrest is the normal state of the non-violent protester. The power of non-violence lies in the insuperable power of innocent suffering. The more deeply innocent, the more powerful the protest. General civil disobedience waits for a well-disciplined population. Beginning before the people are prepared bodes ill. Civil disobedience has two requisites: being undertaken openly and without violence.

73. *Civil Disobedience [2].* Disobedience that lacks civility and intelligent discrimination of circumstances leads to defeat. Among well-disciplined people, civil disobedience nurtures life.

74. *The Right of Civil Disobedience.* Civil disobedience is a natural right. Criminal disobedience is justly put down, but its civil counterpart merely expresses citizen conscience. Where a state is unjust, civil disobedience is a sacred duty.

75. *Aggressive v. Defensive.* Offensive civil disobedience finds laws to disobey as a symbol of rebellion. Defensive civil disobedience undertakes forbidden actions where obedience would offend human dignity. Both must be non-violent.

76. *My Faith.* Gandhi believes in Satyagraha, the pursuit of truth. It excludes hatred. Gandhi refuses to let Britain impose British ways on India without a fight. But his fight will be non-violent. Though the movement has fallen short, a single non-violent protester, if perfect, would throw off British rule. Everyone should so strive for perfection.

**Section Fourth: Vykom Satyagraha.**

77. *Vykom [1].* Vykom laws prohibit untouchables from using certain roads around the temple at Vykom. Gandhi defends the non-violent protesters negotiating with the authorities, even while in the midst of their protests. In this matter, the Satyagrahis are not attempting to remove British rule, as in the general protests, but only a religious prohibition. Rulers who ignore public opinion lose their right to rule.

Gandhi opposes Indians from outside the Vykom area sending financial aid. Such assistance may dilute the impact of the suffering of the non-violent protests in Vykom.

78. *Vykom Satyagraha [1].* Gandhi answers objections to the Vykom Satyagraha. A Christian leader ought not to take the helm in Vykom. Untouchability is the Hindu's sin. They must suffer for it and purge themselves of it. Non-Hindus will only offer an excuse to those who oppose being rid of untouchability. Genuine reform comes from within communities. Satyagraha converts its opponents, not by compulsion, but by warming their hearts. No help should come from outside, pecuniary or personal. Enthusiasts wish to fast to force the hand of the authorities. Gandhi replies that fasting is only to convince one's supporters, not enemies, and then only for reforming those supporters when they have stumbled. Some object to protests in Vykom, because it is an Indian, not British, state. Gandhi argues that untouchability must be confronted wherever it exists. Though these protests are regarding road use, caste abuses must be confronted all over India. These reforms should have limits, not to include inter-dining and inter-marriage.

79. *Vykom Satyagraha [2].* A spiritual leader advised untouchables to scale the barriers and dine with others in the temple. Gandhi responds that this is not non-violent resistance. Still, Gandhi will not call off the resistance. The leaders should keep participants in line, and work toward the conversion of the opposition by self-sacrifice.

80. *Vykom [2].* Goondas, who are orthodox Hindus, attack the Satyagrahis by blinding them with lime in the eyes and stripping their clothing. Gandhi opines that the protesters must endure. Loss of a few hundred Satyagrahis counts little when compared to the freedom of the untouchables. All martyrs must perish without moral stain.

81. *Vykom Satyagraha [3].* The Vykom protesters suffer social ostracism, being denied even family property and family relations. These Satyagrahis fight by suffering. They love their oppressors and do not resent them. May they persevere.

82. *Vykom Satyagraha [4].* God helps helpless and suffering Satyagrahis. Rely on God. No other, including Gandhi, is sufficient. When the protesters feel defeated, that may be the victory, as birth pangs. The sword of the Satyagrahi is suffering without rancor or bitterness. None can resist its edge.

83. *Vykom Satyagraha [5].* Men of conviction are unmoved by rational argument. The Satyagrahi reaches toward the heart, which opens the reason of the otherwise convinced man.

84. *Satyagrahi's Duty.* Forget politics. The Satyagrahi's duty is to seek truth by personal suffering for the great errors of Hindus, which is making some untouchable. Avoid bitterness by knowing many opponents act in good faith based on their erroneous religious convictions. Learn how the opposition sees themselves. That would obviate most of the world's conflicts. Do not question the resistance's decisions. You are soldiers. Obey. All the work of resistance is equally critical. Cleaning latrines matters as much as sitting at the barricades. Satyagrahis have corruption within, just as the opponents. Eradicate selfishness, jealousy, laziness within your heart. Seek and find truth. Remember Sudhanva, smiling as he was executed in boiling oil. He saw God more than oil.

85. *Vykom [3].* Satyagraha works slowly and quietly, yet it is the most powerful and swift way to its ends. Some untouchables threaten to convert if things don't move along. Religion is not clothing to be changed at inclement weather. One confesses a faith because he cannot do otherwise. To convert is to betray one's heritage. God's kindness has a sharp edge. His followers suffer as they are purified and humbled.

86. *True Satyagraha.* The Vykom Satyagrahi, as they sit at the barricades daily, spin large quantities of yarn for cloth. Gandhi recounts their production. The connection between spinning and protest lies in the motivating spirit of the protesters. They show compassion, patience, and persistence.

87. *Vykom Satyagraha [6].* The reform at Vykom was successful in its short term goals: the roads were opened. Its long term goal, however, is to remove all obstacles to untouchables, which is a great sin on Hindus throughout India. On these issues, it is not time for Satyagraha. All less severe methods must first be exhausted. As to the untouchables, while we remove obstacles, we also work with them to make them more presentable in normal society.

88. *Satyagraha v. Compulsion.* An impatient reformer seeks Gandhi's approval for blocking access to temples that refuse untouchables. Gandhi declines this as a form of compulsion. People change when they will. Satyagraha is used by some for veiled violence. Non-violent protest permits no compulsion in ideas or action. It moves gently and avoids inflicting injuries. It grows from compassion and a sense of injustice, not from hatred. It is patient, compliant, and speaks softly. Satyagraha converts others by appealing to their best selves. The acts non-violence undertakes, it takes against the Satyagrahis themselves. Their self-purification wins hearts. Even these non-violent acts can be twisted to become coercive. The evil in humans makes it possible to distort anything.

89. *Religious Satyagraha.* Mixed motives are most dangerous in religious Satyagraha. Those who would change religions must be blameless and avoid intrigue at all costs. Religions change only under the influence of purity which values opponents as much as supporters.

**Section Fifth: Kheda and Bardoli Satyagrahas.**

90. *The Kheda Satyagraha.* Kheda villagers' crops failed. The government sought a tax increase to reduce its resulting shortfall. Gandhi organized non-cooperation, refusing to pay the taxes. Gandhi spent a great deal of time educating villagers about non-violent resistance, and teaching them to view government men as their servants. Once the people lost their fear of officials, though, they ran the risk of becoming uncivil. Non-violent civility is more than outward pleasantness; it entails a wish for the opponent's good. Gandhi instructed Pandya, who longed for arrest, to harvest a field of attached onions, contrary to government edict. He and his friends were convicted and spent a short time in jail. Pandya was given the honorific "onion thief" by the people.

91. *Bardoli's Decision.* The Bardoli region decided to fight untouchability by mass civil disobedience. They agreed to trans-religious unity, non-violence, making and wearing home-spun clothing, making needed sacrifices including death, and relating to untouchables themselves as though the caste did not exist. The government did not interfere with these preparations. Both sides behaved well.

92. *Bardoli on Trial.* In response to the Bardoli civil disobedience, the government terrorized the people and made untrue claims, as is their habit. Satyagrahis must take their losses in stride. It is a small matter to lose houses when honor and justice hang in the balance. Those who intercede on behalf of the protesters must beware. They should not represent the protest as a weakness of the people. The people rightly demand a judicial inquiry into their plight.

93. *Non-Cooperation or Civil Resistance?* Satyagraha includes all non-violent, truth-seeking actions, including non-cooperation and civil resistance. In the Indian work, non-cooperation means declining to work through government channels until Indian self-rule is established. Civil resistance, as at Bardoli, has a specific and narrow objective. In Bardoli, the people seek judicial review of an unjust tax imposed on them, and withhold payment pending adjudication.

94. *Limitations on Satyagraha.* The resistance at Bardoli is non-political, and not a part of the drive to Indian self-rule, except tangentially. Friends criticize Gandhi's position in this regard as impolitic. Gandhi responds that God leads the resistance. What seems political foolishness to us may be God's plan. Bardoli is home to a tough people and a difficult enterprise. Friends should not cower or make excuses. Bardoli has God's protection.

95. *All's Well.* The Bardoli protesters achieved almost all they sought. Now they must collect the data to win their trial regarding the unjust taxation. Constructive work must come to the fore: removing alcohol, village sanitation, education of the children.

96. *Sign of the Times.* Bardoli offers instruction. The government can learn that non-violent protest and cooperation are powers that may greatly strengthen the people and the government too. It is irresistible, and mounting. The people can learn that cooperating with one another is a spirit of unity. They can overcome reticent government. But now they must learn to improve their own lot continually. Non-violence goes on, confronting their own losses and shortcomings, building their community for good.

**Section Sixth: Salt Satyagraha.**

97. *"Never Faileth."* The Indian Working Committee grants Gandhi authority to undertake non-violent resistance as he sees fit. Members of the Congress seek measures Gandhi believes to be coercive. Gandhi has been seeking freedom from this political melee for months, feeling constrained by committee majoritarian decision-making. Following truth, one may have to contradict every other man. Love may demand civil disobedience, which is dangerous, but no more than the violence that prompts it. The only danger is that the non-violent may be tempted to take up violence.

98. *To English Friends.* On the eve of civil disobedience, Gandhi writes to British friends that he knows the government may use violence to end his civil disobedience. Regardless, Gandhi is not Britain's enemy, though he wishes to end British rule of India.

99. *When I Am Arrested.* When Gandhi was previously arrested, demonstrations were non-violent and silent, while constructive works were accelerated. This arrest should be different. Every non-violent Indian should take action as is locally

appropriate. Gandhi has no successor in mind. Congress will choose. Gandhi intends to start the civil disobedience through the Satyagraha Ashram, which has long been preparing itself spiritually. If the Ashram cannot respond, it should be disbanded. Every Satyagrahi must, as this protest gains momentum, take up the cause. Every man should be in prison, doing civil disobedience, or working at the spinning wheel or other constructive work.

100. *Letter to the Viceroy.* Gandhi writes to the British government about the changes he will be protesting to remedy. Gandhi notes that the British government and some who oppose it move toward violence. Gandhi and his ashram will intervene. Gandhi seeks to convert the British people by his non-violence, to melt their hearts as to the wrong Britain has done India. British trade is tainted by greed. India and Britain should act as equals, helping and trading to mutual benefit. If the Viceroy cannot accede to Gandhi's requests, the non-payment of Salt Tax will commence this month. Gandhi does not seek to embarrass the Viceroy and will delay publication of this letter if the Viceroy sends word of his desire to make the changes Gandhi suggests.

101. *Some Questions and Answers. Might non-violence lead to violence?* Yes, but non-violent resistance gives an outlet to frustrations, where, without it, there would be none. One controls the forces of violence by unleashing the force of non-violence. *How will the movement stay peaceful after you have been arrested?* In South Africa, thousands joined after Gandhi was jailed and did wonderfully. *Will non-violence increase the number of factions in India?* Gandhi does not think so. He is an optimist and has confidence that the masses will behave well by instinct. But, Gandhi admits, he may be more optimistic than realities warrant. Still, one never knows how things will go, and this protest is a rare opportunity. *Why is now the time for civil disobedience?* Gandhi says that his internal conflict has resolved. He will be arrested in the Salt protest, and that arrest will lead to a conference of equals to establish a free India. *Did you err with the Viceroy?* No. Previous negotiations failed. We need to speak in a new way, as equals. *Will Gandhi make concessions if the British come part way on the Eleven Points?* It will depend on the spirit in which concessions might be made.

102. *On the Eve of the March.* Gandhi addresses a large crowd on the eve of the salt march to Dandi. After Gandhi is arrested, no violence must be indulged, even if Gandhi and his companions are killed. The non-violent working committee will then take the lead. Gandhi reminds the protesters of the ways in which they may violate the Salt Laws. The protest may be enlarged to include boycott of foreign cloth, liquor stores, and the courts. Government employees should give up their work and devote themselves to Indian independence. All should cease cooperating with the government in as many ways as possible. Satyagrahis prevail, whether in jail or free, because they fail only when they grow violent and cease hearing the voice of God.

103. *Ashram Discipline During the March.* Gandhi insisted on the daily ashram disciplines of spinning 212 yards of yarn, writing in the journal, morning prayers, even during the march. Those who could not manage were invited to visit with Gandhi to readjust their schedules. This march lays the foundations of Indian independence, and so must be a spiritual offering that is as pure as possible.

104. *Duty of Disloyalty*. British foreign rule of India is a despotism that must be resisted at any cost. The means of resistance cannot include injuring the British bureaucrats. When even the best men join an evil organization, they are corrupted. It is not their fault. When one refuses to cooperate with the British, he denies them allegiance, which no evil system survives.

105. *Some Suggestions*. Gandhi sets April 6th as the day for commencing India-wide civil disobedience, which is to be mass, peaceful, and spontaneous. The protesters aim to replace violence with non-violence. The protest will continue even if violence breaks out. Satyagrahi will sacrifice themselves wherever violence erupts. Gandhi rejects resistance of other regulations. If further targets after the Salt Laws are needed, he recommends liquor shops and foreign cloth dealers and opium dens.

106. *Turning the Searchlight Inward*. As the protesters approached Dandi, Gandhi urged them to greater purity. The protesters are weak and subject to stumbling. Some have ordered milk. One's right to criticize the government comes from one's identification with the plight of the poor. If pampered, one's voice carries little weight. And lavish gifts from supporters amount to food stolen from poor India. The protesters are trustees of the hopes of India's masses. The protesters must be frugal. Their protest must extend first to themselves. Ride only when you cannot walk. Gandhi would rather speak with six poor than droves gathered by expensive advertising. A man carried a stove on his head. Gandhi objects. We need no stove. Gandhi is discouraged by the protesters' failures, which he adopts as his own failures. He will, nevertheless, continue. He will not desist.

107. *Notes on the Way to Dandi*. Gandhi describes the effect of the Salt Tax. The tax is 1,000% of the value of the salt. The government destroys untaxed salt, at public expense. The salt tax destroys local salt industry, which is to take food from starving millions. Gandhi answers critics claiming his Satyagrahi are falling ill; a few have difficulties. The youth are somewhat soft. Gandhi encourages exercise, especially walking. Some women coming to protest used spare time to gather trash. Gandhi commends them. All weak points of Indian society must be simultaneously addressed. Gandhi notes that women may exceed men in the work of non-violent resistance.

108. *Remember 6th April*. When mass protest commences, workers will guide, then step back to let the people lead themselves. If violence erupts, Satyagrahi must interject themselves to quell it, even if they die trying. Those who cannot actively march must do other tasks like spin, weave, picket, clean villages, or help families of Satyagrahi.

109. *Hindu-Muslim Question*. A Muslim boy asks if Gandhi needs only Hindu help to achieve Indian independence. Gandhi responds that he requires all men and women from every village and religion, for they are signs from God. Gandhi felt no conviction about resistance until recently, when he became steeled to act. God looks to the heart; men see externals. God wants purity and self-sacrifice of his workers. Gandhi does not oppose the British, only their rule of India. Gandhi is called to end that rule. Someone asked how many seats Muslims will hold in an independent India. Gandhi notes that the Congress has promised all parties will be satisfied. We fight for the poor, whether Hindu or Muslim. Who does not like such efforts?

110. *Barbarous*. Outside Dandi, police seized salt from protesters, without warrant. The entire village appeared, dug salt, and dared the police to arrest the

village, men, women, and children, for digging salt, but the police desisted. The government can take salt, Gandhi says. Arrest the individuals, try them, convict them, and then police can justly seize the salt.

111. *The Inhuman Tax*. The Salt Tax has impoverished the villages of the salt area of Gujurat, where people made money producing local sea salt. Gandhi tells villagers near the sea how to prepare their own daily salt from ocean water. He challenges the government to arrest and prosecute the tens of thousands who protest.

112. *A Survey*. Gandhi encourages protesters to stand firm when police challenge, and if necessary fold their arms and take bullets in the chest, in order to resist salt seizures. Women should let the men fall, then take their place after all the men are gone. The British act without legal authority.

113. *The Black Regime*. Some protesters at Chittagong have planned violent resistance. Protester violence is as wrong as government violence. Gandhi would have the government use arms against such violent men. They impede Indian independence. Non-violent protesters' injuries bring Gandhi joy. When the best and bravest are sacrificed, the universal law of suffering brings victory. The government has no right to use force to seize salt. They must arrest, try, and then seize. Government agents have poisoned some unauthorized salt.

114. *Purity in Account Keeping*. Some enterprising people are selling salt in the name of the Congress and pocketing the money. The local chapters must keep books and have them audited. Since the public now finances the movement, let the bookkeeping be methodical.

115. *Calm Heroism*. Gandhi reports a protester who held a hot salt pan to prevent police seizure, seriously burning his hands. Gandhi praises him. Such will create Indian independence.

116. *Mahadev Desai and His Successor*. Mahadev was arrested for importing a cart of contraband salt. His successor is an illiterate, but devoted, Muslim. Indian home rule recognizes no religious distinctions, nor educational statuses, nor wealth, but includes the disabled and starving people as well.

117. *Goonda Raj*. Gandhi recounts abuses by the British government in taking salt from salt protesters. The people must resist by suffering. Freedom grows from suffering, and moral license from violence. The British exploit India for their own benefit.

118. *Message to the Nation*. Gandhi believes he may soon be arrested. Indian independence comes from the protesters' suffering. Make forbidden salt. Picket liquor and opium and foreign textile shops. Spin and weave. Burn imported cloth. Ignore untouchability. Find a common heart with peoples of every faith. Provide for minorities. Leave government schools and jobs. Devote yourself to serving people. Then comes independence.

119. *The Second Letter*. Gandhi writes to the Viceroy that he will march to Dharasana and seek possession of the Salt Works there. Gandhi recites British abuses of protesters, and propaganda lies of the government. Gandhi complains of government inaction when protesters are attacked. The science of non-violent resistance teaches that great oppression falls before great voluntary suffering at the hands of oppressors. Non-violence conquers violence. Gandhi appeals to the Viceroy to repeal the Salt Tax.

120. *The Great Arrest.* [This account is not written by Gandhi.] The Surat police, with thirty-two officers, arrested Gandhi (because the government viewed his activities with alarm) at 12:34 a.m. on May 12, 1930, while Gandhi slept. Gandhi asked to brush his teeth, reviewed the warrant, sought additional time to pray with the Satyagrahi, and then was carted off in a motorcar. He was thereafter cut off from communication. His followers call him "Great Soul," and anticipate that no jail can contain his radiance.

121. *More About the Settlement.* Gandhi negotiated a settlement with the British. He addressed a large crowd of protesters. Gandhi says that some are disappointed with settlement before all goals are achieved. Satyagrahi make war, but also seek peace. Peace implies terms not too strict or humiliating for the others. The settlement is provisional. If either side fails to keep its part, the non-violent "war" can recommence. For now, have hope and patience, and negotiate rather than refuse to cooperate.

122. *The Congress.* Congress reconvenes soon. Gandhi notes that many members have been in jail. While all should be ready to suffer, suffering is not an end in itself. The protesters' self-purification has not been perfected. Many still accept untouchability. The rich do not live as the poor. The alcohol and drug trades have been impaired, but we have not addressed the addicts themselves. Much fine imported cloth is still apparent. All these will vanish when self-purification progresses. Indian self-rule will arrive from within, not from the British or from talking in Congresses.

123. *Let Us Repent.* The Mayor of Karachi, a strong supporter of Satyagraha, publicly criticized the non-violent movement for creating hatreds, for being intolerant of differences of opinion in its ranks, for using non-violent methods indiscriminately, and for missing the deeper spiritual point of Satyagraha. Gandhi responds that all must listen to the Mayor. Non-violence begins within the mind, and must never be a sham, hiding antipathy. Used mindlessly, Satyagraha leads to societal disintegration and license. There remains great hatred in India. Non-violence must convert the English. If one finds hatred in his heart, he must begin again.

124. *Power of Ahimsa.* A person wrote that the world's indignation has failed to arise, as it would if a woman were beaten by a ruffian, at India's non-violent resistance, which the correspondent takes to be an indication of the inhumanity of the world. Gandhi counters that women are not powerless nor is truth. Non-violence is a weapon of power, but the non-violence of the Indian uprising was weak and merely formal. It seldom grew from the deeps of the human breast. That is shown by fights among the protesters themselves. When non-violence is pure, none can resist, and the world will take note.

125. *Goondaism Within the Congress.* Gangmembers have become part of Congress. They do not understand non-violence, and were inducted because some feared that without them, there would be no volunteers. One Satyagrahi can win the battle, but a million violent persons cannot. Indiscriminate recruiting threatens the movement. We must deal with the ruffians in our midst. We cannot call the police. They are part of us. We must refuse to acquiesce in their demands, as we would any other injustice. We must reform, convert, and love them.

126. *Conquest Over Body.* Despite arrests and hardship, nothing external can conquer the soul. The spiritual person is care-free. He relies on God to provide. We

cannot store up goods; nature opposes that. We should throw ourselves upon God, as we have these last years.

**Section Seventh: Indian States Satyagraha.**

127. *Suspend Civil Disobedience.* When Gandhi suspended civil disobedience in Kathiawad, some criticized. Gandhi replies that those who abandon non-violence because of delays never understood in the first place and are better gone.

128. *Rajkot Satyagraha.* The big error in the Rajkot protests was to allow another group to join so they would have big protests. Non-violence begins by setting its opponents at ease, avoiding panic.

129. *About the Rajkot Award.* The Viceroy awarded Gandhi a sum in a dispute. Gandhi believes that the award makes him a coward and separates him from God. Gandhi threw the award away.

130. *Suspension of Civil Disobedience.* Some protesters feared depression if their protests were suspended. Gandhi advises them to begin again, since they lack the requisite inwardness. The civil disobedience must be suspended. The opponents fear the protesters' numbers. Only a few Satyagrahi will protest, to be more effective. Those who are not jailed must do the constructive work.

131. *Its Implications.* Gandhi sees that the Rajkot protests were not purely non-violent. The admixture has led to government opposition. Gandhi demands more now of Satyagrahi, and those rigors may reduce the number of non-violent protesters. Gandhi does not know how to proceed with only a few, but waits on God. Congress can no longer lead. It is corrupt, has failed to wed the spiritual communities of India, and has allowed ministers without public support to continue in office. Satyagraha is inappropriate now. There are steps of self-purification that must precede it. India's circumstance is precarious. If non-violence does not prevail, anarchy will erupt.

132. *Non-Violence v. Violence.* The Rajkot protesters were tainted by violence. Non-violence is effective only where head and heart coincide. Even now, Hindu and Muslim arm to fight one another. It is our earlier mixed motives haunting us. Gandhi declines to declare all out resistance under these circumstances. It can only lead to violence.

**Section Eighth: Individual Satyagraha Against War.**

133. *No Suppression.* Gandhi does not suppress others from protesting. All are free to declare civil disobedience. They will not, however, have Gandhi's approval. Only when the protesters have the spiritual prerequisites will Gandhi approve. Those who protest without the inner conditions of Satyagraha are likely to doom their causes.

134. *Every Congress Committee a Satyagraha Committee.* Splits among protesters lead some to spin without believing the spinning wheel central to civil resistance. These people want my approval so they may control others, but do not want to follow my path. True obedience engenders enthusiastic compliance. Gandhi calls on the Congress committees to declare themselves for non-violence, to select active Satyagrahi representatives who nurture goodwill, spin, eschew untouchability, wear only homespun cloth, are willing to be incarcerated, keep a daily diary, and do the

constructive program. These persons are to be registered, with reports to Gandhi. Others, unwilling to spin or go to jail, but who nevertheless are supportive of non-violence, are passive Satyagrahi. The world, and Gandhi himself, believes the protesters' intent is violent. Gandhi admits the non-violent protesters' failures. Gandhi will not fight unless the rolls of the Satyagrahi are pure.

135. *The Charkha and Satyagraha.* Some wish to divorce the spinning wheel from India's non-violent protests. Gandhi refuses, for the spinning wheel symbolizes his commitment to the poor of India. Those who do not share the spinning wheel with him, should leave Gandhi. None are wicked by nature; they are no more wicked than we. If one cannot share this attitude, he should leave Gandhi.

136. *Civil Disobedience.* Civil disobedience must convince the opponent that protesters really intend no harm to others by the protests. The British and the Muslim League believe that Hindu civil disobedience is aimed at them in veiled harm. This belief makes civil disobedience very unlikely. The great majority should just spin, wear local cloth, and nurture feelings of brotherhood with all Indians. A few Satyagrahi may protest. Just leave them to their tasks.

137. *Not Yet.* Some not-too-serious Congress people are doing non-violence violently. They think to fill the jails, but without the right attitudes, without participating in the constructive work. This is just violence against the British. Do the constructive work. Leave civil disobedience to the Satyagrahi.

138. *To the Reader.* Gandhi refuses to continue publishing in the Harijan, after the British gagged him from speaking of non-violence. Gandhi was criticized for suggesting that the British let the Nazis overrun Britain, but develop the internal strength to resist them by dying. Gandhi says that the people who have read his column will be fine without it.

## Section Ninth: Miscellaneous

### I. Fast as an Element in Satyagraha.

139. *Fasting as Penance.* In South Africa, two of Gandhi's students went astray. Deeply distressed, Gandhi swore a penance of a one week fast, followed by one meal per day for four and one half months. Gandhi does not think penitential fasting for the failures of students is always advisable, but it is on some occasions.

140. *The Satyagraha Way with Children.* Gandhi fasts because of failings in some children at the ashram for which Gandhi is responsible. Punishing children does not reform, but only hardens, them. Satyagraha entails suffering. Gandhi wants to identify with the humblest people in India and the world.

141. *Satyagraha—True and False.* A friend asks if one can fast to compel payment of monies owed him. Gandhi says no. Satyagraha fasting aims only at the good of others who are close to the faster. Self-interest sullies the fast.

142. *Fast as an Element in Satyagraha.* Some are concerned that Gandhi may harm himself by fasting against untouchability. Gandhi replies that he has fasted often through his life, it is part of Satyagraha, and if he does so, he obeys God. He can do nothing other than obey.

143. *Fast as Prayer.* Fasting supports prayer, bringing it intensity and focus. We crucify the flesh, growing wholly absorbed in prayer, divorced from physical functions.

144. *Is Fast Coercion*? Gandhi answers no. One sacrifices for those he loves. Fasts sacrifice for family and friends. Fasting is integral to Hinduism. Gandhi fasts when his internal agony leads him to the solace of prayer.

145. *Fast as the Last Resort.* Fasting to death is the last resort of the Satyagrahi. Religious literature tells of people who fast to compel God to answer prayer. Many perished, for God answers as he wishes. Still, those who fasted are heroes.

146. *Fast as Self-Surrender.* Some use fasts to evil ends. Still, one must fast for good, even if a few abuse fasts. Christian Protestants have criticized Gandhi's fasts. Gandhi defends fasting as a denial of self, which is the beginning of devotion.

147. *Requirements for Satyagraha Fast.* The disciplines of doing constructive work, of loving opponents, of bridling one's drives, and of forsaking possessions and ambitions prepare one for the inner fast, which is seeking only Truth. Fasting means nothing without these preparations.

148. *Coercive Fasts.* Some criticize Gandhi's fasts as coercive. Gandhi responds that all fasts influence those in their sphere. Truly coercive fasts have selfish ends. One should resist them, even if the faster dies as a result.

149. *Fasting.* Fasting is a non-violent weapon, but those who can use it are few. Gandhi thinks he is made for fasting. Few follow him in fasting. Its use should be very limited. Only those who have trained should fast as Satyagrahi. Most fasts are not fasts, but hunger-strikes. Their lack of spirituality makes them both dangerous and mostly ineffective.

150. *Fasting in Satyagraha.* Non-violent fasting contains power, and should be used judiciously by those thoroughly prepared. Fasters must be directly associated with the person fasted against. Gandhi erred in his Rajkot fast. Gandhi was angry, impatient, selfish, and lacked faith. The result was coercion of a friend. Fasts for purification of body or spirit differ from the non-violent fast.

151. *Fasting in the Air.* Gandhi asks that those who contemplate non-violent fasts should seek Gandhi's permission. This obviates the need for rules during Gandhi's lifetime. Non-violent fasts require one to exhaust all other avenues of redress before fasting. One cannot fast to change things. That brings failure. One fasts because he cannot fail to do so. Fasting is much abused, and ill-considered fasting spreads like disease.

## II. Women and Picketing.

152. *To the Women of India.* Women are better adapted to non-violence than men. With them lies its future. Women exceed men in intuition, self-sacrifice, endurance, and courage. Women should take up the picketing of liquor stores and drug dens. And they should focus on home-spun clothing.

153. *Women in Conference.* In response to Gandhi's call, the women of Gujarat convened, adopted the homespun clothing boycott of mill textiles and picketing of drug and alcohol shops. Gandhi argues that if India is to be independent, she cannot avoid making her own cloth and clothing. The processes are simple. Avoid idleness. Spin and weave.

154. *The Men's Part.* Men have a part in the women's movement. First, they can avoid meddling in their spinning and boycotts. Women know non-violence innately; men know it only by slow learning. Second, everyone can spin. There exist sufficient weavers, but too few spinners creating sufficient thread. Third, men may never use coercion. We non-violently resist our erring friends. When Satyagrahi become violent, Gandhi gets ill. His heart suffers. Gandhi may one day offer a perpetual fast in response to supporters who practice violence and coercion.

155. *Notes. The Frontier Provinces.* People not convinced of non-violence most help Indian independence by declining to participate in the protests. When protesters lapse into violence, Indian independence suffers. Lives are lost fruitlessly as well. *Boycott and Picketing.* Indian foreign cloth merchants are bartering their cloth to avoid the boycott on purchase of cloth. This must stop. A local Congress may have promised Delhi merchants they would stop picketing. If this is so, the pickets must stop. Honoring one's word is a critical adherence to truth. The picketing must be left to women; men are too easily provoked.

156. *How To Do the Picketing.* Ten women per shop choose a leader. They ask the merchant to stop selling, and appeal to customers outside the shop if the owner refuses. Picketers carry banners, wear uniforms, prevent male involvement, avoid ill-language, and eschew compulsion against customers. Men should support the women by organizing marches and printing materials. All monies must be accounted, and those accounts audited.

157. *Some Picketing Rules.* The purpose of picketing is to convert the alcohol, drug, or cloth patrons and sellers. Gandhi lists rules for picketing, which emphasize personal warmth and kindness, not political pressure. Picketers control their good thoughts and deeds, not the outcomes.

158. *A Stern Reproof.* Foreign cloth merchants attempted to award Gandhi a cash prize and honors. Gandhi declines. Gandhi invites them to burn their stocks of cloth or to take back their award.

159. *Picketing.* Critics castigate Gandhi's criticism of some picketers who formed living walls blocking off boycotted stores. This is mere violence, says Gandhi. No living walls are permitted.

160. *When Is Picketing Peaceful*? An inquirer asks if picketing in which buyers are actively engaged to join the boycott is peaceful? Gandhi replies that all pickets without a plainly just cause are violent. They impede individual rights. Pickets should be organized only by responsible organizations, and then only within rigid guidelines.

161. *Picketing and Love.* A critic argues that picketing and love are incompatible. Gandhi agrees they can be at odds. But some picketing is loving, as when family members watch over errant loved ones. Indifferent acts become good or evil by the motives that actuate them.

## III. Satyagraha in Social Reform.

162. *Students' Noble Satyagraha.* Students opposed a feast in honor of the spirit of a departed mother as wasteful and a reprehensible custom. They employed Satyagraha, fasting the day of the event and refusing all food of the party. The event occurred. Changing such things requires much effort and patience.

163. *Limits of Satyagraha.* Old men marry young girls, so fathers get dowries and the old men indulge their lusts. Gandhi notes that direct confrontation will only cause secret marriages. He proposes approaching the girls' fathers and mothers. Social reform is harder than political change. One must be satisfied with small gains in social improvements. One cannot possibly hope to change the lustful habits of old men. Approach the parents.

164. *Satyagraha Against the Colour Bar Bill.* When South African laws injure the Indian citizens, those persons must offer Satyagraha. Non-violence always wins.

165. *The Jews.* As Hitler rounds up Jews in Germany, Gandhi advises mass civil disobedience. Stand up, be counted, and be shot. By so doing, the Jews will win over the German people to human dignity, and offer true religious resistance against Hitler's mechanized inhumanity.

166. *The Satyagraha Way with Crime.* Someone burglarized a villager's home. Gandhi noted only three approaches exist. First, one can report to the police, who may do little and may be corrupt themselves. Second, the village may acquiesce, which is cowardice. Third, the village may practice non-violent resistance upon the thieves. Cure, rather than punish, them. Teach them skills and vocations. Recognize that the criminal is oneself, with only minor changes of circumstances. All aggregation of money beyond one's legitimate needs is theft. Theft would disappear if society better distributed wealth and insisted on social justice. One aims to reform the criminal, not inform the police.

167. *Socialism and Satyagraha.* Humans find their strength in their relation to Truth and the divine. Socialism will never emerge from human action, but only from god. Non-violence is god's force to bring socialism. Socialism cannot emerge otherwise. Non-violence can bring on utopia.

**Section Tenth: Questions and Answers.**

168. *Some Questions. Informing the Government?* Non-violent protests are done openly, with the foreknowledge of the government. *Readiness for Non-Violence?* Young men are prone to violence, despite their best intentions. Gandhi has taken over the non-cooperation protests personally, to relieve Congress of its moral dilemmas in leading. Gandhi is responsible for violence that emerges out of his non-violence, and the British are responsible for the urgency the Indian people feel. Gandhi is gambling that his pursuit of truth will win out. *Hindu-Muslim unity?* The Congress must not accept any independence that is not based on all parties, protecting the minorities. This love has always driven Gandhi. *An Indian army?* Never. Non-violence aims to benefit Englishmen as much as Indians. Personal hallucination? Gandhi's view may be his religious hallucination. He does not believe so. He asks the people to address the wrongs he has patiently enumerated.

169. *On Non-Violence.* The non-violent protester works even when asleep, because his weapon is in his heart. The armed warrior must rest. *Refuse military service?* Yes, but non-violence is much more than that. When we pay taxes or cooperate otherwise, we support the military state. One must be willing not just to avoid fighting, but to be jailed or thrown into the street. *What about non-military service?* Non-military service cooperates with the militarist state. It is as violent as carrying guns. *Allowing other countries to be destroyed?* One should not allow that to happen.

An unarmed country could march *en masse* to the front, and stand before the armies, asking them to fight only by slaughtering the innocents intervening. Such courage is possible. If you die, you did your duty. *Soldiers firing in the air?* Such soldiers would be liars and cowards, and would discredit the non-violent war against war. Non-violent warriors must be morally pure and above reproach.

170. *What are Basic Assumptions*? Unity of all people and complete appreciation of non-violent principles by the masses are not requirements for Satyagraha. What is essential is the conviction that suffering by non-violent protesters can defeat armies. There are no historical precedents. This sort of thing works in families. Mankind is just a large family.

171. *Belief in God. Can atheists be Satyagrahi?* No. They may protest, but they will not be Satyagrahi. A non-violent protester suffers tortures without resentment. That sort of power comes only from god. I am no prophet, but just a human stumbling from error toward truth. You need not believe as I do. Your god may differ. But you must rely on him to be non-violent. *Must one wear khadi?* Yes. Those who decline may participate in the constructive work. My "Himalayan blunder" was to authorize people ill-prepared for the rigors of civil disobedience to resist. Violence ensued. *Foreign cloth?* No Satyagrahi may sell foreign cloth or use intoxicants, which skew his intelligence. *Non-violent protest in jail?* Yes, if required to defend one's dignity. But if one is easily provoked, it would be best not to head to jail in the first place.

172. *Not Guilty*. Dr. Lohia asks Gandhi to extend Satyagraha to programs other than Gandhi's own. Gandhi replies he has always welcomed such adventures, but never yet seen one. Congress has disputes with Gandhi. Non-violence in India's circumstance requires Hindu-Muslim unity, breakdown of untouchability rules, closing the intoxicant shops, and wearing home-spun clothing. Protests by peasants will not be non-violent; these persons have not been trained. Congress could train them, but has not. What is being provided is preparation for violence.

173. *Question Box [1]. Noncompliant Wife?* If one's wife refuses to deal with untouchables, she should have a separate kitchen and rooms. Do as is right. She will do as she pleases. *Congress's Views*. If Congress wishes to commence non-violent civil disobedience at a time when Gandhi disagrees, they have authority to proceed without Gandhi. *Secrecy?* There must be no secrecy. Open plans and books. Gandhi waffled on this before, but is firm now. Some disagree. *Property Damage?* Some maintain that property damage is not violence; they are wrong. Critics claim that I have taught the poor to be disruptive but not non-violent, and that my haste has made a mess. I cannot answer. I err. But I believe deeply in what I am doing. My tombstone may read that I invested much effort but achieved paltry results.

174. *Question Box [2]. Spinning?* Satyagrahi spin daily, unless ill or traveling. *Untouchability?* All Satyagrahi must renounce untouchability and welcome untouchables. This caste curse pollutes India and Hinduism. *Lawyers?* Some lawyers lie, and are impure. They cannot be Satyagrahi. But no profession is excluded from non-violence. *Obstructionism?* Some in Congress oppose measures unless their own party proffers them, and this is wrong. All owe a duty to support wise measures of the majority, regardless of party considerations.

175. *Five Questions. Legal Defense?* Satyagrahis, upon arrest, may offer legal defense. *Class Treatment?* No Satyagrahi, upon arrest, should seek to improve his

prison treatment by seeking to change his arrest classification. *Humane Treatment?* A Satyagrahi, upon arrest, should work to improve the humane treatment of prisoners. *Spinning Minimums?* One hour per day at 300 rounds per hour, unless doing public work. *Waiting Period?* None, but waiting to take the Satyagrahi pledge without cause is dishonest.

176. *The Sermon on the Mount. Should poor tenants give their coat and cloak to rapacious landlords?* Yes. They should abandon the landlord's lands. Giving a thief more than he sought to steal disarms him. This is the genius of non-violent non-cooperation. Jesus understood.

177. *What Can a Solitary Satyagrahi Do?* A lone Satyagrahi in a village conforms his life to that of the poorest members, he serves the villagers, welcomes all children as his own, spends only for strict necessities, and touches untouchables. He wastes no moments, but educates himself, spins, runs an ordered home. The village will be moved to follow. Gandhi says he cannot himself fulfill this ideal. One man making one ideal village may change the world.

178. *Non-Violent Non-Cooperation.* During World War II (1942) Gandhi was asked what he would do if the Japanese invaded. He said India would have to offer non-violent non-cooperation, perhaps at the loss of some millions of lives. But this would be no more than India would lose if resisting with arms.

179. *Sabotage and Secrecy.* A friend argued that government property belongs to the people, so he may destroy it without violence. Gandhi demurs. Such action would cripple government, injuring millions. The problem is men, not infrastructure. We must address the real problem. The friend objects that blowing up bridges encourages the protesters. Gandhi responds that some confused people think they can style violence as "sabotage" and remedy its ills by the name. The friend suggests that organizational secrecy may be strategically important, though personal secrecy is not. Gandhi rejects this proposition.

180. *Satyagraha in Face of Hooliganism.* A friend asked how to prevent gang thefts. Gandhi responds that one should love the hooligans and let them kill you, if necessary. But resist them peacefully. Aim for no result. Just show them love and non-violence while resisting. All Indians should learn self-defense in Satyagraha, which is primarily mental training in non-violence and courage.

181. *The Non-Violent Sanction. How does the non-violent protester cause the rich to do right by the poor?* First, the poor persons resist non-violently. They induce their neighbors to join them. Soon the whole village protests peacefully. Thus, Satyagraha teaches the public how to exercise power. All must learn to eschew hatred of opponents, choose only just causes, and suffer to success or death.

**Section Eleventh: Conclusion.**

182. *My Faith in Non-Violence.* Vanquish opponents with love. India has had failings. Violence has erupted, but the vast majority clings to non-violence. Gandhi can anger, but works hard to restrain himself. Love is like gravity. It works ceaselessly, a power as basic as physical forces, but less explored. Gandhi contemplates that he may be hallucinating about this.

183. *The Future.* A friend asks whether an independent India will adopt non-violence as state policy, and, if so, how India would defend itself from an armed

foreign invader. Gandhi says he does not know, since his education in non-violence is incomplete. Gandhi speculates that it is unlikely independent India will adopt non-violence as state policy. However, a well-trained country of non-violent believers could defend itself. First, the nation could welcome the invader, but refuse to cooperate. Second, the nation could descend upon the invader to die at the invader's hands. Even the worst humans have a heart which will eventually melt. The cost of such non-violence is unlikely to exceed the losses to violent resistance. Love rules mankind. If hatred and violence ruled, man would long ago have become extinct. Successes to date have been mixed. The generous critic will admit the experiments have promise.

## EPITOME 6

**Karen, Robert. *Becoming Attached: First Relationships and How They Shape Our Capacity for Love.* New York: Oxford University Press, 1998.**

*Robert Karen works as a private practice clinical psychologist and associate clinical professor at the Derner Institute of Advanced Psychology Studies of Adelphi University.*

**Introduction: How do we become who we are?** Everyone seeks love. Many encounter difficulties in achieving satisfying relationships. Parents set the stage for the emotional tenor of children. Attachment theory addresses the centrality of love between humans, how its roots emerge in parent-child relationships, how that relationship forms and endures, and the effects of damage to or insufficiency in the relationship. Attachment theory is deeply debated. Eugenics theorists argue children become what their genes dictate. Behaviorists argue that children are infinitely malleable. Psychoanalysts moderated these extremes. John Bowlby shaped attachment theory, arguing that first relationships determine much about future affection. Mary Ainsworth followed up Bowlby's theories with field research on mothers and babies in their homes. She found secure attachment (welcoming, responsive, attuned, and reliable) created emotional health. One-third of American children suffer insecure attachment. Attachment, secure or insecure, influences all of life. It echoes forward through time, affecting even a person's offspring. Insecure attachments can change, with some effort. Some attachment theorists view day care as a threat to child well-being, because the child may become anxiously attached. Feminists have objected to the over-emphasis on maternal influence. Other critics argue that attachment theorists under-appreciate the role of heredity in child and adult behavior. This book considers attachment, the evidence for attachment, and the arguments of the critics of attachment.

### Part I. What Do Children Need?

**1. Mother-Love: Worst-Case Scenarios**. Lacking a mother may cause inability to form relationships or interact with the world with normal emotionality. Mother-love suffers many injuries, any of which may lead to a mother's inability to care for her baby's difficulties. If mother's love is entirely absent, dire consequences follow for children. David Levy studied such circumstances. Children deprived in this way become shallow in affection, indifferent, absent pride of self, unmanageable (including sexual aggression, lying, theft, outbursts), and lacking in friendships. Levy postulated emotional starvation. Loretta Bender's research concurred. The children she investigated suffered emotional deprivation during formative years. In hospitals, concern for sterility led to a rule that none handled babies. Untouched babies failed to thrive and died in droves. When the rule was inverted, and all were urged to hold babies, survival rates soared. Inadequate attention to infant emotional needs damaged intelligence. A potent documentary on infant isolation (*Grief: A Peril in Infancy*) by Rene Spitz shocked child workers. It showed healthy babies collapsing into grief when mothers left them in good care for long periods. Some babies suffered permanent injury or even died.

**2. Enter Bowlby: The Search for a Theory of Relatedness.** John Bowlby's work drew further attention to infant-mother relations. The emotional quality of the home governs. Damage ensues if the infant is separated from its mother for a long period. Damage also ensues if the mother's emotions toward the infant are ambivalent. Personally, Bowlby was affable, but arrogant, and occasionally aggressive with unwanted interruption or dissent. Yet, his good manners helped him keep up relations with opponents. In youth, Bowlby suffered typical British upper-class distance from his parents, and boarding school at the age of eight. As an adult, Bowlby was taken by a fringe view of child-rearing: let them do as they please, and support their learning. Teaching at such a school, Bowlby saw the connection between troubled homes and disturbed behavior in children. Bowlby studied psychoanalysis. He resisted his own treatment. He joined Canonbury Clinic, a family mental health center. There, other workers showed him that a mother's unresolved emotional issues affected her parenting of her infant. They began treating both mother and child. Freud argued that neurosis found its source in childhood sexual trauma, real or imagined (Oedipal complex). Freudian analysts neglected environmental influences, favoring psychological ones. They neglected the real relationships their patients had with parents. Non-Freudians began arguing that humans have a fundamental need for meaningful connection to others, as deep a need as food or sex. Fairbairn criticized Freudian analysis, arguing that psychopathology emerged from early relational disturbances.

**3. Bowlby and Klein: Fantasy vs. Reality.** Melanie Klein developed psychoanalytic play theory. She argued that the maternal relationship becomes a template for adult relationships in every person. Klein found that the infant's imagined mother is more real than the actual mother, and the impact of the fantasy mother on the infant may be poorly correlated with the actual mother's mothering. Infants do not see persons, but pieces of persons: faces, breasts, hands. After six months, whole persons become present for the infant. For infants, the breast is critical, according to Klein. It is a good or evil breast, according to the experience of the infant with it. The infant rages, though not intellectually. Infants have a violent inner life. All future experience repeats this early drama of the good and evil breast. Klein described the "depressive position" that emerges for the child when it recognizes that the evil and good breasts are in fact the one person of the mother. Klein's views were ill-received by many. Klein's own difficult personality (devious and nasty) and ill-considered ethical choices (analyzing her own daughter) compounded the vigor of dissent to her views.

Melanie Klein became John Bowlby's supervisor. Klein immediately refused to let Bowlby treat disturbed children's social setting. Only the child's internalization mattered. Bowlby revolted, seeing clearly that, in his own view, real life experiences were the crux, not something to be regarded as unimportant. World War II intervened. Bowlby served, and Klein's supervision ended. Klein influenced Bowlby to consider infantile fantasy in his clinical and theoretical work.

**4. Psychopaths in the Making: Forty-four Juvenile Thieves.** Bowlby believed that parental response to children's inner conflicts diverted children down a path toward coping with their dramatic emotions or being controlled by them. Defenses bury unwanted feelings beneath consciousness: humor, sublimation, repression, reaction formation, passive-aggression, acting out, delusional projection, and reality denial. Bowlby researched forty-four adolescent thieves at the Child Guidance Center. All had poor or no parental relating in early life. Upon examination, all the parents were very dysfunctional. Bowlby needed a group of normal children and families to compare and contrast. But that lay beyond his resources and so a longitudinal study of these observations could not be mounted. So Bowlby turned his attention to one factor only: early prolonged separation from mother. Among his thieves who were affectionless (psychopathic), twelve of fourteen suffered early maternal disruption. Bowlby argued that symbolically the thefts were attempts to gather the affection missing from early life. The dearth of early affection also worked itself out in adult sexuality. Deprived children imagine their mothers as hateful, and so end up hating themselves. Interrupting this vicious circle perhaps lay beyond the coping skill of most parents. Bowlby's paper on the forty-four thieves was influential. Later research showed that mere separation did not cause psychopathy, but rather unremediated separation, where the child has no opportunity to establish true attachment to anyone.

**5. Call to Arms: The World Health Report.** The United Nations conducted a study of the needs of homeless children after World War II. Bowlby wrote a report on this subject, *Maternal Care and Mental Health*, which amalgamated research from Europe and the United States. Bowlby argued that maternal care was essential to infants, and separations injure both infants and, later, society as well. Institutions cannot provide the maternal care that babies elicit naturally from mothers. Neglected children grow up to become neglectful parents, and are a source of "social infection." Bowlby's report had massive impact. It generated massive response, both advocates and detractors.

**6. First Battlefield: "A Two-Year-Old Goes to Hospital."** In the 1950s and before, hospitalized young children's parents were excluded. These children suffered emotional trauma. Unable to understand the abandonment, young children despair, and become locked into permanent suspicion and alternatives to attachment (such as aggression, jealousy, theft). All suffered permanent insecurity about maternal abandonment. Even short separations (mere days) can cause deep emotional injury. Bowlby took over the Tavistock Clinic children's department. His associate, James Robertson, and Robertson's wife, Joyce, chronicled the emotional problems of young children separated from parents in the hospital ward. Robertsons' research was disregarded by hospital staff. Robertsons made a film of Laura, a two and one-half year old in hospital for eight days. The effects on self-possessed Laura were profound and enduring. Robertsons were savaged by hospital staffs for slandering them. But reviews of the research were generally positive, and deeply influential. A Glasgow hospital allowed one children's ward unrestricted maternal visits, and another would continue to follow the one-half hour twice weekly visitation schedule for parents. The experiment became the rule for the hospital. Robertsons made a follow-up film on going to hospital with mother. The attended child suffered none of the ill-effects of maternal absence. A series of subsequent films followed healthy young children separated from their ill mothers under nearly ideal conditions. All suffered separation anxiety that changed the course of their development somewhat. In one film, Robertsons depicted a seventeen-month old child in institutional care while his mother had another baby. The seventeen-month old suffered the expected damage, and it persisted for months after the nine day separation. Robertsons became alienated from Bowlby, though Bowlby's appreciation of the Robertsons persisted.

**7. Of Goslings and Babies: The Birth of Attachment Theory.** Bowlby encountered the imprinting work of Konrad Lorenz. Goslings imprint upon the first moving object they see after hatching. Ethologists (ethology studies animal behavior in natural settings), starting with Darwin, asserted that each species exhibits specific behaviors, as unique as their anatomy. Bowlby applied this learning to human infants, asserting humans are hard-wired for relationship, starting with mother. A baby's need for an attentive and reliable mother-figure is instinctive, just as providing that attention is instinctive for parents. Bowlby coined the term "attachment" for the constellation of behaviors a baby undertakes to elicit response from his caregivers (cooing, sucking, babbling, smiling, crying at departures, welcoming returns, clinging, following), and the response of the caregivers themselves to that infant. Attachment, in Bowlby's characterization, lies close to love. Having it, an infant prospers. Lacking attachment at critical junctures, depression, anxiety, and suffering follow for an infant. By 1950, most psychologists agreed that a child's earliest relationships are foundational and that mother is preeminent among those. But no one had a convincing theory. Buhler worked on the early facial "talk" between smiling mother and newborns. Balint argued that humans wish to be loved without conditions. If they lack this in childhood, they spend the remainder of life hunting for it. Winnicott's theory most strongly resembled Bowlby's, but they were very different sorts of people, and collaborated poorly. Bowlby delivered three papers. He argued that babies' behaviors aim to elicit care and stimulate parents to provide that care. It is multi-form, and not based solely on feeding. Neurosis derives from disturbances to a child's attachment system. By six or seven months of age, the infant recognizes mother in particular, and rejects parenting by other competent replacements. (The author, Robert Karen, disputes Bowlby on this count, arguing anecdotally that babies even earlier in their development show preference for their parents.) Bowlby called the child's hierarchy of care-giving preference "monotropy." Maternal absence produces astonishing anxiety in the abandoned child. Bowlby believed that attachment-disrupted children grieve as do adults suffering loss. Normal grief resolves. Pathological grief fails to resolve. Attachment disrupted children may never resolve their grief. As Freud developed an entire psychological framework commencing from hysteria, Bowlby started with separation.

**8. "What's the Use to Psychoanalyze a Goose?" Turmoil, Hostility, and Debate.** Some mothers, reading Bowlby's and Robertsons' works, came to dread leaving their babies for even a few hours. Bowlby sought to comfort and reassure these parents. Bowlby sympathized with the pressing emotional and physical demands of having a young child, and warned mothers that when they have babies, they face five years of hard labor. If a substitute caregiver (say, a nanny) spends a great deal of time with the child, she must remain until the child reaches six years of age. She will become the emotional "mother." Bowlby recommended against child hospitalizations, and insisted mothers stay with children who must be hospitalized. When separation was unavoidable, Bowlby recommended the child be cared for by a familiar person who is willing to provide care full-time during mother's absence. Even with such care, the child will be disturbed by mother's absence. Re-attachment will require time and great affection and reassurance. Bowlby created an ancillary furor by asserting that father's parental role was to support mother. His absence at work precluded him providing fundamental security to his children. Bowlby urged mothers never to stint on giving their child attention and affection, for, if absent, one can never really replace what was lost. Over time, Bowlby came to recognize that humans better make up early losses than do goslings. Still, he recommended that mothers take a leave of absence from the workplace until their young children mature (age 3-6). Critics (Melanie Klein and Anna Freud) emphasized that a child's fantasies about maternal inattention were of as much effect as real inattention. Bowlby countered that fantasies find their first brick in reality. Freudian critics argued that Bowlby so focused on human relations as to neglect what was going on in the child's head. Babies are not fish or birds. What distinguishes them is what goes on in babies' heads. Anna Freud and Melanie Klein were dogmatic authoritarian personalities. All who disagreed with them, were, in their view, wrong. Bowlby disagreed, and held all psychoanalytical pronouncements up to experimental scrutiny. Bowlby himself could be utopian, imagining that once parenting disasters were avoided, man would be less tortured and more amicable. Some colleagues believed Bowlby aimed to destroy psychoanalysis. For many analysts, allegiance to Freud's theory was inseparable from their work and identities. Bowlby's theory could not be adapted (or Bowlby would not make the effort to adapt it). The British psychoanalytic conventions at which Bowlby read his papers roiled. Sessions were added to accommodate the extended debates. Bowlby withdrew from the Psychoanalytic Society, so threatened by his work, and interacted little for the next three decades. Some research undercut Bowlby's previous findings. Children responded differently to maternal deprivation. Character deformation proved more complex than mere social disruption. Critics tore apart many studies' methodologies or reporting standards. The case for Bowlby's views sagged.

**9. Monkey Love: Warm, Secure, Continuous.** Harry Harlow at University of Wisconsin had disease-borne deaths among his experimental rhesus monkeys. He separated sixty babies shortly after birth to an antiseptic isolation. The babies bonded to the cloth diapers on the cage floors. Subsequent experiments reproduced Bowlby's child observations in rhesus infants. Cuddling mattered more than breasts. All attached to their woefully defective wire mesh mother-surrogates. All suffered later difficulty relating or raising their own young. Bowlby went to Wisconsin to see Harlow; they remained in touch with one another's work. The United Nations elected to do a follow-up study to Bowlby's 1951 report. Mary Ainsworth drafted the core review. She took apart criticisms of Bowlby's work, and sorted maternal deprivations into three types: insufficiency, neglect, and separation. This resolved many internal conflicts in Bowlby's work. The rhesus monkey work continued, showing results that supported Bowlby's theories. Ainsworth concluded that Bowlby's work was essentially sound.

### Part II. Breakthrough: The Assessment of Parenting Style

**10. Ainsworth in Uganda.** Ainsworth, already a faculty member, followed her younger husband to London, where she answered a help-wanted ad placed by Bowlby. They worked together for more than three years. Later, Ainsworth studied the mother-child relationship in the child's first year in their natural environment in Uganda. Ainsworth observed twenty-eight babies in their familial settings for a period of nine months, visiting each for about two hours every other week. Ainsworth noted the milestones in infant development and attachment in detail, concluding that mother provided a secure base from which a child can, without anxiety, move out to explore her environment. Ainsworth found five phases of attachment development: a) undiscriminating (newborn), b) differential responsiveness, in which the baby shows preference for the mother, c) differential preference at a distance, in which the baby greets or objects to the mother's comings and goings, d) active initiative, in which the infant follows the mother and begins exploring around the mother, and e) stranger anxiety, in which the infant recognizes outsiders and watches them. Parenting style mattered in attachment. Infants failed to attach to distant mothers, but attached to others who were responsive. Five of her twenty-eight (18%) *failed to attach*. Ainsworth struggled to differentiate why some babies did not cry when mothers left them; was it a secure relationship or failure of attachment? Seven babies were *insecurely attached*. These babies initially looked secure and attached, but grew less so as the months passed. Their mothers were dutiful and affectionate, but distracted. Total amount of care provided by extended family did not prove significant. The securely attached infants got the most care, the unattached the least, and the insecurely attached were in between. Ainsworth's book, *Infancy in Uganda*, established the concept of the "secure base."

**11. The Strange Situation.** Ainsworth moved to Johns Hopkins University and divorced. Bowlby learned of her Uganda research and saw its relevance to his work. They became intellectual partners. Ainsworth did a longitudinal study of Baltimore mothers and infants. She chose twenty-six families with babies coming. Her team would make eighteen visits of four hours each over the infant's first year. Ainsworth found all sixteen attachment behaviors the same in Ugandan and American babies (with two cultural deviations). American babies were less insecure than Ugandan about the maternal secure base when at the mother's home. Ainsworth devised a lab experiment to test whether the secure base idea pertained as in Uganda. A lab with three chairs and toys was established. An infant came with its mother to the lab for an eight episode event. A stranger joins them. The mother leaves. The stranger leaves. The stranger returns. The mother returns. This arrangement was called the "strange situation." Some insecurely attached babies experienced great difficulty with the separations, and only slowly reestablished connection with the mother, all the while both wanting and resisting reconnection (ambivalent babies). Others were barely perturbed by the separations, and sought less comfort from the mother. These often expressed some hostility or even anger (avoidant babies). Ainsworth developed a mothering scale: 1) sensitive to baby's signals, 2) accepting of the baby, 3) cooperating with baby's desires, and 4) availability to baby. Securely attached babies have mothers high on these standards. Insecurely attached babies had mothers who scored poorly on these measures. The quality, not quantity, of mothering mattered most. Ainsworth subdivided her three groups (secure, ambivalent, and avoidant) into eight subcategories. These categories became a metric for parenting and attachment. They demonstrated what Bowlby had urged: early parenting behaviors were crucial to a child's emotional development. And Ainsworth's work built bridges, much in decay under Bowlby, back to the psychoanalytic community.

**12. Second Front: Ainsworth's American Revolution.** Young scholars began adopting attachment theory as their base of experiment. These researchers recognized in Ainsworth's approach a shift from counting behaviors to exploring the meaning of a child's and mother's interactions. The unit of study was no longer the individual, but rather the dyad. These young researchers found that attachment styles persisted into the baby's future. Ainsworth and her colleagues taught in institutions with behaviorist orientations. Watson and Skinner were pre-eminent. Consciousness was discounted, behavior lionized. Thought was subvocal speech. All human behavior derived from environmental stimuli; none was inherent. Behaviorists had little patience for Ainsworth's emphasis on relationships and qualitative analysis. And they rejected Bowlby's view that attachment is an inborn need of and structure within babies. The behaviorist faculties declined to fund Ainsworth's ongoing studies. But slowly, as the children evaluated in the Strange Situation labs developed, the attachment styles were correlated with a vast host of behaviors in older children. Ainsworth slowly prevailed.

## Part III. The Fate of Early Attachments

**13. The Minnesota Studies: Parenting Style and Personality Development.** Bowlby used the Ainsworth data to argue that infants who enjoyed sensitive responsiveness to their needs developed secure attachment to a trusted figure, which served, as the infant matured, to make her self-reliant, while still trusting in and collaborating with others. Sroufe conducted longitudinal studies of children with known attachment histories to see what came of secure and insecure attachments. Sroufe believed that secure attachment led to high quality adaptation to the changes and new circumstances maturation brings infants. Securely attached children, faced with a difficult play problem, persisted, better managed frustration, appropriately sought assistance, and sought autonomy. Ambivalent or avoidantly attached children performed less well. Mahler's research showed that toddlers want mother's participation in all they do, but also push mother away for growing independence. Mothers of securely attached toddlers remained deeply involved, but now encouraged problem-solving and independence. They gave just what was needed to keep the toddler exploring and solving. Mothers of anxiously or avoidantly attached toddlers failed to keep their distance or stay involved. At three and one-half years, securely attached children were more advanced in other relationships. Egeland conducted the next set of studies, which involved 267 low-income single pregnant women. Egeland studied child abuse; Sroufe studied attachment patterns. Evaluations of mother's emotional state and enthusiasm for pregnancy predicted the sort of attachment their babies would achieve. One neurological study correlated a predictor with ambivalent attachment (which created a firestorm in later debates). When the children reach age four and one-half, the researchers created a pre-school attended by forty of the sample children. Securely attached children outperformed others in every category of analysis. Secure children were more likely to show empathy. Insecurely or avoidantly attached children were, respectively, more likely to feel personally injured or revel in others' pain. Sroufe identified three avoidant types: lying bullies, shy detached emotionally flat children, and detached twitching daydreamers. Sroufe identified two ambivalent types: impulsive fidgeters with low concentration, and fearful, sensitive, hiding child with low initiative. All seemed to suffer painful feelings of separation; all were highly dependent. Avoidant children, in their lying and aggression and projected false self-confidence, angered teachers. Ambivalent children, who showed insecurity, elicited sympathy and were judged according to lower standards. The Minnesota studies show the influence of early attachment patterns to emotional patterns of adulthood. The studies, however, failed to prove that secure attachment caused emotional health (temperament must also be a factor), and not all children observed followed the predicted patterns at all. The Minnesota studies faced political opposition, coming at a time when women were entering the work force and revising their parenting styles. Attachment theory exposed that western reliance upon mothers as the generally sole instrument of nurturing young children, with paternal absence, is unworkable, given the fragility of life stability in the first place. We rely on mother nurture more than other cultures and more than other times in history. Attachment theory identified mothers as the problem. Critics seized on this.

**14. The Mother, the Father, and the Outside World: Attachment Quality and Childhood Relationships.** As the Minnesota subjects aged into social relations with outsiders, the patterns continued. Securely attached children made sensitive partners, formed friendships, and played creatively. Avoidantly attached children did not want relationships and took advantage of weaker playmates. Ambivalently attached children wanted relationships but proved incompetent in forming them. When avoidant children were matched with ambivalent ones, avoidant cruelty often followed. Securely attached children avoid aggression, withdraw or transform relationships that pose dangers, and use force only as a last resort, and then as little as possible. Empathic, peacemaking children have experienced empathic, peaceful core relationships and export that model to their social environment. In early adolescence, social groups formed from entirely securely attached children. Ambivalent children could not navigate the social requirements of participation without alienating their peers. Among the children, sexual differences emerged. Avoidant boys tended toward violence, lying, and boasting. Avoidant girls tended to internalize their stresses, becoming depressed or feeling shame. Sexual differentiation in behavior was minimal in securely attached children. Insecure girls tend to smile inordinately. Ainsworth believed that the system involved in social relations is more complex than early attachment can explain. Sroufe's longitudinal studies of these Minnesota children may prove that early attachment profiles project far into adult life, affecting even the attachment patterns of children born to the Minnesota subjects.

Researchers began to investigate paternal attachment. Distressed infants prefer mothers, but reach out to fathers whenever mothers are absent and in the same ways they reach out to mothers. Among securely attached children, those most secure and empathetic had secure attachment to both parents. The secondary caregiver, usually father, is not a lesser mother. Fathers, when attached to toddlers, provide exciting play and a bridge to the world beyond mother. Fathers offer something mothers cannot. Fathers provide to sons a model with which to identify. Though fathers often become significantly involved with their children only when they are older, their impact, especially in their satisfaction or dissatisfaction with the mother, proves formative to the partners' children. These powerful observations about the predictive impact of early attachment patterns created a tidal wave in academic psychology.

**15. Structures of the Mind: Building a Model of Human Connection.** Why are emotional habits acquired early in life so persistent and predictive of future outcomes? Early emotional experience becomes a blueprint for future events and relationships. Psychoanalysis dealt with these issues by talk of "transference," but Bowlby sought to clear away the brambles with his "internal working model." Piaget described an infant's flexible learning programs, which, elaborated by experience, develop into adult intelligence. Working from Piaget's research, Bowlby described the internal working model, a mental structure in infants that makes of early relational experience a template for future intimacies, how one views and feels about himself and others. Attachment creates sufficient security to enable exploration. Injured or scared during exploration, an infant returns to the safe haven of the attached adult to recover and refuel. Anxiously attached children have rigid internal working models; their experiences do not update their model as happens in securely-attached children. The anxiously-attached (ambivalent or avoidant) person gives little, distrusts, ignores or misinterprets persons offering friendship, pretends superiority, stands off and backs away. Having done so, his future relationships reflect these attitudes, confirming anxious attachment's predictions. In children, the internal working model is complicated by a large number of distortions and misinterpretations the children suffer, due to their lack of experience. These distorted internal working models may be revised later in life. But the feelings these distortions engender are often repressed, becoming buried and denied. Anxious attachment tends to rob children of the capabilities necessary to work through distorted internal models. Anxiously attached children have reduced ability for self-reflection, less ability to imagine what others might be feeling when it differs from their own feelings, and reduced ability to recall the past accurately. Bowlby's "internal working model" is now viewed as simplistic, failing to take seriously the depth of misery that dysfunctional psychological patterns may inflict on people. But Bowlby's work encouraged cross-disciplinary studies and a vast body of empirical research.

**16. The Black Box Reopened: Mary Main's Berkeley Studies.** Mary Main, who studied under Ainsworth, collaborated in a longitudinal study of forty six-year olds. By showing them pictures of children separating from parents, the group accurately identified attachment style in seventy-nine percent. Securely attached children were able to discuss what the pictured children might be experiencing. Avoidant children, however, struggled to express themselves, and saw few options for coping.

They were flooded with anxiety. Ambivalent children expressed contradictory impulses of wanting proximity and rage at abandonment. They often imagined killing a parent. Disturbed children (a fourth category) expressed intense fear in language that was frequently nonsense. Main's contribution lay in her recognition that attachment styles affect more than behavior. Attachment determines the structure of a child's brain, and affects attention, memory, and thinking. Behaviorists had discredited speaking of the mind because it is a black box from which behavior emerges. All mind talk was gibberish to behaviorists. Main disagreed. She set a student, Jude Cassidy, to studying the tapes of the reunions of the six-year olds with their parents. Slowly, Cassidy found observable differences in how the children interacted with their returning parents. She showed that the internal working model had rooted in six-year olds. These studies moved child attachment theory closer to its roots in psychoanalysis.

**17. They Are Leaning Out for Love: The Strategies and Defenses of Anxiously Attached Children, and the Possibilities for Change.** Insecurely attached (ambivalent or avoidant) children suffer unconscious strategies for coping with their primary caregiver's neglect or unavailability or indecision, and the furious emotions that well up within such a child, once slighted. Given the diversity among people, all generalizations neglect special coping skills of some, special alternative relationships, and mixtures and degrees of relating strategies. Nevertheless, some generalizations seem warranted.

Ten percent of middle class children are *ambivalently attached*. They over-focus on mother, wheedling to get attention, finding dangers to be protected from. In the end, they fail to believe they have what it takes to get what they want from another person. Klein emphasized the roiling emotional life of the insecurely attached child, the rage and aggression, self-loathing and anxiety. Ambivalent children fail to learn that mother can weather their rage while it dissipates, and suffer no ill-effects, while for the child, his rage seems uncontrolled and permanent. Ambivalent children often have unconscious fantasies of grisly retaliations against their love object. Refusal to receive offered love, when that is what is desperately wanted, is a form of aggression. It may relate to anorexia and sadistic emotional injury of others, all coupled with a fatalistic sense of repeating mother's history.

Twenty percent of middle class children are *avoidantly attached*. Such children turn off, seeming to need no love. The child preserves proximity to mother, without really relating to mother. He develops anger toward mother and others, grandiose self-deceptions, feelings of superiority, and detachment. His anger threatens all relationships.

Avoidant and ambivalent attachment arise from unsuitable mothering, ignorance of the damage caused by absences, and premature training for independence, life stresses, overwhelmed parents, and parental psychological dysfunctions. A child with anxious maternal attachment may keep more secure patterns of relating alive if she is able to find an adult who relates to her in a secure manner. Still, the coping mechanisms of anxiously attached children tend to drive away those who might substitute. Where caregivers can persevere through hostility and ill-behavior, some insecurely attached children learn to attach to that caregiver and begin to take care of their intimacy needs. The child may change, but does so more readily when young.

Adolescence and adulthood make all more committed to familiar patterns. A great problem in anxious attachment lies in the child's ability to trigger aspects of the parents' personalities that are themselves disturbed. Anxious attachment is frustrated love. Addressing anxious attachment requires consistent and persistent return to the child, in the face of ill-behavior and rejection, until the child builds up, as from little bricks, a revised interior model. Often, especially when the child's anxious attachment derives from the parent, this proves difficult for the parent, because it flies in the face of the parent's own internal working model. Even the most difficult avoidant child leaves open opportunities for changed relations with parents. But the opportunities are few, and likely to be initially rejected. Karen recounts his own, and another child patient's experiences of anxious attachment, and moving away from it.

A difficulty lies in the anxiously attached child's interpretations of positive emotions. In his experience of mother, she remains outwardly warm, while inwardly demanding and unavailable. The child associates pleasant emotions with hidden coercion. Such a child exemplifies a fourth category of attachment: *disorganized attachment.* He exhibits characteristics of both avoidant and ambivalent attachment.

Lieberman began to treat mother and child in therapy. As mothers of anxiously attached babies were able to recount their own sordid pasts and sufferings, the mothers' ability to attach to their babies surged. After one year of such intervention, none among 100 anxiously-attached mother-child pairs could be distinguished from pairs with initial secure ratings. The Strange Situation test is a research tool, not a forensic measure. It should not be used to assess individual parent-infant dyads.

**18. Ugly Needs, Ugly Me: Anxious Attachment and Shame**. Consistent, reliable care builds self-esteem in children. They believe they deserve love and can affect their world positively. The anxiously attached child views himself negatively, feeling shame at what he is. He may feel the need to hide the ugly distrust, bitterness, and hatred within. The anxiously-attached child learns shame about those aspects of himself that his parents reject or ridicule. Where anxiously-attached children cope poorly with parental emotion and their responses to that emotion, shame emerges. The negative emotions of a securely-attached child get expressed, and parents respond to those communications meaningfully. Mothers of anxiously-attached children tend to ignore the negative emotions of their children. Parental anger, expressed volubly or suppressed, tends to make a child feel worthless. The parent of a securely-attached child expresses anger in a self-restrained manner, aimed to help the child process that anger. A parent whose dependency needs were unmet as a child finds it difficult to tolerate his child expressing that same unmet need. The child meets over-reaction or a dismissive rebuff. Shame may have evolutionary import. We evolved needing attachment; when that need is unmet, shame is attachment's opposite. Childhood attachment quality rings forward through personal histories. There are other influences (intellectual ability, non-maternal attachment figures, resilience, adult choices). But attachment style rumbles beneath all.

**19. A New Generation of Critics: The Findings Contested.** Jerome Kagan criticized all of attachment theory's premises. Anxious attachments reflect, not parental style, but a child's temperament and its learning of parental values. Human intimacy crumbles; we invent mythologies to support it, like maternal nurture in attachment theory. Socially-deprived infants do recover in appropriately nurturing environments, Kagan argued. Kagan's line of thought went like this: Children differ. They change, as their environments change. Why focus on year one? The "internal working model" is an unlikely theory for which there exists little support. Temperament matters most, then environment. In response to Kagan's assertions, Sroufe undertook analysis of children who had shown noteworthy declines or improvements from their early assessments. Sroufe found that shadows of initial attachment formats remain, even where there is overall improvement. And there are instances of marked decline from formerly secure attachment. Longitudinal studies by Crowell and Waters show that among the earliest tested children, now adults, 69% retain their Strange Situation classifications, and when adjusted for untoward life events (death of mother), 77% retain those classifications. Karen concludes: a) attachment patterns exist, b) they show up as early as year one, and c) they affect people later in life, often deeply, becoming a component of our individual psychology. Having occurred pre-lingually, they are deeply buried and difficult to access. The attachment process continues past the first year. But the first year is critically important. All should want mothers and their babies to get off to a good start in those crucial early months.

The Grossman longitudinal studies in Germany (Bielefeld) failed to replicate the American findings in very young children. Many more were avoidant (two-thirds insecure, and one half avoidant), which Grossman's attributed to German cultural value for independence. Mothers pushed away infants as young as ten months, wanting them to begin self-restraint. A second study (Regensburg) closely matched the American results. Grossmans found that securely attached children profited from that orientation. The mothers of securely attached children were "less" German in their expectations, and better adapted personally. The northern German mothers were less rejecting than rejecting American mothers. There were more reversals of orientation in the German children.

Michael Lamb's critique of Ainsworth's studies cuts to their core, and his tone was insolent. Professional colleagues declined even to comment in response to his articles. Lamb's critique, however caustic, made points: the Strange Situation studies addressed small numbers of individuals, there were few cross-checks, and replication studies were few. Karen finds these issues relevant and lingering.

## Part IV. Give Parents a Break! Nature-Nurture Erupts Anew

**20. Born That Way? Stella Chess and the Difficult Child**. Advice on child-rearing mutated from the "do-not-coddle" position of Watson to permissiveness in the 1950s. Benjamin Spock noted pervasive confusion and problems raising children. Stella Chess noted that attachment theory made mothers feel encompassing guilt about their children's problems. Chess believed that children have temperaments, and these interact with nurture to produce personality traits. David Levy too found that maternal style interacted with the underlying predilections of the child. Chess conducted a longitudinal study of temperament's effect on later problems. She assessed 136 infants for activity level, the reliability of his or her biological rhythms, whether the child favored or disfavored new experiences, how the child adapted to new events over time, the intensity of reaction to discomforts, how intense new experiences have to be before eliciting response, general mood, distractability, and length of focus on an activity. Chess, from these characteristics, defined four types of temperament: difficult, slow to warm up, easy, and mixed. Some parental temperaments match poorly with their children's temperaments, with expected poor outcomes. As Chess's study progressed, some seventy percent of difficult temperament children suffered problems requiring therapeutic attention. In Chess's view, temperaments interacted with environment to produce personality traits. Differing parental responses produced markedly different outcomes for children of like temperament. Culture and the wider social circle also produced effects. Chess's research, which continued for three decades into these children's lives, emphasizes that one size does not fit all. Parents must adjust their approaches to the temperaments of their children. Chess's colleagues disparaged the attachment theorists, and vice versa. Attachment theorists criticized Chess's timing, reliance on parental self-reports, typology of temperaments and the underlying characteristics, and emphasis on fit between parent's and child's respective temperaments. The parties polarized, then warred.

**21. Renaissance of Biological Determinism: The Temperament Debate.** Both Bowlby and Ainsworth recognized infant temperament differences, but did not emphasize them. Genetic studies, however, showed massive hereditary influence on personality, as demonstrated by separated identical twins studies. These studies showed twin convergence on matters often deemed mere historical or cultural trivia. Twin studies had extensive influence. Physiological studies confirmed twin similarities on a deeper biological level. Kagan's research on fearful toddlers led him to believe that people come in breeds, like dogs, and do not change their breed. Families have influences, but they are influencing the outcome of a genetic basis.

Behavior geneticists attacked attachment theory in two ways. First, they assaulted the blame of mothers and the neglect of the idea of "poor fit" between mother's and infant's temperaments. Second, the behavior geneticists attacked the research underlying attachment theory, arguing that it in fact measured temperament, not attachment. Avoidant and ambivalent babies became the core dispute, each side arguing that the observed behaviors related to temperament or maternal attachment, depending on ideological commitments. Researchers turned to studies. Van Boom chose 100 babies classified highly irritable at birth. Fifty mother-baby pairs were given six hours of counseling about how to relate to a fussy baby. The other fifty received no such counseling. More than twice as many of the irritable babies whose mothers received counseling were classified as securely attached at one year. Clearly, maternal style was a critical, but not sole, determinant of secure attachment. Intense irritability in babies (temperament) also played a role. Behavior geneticists have found genetic influences, much to the detriment of environmental ones. Heralding genes and temperaments, they have neglected environmental influences, even when those are patent. Despite geneticist claims to the contrary, first relationships remain potent influences on the person's ultimate ability to form lasting, meaningful relationships. Babies attune to their caregiving environment. What we have assumed to be temperamental, may in fact be environmental caregiving mismatch. The debate has been beneficial to both attachment theorists and behavior geneticists. Each is coming to grapple with the data of the other.

**22. A Rage in the Nursery**: **The Infant Day-Care Wars**. Attachment theory raised questions about the monumental social shift of women from homes to the workplace. Was mother work injuring infants? Was daycare imperiling future attachment? Non-attachment theories and feminists attacked the attachment findings. Research comparing daycare to home care was contradictory. The studies of daycare placements suffered from massive circumstantial differences and some poorly structured investigations. Bowlby asserted, in his blunt style, that mothers should be primary caregiver for their children and not work until the child was ready to go to preschool (age three). This made Bowlby the feminist demon, until Belsky took over the job. After initially resisting the data, Belsky opined that more than twenty hours per week in daycare for a first year child created an increased risk for anxious attachment and its behavior problems. Feminist political operatives and their academic supporters scourged Belsky for questioning their orthodoxies. Regardless the political fallout, the data showed that the Strange Situation identified insecure attachment in just the sort of curve one would expect: descending insecure attachment as one progresses from abused children, to children of depressed mothers, to children spending more than twenty hours per week in daycare, to children from stable homes with less than twenty hours per week in daycare. Belsky's predilection for blunt talk and seeking volatile venues (Good Morning America) partly explains his demonization. Belsky's research, despite making him a pariah, brought the issue to the fore. Does daycare harm infants? Studies of daycare show dramatically low quality care (9% offer high quality care). In Vandell's study of Dallas third-graders, children who as infants had thirty or more hours of daycare scored lowest in emotional well-being, work habits, relationships with other children, and compliance with teachers. Bates's study found a direct correlation between infant hours in daycare and problems with aggression at age five. European studies, where quality of care is high, show that such high quality care can not only match, but may outperform, parental care. Such high quality care is rare in the United States. But in the media, there is reticence to say so. And the business culture of the United States fails to accommodate the needs of parents without attendant loss of career possibilities. The attachment community of scholars seems to have reached consensus that parents can put infants in high-quality alternative care and not injure that baby. Still most developmental psychologists believe that a parent should stay home with his or her infant for a period of months following birth. Nanny care has the same problems as daycare in increasing insecure attachment. Government policy should make high quality day care available to all citizens. But there is a lack of political will in this regard.

**23. Astonishing Attunements**; **The Unseen Emotional Life of Babies**. Babies are born social. They recognize faces, prefer mother's smells, and remember emotions. Mothers attune to their babies, giving them security in the midst of their vulnerabilities. An infant's emotional health is erected upon the scaffold of his mother's attuned involvement for an extended period of that child's infancy. Mother-child relational exchanges came under examination. Researchers found an intricate skein of mother-child interactions in which the child led and the mother followed, but elaborated in variations of intensity, timing, and length. Mothers who synchronize well with their infants create secure attachment. Intrusive mothers foster avoidant babies. As language develops, the mother's interaction serves to delimit the range of acceptable behavior and expression. Research shows that ambivalently attached children have mothers mis-attuned except as to baby's fears. Mothers of avoidant babies mis-attuned to babies' negative feelings, but gloried in their play. Well-attuned mothers lose themselves in their babies for a time, but slowly emerge from their monomania to broader life, just as the infant himself seeks greater autonomy. He comes to see others having lives independent from his own. Infants at this stage adopt transitional objects (teddy bear, doll, favorite blanket). No mother is perfect, nor should she be. Mothers should be "good-enough," as Winnicott put it. The attachment patterns of a person tend to project into his or her own parenting.

### Part V. The Legacy of Attachment in Adult Life

**24. The Residue of Our Parents: Passing on Insecure Attachment.** The parent-child dyad elicits powerful emotions, akin to new romance in intensity. Some of these emotions are negative: jealousy, hatred, or resentment, for example. In parents, when suppressed, these emotions later emerge veiled, recapitulating the parent's childhood emotional experience of home. Mary Main studied transmission of attachment styles from parent to child in a Berkeley study. Main found that adults' recollections of their attachment childhood fell into three categories, reflecting the Strange Situation categories:

1) Secure-autonomous (= secure attachment). These parents speak with ease and perspective about parents and childhood, and rely on important relationships. A great majority of their children are securely-attached.

2) Dismissive-of-attachment (= avoidant attachment). These parents speak haltingly of childhood and parents, and feel compelled to respond to the interviewer's impertinent questions. Such parents have recollections that contradict their representations of their parents and childhoods. Three-fourths of the children of dismissive parents are avoidantly-attached.

3) Pre-occupied with early attachments (which is ambivalent attachment). These parents are still actively engaged with their childhood parental lapses. They suffer little appreciation of their own role in failed and failing relationships. The great majority of their children are ambivalently-attached.

Fonagy's research with mothers before birth enabled him to predict with seventy-five percent accuracy the attachment style of the subsequently-born child in the Strange Situation. These mothers' interviews showed that they were projecting, often unconsciously, their own childhood experiences upon the as-yet-unborn experience of their infants. The degree of researcher subjectivity in rating adult subjects is substantially higher than among Strange Situation researchers.

Fonagy and Main found that what differentiates secure from anxious adults is the ability to understand their own and others' inner motivations. The avoidant mothers were distant, un-insightful about their own feelings, and failed to lead their infant into comfort with the child's inner world, just as the parent remained uncomfortable. The avoidantly-attached mother keeps the baby at a distance, because proximity re-opens the mother's own infancy, so filled with pain and anxiety. Mothers of anxiously-attached infants may perpetuate their child's anxiety by being inconsistently available. This theory explains much. But it also fails to explain much. Why do some children have anxiously-attached parents but grow up secure? What role do fathers play in attachment types?

Parents, in order to avoid reproducing their own insecurities and attachment defects in their children, need to face their own histories and its effects upon their own psychologies. And that is painful.

**25. Attachment in Adulthood: The Secure Base vs. The Desperate Child Within.** Karen tells the tale of an avoidant, but talented, judge who goes berserk after losing his adoring mistress, and ends up in jail. Bowlby believed that attachment style governed the emotional tenor not only of parenting, but of all of a person's emotional life. Studies find that emotional health creates self-reliance conjoined with appropriate dependence on trusted others, and derives from a home with two loving, emotionally-available parents and a mother devoted to the child's security in infancy. Solitude is healthy only when one departs for a time from a secure social base, to which one returns after an appropriate period. Ambivalent or avoidant persons experience debilitating loneliness, and tend to grow addicted to people (for ambivalently-attached persons) or to work things, promotions, and obsessions (for avoidantly-attached persons).

Loss of an attachment figure can debilitate even adults. Those who suffer such griefs slowly restructure their emotional lives to rely on new attachment figures. But avoidant persons fail to appreciate the damage losing important relationships will inflict upon them. Ambivalent persons grow panicked about separations and resist them.

Hazan and Shaver studied self-reported attachment styles in adults. In romantic relationships, secure partners trust their lovers and accept their flaws. Avoidant partners fear intimacy, reject feelings of love, and suffer jealousy. Ambivalent partners obsess over their lovers. In adult exploration of life, secure persons explore and prosper. Ambivalent persons procrastinate, lose focus, and fuss over interpersonal matters. Avoidant persons work too much, letting tasks abort social relations, but prosper financially. But there are limitations to the Hazan and Shaver methodology. Self-reports may be inaccurate, and the romantic reports may reflect more the current love interests of the interviewees than their long term attachment styles. Adult attachment may be substantially more nuanced, with alcoves of different relating styles for different circumstances. Some researchers believe that the three categories are too simple and fail to comprehend mixed states and complex, changing relationships.

Psychoanalysis has begun reintegrating attachment theory, revising the pre-oedipal states to accommodate the attachment research. There is some correlation between attachment states and psychiatric diagnoses. Nevertheless, attachment styles are not pathological in all circumstances, but rather broad, general observations of relational styles. Anxious attachment may, for some, become pathological, especially under severe stresses. Karen draws explicit links between severe anxious attachment and narcissism, compulsive personality, schizoid personality, and borderline personality. Karen appreciates Roger Kobak's attachment continuum, which links normal experience of attachment issues to pathological states as degrees of experience.

**26. Repetition and Change**: **Working Through Insecure Attachments**. In transference (a psychoanalytic term) a patient projects childhood roles upon his therapist: parent, friend, lover. Attachment theorists find people transferring in many circumstances, especially when the emotional trigger is potent. Sullivan argued that we each have a self developed response to some primary figure in our infancy, and we play out those various selves throughout life. Freud believed that we prefer relationships that recapitulate our early models, even when those relationships are unsatisfying. Freud called this "repetition compulsion." Bewitched by failings of parental attachment, the adult repetitively seeks the same sort of pain experienced as an infant. Worse, the person caught in such a pattern rejects better loves because they feel strange to him. Especially in sexual relationships, the ambivalent or avoidant adult plays out dramas of rejection, though secure relationship may be offered. Shame recurs. Ambivalent adults feel shame. Avoidant adults evade and suppress shame. Adults may find other models from childhood that assist them in coping with anxious attachments. Therapy may help, providing insight and safe conversation from which to begin to cope. The clean and simple world of the therapeutic relationship can provide a venue in which to experience self-sympathy and self-love, leading eventually to a reappraisal of one's thwarted early attachment needs and self-reflection that is healing. In secure love relationships, people go over and over things that could not be addressed with parents, sometimes resolving persistent emotional tangles. The marriage becomes a secure attachment at the core of life. To break the intergenerational cycle of transmissible emotional damage of anxious attachment, one needs a secure attachment figure in childhood, or in-depth psychotherapy, or a stable and lovingly responsive spouse. With these helps, anxiously attached people may not engender anxious attachment in their children and associates. For some, having a baby offers opportunity to cope with anxious attachment issues. We may respond to parental inadequacies in two ways, neither of which is very helpful: first, we feel they are not to be criticized, since, despite their flaws, they provided for us, or, second, we rage against their flaws. Karen believes one must experience the injuries parents inflicted in one's childhood, but move past them thoughtfully. Though childhood cannot be improved once its time has passed, one can adjust one's attitudes now, re-examine both oneself and one's parents from an adult perspective, and adequately mourn the losses one experienced as a child.

## Part VI. The Odyssey of an Idea

**27. Avoidant Society**: **Cultural Roots of Anxious Attachments**. Pre-modern society consisted in community life: families, towns, guilds, extended friends and support, churches. Despite interpersonal bickering and absence of personal freedom or social mobility, people were secure and knew they were part of their community. Their many intimacies were attachments. In the modern era, industry and politics combined to erode that sense of place and safety. Competition replaced cooperation. The sphere of attachment shrank dramatically. People were not sure they had a place in society. Children lost their many associates, and were left with two (possibly, one) attachment figure: the parent. And that parent became unsupported by family and friends in many instances. People moved, dousing reciprocity (how can you help me if you will be across the country thirteen months from now? So, why should I help you now?). Life's pace accelerated, leaving less social interaction. Every member of modern society became anxiously attached to that society.

In primitive Yequana society (Venezuelan jungles), Leidoff, who lived with the tribe for more than two years, found a world of attachment. Babies were carried by mothers constantly, until they crawled. Children were securely-attached. Attachment affections persevered throughout adulthood. Leidoff concluded that modern society has lost much, including natural child-rearing processes. She urged recapture, with mothers staying home with babies, carrying them, instant response to distress, and sleeping with infants and young children. Leidoff's study, and others like it, instill a sense of loss when reflecting on modern society. Many are attempting to re-introduce some of the Yequana child-rearing practices into their modern lives.

Karen advocates introducing greater simple helping and support structures in our society. In longitudinal studies, the children of poor families provided such supports show far fewer dysfunctions ten years out. Poverty itself does not generate anxious attachment. But early neglect in the parents' own lives and scant support structures dramatically increase the likelihood of anxious attachment, even learning disabilities. Experts recommend paid family leave, strong day care standards and financial supports, comprehensive public health care, income support for poverty-stricken families, and appropriate therapeutic interventions. Age isolation should be met with giving children regular opportunities to relate to younger and older persons. And teachers should be trained not to worsen insecurely attached children by meting inappropriate discipline. All these programs would be very expensive, and really cannot provide what can only come from caring individuals. We need structures that support and improve the chances of intimate, caring human relationships. Nevertheless, our current pattern of moral condemnation, incarceration, and disgust fail to address the underlying problem. Investing in attachment, society will generate fewer problematic personalities at a cost, but will reap the benefits of having better overall life conditions for most.

**28. Looking Back**: **Bowlby and Ainsworth**. Late in life, Bowlby wrote a psycho-biography of Charles Darwin. He painted Darwin as a study in spoiled attachment, having lost his mother at age eight (and hence sent to boarding school) and tormented by a distant father. Darwin suffered debilitating anxiety his entire life. Like Darwin, Bowlby loved his friends. But Bowlby did not want intimacy with them. Bowlby was avoidant. He was gratified that some of his concepts won the intellectual day. The analytic community has come to accept Bowlby; some even embrace him.

Ainsworth, like Bowlby, had avoidant features in her personality. She and Bowlby were friends and admired one another's work. Ainsworth had a keen mind, and wrote well. Ainsworth's research worked a revolution, challenging the fervent desire among feminists that both parents be able to work without damage to children. Unlike Bowlby, Ainsworth was shy. She just loved the details of her work.

Both Ainsworth and Bowlby failed to include some features of infant life in their theory: fantasy, sexuality, aggression. Fathers were neglected. Later adolescent adaptations did not command attention. So too, attachment to non-parental others. How does attachment affect character? Does insecure attachment lead to neurosis? What other systems are developing in children as they age, and how do those relate to attachment? All classifications fail to encompass the complexity of individual life. Attachment styles are no exception.

Both Bowlby and Ainsworth sought reform, political and social, regarding children and the way we think of them. Loving attachment to a reliable caregiver is a primary motivation. This fact flies in the face of much in our culture. We are distracted. Still, our need for closeness, affection, touching, understanding, our desire to work through losses: these are biological demands. We cannot avoid them by denying our feelings about them.

**Appendix: Typical Patterns of Secure and Anxious Attachment.** Karen charts short descriptions of secure, ambivalent, and avoidant attachment at various developmental phases through individual life.

## EPITOME 7

**King, Jr., Martin Luther. *The Autobiography of Martin Luther King, Jr.* Edited by Clayborne Carson. New York: Grand Central Publishing, 1998.**

*Martin Luther King, Jr. (1929-1968) worked as a Baptist preacher. King is praised for his non-violent political agitation seeking racial equality in America. King's visionary oratory and personal flaws render his story complex. King headed the Southern Christian Leadership Conference, which he helped found, and helped organize the March on Washington in 1963. During that large protest, King delivered his iconic "I Have a Dream" speech from the steps of the Lincoln Memorial. This massive protest influenced passage of the Civil Rights Act of 1964. King was assassinated in 1968.*

1. **Early Years**. Martin Luther King Jr. described himself as religious, the descendant of a family of preachers. King was born at the leading edge of the Great Depression. His family was loving, his community middle class, and he was gifted physically and mentally. For these things, King was grateful. King's mother was quiet and devout. She countered racial discrimination by teaching her children, including King, that they were somebody, in no way inferior. King's father sought education, despite many obstacles. He was deeply moral, and spoke bluntly about circumstances. King's religious life was a constant support from childhood. His grandmother's death shook King. Being excluded from a white friend's life at age six shocked King, making him hate all white people. King's father resisted segregation, and spoke against it. As a youth, King won an oratory contest, speaking on the negro and U.S. Constitution. On the bus home, he and his teacher were forced to stand for ninety miles to let whites sit. King learned that poor whites were as economically oppressed as blacks.

2. **Morehouse College.** King entered Morehouse College at fifteen years of age. His professors discussed race issues frankly. King read Thoreau on civil disobedience, reaching conviction that noncooperation with evil is as essential as cooperation with good. King's racial hatred moderated to willingness to cooperate with some whites. King came to question much in his religious heritage as he encountered historical criticism of biblical texts, even as he moved closer to choosing a vocation as a pastor. King, following his father's example, entered seminary at nineteen.

3. **Crozer Seminary.** King tried to live in a manner that contradicted stereotypes about negroes. King developed understanding that individuals and societies are linked, and that one cannot fix one without fixing the other. He understood himself as preaching a social gospel. King read Marx and Lenin, concluding their materialism, atheism, dismissal of ugly means if the ends were deemed glorious, and totalitarianism made both unpalatable. King appreciated communism's roots in the outcry of the poor, its hatred of classism, its action to end income maldistribution, and its critique of capitalism as profit-mongering at the expense of collective well-being. Marxism does justice to man's collectivity; capitalism sees man's individuality. King

despaired of peaceful settlement of American race issues; war would be necessary. Love worked, King then believed, but only in individual relationships.

Then King heard a lecture on Gandhi's non-violent non-cooperation. King adopted Gandhi's nonviolent resistance as his approach to social ills. King abandoned his earlier fundamentalism, in favor of a liberal view of scripture. He eventually grew critical of liberalism's rosy view of man, which did not accord with King's experience of southern racism. In the end, King settled toward neo-orthodoxy. Human reason is compromised. It justifies evils. Reason peers darkly through sin. Collective evil protrudes like a cancer. Faith is necessary to cope with these shortcomings in man.

Niebuhr's rejection of pacifism argued that nonviolence harms where there exists no reason to believe that its tactics will succeed. Some lack moral conscience. Nonviolent suffering will not move those persons. King rejected Niebuhr's criticism. Niebuhr saw nonviolence as acquiescence in evil, not active opposition to it without violence. King settled in a realistic pacifism, seeing the involvement of all men in collective evil. King praises religious faith as that which gives life meaning. He savored nature, which reveals God.

4. **Boston University.** In his doctoral studies at Boston University, King modified his liberalism by affection for the corrective of neo-orthodoxy. Though Niebuhr held too dim a view of human nature, King balanced that with a bright view of the divine. King encountered personalism, and ultimately wrote a dissertation comparing the god-concepts of Tillich and Wieman. King came to the conviction that he wanted to base his life on the biblical god, not on passing fads.

5. **Coretta.** King met Coretta Scott in Boston. She was at that time involved in justice and peace issues. They married in 1953. Coretta came from Alabama, studied at Antioch in Ohio, and later studied music at a Boston conservatory. Her father ran several businesses, and endured threats from white competitors without becoming bitter. Coretta's mother was shy and attractive, deeply committed to caring for her family. King wrote appreciatively of Coretta's support. He lamented his absence from family life, and felt he failed in those duties.

6. **Dexter Avenue Baptist Church.** King finished his PhD, and ultimately accepted a call to Dexter Baptist Church in Montgomery, Alabama, which church stands across the square from the state capitol where Jefferson Davis took his oath of office for the Confederacy. King, being vetted by the Dexter Baptist congregation, preached on life's three dimensions: personal, social, and divine. King and Coretta had reservations about returning to the South, and raising children there, since segregation still ruled. And King had other offers in the North. King continued work on his dissertation, and preached monthly at Dexter Baptist. King Sr. preached King's installation sermon. King turned Dexter Baptist toward social justice issues. All members registered to vote; all joined the NAACP. King became vice president of the local NAACP, and joined the Council on Human Relations. Daughter Yolanda was born.

**7. Montgomery Movement Begins.** Rosa Parks was arrested for refusal to relinquish her bus seat to white riders on December 1, 1955. King became associated with Ralph Abernathy, a young black preacher in Montgomery. Black leaders met at Dexter Baptist Church; they decided to boycott the Montgomery buses on December 5, 1955, the day of Parks's trial for her bus seat segregation violation. King recast the boycott as noncooperation, after Gandhi and Thoreau. Montgomery's blacks avoided buses; compliance was near 100%. The Montgomery Improvement Association was formed that afternoon; King was elected president. Leaders discussed whether to continue the bus protest. The mass meeting supported continuing the boycott, attended by thousands. Abernathy read a resolution, seeking new courtesies for bus riders, and lesser discriminations. The resolution was unanimously supported. The cradle of the Confederacy was becoming the cradle of the civil rights movement.

**8. The Violence of Desperate Men.** King threw himself into planning the bus protest. King turned to many, first among whom was Ralph Abernathy. King modeled the Montgomery bus boycott on the previous protest in Selma. Private car pools were organized. Many protesters offered their cars for protest use. The police cut off the taxis by enforcing the minimum fare ordinance. But many blacks walked despite the available rides. Walking was symbolic protest. White housewives drove their black maids. The people of Montgomery became aware of Gandhi and nonviolent noncooperation. Christ moved the blacks; Gandhi provided methodology. Some disapproved, wanting to kill aggressively or asserting their right to self-defense. Many just went along, trusting their leaders. King met with city leaders; they declined to budge. Segregation exists to exploit and oppress; none gives up such ideas merely because asked. Powerful opposition is needed. White opponents sought to discredit the Negro leaders, gossip about them, and sow dissent among the blacks. King offered to resign as leader, fearing he was an obstacle to settlement. The black community refused him. A newspaper disinformation campaign announced settlement of the boycott. The MIA thwarted it by a word of mouth counter-campaign. The police began arresting people on pretexts. The number of private drivers fell as fears rose. King was swept up for speeding, and jailed. Abernathy sought cash bail, but the milling crowd outside convinced the jailers that they would be better off with King on the street. Threats against King and his family ensued. King faltered. He prayed and found Jesus telling him to battle on. King's home was bombed, with Coretta and the baby inside. King urged calm and non-violence. King learned his family was uninjured. A militant armed crowd grew around the parsonage. Coretta's father arrived to take her and the baby to Atlanta; she declined. Many wanted armed protection for King and his family; they declined, and got rid of the gun they owned. Violence robs protesters of their moral momentum, and makes them little different from the oppressors they would resist.

**9. Desegregation at Last.** When violence failed, opponents used mass arrest, employing an old anti-boycott law on the books. A grand jury indicted King and a hundred others. The boycott was now thirteen weeks old. King's parents worried, advising him to avoid Montgomery. King declined. King's father called a conclave of elders, who advised King to stay out of Montgomery, but relented when King argued otherwise. On his return, King was arrested, and in short order convicted.

Lawyers appealed his cause. King was proud of his crime, as were most protesters of theirs. They resisted evil. Opposition tactics welded them into a unified force, mutually reliant. Fear paralyzes. Where fear melts, lifting up humanity becomes possible. King preached that segregation must die, that separate but equal is never equal. Human psychology wants actual, not faux, equality. The city appealed to the Supreme Court. The bus boycott wore on. Montgomery insurers refused black vehicle insurance, so they turned to Lloyds of London. Finally, the city sought to enjoin the car pool itself. As the hearing on the car pool proceeded, the U.S. Supreme Court declared Alabama bus segregation unlawful. Despite this ruling, the Montgomery judge ruled against the car pool. New threats emerged. The Ku Klux Klan rode, but the negroes of Montgomery refused to hide. The black community worked hard to prevent violence as the integrated bus seating was implemented. The white community, including its pastors, did nothing. The Supreme Court order arrived. A meeting was called. King addressed the protesters, urging them to make friends of their enemies when they returned to the buses. King rode the first Montgomery integrated bus. Integration proceeded with minor mishaps only. So, the weapon of nonviolent resistance was honed. It demoralized opponents without immoral means. It gave voice to previously muted angers.

**10. The Expanding Struggle.** Opponents bombed Abernathy's home and several Negro churches. Black leaders asked President Eisenhower to speak in the south urging compliance with desegregation rulings. They formed the Southern Christian Leadership Conference (SCLC), and elected King president. King asked God to take him, not others, if someone must die. New bombings occurred, and an unexploded bomb was found at King's residence. King spoke, urging nonviolence and the idea that unwarranted suffering redeems others. The city arrested seven whites with respect to the bombings. Despite written confessions from all, the jury acquitted the seven. King became a sensation in the nation's eye. He spoke across the continent. He struggled to be as good as people deemed him. King worried about the future, about encore performances to the Montgomery victory. *Brown v. Board of Education* made segregated education illegal. King saw the American black struggle as part of a global struggle to throw off imperialism. At the Prayer Pilgrimage to Washington D.C. (1957), blacks called for voting legislation and criticized the federal government and both parties. In the summer of 1957, SCLC promoted the Crusade for Citizenship, attempting to register black voters and get them to vote. In September 1957, Eisenhower sent federal troops to insure that blacks could attend Little Rock High School. King thanked Eisenhower, but criticized his interest in fighting communism abroad more intently than segregation at home.

**11. Birth of a New Nation.** When the British imperium released Ghana to independence, King wanted to see that event. King traveled to Ghana for the birth of independent Ghana with people from across the planet. Prime Minister Nkrumah said that Ghana faced challenges, but he preferred those dangers to the quietude of servility.

**12. Brush with Death.** A mentally ill woman knifed King. King attributed his calm during the near fatal ordeal to God removing bitterness from his heart. To be nonviolent means to suffer the violence of others without retribution, hoping your pain will redeem the situation.

**13. Pilgrimage to Nonviolence.** King and Coretta traveled to India, where they were well-received. King spoke to thousands; Coretta sang spirituals for them. King's travels led him to question the U.S. military budget. Indians were divided on development. Some wanted better standards of living by industrializing. Others feared losing the Indian soul to Yankee factories. King was impressed with the Bhoodan movement for land reform. The Bhoodanists urged landholders to give land to the landless, to create self-sufficient villages that bartered with surrounding villages. This would stem the tide toward urban centers. It met with moderate success, but lacked centralized organization. King asked the Indian people to take the lead in disarmament. He praised Gandhi's public self-criticism. King took the non-violent revolution that freed India from British rule to be one of history's most important events. King argued that willingly suffering violence, rather than inflicting it, may strike the opponent with shame and change his heart. Gandhi hated untouchability; King recognized that he and America's negroes were untouchable to white America. Gandhi adopted an untouchable as his daughter, over Gandhi's wife's protests. Gandhi fasted, almost to death, to get Brahmins and untouchables to abandon their prejudices. And India outlawed discrimination against untouchables, instituting affirmative action and other atoning policies. King thought that India had made more progress than America in class matters.

**14. The Sit-In Movement.** King and family moved to Atlanta, in part to address King's need for some time to reflect. Atlanta did not, however, afford him that. The sit-in movement challenged segregation frontally. Students in thousands opposed administrations, and went to jail, and walked out of classes. King was indicted for tax fraud. An all-white jury, and all-white court, acquitted King. His negro northern lawyers convinced the prejudiced jurors to heed a black man over his white accusers.

**15. Atlanta Arrest and Presidential Politics.** King recounted his meeting with then-Senator John Kennedy, who was seeking the presidential nomination. Kennedy was compliant, but not emotionally committed to the civil rights movement. King was arrested during a lunch counter sit-in in Atlanta. When all 240 arrestees refused bail, the merchants dropped their charges. Released, King was arrested for violating his probation, of which he knew nothing. He had been arrested for having an Alabama driver's license in Georgia, and his attorney had pled guilty on his behalf. After trial, King was sent to four months hard labor a great distance from Atlanta and then-pregnant Coretta. John Kennedy intervened. Robert Kennedy got King released on bond. This intercession swayed King toward Kennedy and away from Nixon. King said, if Nixon was not sincere, then he was the most dangerous man in America. King never endorsed Kennedy, and found things to like and dislike in both Kennedy and Nixon.

**16. The Albany Movement.** The Kennedy administration took minor actions supporting civil rights. But the negro communities wanted immediate action. Broad protests erupted. King was arrested and jailed in Albany, Georgia. Freedom Rides sought to compel integration, already ordered by federal officials, of bus terminals and interstate transportation. The Albany Movement was multi-focal, addressing schools, voting, speech and assembly, and travel by means of sit-ins, jail-ins, boycotts, lawsuits. 700 were arrested; merchants urged their release. But the City ignored its agreements. Protests resumed. King and Abernathy were jailed, but after two days, some anonymous person paid their fines. They were released. The protests resumed. The police and crowds grew violent against protesters. Negroes retaliated. King halted demonstrations while he urged the black community that no resistance would be acceptable. King was arrested again, this time for praying in front of city hall in Albany, Georgia. The police chief tried to get King to leave; someone put up cash bail. King refused, asking to serve his sentence. The Albany Movement leaders kept up the pressure of legal challengers, demonstrations, boycott, and voter registration. The Albany Movement ended without the hoped-for results. King blames his own bailing from jail and human weaknesses for that failure. King thought their general protest against segregation should, in hindsight, have chosen a particular practice as its focus. Albany's segregation laws were repealed. The library was integrated. In the fall a moderate defeated a local racist in elections. But the successes were mixed. Lunch counters remained segregated. Overall, Albany was a learning episode.

**17. The Birmingham Campaign.** Birmingham was a racist stronghold. Segregation replaced slavery, and was every bit as degrading. Blacks were assaulted and killed with impunity by racists. Fear prevailed. George Wallace was Alabama's governor; he promised segregation forever. Birmingham was the most segregated city in the United States. Fred Shuttlesworth, a local pastor, organized protests, and was bombed, stabbed, and beaten for his efforts. Project C (for confrontation) was planned. Learning from the Albany diffuseness, they focused on the business community, which was vulnerable. The protesters waited until after municipal elections, to avoid becoming an issue in that race. The election loser, a virulent racist (Bull Connor) refused to vacate office. Freedom songs lay at the heart of the movement's soul. The Birmingham black community was not united. King and Shuttlesworth blitzed Birmingham, seeking to gel the community behind the protests. Birmingham blacks responded and got behind SCLC efforts. Bull Connor got a court injunction against the demonstrations. The SCLC disobeyed the court order, a first for the organization. The city changed the criteria for bail bondsmen, effectively putting the SCLC's bondsman out of business. So, going to jail might mean very long stays. King and Abernathy decided to go, regardless of the unknown outcome. King endured solitary confinement. Coretta called the Kennedys, and Robert intervened. John Kennedy called Coretta a few hours later. Harry Belafonte raised $50,000 for bail bonds.

**18. Letter from Birmingham Jail.** King wrote on scraps a letter responding to other pastors critical of the Birmingham protests. King notes he seldom responded to criticism, for by so doing he might seldom do the work before him. King is no outsider; he works for SCLC and is an American. Injustice anywhere injures justice everywhere, due to human mutuality. Birmingham is racially rancid. King explained the timing of the demonstrations in Birmingham. The purpose of non-violent demonstrations is to create tensions that bring parties to the negotiation table. Pressure opens the door to change, which never occurs voluntarily in the intransigent. Groups, especially, welcome immorality. The American black has been patient for 340 years. Now the civil rights movement opposes unjust laws, those laws failing to conform to God's morality. Protesters break laws, and willingly accept punishments for those transgressions. King expresses disappointment in white moderates, who mouth agreement, but oppose King's tactics. Virulent opposition is more welcome than tepid support. When one opposes evil, evil men do violence. Do not blame the protester. Others condemn the civil rights movement for its hurry. Time aids the recalcitrant. One must strike while the iron is hot. The silence of good people distresses King. But he is convinced that oppression cannot prevail. King reluctantly accepts the name "extremist," but only if Jesus, Amos, Paul, Martin Luther, Bunyan, Lincoln, and Jefferson were extremists. King expresses disappointment in the church. Many are ensconced behind their stained glass in a stupor. If the church is Christ's body, we have terribly mutilated him. The church gives itself to conformity and the status quo. Perhaps a nugget lies within it, the true ecclesia. Praise for the Birmingham police is misplaced. They have been brutal. And to the extent the police have been patient, their patience served segregation. Ends must be pure; moral means do not cleanse filthy ends. The civil rights movement is a signal moment in American history; its leaders promote the best of our heritage. King's letter from jail is long, but what else has a prisoner to do with his time? Long letters, long thoughts, long prayers.

**19. Freedom Now!** King and Abernathy bailed out of Birmingham jail after eight days. King brought students into the Birmingham action. The youths responded in great numbers, and the protesters filled up the jails. Sympathy with the protesters grew nationally and locally. Birmingham whites stood the sidelines in the battle, which heartened the protesters. The federal government sent officials to negotiate between the parties. In secret, the SCLC and Senior Citizen's committee initiated negotiations. Police violence (and a few protesters' violence) continued throughout the negotiations. After initial intransigence, the business community moved toward settlement. King called a truce for twenty-four hours. An agreement was reached that effectively ended segregation in Birmingham. Adamant segregationists bombed several locations in response. A Saturday night brawl ensued, after bar closings. George Wallace's state police moved in and sealed off the negro areas. Kennedy ordered 3,000 federal troops to Birmingham and federalized the Alabama national guard. The school board suspended or expelled the protesting students. The SCLC took the student issue to court. A federal district court judge upheld the board, but an appeals judge overturned the ruling that same day. The next day, the Alabama Supreme Court ruled that Bull Connor and his cronies held office illegally. The segregationists continued opposition, but their cause was lost.

**20. March on Washington.** Birmingham inspired people to protest. They did so, in their millions. The March on Washington brought 200,000 blacks and whites to the Lincoln Memorial. Media coverage of the March brought to millions of Americans their first view of negroes engaged in important, organized business, to the detriment of stereotypes.

**21. Death of Illusions.** Inhumanity finds its source in ugly action of bad men, but also in the passive inaction of good ones. Four girls in Sunday School were killed by a bomb. No white officials attended their funerals in Birmingham. King's funeral sermon castigates lethargic clergy and sideline negroes, calls for an aristocracy of character, rather than color, and expresses hope in life after death. Kennedy summoned King and the Birmingham white leadership to confer. But the administration met separately with black and white emissaries. King objected; nothing was accomplished. King criticized failure to apprehend racist assassins. John Kennedy was assassinated. King thought Kennedy two men, one before 1963 began, another after. King lays the reason for John Kennedy's death to an unkind moral climate. Kennedy's death also killed many happy illusions. Hate spreads, even to the highest echelons of society.

**22. St. Augustine.** 1963 and 1964 were the crux of the civil rights movement. St. Augustine, Florida, held vigorously to segregation policy. The SCLC asked for accommodations to that policy, and was rebuffed. SCLC began its nonviolent agitation: legal action, marching, boycotts, nonviolent suffering. The Civil Rights Bill of 1964 passed Congress; St. Augustine officials said they would comply, but did not. Johnson followed Kennedy's policies and enhanced them. He started a war on poverty, which helped blacks emerge. Civil rights legislation was passed by Congress, but written in the streets by protesters.

**23. The Mississippi Challenge.** King broke with his policy of political neutrality to oppose the Goldwater nomination. King opined that, while not personally a racist, Goldwater's campaign gave racial hatred a haven and hope. King was offended that Goldwater shook Strom Thurmond's hand. King urged all negroes to vote with the Democratic Party. Mississippi was the testing ground. Nowhere were negroes more oppressed politically and economically. But the negroes were determined to free themselves. King's life was threatened, but he persevered. Only 1,600 Mississippi negroes were registered to vote in 1964. An alternative political party, the Freedom Democratic Party, sought to be seated at the Atlantic City national convention. Two members were seated, in a losing compromise for the renegade party. Johnson won the election, but lost all the southern states to Goldwater. Congress was still compromised with racist members.

**24. The Nobel Peace Prize.** King was admitted to a hospital for rest and a physical. While there, he received notice that he had been awarded the Nobel Prize for Peace. King took this to be an award for the thousands on the ground of the civil rights movement. World opinion favored the negro civil rights movement. King sought economic sanctions against South Africa. King vowed to live a better personal life. He called for the wealthy nations to lift up the poor, mostly black, nations. After the award, the SCLC turned its attention to the American north, and to global racism, poverty, and war. King advocated a national boycott of Mississippi goods, and that the Mississippi congressional delegation not be seated for the state's failure to make negro voting possible.

**25. Malcolm X.** King met Malcolm X for one minute at a press conference in Washington. King wished Malcolm would speak less of violence, and articulate a creative alternative way of life. Negroes could not win a race war. The only viable alternative is nonviolent protest. Negroes threw eggs at King; King believed that was Malcolm X's doing. King believed that the Black Nationalist groups failed to understand his message, took him to be an Uncle Tom, and did not distinguish between acquiescence in evil and non-violent resistance. Malcolm X's hatred grew from the hatred he experienced. He could have become a master criminal, but turned instead to religion for guidance. He was doing so to his death. Malcolm spoke at length with Coretta, while Martin was in jail in Selma. He could not then renounce violence. He died violently, as he advocated. King noted that negroes cannot afford to kill their men of talent. Those are too few to fall to envy and rivalries. Violence does not work. Black supremacy is no better than white supremacy. Both tyrannies crush humans. Only brotherhood works.

**26. Selma.** President Johnson told King he wanted to delay the Voting Rights Act, in favor of other elements of his Great Society program. Two months later, the Act was passed. King credits the protests of black communities for this result. Obstacles to black voting were police brutality, restrictive mass meeting laws, intentionally dawdling registrars, and literacy tests. In Selma, Alabama, the SCLC organized registration days and protest marches. King and thousands were arrested. King, upon release, met with Vice President Humphrey and the Attorney General urging federal intervention. The Selma demonstrations happened to pressure the federal government into action. State police violently suppressed a march in Selma. King led a responsive march to Pettus Bridge, where troopers blocked the street. The marchers came up to them, and departed. James Reeb, a white protesting pastor, was murdered. King argues that segregation seeks to control white, as well as black, opinion. The SCLC won the right to march in federal court, so they did march from Selma to Montgomery. King likens this march to Gandhi's March to the Sea. The march proceeded peacefully. Thousands of federal troops stood by insuring safety. In Montgomery, the protesters petitioned Governor Wallace. King preached endurance, peace, and friendship with white men. How long? Not long. The SCLC went to Selma with limited objectives. Police brutality made the issue national. The Voting Rights Act ensued.

**27. Watts.** King turned his attention from southern segregation to northern riots. Watts in Los Angeles had erupted in violence. King deplored the negro violence, but called all to accept responsibility for permitting the underlying causes of the unrest. King portrayed looters as protesting poor people; looters wanted work and dignity. White conspicuous consumption prodded negroes to envy and resentment. The Watts riot was a mass temper tantrum, according to King. King condemned rioting as a theory; it serves only to justify reaction. King asserted that poverty and humiliation hurt people as much as batons. King demanded creative leadership. Such was absent in Los Angeles. Matters worsened in the city. California repealed laws prohibiting housing discrimination. King asserted that economic participation is the root of what it means to be American, which was a somewhat embarrassing admission for King as a pastor.

**28. Chicago Campaign.** The SCLC chose to address the ghetto pathology and problems of Chicago blacks. It joined a non-violent coalition seeking to address black slums and poverty, starting with poor education. King moved to Lawndale, a slum. Laws and restrictive covenants made it impossible for negroes to buy affordable houses. So, they were restricted to Lawndale. Landlords exploited the poor. To go on welfare meant one could not own a car or house. So employment proved difficult. King's own children developed behavior problems in Lawndale. King, for the first time in his career, was booed by angry black men. King saw that his rhetoric had promised more than he could deliver. Many were disappointed. The Chicago riots of 1966 grew from large numbers of poor with no stake in the system. After the riots, some attempted to blame King and his activists. They stepped up activities. Neo-nazis threw bricks and bottles. The crowds of opponents were the most hostile King had ever encountered. King styled the Chicago agitators as social physicians, pointing out the cancerous state of community life. The protesters worked out an agreement with the leaders of Chicago and the real estate community. Protesters then formed tenant unions, got neighborhood rehabilitation of buildings in dilapidated condition, and boycotted to force employment equity. King sought negro advantages in negro-dominated business. Jewish landlords exploited negro tenants in Lawndale. King argued with both angry parties. Negroes should not indulge anti-semitism. Jewish landlords should not exploit. The Chicago Housing Authority dragged its feet in implementing the fair housing agreements of the year prior. King gave effort to teaching non-violence to Chicago black gang teens. Some joined southern protests, and performed admirably.

**29. Black Power.** A sniper shot, but did not kill, James Meredith while on his March Against Fear voting protest. The SCLC decided it must take up leadership in Meredith's absence. While King visited Meredith in the hospital, Stokley Carmichael came to visit as well. All black civil rights organizations were invited to join in the continuing March. As they marched, some younger men expressed racial bitterness. King reasoned with dissenters to nonviolence. Violence would muddy the waters, and insisting on blacks-only would be racist. One builds inter-racial understanding a bit at a time by contact and effort. King prevailed, in this one instance at least. In Greenwood, Carmichael called for "black power." This divided the marchers; King's followers wanted to chant "Freedom Now." King and Carmichael met to discuss the Black Power slogan. King advocated strongly against its use, since its connotations were violent. The SNCC leadership remained adamant. All compromised by agreeing to chant no slogan in the remainder of the march. The slogan "Black Power" expresses some positive thoughts. Black Power expresses disappointment with the broken promises of white power-brokers. Black Power calls black people to gain legitimate economic and political power. Black Power calls for black people to pool their financial resources to better the plight of black people. Black Power calls blacks to manhood. History books ignore black contributions. Despite these positive features of the slogan "Black Power," it could not serve as the basis of the civil rights movement. The slogan expresses despair about changing America. It is nihilism, eschewing hope. Yet hope is the core attribute of all change. King spent long sessions with Black Power advocates, arguing into the night for nonviolence over against

Fanon's Algerian praise for violence as a legitimate tool for oppressed peoples. Armed insurrection would result in thousands of negro casualties. One cannot prevail against racial prejudice by violence. Whites of good faith need their fears assuaged by blacks of good faith. Then integration and power sharing can proceed. Even if most blacks prefer violence, King declined to lead them. Genuine leaders shape opinion, not follow it. Black Power invited negroes to fashion themselves after the worst people in America. King asked people to be concerned with outcomes, but also to be concerned about their moral inwardness. King sought a new man, new power, and a new day.

**30. Beyond Vietnam.** King privately urged peace in Vietnam, but did not protest. When he began making anti-war statements, he was roundly criticized in the black and white press for involving himself in matters he poorly understood. King came to a crisis when he realized the American government talked peace, but intended to make military victory at any cost. King spoke, and organized protests. He could no longer condone by his silence. King linked the paltry war on poverty with the expense and distraction caused by the intent to destroy Vietnam. A disproportionate number of blacks fought and died for democracy in Vietnam when they found none in Georgia. The United States purveys violence; none excels America in this. God gave King his calling; that calling exceeds the interests of one nation. America is on the wrong side of revolution. We must change from money to people in our values. To spend more on war than on social healing portends spiritual collapse. Mankind can no longer preserve his local culture by loyalty to it; we must support mankind to save ourselves. The NAACP opposed a position King never iterated. King criticized them. President Johnson was a man who could not admit wrong, in a statesman-like fashion. King told Johnson so. King stated he would not fight in Vietnam if he were drafted. He encouraged every young man to search his heart, and refuse to fight.

**31. The Poor People's Campaign.** The SCLC decided to take on financial opportunity in America by means of a poor people's march on Washington. They would persist until the federal government acted to end poverty. The government had failed to address any of the root causes of the summer riots of 1966 and 1967. Instead, Congress tinkered. So, the SCLC organized demonstrations in Washington. Racism will be confronted. King looked to Jesus for example. He was the true revolutionary, not Marx. King joined the Memphis sanitation workers' strike. America will go to hell if it does not end poverty. King admitted that he got discouraged, but he found solace in his faith.

**32. Unfulfilled Dreams.** Life often disappoints dreams. At the heart of the universe, evil and good struggle. The struggle extends to our own hearts. God judges a man by the tendency of his life, not incident by incident. God wants your heart to be good. God wants us to try. Of all of human history, King wished to live in no other than his present; for God is at work in the world now. Negroes have grown determined to be men. King encouraged followers to develop a dangerous charity. Do not fear. Project yourself into the shoes of others. Stand with the sanitation workers. When the demented woman almost killed King, newspapers reported that if King had sneezed, he would have died. King received letters of condolence. Of all those,

King remembered best that of a ninth-grade white girl, who was glad he had not sneezed. King too was glad he did not sneeze. He recounted the events of his life, with gratitude. When King dies, he wants to be remembered for serving, loving, opposing the Vietnam war, clothing the naked, visiting some prisoners, and serving humanity. King wanted to leave behind a committed life. That is all.

## EPITOME 8

**Kurlansky, Mark. *Nonviolence: The History of a Dangerous Idea.* New York: The Modern Library, 2006.**

*Mark Kurlansky (born 1952) works from New York City as a freelance writer and lecturer. Kurlansky's works address nonviolence, food and culinary works, children's books, science, Basque history, Judaism, and the Caribbean culture. Mark Kurlansky is also an artist, and illustrates some of his books personally. He refused to serve in the military during the Vietnam War and received early education in nonviolence.*

**Foreword by His Holiness the Dalai Lama.** The Dalai Lama's daily practice cultivates nonviolence and compassion, which helps create deep relations with others. Nonviolence exceeds mere lack of violence. Nonviolence leads one to intimacy that results in feeling responsible for others' well-being. Violence leads to more violence, and is seldom warranted. We should aim to resolve conflicts by talking and listening, rather than through coercion.

### I. Imperfect Beings.

No proactive word for nonviolence exists. The only word available is the negation of violence. Proponents of nonviolence have been marginalized because nonviolence threatens state militarism. The victors of wars write the histories of those wars. Nonviolence differs from pacifism. Nonviolence seeks to persuade its opponents. Its core conviction is that persuasion is more effective, as a political strategy, than violence. Gandhi's word for nonviolence, *satyagraha*, has never achieved popular usage.

Hinduism does not advocate nonviolence, though strains of nonviolence run through its history. Man is stained by violence, and remains obligated to attempt to remove the stain. Nonviolence emerges from spiritual strength.

Nonviolence entered Chinese culture through Buddhism. Buddhism avoids taking life, but its strictures suffer many interpretations. Chinese Confucianism endorsed armies, but is ambivalent about their proper uses. Confucius advocated neither pacifism nor nonviolence. Mozi wrote against Confucians, advocating universal love, pacifism, and the Golden Rule. In Taoism, Lao Tsu advocates only defensive wars, which is but half-way to nonviolence.

Judaism's sixth commandment forbids murder, but the tradition has many strands that evade or redirect the rule. The prophet Isaiah foresaw a day when God's people cease war.

Many religions forbid violence, but have been coopted for political and violent ends. Kurlansky notes the perversion of Zen Buddhism in the hands of Japanese ninjas or the celebration of the Maccabean Revolt (Chanukah) in the hands of Zionists. Rebels who insist on nonviolence are killed, then canonized, as was Jesus. States prefer saints to revolutionary martyrs.

## II. The Problem with States.

Jesus advocated a thorough-going nonviolence, including emotional nonviolence. The early church, sundered from its Jewish roots, became a Roman anti-war cult. Origen (Alexandrian third century A.D. Christian philosopher) argued that Christians should submit to the emperor but decline to fight his wars. Origen did not reject armies, only Christian participation in them. Christians targeted converts among the Roman legions, impairing Rome's ability to war. Christianity's control of the Roman world was, for the church, its greatest disaster.

Constantine I, believing he needed a powerful divine partner in battling to become emperor, painted crosses on the shields of his soldiers. When they won, Christianity was coopted into the service of Roman wars. The Edict of Milan decriminalized Christian faith. So, Christianity, like all great religions, was turned to serve state power and the wars by which it is maintained.

The erosion of the church commenced almost immediately. Accommodations of state violence led, in Augustine's work, to the just war concept, which emphasized not the killing of others, but the motives of the killers in killing others. Some objected. Martin, a Roman soldier of two years, put down his sword and refused to fight. He offered to lead the phalanx into battle unarmed, and would have been slaughtered but for a rapid peace on the field of battle. Martin became St. Martin of Tours. Saints are of use to the state. Rebels are not.

## III. The Killer Peace Movement.

Involved in war, the church began to interfere in state war-making. The Crusades sought to effect theological ends by military means. Just war theory prevailed: the State declares a bad guy, whom good guys must kill. The Truce of God required kings to lay down arms every Sunday, and half of all days in the year (the holy days). The church organized peace militias to attack lords who violated the Truce of God. The kings retaliated. By the eleventh century, the church argued that killing criminals and aggressors pleased God. This was malicide, killing of bad people, not homicide, killing of the good.

Islam, in its origins, emphasized peace. Mohammed's attempt at utopia in Mecca required no violence. But when Mohammed was put to the task of defending Medina, after Mecca rejected him, "just wars" ensued. Mohammed conducted nineteen campaigns, even while arguing that nonviolence was preferable. Jihad originally meant intense struggle to convince others nonviolently. It was subsequently bifurcated into spiritual struggles and martial struggles, the greater and lesser jihads. A just war theory prevailed, when it became apparent that Islamic soldiers would prove unable to conquer Europe.

Pope Urban II declared the first crusade in 1095, a holy war to liberate Jerusalem from Saracen domination. This was a time of apocalyptic frenzy in Europe. The church demonized Islamists. Taking the Muslim world by surprise, the first crusade was alone among the six invasions in military success. Islam eventually mounted a counter-crusade, driving the west from Jerusalem, demonizing the "Franks." War makes one like one's demonized enemy. The imagery associated with crusading echoes through all subsequent wars.

## IV. Troublemakers.

Most dissenters from the militarization of the Church fled to monasteries, which remained intellectual refuges. The Cathars, adopting Manichean dualism, rejected violence, individual and state. They rejected the sacraments, and refused to support the church financially. The church demonized the Cathars (the church's designation for the sect, which means "kissers of cat anuses"), spread rumors that the Cathars ate cremated baby remains, and held orgies for anal intercourse. A 100 year crusade resulted in the death of every Cathar. Where the nonviolent become violent, they always lose their argument. Other small sects of nonviolent originalists emerged: Waldensians, Taborites, Hussites, Mennonites, and Anabaptists. A Taborite writer, Petr Chelcicky, wrote that war resides in the logic of power. Renouncing power politics, that is both war and imprisonment, would be sufficient to beckon world peace. An Anabaptist leader named Michael Sattler defended himself at trial for refusing to kill Turks, arguing that Turks knew nothing of Christ, but those from Europe who killed Turks knew Christ's prohibitions on murder but rejected them. Sattler preferred to fight the Europeans. Sattler suffered execution. After the Thirty Years War, Spiritualism, Pietism, the Diggers, the Quakers, and the Dunkers evolved, all embracing pacifism and opposing war.

## V. The Dilemma of Unnatural People.

Quakers and other pacifist Christian communities flocked to America, and received diverse welcomes. By 1658, four Quakers had been executed in the Massachusetts and Plymouth colonies. Pennsylvania, however, was formed as a pacifist haven.

Political warmakers enlist intellectuals to create rationales for their ventures. None fabricated more creative war theories than the English. Alberico Gentili, then at Oxford, invented preventive war theory, arguing that one may preemptively attack those one fears may attack you in the future. John Selden argued that extending empire was itself a justification for war, because all men are acquisitive. Thomas Hobbes argued that war was the natural human state. Jean Jacques Rousseau extended that sentiment to nation-states. All naturally war. John Locke enthused about colonialism and asserted the right to take slaves.

Other thinkers disagreed. William Penn's supporters established Pennsylvania as a pacifist enclave out of line with British foreign ventures. Non-pacifist Pennsylvanians were given western lands, and Quakers eastern lands (the more fertile soils). Tensions rose. In 1756, the pacifists lost control of the legislature, and nonviolence ceased to be Pennsylvania's guiding principle.

Some indigenous peoples attempted pacifist or nonviolent approaches. After initially fighting, the Cherokee nation sued and won before Chief Justice John Marshall their rights as a sovereign nation. President Andrew Jackson circumvented this ruling, and forced the Trail of Tears, during which forced march 4,000 Cherokees perished. The Maori of New Zealand, after offering armed resistance, followed Te Whiti, the leader of a village called Parihaka. Te Whiti taught nonviolence, self-reliance for necessary goods, and peaceful negotiation. The Maori flocked to Parihaka. They made agreements with neighboring Maori and retained ownership of their lands, though they let whites settle there too, without selling. Then they plowed the land. When whites objected, police arrested ploughmen, who did not resist. Te Whiti encouraged his ploughmen, wearing a white feather to identify themselves, to remain calm. Five per day were sent to plow. Five were arrested daily. Te Whiti encouraged them to use the tongue as their weapon. Eventually, Te Whiti himself was arrested. Settlers destroyed homes of natives in Parihaka. Thousands of Maori died. No responsive violence ensued.

**VI. Natural Revolution.**

Most Americans of the revolutionary period could not imagine order without coercion. Still, 80,000 pacifists inhabited the colonies. The Continental Congress permitted conscientious objection provided the resisters paid their taxes and a penalty. But some wanted war with the British. War is more durable than peace. To break peace, one merely fires shots. Debate ends. Fighting begins.

Americans had waged nonviolent contest with the British. The upper classes pamphleteered. The lower classes rioted. Both were commonplace. The colonies had become so unruly as to be unprofitable. The English attempted to remedy this problem with taxes, which proved unworkable. Nonviolent acts ensued: the 1773 Boston Tea Party, and the 1774 blockade of the British puppet judiciary in Massachusetts. It would appear that the American Revolution was a *fiat accompli* before hostilities commenced. Why then war? Perhaps war proved necessary because none could imagine achieving independence peacefully. War may have been necessary to galvanize and consolidate the already-accomplished revolution.

Once fighting commenced, unsupportive citizens were branded loyalists. In New Jersey, 105 were sentenced to death. All but four recanted and fought. The recalcitrant four hanged. A Connecticut pacifist was tarred, covered in pig dung, forced to eat the same. An accused Delaware loyalist was hanged, then drawn and quartered while alive. Benjamin Franklin's son was incarcerated in a dungeon. Franklin did nothing to help. Pacifists, vilified as British loyalists, found no safe harbor.

The American Revolution has been mythically sanitized, home to founding fathers and blessings of liberty. The conflict was, rather, a brutal civil war, as well as an international one. So many colonists behaved unconscionably during the war that no critical history was written during the lives of the participants. Nonviolent pacifists insist war always leads to more war. The War of 1812 followed hard on the heels of the American Revolution.

**VII. Peace and Slavery.**

Peace activism rose after the Revolution. David Low Dodge argued that keeping armies leads to wars, that war is an economic disaster, and that war most injures the poor who pay higher prices from depressed wages. Noah Worcester characterized war as the mass delusion obsessing a guilt-ridden world. Peace societies grew in number. Charles Whipple revised the revisionist Revolutionary histories. Abolition and nonviolence groups united in common cause. William Lloyd Garrison led antislavery forces, calling for immediate freeing of all slaves and boycott of elections until emancipation was completed. Garrison burned a copy of the American Constitution and called for the North to secede from the Union because Southern slavery was guaranteed by Northern armies. Garrison was accused of fomenting Nat Turner's slave rebellion in which fifty-five slave owners died. Harriet Beecher Stowe's *Uncle Tom's Cabin* sold 300,000 copies in its first year. Lydia Maria Child joined Garrison's nonviolent movement and wrote forcefully for abolition. For her book *An Appeal in Favor of That Class of Americans Called Africans*, which discussed the state of black slaves, blamed North and South equally, and treated interracial sex, a taboo subject, Child lost her job, her fortune, and her career as a novelist. Elijah Lovejoy was assassinated by pro-slavery mobs for printing abolitionist tracts. Haitian blacks overthrew two French armies to form a free black society, but the savagery of that war has lingered in their culture for two centuries. The Haitian experience led Congress to forbid further importation of slaves, and the British and French to outlaw slavery altogether. In America, a battle of terror raged between blacks and slave-owners.

John Brown espoused violence to end slavery. He and several sons moved to Kansas in hope it should become a non-slave state. They tortured five pro-slavery men to death by swords. Brown assaulted and took the federal arsenal at Harpers Ferry, Virginia, hoping to lead a slave rebellion. Robert E. Lee captured him the following morning. Brown was hanged, convicted of treason. Many in the abolitionist nonviolence movement teetered toward Brown's sentiments concerning violence. C. K. Whipple continued to encourage nonviolence, and asked for all slaves to stop cooperating with their owners. But once the Civil War shooting commenced, the nonviolent activists were silenced. Some condoned the violence. Garrison argued that once the shooting began, nonviolence was unworkable. The dissenters would merely be pushed aside and ignored. So, Garrison abandoned nonviolence for pragmatic reasons.

The Lincoln administration finessed the question of slavery, since its top priority was to restore the Union. The Emancipation Proclamation freed slaves in rebellion states, but not in the Northern states. In short, the Proclamation freed no slaves. More Americans died in the Civil War (around 650,000) than in all other American wars combined. Slaves were freed legally, but not actually. After Lincoln's assassination, Andrew Johnson, a Tennessee citizen, appointed pro-slavery governors in the seceding states. Black codes and voting obstacles were passed. The task of making abolition a reality in the daily life of southern blacks remained for another century to attempt.

**VIII. The Curse of Nations.**

In 1867, Victor Hugo predicted the decline of the nation-state and war, in favor of a peaceful global community. He was wrong. Wars lead to wars, each tilling the soil of the next. The socialists boycotted the next pan-European peace conference. People seeking power distrust pacifists.

Kurlansky recounts numerous peace conferences running up to World War I. The United States began wars of colonization (Mexico, Philippines), with many, including Samuel Clemens, dissenting. As is usual, when the shooting began in Europe, criticism was stifled. Bertrand Russell found his neutrality support waning. The labor movement argued that a bayonet was a weapon with a worker on each end.

The losses in World War I were unprecedented. As hostilities dragged on, opposition rose. So many British died that the country imposed a draft. Drafted conscientious objectors were treated badly, set to punitive hard labor. Clive Bell, in his

*Peace at Once*, savaged the paltry rationale for World War I and warned that humiliating Germans would not be good for Europe. Dissenters were punished. Bertrand Russell was given six months for opposing a U.S. military base in England. He lost his lectureship at Cambridge as well.

In the United States, anti-war sentiment was criminalized as spying, and 142 life sentences and seventeen death verdicts were rendered. None of the executions was enacted.

Military desertions spread in all involved armies. In the end, ten million died and twenty million were injured.

**IX. A Favorite Just War.**

Remarque's *All Quiet on the Western Front* encouraged a flurry of anti-war sentiment and writings. The Court of International Justice was formed, and the League of Nations. When Hitler came to power, Remarque fled Germany and his novel was burned.

In Hitler's early years, the United States supported Hitler and provided armaments. British prime minister Neville Chamberlain appeased Hitler in the Munich Pact (1938) by giving Germany the Germanic cultural zone of Czechoslovakia, without consulting the Czechs. Critics of appeasement tend to forget that appeasement was popular in the decade preceding the Munich Pact. In America, conscientious objectors were sixteen percent of the U.S. prison population. These imprisoned pacifists worked to integrate prison mess halls, one of the first events in the American civil rights movement.

Gandhi encouraged German Jews to rise up in nonviolent protests. More Jews were saved in Germany by nonviolence than by violent resistance. Kurlansky recites the nonviolent resistance to the Nazis in Denmark and Bulgaria, where most Jews were saved, and the dismal statistics from nations where Jews resisted by force of arms. Throughout the war, British and American allies knew of the Holocaust, but declined to do anything. The Holocaust was, militarily, unimportant. And the U.S. was sensitive to German propaganda that Jews were insidiously leading American government. Saving Jews was politically unpalatable.

Warmongers use World War II as an example of a just war. Stephen Spielberg and Tom Brokaw proclaim soldiers to be acting ethically and saving the world. Winston Churchill did little but encourage warfare. The Allies were good; the Germans and Italians and Japanese bad. It was that simple. War makes an army become like its enemy. When Germany bombed the civilian center of Coventry, the British took to bombing German population centers, which may have prolonged the war. The U.S. continued this policy by producing and then deploying nuclear weapons on the civilian populations of Hiroshima and Nagasaki.

**X. The Rule of Thugs and the Law of Gravity.**

The twentieth century was a time of war extremes, but it was also the greatest century for nonviolence in history. Gandhi, influence by Tolstoy and Thoreau, freed India. The nonviolent advocate was then elevated to sainthood and ignored by nuclear India. Gandhi valued self-denial, nonviolent non-cooperation, and force of will. Gandhi espoused nonviolent resistance, not passive impotence. Kurlansky recounts Gandhi's biography briefly: satyagraha, the South African protest years, and Indian independence strikes and actions. Gandhi recruited a Pathan leader, Abdul Ghaffar Khan, who had been violently opposing the British in northern India for decades. They formed a nonviolent army and took up nonviolent non-cooperation. Gandhi's import lies in creating a template for nonviolent resistance.

Gandhi's example deeply influenced Americans. Kurlansky tells of Richard Gregg's book, *The Power of Nonviolence*, George Houser's pacifist union work, Muste's Fellowship of Reconciliation, Houser and the Congress of Racial Equality. Leaders accepted beatings in nonviolent fashion. They accepted prison terms for refusing military service. Martin Luther King Jr. was turned from his insistence upon armed revolt to a path of nonviolent non-cooperation by Muste's rhetoric.

Anti-nuclear activists opposed the weapon that rendered the fundamental equation of war antiquated—a weapon for which no political end could justify its use, since it would result in annihilation of the user as well as the target. Still, the Cold War justified around 130 shooting wars in the next forty plus years, but no nuclear exchanges. Nonviolence suffered. Stokely Carmichael took over the Student Nonviolent Coordinating Committee with his Black Panther Party, a violent radical group. Students for a Democratic Society took beatings without retaliation, but refused to categorically rule out violent responses. David Dellinger, a nonviolent activist, found most opponents of the Vietnam War criticized this particular war, not war generally. The Weathermen violently terrorized domestic corporations.

Violence is rationalized, and we reject the rationale only if the violence fails. Violence infects and spreads like a disease. Nonviolence wins only if it has the moral rigor to escape the control of thugs and remain simply nonviolent. Violence makes people afraid; fearful people seldom behave well.

**XI. Random Outbreaks of Hope.**

Will and Ariel Durant calculated that of the last 3,421 years, only 268 passed without war. Still, nonviolence has had some seminal moments. The Mexican rightists were removed by years of gentle pressure. The Soviet Union fell, largely due, not to Reagan arms and rhetoric, but due to nonviolent resistance in Eastern Europe. The secret power of nonviolence is patience. Nonviolent resistance to the 1968 Soviet invasion of Czechoslovakia became a turning point, according to Mikhail Gorbachev. Governments function by public opinion; when it turns against an administration, that administration can accomplish nothing. The Argentine junta fell in part because the *Mothers of Plaza de Mayo* met every Thursday in the square to protest. Beaten and killed, they persevered. Nonviolent dissent played its part in toppling Marcos's Philippine dictatorship. In South Africa, nonviolence alternated with violence, Gandhi being followed by violent Mandela, followed by Desmond Tutu. The most effective resistance was not guns, but economic boycott of white businesses by blacks.

Soldiers are not killers, but can be trained to kill. PTSD is the result. Kurlansky tells the stories of two U.S. military deserters facing deployment to the Iraq or Afghan fronts.

Anatole France said that war will cease only when people refuse violence and suffer what comes of their refusal. This movement has begun.

## EPITOME 9

**Thucydides. "The Melian Debate" in *The Peloponnesian War*. Translated by Rex Warner. Baltimore, Maryland: Penguin Books Inc., 1959.**

*Thucydides (455-400 B.C.), as a young man, fought in the early stages of the Peloponnesian War (431-404 B.C.). He was afflicted by, but survived, the plague, after which he was appointed general. He arrived too late with a fleet to save Amphipolis from the Spartans, and was, as a result, sent into exile for twenty years. He likely wrote* The Peloponnesian War *during the years of exile, from which he returned only four years before his death.*

**Book Five, Chapter 7: Sixteenth Year of War. The Melian Debate.**

The fleet of Athens dispatched thirty ships and support troops to the island of Melos, which had been settled by Spartans and was loosely aligned with them. Melos had remained neutral in the Peloponnesian War to this time. The Athenian generals sent a delegation to the Melians to demand their surrender. The Melians would not permit the Athenians to speak with the Melian population, but only to chosen men.

The Athenian delegation sought an ordered discussion, to which the Melians agreed. The Melians objected that open discussion is inconsistent with Athens' intent to war on Melos, should talks fail. The Athenians responded that justice leans on the power to compel; the strong do as they wish, and the weak do as they must. The Melians objected that to so argue abandons justice altogether. Fairness and good faith are concerns for all. Today's victors are tomorrow's vanquished, themselves seeking justice. The Athenians responded that Melos need not trouble itself with Athens' well-being. Athens speaks today to peaceably bring Melos into the empire. To fight is expensive for Athens and risks utter destruction for Melos. Better to make an arrangement.

The Melians offered their neutrality. The Athenians rejected Melos' offer because other villages will think Athens weak if she tolerates Melian ambivalence. The strong compel submission, and where they fail to do so, they are deemed to fear to do so. Such rumors make an empire insecure. The Melians argued that in conquering weak little Melos, Athens will nurture rebellion in all its small neighbors, who will know their time too shall come. The Melians argued that to destroy Melos is shameful, and to resist enslavement honorable. The Athenians responded that hope comforts those in peril, clouding their judgment of peril. The Melians asserted that gods may intervene to balance power between Melos and Athens. The Athenians replied that Athens acts as do gods; where one can rule, he does so. The Melians asserted that Sparta may defend them. The Athenians reply that Spartans think what they like is honorable and what serves them is just. Spartans are not risk-takers when it comes to living honorably or finding justice. Sparta always looks for powerful allies. Melos is not such. The honor and sense of justice the Melians vaunt may well bring utter destruction to Melos. Abandon pride and survive. The Athenians stated their terms: ally with Athens and pay annual tribute; then Melos can otherwise enjoy her property and usual occupations.

The Athenian delegation withdrew, asking the Melians to reconsider their position. Melians, after deliberation, responded with another offer of neutrality.

Athenians responded that Melos deludes herself in thinking that Melian hopes are more potent than Athens' army.

Athens erected a siege wall around the perimeter of Melos. Ultimately, Athens killed the fighting men of Melos and sold her women and children into slavery. Melos was repopulated with a settlers from Athens.

## EPITOME 10

**James, William. *Essays of Faith and Morals*, "The Moral Equivalent of War." Edited by Ralph Barton Perry. Cleveland, Ohio: The World Publishing Company, 1962.**

*William James (1842-1910), brother of novelist Henry James, taught physiology, psychology, and philosophy at Harvard University. His philosophical pragmatism and thoroughgoing empiricism deeply influenced subsequent American philosophy.*

We must wage war against war. We are confused about war. No one would undo the Civil War. Yet no one would vote for having another. We tend to war when compelled. Men of prehistory did otherwise. They warred to profit and glory. We plunder by trade, but still yearn for glory.

History details little but carnage. Consider the Trojan War, the Peloponnesian War, Alexander's conquests, Rome's supremacy. War made us into societies. If there ever were peaceful men, they have been exterminated.

States now call their war preparations peace. But, today, peace means war. No rational actor would war to resolve conflicts. But one must believe such common sense possible in international affairs.

I am a pacifist. I will argue against the virtues militarists vaunt. War may be one way-station in man's journey, not his destination. We might out-grow war. Militarists recoil. They proclaim: "War is man at his ultimate. War benefits the victor and the vanquished. A warless world would be a herd of grazing cattle."

All in some part of their hearts agree with the warmonger. Militarism breeds hardiness. It bursts our weaklings. Militarists view war mystically. War springs from man's psyche and sociology. War must come. Its justifications are always fictions. Militarists believe war is a moral necessity. General Lea believes that Japanese power might take the islands, Alaska, Oregon, California. Steinmetz finds war the winnow of God, by which He sorts nations. The righteous prevail.

Militarist rationale exhibits two fundamental resistances: 1) unwillingness to terminate military life and settle for incrementalism, and 2) pause at the prospect of deleting from human experience the ultimate in strenuousness and the virtues that instills. Pacifists convert no militarists because they refuse to enter the militarist mind. Pacifists harp on the expense, the horror of war. Militarists agree, but find expense and horror the price of higher values. Pacifists must suggest an adequate ethical alternative to war if they wish to win over the war-party. Contemporary pacifist arguments are little more than feeble whining to militarists. A man gains dignity when his community needs him. War accomplishes that for many.

James's own utopia requires nations and individuals to replace war thirst with reasonable claims, and to outlaw acts of war. Nevertheless, war virtues must find their home, for they are a permanent good. We must create a morality of civil honor the equal of military honor. We must fight civil defects as we now fight for our freedom from subjugation. Then pacifism might prevail. Our social influence upon one another is inescapable. One might create a civil morality by conscripting all youths into a civil corps to do public works with military discipline. Besides the good done, the conscripts would be taught adult skills and get some silliness stripped out of them.

Historically, only war disciplines entire communities. A civil alternative must rise. One can imbibe martial virtues without war. We must inflame civic sentiment for peace and against war. The gap is wide, but not so wide as that which separates the primitive from the modern man.

## EPITOME 11

**Kant, Immanuel. *To Eternal Peace.* Translated by Carl J. Friedrich. In *Basic Writings of Kant*, Allen W. Wood, ed. New York: The Modern Library, 2001.**

*Immanuel Kant (1724-1804 A.D.) wrote a pivotal ethics in multiple parts. The first is* Critique of Pure Reason. Fundamental Principles of the Metaphysics of Morals, Critique of Practice Reason, *and* Critique of Judgment *followed. Kant's* Critique of Pure Reason *erodes exaggerated Enlightenment confidence in human reason, and castigates unbridled metaphysical speculation. Kant was a warm conversationalist and popular lecturer in Königsberg, Germany, and a Pietist by religious sentiment. Some believe Kant's work represents the transition point between Enlightenment and modern philosophy. Kant wrote* To Eternal Peace *in 1795.*

A Dutch innkeeper painted the title of this essay above an image of a graveyard. Kant worries that savage interpreters may disparage him for the opinions contained in this essay.

**First Section: Which Contains the Preliminary Articles of an Eternal Peace between States**. 1. Peace means that parties retain no materiel for future wars. The peacemaking States lay aside all claims of past wrongs. Power-seeking cannot be the purpose of peaceful states. 2. No State shall lay claim to another by any means. States are self-governing human societies, and cannot be bought, sold, or commandeered by another State. 3. States must cause standing armies, preparations for war, hoards of money for war-making, and defensive alliances to atrophy, since all make war more likely and pose threats to other States. 4. States may not loan money to another State to fund war-making efforts, for such arrangements make war more likely. 5. States shall not interfere forcibly in the internal affairs and government of another State. States may, however, aid one party interior to another State that is gripped by civil war, which is an anarchic condition. 6. No State shall employ means of conflict that preclude future establishment of peace. This principle excludes assassination, poisoning, refusing to take prisoners, and fomenting treason within the opposition State. Unfettered war, such as genocide, can have no conclusion other than the total annihilation of mankind.

**Second Section: Which Contains the Definitive Articles for Eternal Peace Among States**. War is the natural human state; one fights or flees or expels the other. Peace, being artificial, must be constructed upon a foundation. This foundation is constitutional law. Constitutions govern individuals within a State, relations among states, or relations among global humanity. *First Definitive Article of the Eternal Peace.* All States should be republics, allowing every citizen freedom and civil equality guaranteed by a single legislative body. Republican government saddles all citizens with the costs and deprivations of wars, and so makes wars less likely. The essence of republicanism is to segregate executive from legislative functions. Despotism unites the two in a man. Democracy makes of every man a despot. *Second Definitive Article of the Eternal Peace.* Every State should require of every other State that all form a federal union among all States to regulate the relations of States by law. Men are by nature evil, as unregulated relations among States prove. The very existence of law proves that there hides in the human heart a dormant longing to master evil and establish peace. But winning a war never ends war, but rather merely sets the stage for a fresh conflict. Nations must establish a pacific union, not mere peace treaties, for the latter end a war, but the former ends all wars. All States need not agree at the same moment. Republics can join in pacific federal unions, and invite, over time, all others to join their warless relations. Those who dissent can decline to join and cast themselves into that wide grave that yawns to receive violent men. The federal State comprising all peaceful nations can slowly expand its membership, finally encompassing all of mankind. *Third Definitive Article of the Eternal Peace*. Hospitality must govern treatment of foreigners. No peaceful alien shall be persecuted, for he shares with every nation the earth's surface. So, all must tolerate one another. All land belongs to mankind. The world (cosmopolitan) constitution requires this result. Violations of law anywhere affect every man everywhere. Man needs universal constitutional law among States. Then eternal peace may blossom.

**First Addition: On the Guarantee of Eternal Peace**. Nature works to eliminate human war. Human reason has its limits, and so men cannot understand all things. Nature sees more. Nature drove men to all corners of the habitable globe, and, by war, compelled them to form relations something like law. War springs from human nature. War perpetuates itself, each conflict generating more warlike people than died in the conflict. 1. By war, nature coerces men into constitutional governments. Men agree to avoid the results of constant warfare. Rational men establish constitutional restraints on rapacity, compelling themselves to be good citizens. Peace ensues. 2. Federation prevails over global government because the larger the collective, the less effective its laws. Language and religions segregate peoples into nations, which also then drive men toward peace and understanding to avoid wars. (There is only one religion of man, though there exist many vehicles of religion, with their historical and local differentiations.) 3. Commerce, which matters to men as much as war, cannot coexist with wars. So, nature pits man against himself, requiring that he choose between war and commerce.

**Second Addition: A Secret Article Concerning Eternal Peace**. Any nation considering war should recur to the maxims of philosophers concerning war. Philosophers should not be precluded by law from speaking on war and peace. Their views need not rule the day, but should be heard. Philosophers inquire whether existing laws need improvement; jurists merely apply laws as they are. Make no philosopher king, nor require kings to philosophize. Power corrupts inevitably. Let philosophers speak, as counterpoint.

**Appendix.** *I. On the Disagreement Between Morals and Politics in Relation to Eternal Peace.* Political and moral considerations conflict only when expediency in politics excludes morals from its deliberations. If no man is free, then morality is empty clanging. A moral politician seeks, when constitutional defects emerge, to promptly remediate those difficulties. Politicians who do less seek personal gain. Self-motivated politicians trick people with justifications and evasions and strategies, such as "one must act, then make excuses" or "do what seems best, then deny you did it" or "blame the people" or "divide and conquer." In the end, such men seek only to increase their power, regardless of the means employed. But right and law prevail. Amoral politicians rely on force, not right. They have it backwards. We must rely on right to make power. Right laws rely on this principle, which is a universal dictate of pure practical reason: act only so you might wish your act to become a law for all men. In framing laws, we look not to their effect, but only to their derivation from pure practical reason. Right laws lead, slowly but inexorably, toward better societies. Conflicts of morals and politics spring from human selfishness. We find selfishness within our hearts, and recognize it as well in others. But restraint is possible. Just societies can be created. But morality must prevail over politics, when conflicts between them occur. The natural rights of men count most. *II. On the Agreement between Politics and Morals According to the Transcendental Idea of Public Right and Law.* Right action welcomes publicity. Wrong acts pray for secrecy. 1. Can oppressed citizens overthrow their tyrants violently? No, none would consent to a constitution which permitted occasional rebellions. So, the principle fails the publicity test. 2. Can States breach agreements with one another? No, for if all knew beforehand such was the rule, then none would enter such international agreements. Can small States preemptively attack larger ones, if they fear the larger State's power and ability to dominate? No, because if publicly announced, none would agree to such a rule. 3. As to world laws, the same considerations apply as those of international law. For any such laws to exist, there must be an international State to make those laws. Morality and politics can agree only within such a federative union of States. Charity and respect toward others is a moral obligation, both of which politicians prefer to ignore. Publicity of philosophical maxims would prevent abuses. So, men should require publicity of proposed political acts to determine their propriety. Eternal peace can be realized, but only if we recognize that truces are mere preludes to further war. Eternal peace emerges from steady progress in resolving conflicts. Persevere in small, but steady, steps toward eternal peace.

## EPITOME 12

**Stone, Douglas, Bruce Patton, Sheila Heen. *Difficult Conversations: How To Discuss What Matters Most.* New York: Penguin Books, 1999.**

*Douglas Stone studied law at Harvard Law School, where he worked for ten years in the Harvard Negotiation Project. Bruce Patton co-founded the Harvard Negotiation Project, and teaches negotiation at Harvard, from which law school he also graduated. Mr. Patton co-authored* Getting to Yes. *Sheila Heen lectures at Harvard in negotiations and writes on conflict management and communications.*

**Introduction.** Difficult conversations are those you find it hard to have. Whether you avoid or engage the talk, you run risks. You cannot soft-pedal a difficult conversation. Tact is not what's missing. The Harvard Negotiation Project has helped thousands make such conversations more productive and less stressful. Everyone has a difficult conversation to have.

### I. The Problem.

***Chapter 1: Sort Out the Three Conversations***. Difficult conversations share underlying structure: 1) factual, 2) emotional, and 3) meaning. Talk about the facts frequently bogs down in the assumption we know the truth, we know another's intentions, and we can assess blame. Disputed facts seldom make conversations difficult; rather, conflicting perceptions, interpretations, and values cause the problem. We do not know the intention of others, unless they tell us (and then they may still be wrong). Blame deflects people from understanding causes and making changes. Difficult conversations are mostly about feelings. Meaning in conflict usually touches identity: who am I and who are we together? Fears and anxiety about these answers may cause you to become unstable, which impedes constructive conversation. Avoid persuading or coercing. Seek to understand the other's viewpoint. This will foster openness. Difficult conversations can be opportunities for learning about another person, rather than an argument.

### II. Shift to a Learning Stance.

#### The "What Happened?" Conversation.

***Chapter 2: Stop Arguing About Who's Right: Explore Each Other's Stories.*** Arguing fails. We think, "You are causing this problem," and so assert, impute, and blame. As we do so, the other person does the same. Each person's story makes sense, within their own framework. We tend to trade conclusions rather than comprehend the reasons beneath assertions. Insisting on change makes that very change less likely. People have perspective; they see the world in their own way. Each has information, interprets that data, and draws conclusions. But we have different information, because we tend to notice and ignore different things. And both parties lack all the relevant information. Assuming we know all that is needed is a problem; assume you need to learn critical information from the other party. Our interpretations of experience depend on past experiences, which experiences form rules we live by. The conclusions we draw from interpretation of experience reflect self-interest. We have ample reason to be humble about how right our version of any story may be. Instead of arguing about our certainties, we are well served by choosing a stance of curiosity—toward the other, and toward ourselves. There are parts of our own story we know poorly. Accept both stories, even in their conflicted facts. This is the "And Stance." Understand the other's story. Use your imagination to stand in their shoes.

***Chapter 3: Don't Assume They Meant It: Disentangle Intent from Impact.*** In argument, people frequently think they know the other's intentions. They don't. We assume intention from negative impact on us (though we tend to give ourselves a break under similar circumstances). One may occasionally encounter a bad actor, one whose intentions are bad, but seldom. If we assume bad intent, we frequently proceed to impute bad character, which, when the other hears our view, generates defensiveness. That affects how the other treats us, and not for the good. Once the other explains his good intentions, he frequently believes that his good intentions sanitize his bad impact and hurt will automatically subside. It doesn't. Further, having some good intentions does not mean one does not simultaneously have poor intentions. Our motivations are complex. To avoid all this, *disentangle impact from intent*. 1) Clarify for yourself what happened, its impact on you, and your hypothesis about the other's intention. 2) Tell the other what happened, its impact on you, and your hypothesis about why they did what they did. Ask their intentions. 3) Expect some defensiveness. If you are the person being talked to, tolerate accusations so you can plumb the feelings of the other person. Explain your motivation/intention, then openly reflect on the other possible motivations that might explain your actions.

***Chapter 4: Abandon Blame: Map the Contribution System***. Blame reduces an errant person's ability to change the errant behavior by making them fearful of consequences. Contribution examines the contribution of each player to failure and asks how to change so a negative outcome does not again occur. Blame is costly; it makes people less forthcoming, resistant to needed change, and frequently misses the system interactions that created the entire problem. Mapping contribution to problems does not mean avoiding your feelings, or focusing only on your own contribution, or blaming the victim. We frequently contribute to problems by 1) avoiding them, 2) being unapproachable, 3) failing to notice that our pasts intersect with another's past in incompatible ways, and 4) tolerating dysfunctional roles we play. If you cannot find your contribution, reverse roles or seek objective perspective. Seek a balanced view of contribution. Shifters think they did not contribute to a problem. Absorbers think only their contribution to a problem mattered. Admit your contribution early in conversation. Encourage the other to find their contributions. Be clear in your explanations and explicit about what you and the other person should do differently in the future.

**The Feelings Conversation.**

***Chapter 5*: *Have Your Feelings (Or They Will Have You)*.** Feelings are powerful and are expressed whether we want to or not. Bottled feelings poison relationships. Difficult conversations must address feelings. Frequently, feelings are the substance of the problem. Avoided, they leak (or burst) into conversations. Also, unexpressed feelings block effective listening. Share your feelings with skills. Start by 1) sorting your feelings, 2) negotiating with your feelings, and 3) sharing feelings (not judgments). To sort feelings, first you have to find them. Learn the contours of your own emotions. Recognize that feelings are normal, good people have bad feelings sometimes, your feelings are as important as those of others, "simple" feelings often need unbundling, hidden feelings can mask others, and accusations hide strong feelings. Negotiate your feelings by amending your thinking. Reassess the facts, look into your assumptions, map your contribution to the problem. Your feelings will shift toward openness. Once identified, express feelings carefully by a) putting them into words because they are important, b) speaking of their full spectrum (not just anger, but anger, shame, uncertainty, longing), and c) don't evaluate your (or the other person's) emotions. Just listen without judgment or monopolizing. After expressing the emotions, the other party must acknowledge that your emotions are important to you and have been heard.

**The Identity Conversation.**

***Chapter 6: Ask Yourself What's at Stake*.** Difficult conversations confront others, but also us. Our identity is challenged. Common identity issues are: 1) competence, 2) goodness, and 3) lovability. Identity struggles define life and growth. They cannot be avoided, and are frequently painful. To cope better with the identity struggles in difficult conversations, a) avoid all-or-nothing thinking (I am competent or I am not competent), b) avoid denial, c) avoid hyperbole, and d) avoid letting criticism serve as the only information defining you. Ground your identity by knowing your identity issues and accepting yourself: mistakes, mixed intentions, and contribution to problems. To regain balance when your identity is shaken, i) don't try to control the other person's response, ii) prepare for their likely response, iii) get perspective by thinking of yourself months or years in the future, long after the conflict has subsided, and iv) take needed breaks. Remember that the other person is simultaneously having their own identity struggles with the conversation. Consider raising the issue expressly.

## III. Create a Learning Conversation.

***Chapter 7: What's Your Purpose? When to Raise It and When To Let Go.*** Which difficulties warrant having a difficult conversation? There is no right answer; attempt to think clearly. Process the three issues: feelings, identity, and distortions or gaps in your perception. Avoid difficult conversations if: 1) the real issue is inside you, 2) the problem is better solved by changing your actions than talking, or 3) your purpose in having the conversation is not clear or achievable. Conversations may fail if a) you want to change the hearer rather than influence him, b) sacrifice long-term benefit for short-term peace, or c) you hit-and-run. Give important conversations substantial time. Some relationships cannot be saved. Then one must let go. This is a complex process, different for each person. Some liberating ideas: i) You do not have to fix things, just do your best, ii) the other person is probably struggling too, iii) this conflict is not who I am, and iv) letting go does not mean you do not care. In difficult conversations you decide to: 1) learn the other person's story, 2) express your thoughts and feelings, and 3) work on solving the problem together.

***Chapter 8: Getting Started: Begin from the Third Story***. Don't start a difficult conversation inside your view. The other side thinks that your view is the problem, not the solution, and it triggers defensiveness. 1) Start in the third story, the story an objective third-person might tell, for example, a mediator. Mediators characterize the parties' stories as different, not right or wrong, better or worse. 2) Invite the other person to reach mutual understanding and engage in problem-solving. Make them a partner in solving the problem. Be persistent. When delivering bad news, say the bad news up front. If asking for something, do not demand. Invite an exploration of an idea. If past conversations have gone wrong, talk about how to talk about the topic. Use this map for difficult conversations: 1) third story (objective), 2) their story (facts, impact, contributions, feelings, identity), 3) your story (facts, impact, contributions, feelings, identity).

***Chapter 9***: ***Learning: Listen from the Inside Out***. Humans need to be heard. Listening well helps others listen to you. Good listening is authentic; the listener says "I need to understand," not "I understand." Skills of good listening: ask questions, paraphrase, repeat, acknowledge, sit attentively, and keep eye contact. None of this will matter, if the other does not believe you care and are genuinely curious. Authenticity is critical. Listen to your internal voice: be aware of it, negotiate with it, and occasionally stop the difficult conversation if you find your internal voice too loud to continue. *Inquire*. Avoid rhetorical questions, and questions intended to make a point. Use open-ended questions, and follow up for more information. Invite the other to answer; do not demand. *Paraphrase*. Paraphrasing lets you check your understanding of what the other is saying, and lets them know they have been heard. *Acknowledge*. Every person wants to have his or her feelings acknowledged. Acknowledge what the other is feeling before problem-solving. Acknowledging another's feelings is not agreeing with them. The empathetic listener struggles to understand another from that person's perspective.

***Chapter 10***: ***Speak for Yourself with Clarity and Power***. Self-expression begins internally. One must negotiate with yourself that your views and feelings are as important as those of others and deserve to be heard with respect. We can sabotage ourselves by trying to speak without doing our best. Failure to express yourself precludes important relationships. If you struggle to express yourself, it is something to work on. Start with what matters most to you, what lies at the heart of the matter and what is at stake. Speak directly; don't sidle up to the point or ease in. When you have complex feelings or perceptions, state each, despite their conflict. Don't leave pieces out. To be clear: 1) avoid stating your view as truth, 2) share the basis of your view: information, experiences, interpretations, and 3) don't exaggerate frequency. Avoid "always" and "never." Help your listener. Try to give them your story in a manner that works for them individually: visual, auditory, charts, metaphors. Ask for paraphrase. Ask how and why they disagree. Confidently express your own story.

***Chapter 11*: *Problem-Solving: Take the Lead*.** Take the lead in difficult conversations. Reframe unhelpful expression. Reframe truth statements as different stories. Reframe accusations into intentions and impacts. Reframe blame as mutual contribution. Reframe judgments and characterizations as feelings. Reframe "what's wrong with you" statements as "what's going on for them" statements. Choose the "And Stance." Validate the other's view, and explain the importance of your own. If the conversation gets stuck, listen. Persist in listening. Stubbornly hear the other and seek to be heard. If nothing works, name the dynamic that is happening. Say something like, Each time we get to this point we seem to get stuck. I feel like you get angry and divert the conversation. To solve problems, 1) recognize each must persuade the other to agree, 2) suggest a fair test to divergent assumptions, 3) say why you remain unpersuaded, and remain open to being persuaded, and ask what would persuade them, 4) ask the other's advice. Do joint brainstorming about difficult issues. If no solution is reached, ask what standards ought to guide such an issue. People's differences make compromise necessary. Finding solutions that accommodate both parties affirms the fundamental principle of mutual caretaking. If no agreement emerges, be clear about the choices you are making and be willing to accept the consequences of your decisions. Most difficult conversations are really a series of conversations.

***Chapter 12*: *Putting It All Together*.** Prepare for a difficult conversation: 1) Imagine What Happened?, Feeling, and Identity conversations. Your confidence about knowing the other person's viewpoint should be shaken. 2) Decide whether to have the conversation. 3) Start with the objective viewpoint of a mediator, framing the problem. 4) Explore both stories. Reframe as needed to keep the talk constructive. 5) Brainstorm solutions. Address issues sequentially, if possible. If no agreement is reached, address standards for what a solution should look like, with mutual caretaking in mind. Keep communication open.

## EPITOME 13

**Gottmann, John M. and Joan DeClaire. *The Relationship Cure: A 5 Step Guide to Strengthening Your Marriage, Family, and Friendships.* New York: Three Rivers Press, 2001.**

*John Gottmann (born 1942) teaches at the University of Washington, and codirects the Gottmann Institute. Dr. Gottman's research includes an apartment lab where human relational interactions are recorded and analyzed. Joan DeClaire works as a freelance writer and lives in Seattle.*

**Preface.** This book discusses the basic principles that regulate how human relationships work and how conflict can be regulated. Emotional awareness guides us in finding meaning in our lives.

### Chapter 1: How We Connect Emotionally.

1. *Bid by Bid: How to Build Better Relationships One Step at a Time*. People need to share emotional information to feel connected with one another. The "bid" is the fundamental unit of emotional communication. A bid may be an inquiry, movement, gaze, touch, or anything that communicates the actor's desire to build a positive connection with you. A response to a bid is a positive or negative act that invites further bidding or declines further bidding.

2. *Turning Points: The Choices We Make in Responding to Bids*. Relationships build bid by bid. Positive responses to bids lead to further and more intense and frequent bidding and responding. People almost never re-bid when a bid is rejected. There are three responses to a bid: a) Turning Toward. This bid response invites further bidding. b) Turning Against. This bid response expresses hostility, and is usually followed by repression of emotions. This hostility destroys a relationship. c) Turning Away. This bid response ignores the bid. This ignoring also destroys a relationship.

3. *Unrequited Turning*. Rejected or ignored bidders generally never try to connect with a person in the same way again.

4. *Disconnected: The Consequences of Living Without Emotional Bonds*. People satisfy three needs by bidding to relate to someone: 1) to feel included, 2) to feel in control of one's life, and/or 3) to be liked.

- When Parents Fail to Connect. Emotional bonds with one's child set a pattern for their future relationships. Infant cries are bids, and the response sets expectations concerning what to expect from people. Children raised in conflict-ridden homes have chronically elevated stress hormones.
- When Couples Fail to Connect. Even if one has failed to make emotional connections well, the skill can be learned at any age. Unhappily married people get sick thirty-five percent more often than happily married couples, and live an average of four years less.
- Trouble Connecting with Friends and Siblings. Good friends extend life, reduce stress, increase infection resistance. Some studies indicate that longevity is more related to friendship than genetics.

- Trouble Connecting on the Job. Workplace harmony makes worker lives better. But ignoring worker emotions may be profitable. The downside of such neglect is the fractured workplace.
- The Good News about Connecting. Emotional connection is a skill to be learned, practiced, and mastered. Even hobbled relationships can be improved if both parties persevere, give attention, and correct mistakes.

**Chapter 2: STEP ONE: Look at Your Bids for Connection.**

Bids are not exciting talk; they deal most frequently with the mundane.

1. *How Bids Work.* People bid because they want to be connected to another person. The closer the relationship, the more frequent and intense the bidding. The ladder of bidding looks like this: small talk, humor, friendly gossip, affection, support, problem solving, and heartfelt subjects like future goals, worries, values, meaning.

2. *What Do Bids Look Like?* Bids come in bewildering variety. They may be verbal or non-verbal. Many bids are ambiguous.

3. *What Causes Fuzzy Bidding?* Fear of emotional risk and poor communication leads to fuzzy bidding. A fuzzy bid is often a trial balloon. People turn toward, away, or against the bids for connection from others.

4. *Choosing to Turn Toward Bids for Connection.* Responses to bids may be nearly passive, low-energy, attentive, or high-energy. Turning toward a bid leads to healthy relationships, and one must turn toward the other in all sorts of circumstances. Low conflict families build better environments for children. Playfulness is good for relationships. To build a deep relationship, turn toward that person as often as possible.

5. *Choosing to Turn Away From Bids for Connection.* Turned away responses may be preoccupied, disregarding, or interrupting. The usual reason for turning away from a bid is mindlessness. When intentional, the turner may be seeking more autonomy. When a partner turns away, the rejected bidder crumples and rarely rebids. "Habitually turning away can eventually destroy relationships." Preoccupied wives are frequently more dissatisfied with their marriages than are preoccupied husbands. There are gender differences in bidding and responding.

6. *Choosing to Turn Against Bids for Connection.* Turning against a bid may be contemptuous, belligerent, contradictory, domineering, critical, or defensive. Creating an emotion log of your emotional experiences may help you become more aware of your style in bidding and responding to bids. Use a blank book.

7. *Difference between Men and Women.* Husbands in happy marriages turn toward their wives more frequently than husbands in unhappy marriages. Unhappily married wives turn toward their spouses with the same frequency as happily married wives. When turned against, husbands become hostile or repressed. Wives only become repressed. (Bidding analysis worksheets. Love map exercise.)

8. *Better Bids Ahead.* Once you become aware of your style, there are patterns to avoid that otherwise might obstruct closer bonds with others. You can improve your relationships.

**Chapter 3: Six Bid Busters and How to Avoid Them.**

1. *Being Mindless Rather Than Mindful.* Generally, people are not deeply aware of other's emotional needs. Learning to share the feelings of others creates a shared journey of discovery. Set a goal to learn the other's feelings. Collect moments of emotional poignancy. See life as a string of these collected pearls.

2. *Starting on a Sour Note.* The "harsh startup" is a bid that begins with a negative, blaming, or critical introduction. Start bids softly.

3. *Using Harmful Criticism Instead of Helpful Complaints.* Complaints concern a specific problem, and address behavior. Criticism judges, addressing character. Criticism hurts people's feelings, increases tension, defensiveness, resentment, and leads the other to shut you out.

4. *Flooding.* Emotional stress can become so intense that one grows emotionally and physically incapable of responding. Thinking is muddy. Men flood more easily than women. If flooding happens, take a break from the conversation and soothe yourself for at least twenty minutes. (Relaxation, flooding, and emotional literacy exercises.)

5. *Practicing a Crabby Habit of Mind.* Crabby people grow fixated on making situations perfect and pointing out the faults of others. Their tendency is to turn against bids. If you are such a person, redirect your attention to things in your world that please you, that make you want to offer praise. Children of crabby parents learn to turn away from those parents. (Thanksgiving exercise.)

6. *Avoiding Conversations You Need to Have.* Most often, damage to relationship derives not from what was said, but from what was avoided. If there is conflict on the horizon, only three choices lie open: a) attack and defend, b) avoid or deny, and c) self-disclose and connect. Tell the person about how you feel now. Do not try to resolve events of the past. This is not always possible. Both parties must choose self-disclosure and connection.

7. *Looking Ahead.* Our lives can become an ascending chain of improved emotional insight and improving relationships.

**Chapter 4: STEP TWO: Discover Your Brain's Emotional Command System.**

1. *Panksepp Research.* Jaak Panksepp is a neuroanatomist who studies the human emotional brain systems. Panksepp argues that at least seven deep emotional brain structures govern large portions of human behavior, and these structures are ancient and aim to protect us. They constitute genetic learning. People differ in the comfort they experience when different systems are stimulated. Some people prefer one system over another, though all employ all systems. Knowing your own proclivities is important self-awareness, and also important for how you relate to others who do not share your preferences and inclinations. Being overstimulated or understimulated in emotional control systems can make a person uncomfortable in a circumstance, and if the unwanted stimulation (or lack of it) becomes chronic, it can alter your personality.

2. *The Seven Systems and How They Affect Us.*

- Commander-In-Chief. This system coordinates dominance, control, and power urges.
- Explorer. This system coordinates searching, learning, and curiosity.

- Sensualist. This system coordinates sexual and reproduction urges.
- Energy Czar. This system coordinates rest and food requirements.
- Jester. This system coordinates play, recreation, and diversion.
- Sentry. This system coordinates worry, fear, vigilance, and defense of self.
- Nest-Builder. This system coordinates affiliation, bonding, and attachment.

3. *Command Systems Often Act Together.* More than one system frequently coordinates in meeting a specific need of an individual.

4. *What Determines How You Use Your Command Systems?* Your individual emotional orientation with regard to emotional command systems is influenced by: a) genetic heritage, b) gender (men more likely to prefer the command, jester, and sentry systems; women more likely to prefer the nest-builder system), c) life experiences generally, and 4) lone experiences of great intensity. Emotional command systems are malleable over time, and a natural part of human survival.

5. *Evaluate Your Emotional Command Systems.* You should become aware of your own emotional command system needs and preferences, so you can care for your own emotional needs, improve your ability to bid and respond, and help you understand others. (Emotional command system exercises.)

6. *Putting Knowledge To Work.* When we make decisions that conform to and cooperate with our emotional command system needs, our sense of well-being grows and life improves.

7. *Accepting Ourselves and Others.* Your brain differs from others' brains. Knowing this makes compassion easier. This mental framework helps people know how to compromise with others.

8. *Expect Mismatches and Work with Them.* You will experience people with whom your emotional command preferences collide. You can celebrate the differences or complain about them.

9. *Bidding Across Emotional Command Systems.* Gottmann offers a long section of exchanges between persons with differing emotional control system preferences.

10. *Still More Connections.* Emotional command style is not all the difference between people. Their experiences also complicate matters.

**Chapter 5: STEP THREE: Examine Your Emotional Heritage**.

One person frequently responds and feels differently about experiences than does another. A person's emotional history impacts their ability to connect emotionally with others.

1. *What Our Experience Tells Us.* Past experience influences future emotional experience, which can affect your ability to connect with others. Brain pathways are plastic to an extent. Events can influence them. (Emotional history exercise.)

2. *Your Family's Philosophy of Emotion Matters, Too.* Each of us (and our families) has a philosophy of emotion. We take on beliefs and expectations concerning how our emotions should be. Families generally fall into one of four approaches to handling emotions: a) coaching, b) dismissing, c) laissez-faire, or d) disapproving. "Coaching" families accept expression of emotion and help one another cope. "Dismissing" families discourage expression of negative feelings. Feelings are ignored or minimized. Little help with emotions or instruction about emotions occurs. "Laissez-faire" families allow emotional expression, but do little to help one another cope.

"Disapproving" families also hide negative feelings, but suffer active hostility to their expression. (Family philosophy of emotion exercise.)

3. *The Emotion-Coaching Philosophy.* Emotion coaching families turn toward one another during a member's feelings of sadness, anger, or fear. They empathize and help. They set limits on expression of negative emotion. Emotions have value, even negative emotions. They teach self-soothing to one another.

4. *The Emotion-Dismissing Philosophy.* Emotion dismissing families discourage expression of negative feelings. They ignore or disregard emotional expression. They often fear emotions will overwhelm the family and lead to catastrophic results. Some members may avoid emotions because they feel too responsible for fixing the underlying problems. Dismissing emotions causes lost opportunities for connection, and deeply injures children. Opportunities for teaching children to care for themselves when upset, and how to problem-solve, are also lost.

5. *The Emotion-Disapproving Philosophy.* Emotion-disapproving families often see emotional expression as an unfair strategy to manipulate toward an outcome. Emotional expression is countered with threats. Such families have not learned to tolerate negative emotions and see them as bids for connection. We can accept people's emotions, empathize, all without adopting the sufferer's position.

6. *The Laissez-Faire Philosophy.* Laissez-faire families view emotions as letting off steam. When the emotional outburst is over, it is over. There is no more work to be done. Often, parents with this philosophy came from abusive or chaotic homes, and have sworn off that approach. But they do not know what to do. So, such parents eventually feel helpless. (Emotional philosophy exercise.)

7. *Which Philosophy Works Best?* Emotion-coaching families prosper. Their lives are more successful and fulfilling. The other approaches do not work.

8. *Emotional Intelligence Versus Detachment and Denial.* Emotions are diverse; people are healthiest when they express, identify, and cope with emotional breadth. The pain of negative emotions is real, and many fear it. But failure to welcome your own emotions, even the negative ones, leads to inability to understand yourself and consequent inability to understand others. You will connect less often. Bonding becomes difficult.

9. *Understanding Enduring Vulnerabilities.* An "enduring vulnerability" is a life event so powerful that it is not possible to move past its effects. Such events may, for example, be deaths, abuse, rape, seeing violent acts, being victimized, marital problems, job loss, hazing, illness, depression and suicidal ideation, substance abuse, or war. Enduring vulnerabilities may hinder attempts to form new relationships, because they affect our behaviors and erode self-trust. (Enduring vulnerabilities exercise.)

10. *What Awareness Offers.* People able to speak of their enduring vulnerabilities with others help their relationships get over the hurdle the vulnerability presents. The others need to listen carefully when the vulnerable person tells their difficult story from which the enduring vulnerability derives.

11. *Back to the Future.* Learning about your emotional history helps you differentiate yesterday's problems from today's opportunities.

## Chapter 6: STEP FOUR: Sharpen Your Emotional Communication Skills.

We can learn emotional communication skills throughout life, though childhood is the primary classroom. You can become a person who detects unspoken difficulty and views it as a bid for connection, turning toward it with compassion. Many cues are unspoken: expressions, posture and gestures, tone. Others are verbal: word descriptions and metaphors. Building these skills makes heart-to-heart exchanges more likely.

1. *Pardon Me, But Your Feelings Are Leaking.* Many people avoid expressing negative emotions because they fear them, or don't want to burden others, or because they lack vocabulary to say what is happening, or cherish privacy. But people's true emotions leak through to others, even when they actively seek to hide them. And people believe the non-verbal cues one gives over the words one says.

2. *Understanding the Face.* Thirty-three muscle groups in the face are dedicated to communicating emotion via changes in the shape of forehead, brows, eyelids, cheeks, nose, lips and chin. Basic facial motions are universal, always expressing a given emotion. These movements are genetic and not culturally determined. The seven basic emotions are: sadness, anger, fear, happiness, surprise, contempt, and disgust. These expressions may be mixed with one another. To read another's emotions facially, a) learn their face's neutral state, b) keep in mind that more than one emotional state may coincide and be expressed, c) avoid interpreting physical features of a face as emotional expression, and d) watch carefully because many of the facial expressions are fleeting. People frequently mis-report their own emotions. The careful observer can listen past the error and detect authentic emotion. (Facial expression exercise.)

3. *Reading Movements and Gestures.* The face tells what a person is feeling; bodily actions tell you how strongly they feel it. Factors to consider are a) universal gestures (fidgeting = non-interest; relaxed forward leaning = respect and attention; copying posture of other = affiliation; arm or leg crossing = opposition), b) distance from another, and c) eye level (equal level means openness). (Movement-gesture exercise.)

4. *The Language of Touch.* Touching is important for our wellbeing (consider the research on depressed mothers massaging their babies), but is subject to misinterpretation. Touching may express attachment, power, sexual interest, or other sentiments. The appropriateness of forms of touching is culturally determined, and may evoke strong responses. (Touch exercise.)

5. *What the Voice Reveals.* Voices communicate emotions by changes in pitch, rate, and volume. Fear and tension cause halting or broken speech. (Voice exercise.)

6. *Putting Feelings Into Words.* Some people can talk easily of their emotions; others lack understanding and words to express emotion. Identifying and conversing about one's emotions gives a sense of control over them, helps one connect with others, and opens the door to input from others. (Identifying feelings exercise. Emotional vocabulary list.) (192)

7. *Metaphorically Speaking.* The metaphors by which people speak of their emotions may reveal their experiences and histories. One may shift feelings by changing metaphors. You might adopt the metaphorical language of a person with whom you want to connect. (Metaphor exercise.)

8. Above All, Just *Listen*. To connect with others:

- Focus on being interested in others, not interesting to them.
- Start by asking open-ended, but reasonably specific questions.
- Ask questions about people's goals and visions of the future.
- Look for and express your commonalities with others.
- Tune in with all your attention to what the other is saying. Do not plan what you will say next while the other is speaking.
- Respond with an occasional brief nod or sound.
- From time to time, paraphrase what the speaker says.
- Maintain the right amount of eye contact. More when listening, less when speaking. Lack of eye contact indicates disinterest, nervousness, lack of confidence.
- Let go of your own agenda. Listening requires patience and a willingness to forgo action for the present. Engage in open receptive listening. Reach for a place where you can honestly say, "I understand."
- Turn off the television. TV reduces people's ability to connect, especially for children. Limit TV watching. Watch something together, then discuss it afterwards. (Emotional communication game.)

**Chapter 7: STEP FIVE: Find Shared Meaning.**

Shared meaning supports emotional connections. Supporting another's dreams is very good for relationships.

1. *People in Conflict as Idealists*. Irresolvable conflict is usual and normal. 69% of marital conflicts never go away. Most conflicts grow from different meanings attached to common circumstances. Uncovering the dream takes the edge off conflict.

2. *Become a Dream Detector*. Find out the meaning a person's position holds for him or her. Such conversations reveal meaning, not positions, and expose what really matters to a person.

3. *Sometimes Dreams are Hidden*. The dream-conflict connection is not always obvious.

4. *Listening to Dreams*. Look for the other's dream when in conflict.

5. *Trust the Process and Offer Support*. Zero-sum conflicts eradicate the possibility of connection between people. We must honor the dreams of others. We can do that by asking questions, offering empathy, offering validation, and participating in the other's dream at an appropriate level. (Dreams exercise. Ending gridlock exercise.)

6. *Explore the Rituals You Share and Create New Ones*. Shared rituals create structures within which bids for emotional connection occur on a regular basis. Rituals symbolize meaning and values we share. Rituals combat the excuse of lack of time to connect emotionally. Rituals help people normalize relationship after or during conflicts.

7. *Consider Emotional Command Systems*. Different rituals may appeal to different parts of our emotional makeup.

8. *Re-create and Update Rituals in Healing Ways*. Examine your rituals and adjust or delete or create them to be meaningful to you now. (Rituals exercise.)

**Chapter 8: Apply What You've Learned**.

Building better connections to others does not prevent conflict, but it helps relationships better weather conflicts that do occur. Gottmann and DeClaire apply their five steps to marriage, parenting, friendship, sibling, and co-worker relationships.

**Chapter 9: In Conclusion**.

Make bids toward the others you want in your life in simple and positive ways. Learn to recognize and respond to the bids of others. Be patient, observant, and optimistic. Deep bonding will follow.

# EPITOME 14

**Lederach, John Paul. *The Moral Imagination: The Art and Soul of Building Peace.* New York: Oxford University Press, 2005.**

*John Paul Lederach (born 1955) received his Ph.D. in sociology from University of Colorado. Lederach has taught at Notre Dame and Eastern Mennonite University. Lederach has participated in conflict resolution in Somalia, Northern Ireland, Nicaragua, Columbia, and Nepal. Lederach's emphasis on non-violence leans upon his Mennonite faith.*

**Thoughts for a Preface.** Lederach writes for colleagues involved with "conflict transformation," by which he means mediation, restorative justice, and peacebuilding. Lederach's previous book, *Building Peace*, concerned engineering social change, in particular, peacebuilding. There exists a tension in social structures, and in Lederach's own personal psychology, between violence and constructive engagement. This present work addresses that tension. Lederach does not seek objectivity. Eliminating personal intuition robs us of understanding. He seeks to explore the "messiness of innovation." He seeks the deep reason and art of peacebuilding, which is both an art and skill. Moral imagination guides constructive change. One must recognize what is, but seek what is not yet. Lederach calls this a "messy process." The present work is not a technical manual. It aims at deep questions of why do the work and what nurtures that effort. Many of Lederach's insights spring, not from analytic rigor, but rather from serendipitous accidents.

**ONE. On Stating the Problem and Thesis**. A core question: How does one surmount community violence while living within the community? Lederach proposes: Moral imagination transcends violence. 1) We imagine ourselves embedded in a community that includes enemies. 2) We remain curious about complexity without recurring to polarities. 3) We rely on creative acts. 4) We embrace the risk of entering a mystery beyond violence. Moral imagination requires the genius of art more than the rigors of the academy.

**TWO. On Touching the Moral Imagination.** *Four Stories.*

- *Ghana*. 90s. Northern Ghana. Muslim-Christian tensions. Two tribes, the Konkombas (Christian) and Dagombas (Muslim), fought over land in one town. Violence threatened to spill to the entire region. Mediators called a session with the disputants. The Dagomba chief asserted ascendancy. But a Konkomba young man (for they had no chief), responded to insults with humility, calling the Dagomba chief "father." The chief relented and apologized. The key was **humble demeanor** in the face of hubris. Peace required much work, but that day conflict took a new tenor and direction.
- *Wajir, Kenya*. Somali clans in Kenya fought, and the culture devolved into lawlessness. Women gathered to seek a solution. They started

change by making the public market safe for women of all clans. They expanded to broader issues, including providing employment for the bush fighters. The key was **direct engagement** with people before violence spiraled.

- *Colombia*. Peasants in central Columbia faced grave pressure to join in the fighting of government, leftist, and drug armies. They resisted and formed an association for non-violent resistance. Their watchwords were: solidarity, public meetings, sincere dialogue, negotiate with anyone (no enemies), support one another, and transparency. Their key was to **approach every person as an individual**, not as representative of an institution.
- *Tajikistan*. The Tajiks negotiated an end to their civil war. Commencing mediation between the Mullah commander and his opponents proved difficult. A professor met with the Mullah, and they spent several months discussing philosophy and Sufi theology. When trust had been built, the professor asked the Mullah to consider putting down his weapons to discuss peace. The Mullah sought guarantees of his safety. The professor promised to die alongside the Mullah, if they were betrayed. The professor and the Mullah built **personal bonds**. The path to dialogue is seldom straight. Tajik peace was negotiated. Lederach sees in each of these stories surprising acts of moral imagination.

**THREE. On This Moment**. Peacemakers promise more than they deliver. We cannot remedy human conflict globally by merely solving humanity's problems. We require moral imagination. The concept of moral imagination has deep roots, and has graced the titles of many books in diverse disciplines. These authors share the idea that moral imagination: 1) pierces to levels deeper than initial perceptions, 2) is a creative gesture, and 3) transcends the usual, refusing to labor in worn ruts. The "moral" is not religious, where morality often devolves into dogma. Such moral stasis is the death of moral imagination. The moral imaginer creates what did not before exist. Violence grips those who can imagine no better solution. We dwell in a violent context, but forge new patterns with an enemy. Lederach coined the word "justpeace," which is the goal sought by conflict approaches that seek simultaneously to reduce violence and increase justice in human relationships.

**FOUR. On Simplicity and Complexity**. Disputes are complex relationships. At the root of complexity lies simplicity. Lederach advises to embrace the complexity of a conflicted situation fully. Only when one plumbs a morass can one innovate a better solution. Simple dynamics lead to complex conflicts. Identify those simple patterns, for "simplicity precedes complexity." *Relationships*. Core convictions of peacebuilding are: 1) Since nothing lives alone, relationships govern all. The violent believe they can achieve their goals outside their relationships, and their violence ceases when they recognize themselves as relationally interdependent. 2) Contestants can come to see themselves situated in the relational web they share with opponents. With this insight, violence collapses. One's own well-being depends upon that of the enemy. *Paradoxical Curiosity*. Moral imagination rises above dualistic polarities. It seeks values that lie beneath the overt conflict, values "where meaning is rooted." *Creative Acts*. Creativity sees possibilities in a circumstance. One makes interior space for creativity by believing in its availability, despite obstacles. "The future is not the slave of the past and the birth of something new is possible." *Risk*. One moves into the future without foreknowledge of what will transpire. The path is mysterious, and possibly dangerous.

**FIVE. On Peace Accords**. Mediators know more about how to end violence than how to build justpeace. In communities mired in violence, fear and love are present. Outcomes hinge on which predominates. Opponents reach accords and sign them. The harder task is post-accord. Accords seldom end violence all at once. Time helps parties to see that their conflict continues, but under new conditions. There remains much psychological work to be done (which Lederach calls "the deeper epicenter"). When the shooting stops, space opens to do other constructive things to mend relationships. One hopes to create an ongoing platform where adaptive change emerges; that requires genuine engagement of others, especially opponents. Accords without deeper change boomerang back into violence.

**SIX. On the Gift of Pessimism**. Lederach's work in Columbian civil wars induced forgetfulness in him, a chosen lack of memory. Peace negotiations suffered from myths and lies, jumbled with half-truths. They also limped because of technique-oriented peacemakers, who rendered the process inauthentic. The idea of post-agreement context may lack application in Columbia, because the region suffers serial wars, not a single conflict. To learn of constructive social change, one must listen to people who live through transitions from war to peace. Such persons, who live amid violence over which they exercise no control, learn a constructive form of pessimism. It becomes a gift for survival, a kind of grounded realism. Authentic change rises in communities. Only there do people come to believe in change. People, in order to accept change, have to be in proximity to and converse with the enemy. An opponent's words and behaviors must match if the other is to judge the exchange authentic. *Realpolitik* destroys these premises of authentic change, since *realpolitik* recognizes only political and economic factors. It misses community. Moral imagination seizes different relationships, rejects dualisms, expects the unexpected. Peace builds relationships with those who are feared.

**SEVEN. On Aesthetics**. Lederach finds in poetry a metaphor for peacebuilding. One embraces complexity through simplicity. Lederach discusses Japanese haiku. Excellent peacemaking follows the gut, side-stepping (or, at a minimum, augmenting) what one learns from technical approaches. Like haiku, intuitive core moments of change capture complexity simply. Fewer words; more deep listening. Lederach takes no notes in meetings. Instead, he doodles images that metaphors in conversation suggest, and captures occasional phrases. Mediators create; they are artists recognizing and sustaining something new.

**EIGHT. On Space**. When a setting stabilizes, relationships form its center. Lacking this relational web, matters deteriorate. To achieve "constructive social change," we look to "the quality and nature of people's relationships." Untangling a conflict is not so much a matter of technique (know-how), but rather a matter of reconnecting disrupted partners in a web of relationships (know-who). Lederach describes his fascination with spider webs, as a metaphor for conflict resolution. Like spiders, the mediator grasps his social geometry, finds unlike people to interact, and then puts them in position to relate creatively. Adaptability governs.

**NINE. On Mass and Movement**. To create constructive change, one seeks not large numbers of adherents ("critical mass"), but rather multiple cross-linked groups of people who share a perspective. One asks not "How many?" but "Who needs to connect with whom?" Lederach teaches peacemaking lessons from baking bread. There "critical yeast" is the watchword. Lederach draws peacebuilding lessons from yeast in the bakery: 1) Change agents need not be numerous, but rather well-positioned. 2) To facilitate constructive change, change agents need quiet, separate, safe locations to nurture that change and one another. 3) Change agents inject themselves into conflicted situations only when they are sufficiently potent. Then they must act at various locations simultaneously.

Change in the idea of mediation is needed. Mediation is a quality of social relations, not a role in conflict resolution. In violent communities, there remain social spaces where opponents relate out of necessity (schools, hospitals, marketplaces, transportation). Constructive change emerges when a community moves beyond agreements of representative leaders. The community, in its relational web, revises itself from violence to cooperation and interdependence. This is the essence of moral imagination: re-imagining relationships, resisting dualistic polarities, creating afresh from old materials, and tolerating risk.

**TEN. On Web Watching**. Lederach returns to his interest in spiders. Watching spiders' webs requires special skills: caution, patience, moving in tiny increments of distance, seeing what may be mostly invisible. As applied to social change, one must adopt "soul-based disciplines," skills that enable one to pierce the noise and hear the hidden voices, patterns, rhythms behind and within violence. These soul disciplines are three. *Stillness*. Lederach calls stillness the "zen of going nowhere." This meditational posture leads one to patient, careful, intense observation. Being still, one is positioned to see what is, and to imagine potently. Lederach identifies the guideposts of stillness: "Slow down. Stop. Watch what moves around you. Feel what moves in you." *Humility*. Spider web-watchers explore the empirical with respect and connectedness to their arachnid subjects. To bring less may destroy what is observed. "The soul of place" identifies the deep relational location in which one discovers identity and role. Humility calls one to recognize that she plays a bit part in a larger whole, but from that small place makes a meaningful contribution. Humility undergirds learning and adaptation. One needs to help create adaptive processes so that change does not derail steps toward peace. *Sensuous Perception*. Moral imagination requires that one uses senses beyond hearing and seeing, which constitute the world of words. We move gently, as if our relationships were spider webs, so as not to destroy what we seek to improve.

**ELEVEN. On Serendipity**. Moral imagination leans on serendipity, that is, discovering wisdom that you never sought. Such discoveries can lead to "accidental sagacity." Serendipity strikes when one is willing to move sideways or even backwards, in order to move forward. Formal training in conflict resolution tends to create tunnel vision, which afflicts one by assuming a static conflict environment and failing to emphasize the peripheral. Processes become rigid, and incapable of adaptation. Max Weber (1947) taught that social institutions grow solid, then rigid. Their goal becomes continuation, not their originating purpose. Conflict resolution requires smart flexible platforms, rather than institutions that are politically cognizable. Smart flexible platforms weave purpose with flexibility to survive and help. Our structures must support innovation in process and response to change. Lederach likens such process structures to skin or rivers.

**TWELVE. On Time.** Utilitarian views of time find it something to be expended, controlled for a purpose—and then gone. Others, on ancestral time, view time as a field on which life plays out. It extends backward to the past, and forward to the future. What we do now derives from generations past. What we do now changes what will come in the future. Ancestral time is occupied by those born but now dead, and those unborn and so not yet capable of dying, as well as we the living. Some indigenous cultures conceive time as the past that lies before us, known and peopled with persons we know. We walk backward into the future, which is unknown and filled with unknown persons. Moral imagination needs to grasp the "past that lies before us." Lederach styles this non-linear conception of time as "polychronic spacetime." In moral imagination of conflict resolution, one dwells in multiple spheres of time and space.

**THIRTEEN. On Pied Pipers**. Lederach recounts the tale of the pied piper, and its moral that one had best keep promises. He notes his changed perspective, later in life, that the point of the pied piper tale is, rather, the power of music to change communities. Reconciliation requires, not forgiving and forgetting, but rather remembering and changing. Artistic moments can transform the negotiations of adversaries, which Lederach styles "artful change." Lederach cites four stories in which art redirected conflict. Conflict resolution sparks the sense of art in participants. For art is a kind of love, expressing beauty and human connection in our lives. Conflict resolution has lost itself in analysis and technique. Practitioners have failed to nurture the artist in themselves and others.

**FOURTEEN. On Vocation**. Building relationships brings risks. We venture into unknown precincts, vulnerably so. Peacebuilding is a "mysterious journey toward the sacred." It is a vocation (which is not a job), a heeding of the deep voice that guides us home. Lederach tells the tale of Rose Barmasai, to whom his book is dedicated. She walked and talked (a voicewalker) throughout the Kenyan Rift Valley, soothing tensions and making space to change without violence. She took risks. She helped.

**FIFTEEN: On Conclusions**. Lederach styles the point of his book as "how to invoke the moral imagination in the midst of human conflict and violence." Post-2001, world peace has suffered substantial deterioration. Our theories of conflict management hobble the moral imagination. Our peace has become violent. Four pathways to innovative coping with violence are: a) Abandon isolation and domination, in favor of building interdependency. Include the enemy; b) Avoid dualisms; c) Seek creativity; and d) Risk engaging what we fear, as a means to create genuine community. Lederach wonders what would happen if conflict resolution moved to a model of nurture, if professionals reconceived themselves as artists, if serendipity were welcomed, if art was given a place in the process, if conflict workers thought of their work as a vocation rather than a profession, if leaders invited artists to contribute before problems explode, and if leaders were invited, perhaps for one week per year, to a school for moral imagination. Its mantra might be: seek those you fear, welcome complexity, imagine what has never before happened, and dare vulnerability a bit at a time.

**EPILOGUE**. Lederach offers the wisdom of many players who have appeared in the course of his book on moral imagination.

## EPITOME 15

**Taylor, Michael. *Community, Anarchy, and Liberty.* Cambridge: Press Syndicate of the University of Cambridge, 1982.**

*Michael Taylor (born 1942) received his Ph.D. from University of Essex, United Kingdom. He has taught at Yale, Stanford, Netherlands, Vienna, Florence, and Canberra, and University of Washington in Seattle. Taylor's work has emphasized community, anarchy, cooperation theory, and critique of rationality.*

### 1. Anarchy and Community.

**1.1. Introduction: the scope of the book**. The great challenge to anarchy is whether members of such a society can maintain basic personal and property security. Some anarchists slide silently past this question, relying upon the future transformation of human nature or market solutions. But some will forever militate or free ride, and the market insufficiently bonds members to cause stateless society to cohere. Anarchy requires human community, which entails direct and multi-form relationships among members and a very rough economic parity among members. Such anarchic community is the human norm, dominating the last 50,000 years. To have smaller states, community must be revived.

**1.2. Anarchy: what it is**. States concentrate some force and attempt to limit which other actors may use force. Pure anarchy, which never exists, perfectly disperses force among members. Practical anarchy concentrates some force and permits some political specialization, but permits no enforcement of collective decisions. Anarchy presupposes roughly equal participation in all political decision-making. Practical anarchy resembles Rousseau's social contract.

**1.3. Power, authority, and what anarchy is not**. Anarchists have seldom analyzed the concepts underlying their political theory. One induces another to do something he would otherwise have avoided by: 1) power/coercion, 2) force, 3) persuasion, 4) activation of commitments, and/or 5) authority. *Power* alters incentives, making a different choice rational for an actor, by means of threats, offers, or mixed approaches (*throffers*). Offers reward compliance. Threats punish for non-compliance. Coercion describes only threats. Taylor considers Nozick's analysis of coercion. The prime difference between threats and offers is that actors welcome offers and shun threats. Communities present low-level throffers relating to reputation (praise or gossip) and mutual assistance (help or hindrance). *Physical force* removes the victim from causation. Victims of force become instruments of their violators. They have no choice. *Persuasion* changes another's choices by altering the decider's attitudes in a transparent manner. *Activating commitments* urges a decider to follow rules he has previously acknowledged, such as laws and morals. *Authority* operates when a decider accepts the decision of another, whom the decider believes could (but does not necessarily actually) offer good reasons for compliance. *Manipulation* induces a change of choice in a manner that leaves the decider unaware of the cause of his new thought. In light of these considerations, anarchy cannot be lack of power or authority. No society could function without some power and some authority. Anarchy, rather, lacks concentrated force and political specialization, and is defined by these societal traits.

**1.4. Community**. The idea "community" admits many uses, but Taylor focuses on three characteristics of communities: 1) their shared values, 2) their direct relations in a large number of aspects, and 3) their reciprocity in mutual aid, sharing, and cooperation. The core social relationship in community is friendship. However, neither love nor friendship (as in Aristotle) nor a shared sense of transcendence (as in Buber) are universal characteristics of community. So, Taylor concludes that communities must be stable and small to retain these characteristics. Largeness and instability attenuate communal interactions.

**1.5. Anarchic communities**. Acephalous societies (lacking a head) are the human norm. They lack concentration of force, except in ad hoc circumstances, and have little division of political labor. Acephalous societies have been replaced only lately by anonymous, hierarchical states. Even chiefdoms and big-man societies may be anarchic, provided power is not concentrated. Some peasant communities, dwelling within states, function as quasi-anarchies. They are responsible for regulating their own internal affairs, and do so without formal power or authority. Taylor calls such "closed corporate peasant communities." Intentional communities (such as utopian communities, secular family communes, and kibbutzim) function in quasi-anarchy, though embedded in a state.

## 2. Social Order Without the State.

Social order requires, in addition to socialization, ritual, and social exchange, a modicum of coercion. This is due to social order being a public good.

**2.1. Social order and public goods**. Public goods are those indivisible goods that, when consumed by one citizen, may also be consumed by another (clean air, security). Private goods are divided among individuals, and once consumed, cannot be consumed by another (peaches, cows). Goods may be partly private and partly public. The public may be excluded from some public goods (toll bridges). With respect to non-excludable public goods, free riders may consume without contribution. If all members choose to free ride, the public good will not be available at all, since the free rider seeks to consume without producing. Social order is security of person and property from violence or damage. Hobbes argued for this view of social order. Other views deem social order predictability or conformity to norms. Taylor considered social control in creating these social orders.

Members are tempted to free ride when their contribution to the cost of a public good exceeds their benefit, which outcome is more likely in large than small public domains. In fact, such decisions are faced over and over through time, so people make conditional commitments. In small groups, where members are known, conditional cooperation, as an alternative to free riding, increases in likelihood. Still, without more, public goods will be fragile and may collapse.

**2.2. Social order and the state**. One justification for the state's existence (which Taylor calls the "liberal theory") is that only by state coercion can free riders in large populations be compelled to contribute. This is, at its essence, Hobbes's argument. None contributes willingly; all must be compelled. But Hobbes grants that such logic applies only to large, anonymous populations, and not to tribal communities. Taylor offers three arguments against Hobbes's theory of the necessary coercive sovereign: a) lack of altruism in large populations grows because States quash altruism; b) States undermine community, which presents an alternative and independent source of societal authority, which community is the only viable alternative to the anonymous State. States forestall the fission by which small communities remain small, and so necessitate that the forces that make community work will become attenuated; and c) The State may not be the only means of providing for common contribution to the public good of social order.

Three forces may create social order: the State, the market, and community.

**2.3. Social order on the market**. Taylor discounts the possibility that markets might replace all components of social order, without an intervening State and community. Libertarians tend to neglect and brush past the problems of free riding. As Nozick argues in *Anarchy, State and Utopia*, minimal states would emerge from private protection contracts, as consumers sought protection from the largest provider, crowding out other providers. Taylor considers private security providers in England, and finds the arrangement wanting both practically and theoretically. Others benefit from the deterrence of private providers, and so some free ride. Large private security companies become proto-states.

**2.4. Social order in stateless societies**. Community is the adequate basis for social order in stateless society. In primitive communities, personal reciprocity creates and sustains social order. Reciprocity attenuates as kinship distance grows, leading to less positive relationships and diminished social order. Kinship groups exchange food reciprocally. Tribes exchange women as spouses reciprocally. Marriage exchanges cut across local bonds, creating mixed loyalties that reduce conflict. Clans and age-affiliations also cross-cut loyalties, reducing conflicts. Matrilocal systems suffer less conflict than patrilocal systems. In community life, deviant behavior disrupts much besides the matter directly at issue. All normal social life stutters, and the deviant's acts become a focus. Socialization and education, though important, are insufficient to generate social order. Nor are initiation rites sufficient, by themselves.

In primitive societies, social control arises from threats of retaliation. Social control also emerges from reciprocity, which is conditioned on good behavior. Ostracism and excommunication (exclusion from rituals) are sources of control. Expulsion is a seldom-employed option for social control. Even approval and disapproval serve social control functions. In primitive societies, threats of witchcraft and sorcery and divine sanctions play a part in social control.

Peasant societies have similar social controls, as do contemporary intentional communities. Both, however, live in the shadow of states and their laws. Free riding frequently causes intentional communities to collapse.

**2.5. Community and stateless social order**. Where communities remain small and stable, four sorts of social controls predominate: 1) retaliation, 2) reciprocity and threat of its withdrawal, 3) approval and disapproval, and 4) witchcraft and threats of divine punishments. Communities remain small by fissioning generated by overpopulation or persistent internal conflicts. Consistent cooperation requires a small, known, stable group of cooperators, who reliably contribute.

## 3. Equality in Anarchy.

**3.1. Is equality unstable in anarchy**? Gross economic inequality among members erodes community. Any approximate equality of initial conditions will perish at the hand of member choices, luck, and differential skills and ambition. Equality would rely upon persistent government redistributive coercion, to the detriment of liberty. Taylor recounts Nozick's tale of how Wilt Chamberlain would become rich, given equal initial conditions. Taylor counters that, were conditions actually equal overall, communities might well resist wealth aggregation. Some societies have maintained rough economic equality for millennia without state interference. There are informal social sanctions for wealth accumulations, and so the equality is not strictly voluntary. Rough economic equality within a community can be maintained, but only where small, stable community exists. In addition to economic equality, rough equality of participation and power are also requisite to community. Some of the controls are innate; one feels embarrassed if one takes advantage of or stints friends one sees daily.

**3.2. The control of inequality in stateless societies**. Taylor considers cultural practices that level economic inequality. A) The "domestic mode of production" (DMP) distributes labor to produce needed goods. In "acephalous" (that is, headless" societies like families) sex determines productive behavior, and sharing entails rough communism (which sharing extends to kinship relations). Groups have limited rights in land, but own their own implements. The limited objectives of DMP groups are to satisfy (not maximize) needs and share excess. B) In chiefdoms or big-man arrangements some goods flow to the leader, then back out to the members, in redistribution to the community by way of providing support in times of scarcity, providing public buildings, and supporting needed crafts. This arrangement, conjoined with common use of land and resources, creates substantial financial equality. Power remains relatively equal; status depends on character and ability. None coerces by societal agreement; society remains egalitarian. Big man societies acknowledge charismatic leaders, but grant them no formal recognition. Primitive societies use public opinion, threat of withdrawal of reciprocity (including expulsion), and accusation of demonic activity to deter inequality (how else might one become wealthy?). C) In peasant societies, power and assets are less-equally distributed. Active, wealthy members take the lead in decision-making. But the community owns the land, and periodically redistributes it. Andean peasant communities also required wealthy members to pay for religious ceremonies for all, and divided land among offspring, breaking it down into small pieces. Southeast Asian peasant communities premised social life on required reciprocity and a right to the means to subsist. The more open a peasant community, the more inequality is tolerated. Redistributive schemes may create free rider problems. One wishes equality, but on another's dime. A different free rider problem emerges in communist societies distributing according to need without reference to contribution, where one elects to malinger. This problem vexed Israeli kibbutzim and shitufim. Communities that formalize response to free riding tend to survive longer. Where a society is a community, wide political participation and collective decision-making inhibit inequality. Anarchy can retain economic egalitarianism if it functions in communities.

**3.3. The birth of the state**. Stable anarchy depends on community. To persevere, anarchies must maintain rough economic and political equality among members. Humans lived in stable anarchy for all of human history until the emergence of the state. Under state regime, acephalous independent anarchic communities have mostly disappeared.

Secondary states would emerge from the threats posed by primary states. How did the first states emerge, without a pattern to follow? Marxist theory states that surpluses led to middle men brokering those surpluses, which led to classes and to oppression. Taylor rejects Marx's analysis. Domestic production never produces surpluses, since these cannot be marketed or preserved. Only central political leadership compels excess production, and the excess work that attends it. Contrary to Marx, investigation reveals no class conflict and no organized repression of dissent. Taylor presents his version of state origins (following, but augmenting, Service's argument). Competent chiefs aggregate supporters. In a threat-filled environment, defensive force would be concentrated under the trusted head. The central chief resists natural communal fissioning (due to overpopulation or conflict), since the departures weaken his domain. But such a chief's defense policies (in keeping a community together when it should fission) weakens community generally, and the communal forces that keep community egalitarian and peaceful erode, being then replaced by centralized force and artificial social controls. Fissioning new communities becomes an unattractive option, since these communities would be weak, and the threats to them increasing. Threats may not only prevent fissioning, but may cause communities to fuse to protect themselves. Carniero presents an alternative theory. A geographically-delimited group, when its population exceeds the land's carrying capacity, intensifies agriculture. Conflicts emerge, with victorious groups banishing losers or incorporating them. Political units fight one another, and the necessity of defense brings the state into existence. None of these state-emergence theories makes one hopeful that anarchies might now emerge and survive in the morass of states that now occupy the planet.

## 4. Community and Liberty.

Communities exercise powerful constraints upon acts its members would otherwise have undertaken. Is community compatible with individual liberty? Most liberal thinkers argue that community quashes liberty. Taylor argues that community need not do so. Taylor weeds some confusions from the morass. Three notions of liberty are distinguished: a) pure negative freedom, b) freedom from coercion, and c) autonomy.

**4.1. Pure negative freedom, freedom from coercion, and autonomy**. Pure negative freedom means that one can do a desired act without positive restraint by others. If the act preferred is possible, even though daunting sanctions might be imposed, then one remains free. Neither threats nor offers limit pure negative freedom. One can undertake any act, and suffer the consequences, good or ill, that attend it. Offering reasons (persuading), transforming perspective (changing the actor's beliefs), or making threats (changing the utility of a given choice) need not deter a member. If they do, the result lies as much in the choosing member as in the outside intervention. Autarchic persons can resist suggestion or threat. Heterarchic persons cannot, usually for some neurotic or brain-impairment reason. These lack the ability to resist. Another liberal criticism alleges that community defeats autonomy. Autonomy consists in rationality and authenticity. Authentic acts express one's coherent core self critically affirmed.

**4.2. Are community and liberty incompatible**? Comparing the freedom of individuals or groups proves problematical. Regardless how much restraint limits a person, he retains numerous pure negative freedoms, and those freedoms are variously valued by various individuals. So, comparisons prove difficult, except where the freedoms on one individual prove a subset of those available to another. Freedoms are not a zero-sum game; one may have more without diminishing freedoms of others, provided the material means supporting the freedoms are available. Reciprocity agreements to share tools increase the freedoms of members making them. Coercion, in various forms, influences individuals, but reduces pure negative freedom only when its threats are enacted. (In an aside on privacy, Taylor argues that community invades privacy to the extent necessary to create direct, many-sided relationships, but otherwise does not senselessly invade.) Community precludes some of what liberals mean by autonomy. The community member is not free to ignore the opinions of other members. But in secular family communes (Taylor's term for communities which institutionalize friendship), friendship is a tenuous relationship, subject to many deteriorations. Great dangers lie in reification (valuing the community structure more than the friend) and ideology (valuing community ideas over one's own, and conforming to them). Liberty appears to flourish in some secular family communes. So, contrary to the aspersions of liberal critics, liberty and community are not inimical.

## 5. Epilogue: the future of community and anarchy.

Communities may sustain anarchic social relations. Inter-community relations must mirror those conditions within communities to remain anarchic. Rough economic equality must prevail. Taylor believes that the social controls effective within communities (approval/disapproval, reciprocity, and threats of supernatural sanctions) cannot work between communities. Most anarchist theorists adopt federalism among communities, with contracts and ad hoc relationships emerging to achieve common goals. Federal relations would address specific problems and have no control over force. Taylor notes that growing up in a community does not make it more likely that one will feel cooperative toward strangers. Taylor doubts that federalism among communities would in fact work. But relations among small independent communities would never be so threatening as are relations among nations. The transition from states to a welter of small independent communities is perilous. Community anarchism crumbles before state threats. Taylor is not optimistic about the anarchic possibilities. The efforts at the time of Taylor's writing were a) attempts to build whole anarchic communities (kibbutzim and utopian efforts), and b) attempts to introduce anarchic practices into less expansive cooperations (such as neighborhood associations and economic collectives). Wherever human social relations deepen reciprocity, cut out state offices, widen political participation within the group, and build toward less specialization, then anarchic community begins to root. One must take care that economic cooperations do not cut at the root of community by producing goods antithetical to community, such as cars or nuclear energy.

## APPENDIX A

### EIGHT INEFFABLE RULES OF AMITY, NONETHELESS WRITTEN[506]

1. **Community.** Our community is its web of relationships among members. Keep our community relationally complex, but otherwise simple. If young children fail to understand how our togetherness works, our life together is too complex. Amity governs.

2. **Relating to Others.** Speak well of members. Speak well to members. You need them; they need you. Every member is massively more complex than our understanding of him or her. Be kind and humble and helpful. Undertake tender acts daily. Offer no pointless offense to any person, but create principled offense when members injure themselves or others or our community. Treat non-members as provisional members.[507] Welcome them; offer, but do not insist upon, frank sharing.

3. **Possessions.** Keep what you need, nothing more. Some members prefer more material goods than others. If you are materially-laden, do not preen. Your wealth is a blemish in your character. If you lack material goods, flee envy. Take care to provision yourself and your community. Respect the choices of others, except when errant choices cause tangible (not merely potential) harms.

4. **Activity.** Labor at what you do best for the community. The labor of every member belongs to the community, adding to our shared generational legacy. Provide fully for every member's needs. Provide also for yourself. Measure yourself by relational wealth, not material excess. Some members produce less, others more. Produce what you are able. Then produce yet a bit more and expend that excess constructively to enrich our community or that of others. Compensate for the shortcomings of others. Metaphorically, drop no trash; pick up trash.

5. **Community Adaptation.** Welcome change. All organisms, including our social organism, adapt. Take heart. Embrace changes. Misdirected change may annoy, but does not imperil, our life together. Our community will discern and adjust. All *lethal* mistakes are relational, not strategic.

---

506 Oddly, I express what cannot be adequately rendered in language, since these communal rules flex to the persons and circumstances of their applications. Sometimes, their application appears at odds with what the words say, even their opposite. To write immobilizes these rules of amity unnaturally, as one might discover a busy bug, snatched amid its vital efficiencies, trapped in amber, and, therefore, long dead. Please note how deeply, in this respect, amity differs from laws, which begin dead and pertain to coercing strangers. In amity, friends adapt to life with friends. "There is no one norm, stated as a rule, that resolves conflicts in [Navajo] peacemaking. The emphasis is upon relation-based and affective process rather than the application of rules by a neutral third party. Outcomes are driven by relationship and needs." Zion and Yazzie, "Navajo peacemaking," 153.

507 Civility is little else than amity lavished upon outliers.

6. **Member Adaptation.** Our community intervenes when members injure themselves or others or our community. Our community adapts its rules to an errant member's capacity to conform. Speak privately with erring members. Encourage, but correct, errant members, as is appropriate under your circumstances. Remember to speak of your own errors and responsibility during corrective conversations. Acknowledge that the community's long-cherished standards may themselves be errors. Invite mutual discovery of answers to these issues. Discussed mistakes lead toward intimacy. The purpose of adaptation is to avoid enmity, and restore amity, within our community and among our members.

7. **Consensus.** Seek consensus. Be patient. Face disagreements squarely. Disputes, well-managed, enrich our community. Speak fairly and promptly. Listen intently. Avoid outbursts. Plunge into the perspectives of disputants. Be supportive and hopeful. When consensus proves impossible, keep talking. If circumstances prohibit patience, choose reluctantly. Let dissenters' concerns ring in communal ears as disputed matters progress. For dissenters may be right. Affirm affection for dissenters, and praise their value.

8. **Purpose.** Our community shares purposes. These common goals change over time. Members are unique but share life. We share values, which change infrequently. Some persevering values are amicable affection, adaptive resilience, meaningful existence, our particular historical legacy, and thirst to plumb life's deeper recesses.

Considered together, these rules point toward life in amity.

# APPENDIX B

## TWELVE STEPS TOWARD AMITY

### STEP ONE
### ABANDON COERCION

To foster amity, one abandons coercion. Do something other than litigate. Speak no ultimatums. Relate without threats or intimations of consequences to be had. The big questions are these: What am I accomplishing? What good emerges from the hours I spend working? Are people's lives improved? Are the neighbors with whom I interact professionally happier and better able to cope? Is their social world more stable and meaningful? Or are clients transported to a new location, but one that is no better, or possibly even worse, than they occupied before I stumbled into their existence?

> NONE MAKES PEACE BY WARRING.
>
> COERCION BREEDS RETALIATION.

In a lawyer's mind, amity cohabits with litigation as oil welcomes water. I doubt these two antiphonal worldviews can share a symphony. Law demands more of a person than "thinking in a mode" for a few hours daily. Values, interests, commitments, and even identity follow one's practices. One becomes a peace-maker or a litigator, but not both. If I am right, one must choose, as a lawyer, between amity and courthouses, between friendship and recompense. Your brain and your heart are not big enough to make a home for both.[508]

The choice daunts. What about making a living? What about the sunk costs of law school? What about those thousands of hours and garbage bags full of money which, after years, enabled me to write a decent appellate brief? What about my colleagues' expectations? Who will deem me brilliant if I set about helping my neighbors speak again? What of my exuberance when I wax rhetorical, intoning arcana of law to that itty-bitty audience who can appreciate my flourishes? What about American traditions? What of the grand aspiration at common law, that intelligent people acting prudently might incrementally, over centuries, deflect society toward enhanced humanity?[509] What about all those clients who

---

[508] Perhaps your brain and heart are sufficient, and I speak only of my own inadequacies.

[509] Common law has grown into an obstacle to a fair world, rather than its harbinger. Every appeals decision renders law a bit less accessible, a bit more distant, from the people law intended to serve. At law, expense, arcana, hypertrophic procedure, and the culture of medieval jousting bury the pedestrian task of shaping resolutions. Those in the know in the restorative justice field argue that an amicable theory of justice is a "form of insurgency because it 'competes with' the state,'" and is fundamentally subversive of the common law system. Sullivan and Tifft, "The healing dimension of restorative justice: a one-world body," 5. Sullivan and Tifft further argue, following Marshall McLuhan, that humankind has, from the advent of the telegraph, begun the process of exteriorizing our nervous system. It reaches now, almost instantaneously, around the planet and into the cosmos. This is but one aspect of interpenetration among

hunger for opponent carnage, wagering more than they ought to achieve less than they expect?

To abandon coercion, one must find equipoise. The best lives are tranquil—active, but centered and calm. Seneca helps comprehension with thoughts on finding tranquility. From his perch in first century Rome, he offers thoughts from the Stoic school, made more poignant by his personal collision with imperial power.

Nero Claudius Caesar Augustus Germanicus (37-68 A.D.) ascended to Rome's imperial throne at age sixteen, carried on winds of fortune and maternal ambition. It helped to be adopted by his great-uncle, Emperor Claudius. His childhood tutor was Lucius Annaeus Seneca, a worldly Stoic philosopher and politician of first century Rome. When Nero rose to emperor, Seneca and Sextus Africanus Burrus, prefect of the Praetorian guard, advised him, running the Empire, with the help of Nero's mother Agrippina, for perhaps the first decade of Nero's reign. Seneca wrote Nero's first speech before the Roman Senate. Nero became a tyrannical and fiscally profligate ruler. High taxes alienated those who paid them. Several attempts were made upon Nero's life. Nero proved indecisive. He relied upon others, among whom was Seneca. In 59 A.D., four years after becoming Emperor, Nero ordered his mother, Agrippina, killed. He sent her to travel and arranged a shipwreck. When Agrippina managed to swim to shore, a Neronian minion murdered her and reported her death as a suicide. Nero divorced his wife, Octavia, alleging she was infertile. Banished, Nero accused her of infidelity with the murderer of Agrippina, and had Octavia executed. In 64 A.D., the great fire of Rome swept the city, burning for a week. The inferno razed three and damaged seven others among the fourteen districts of the capital. Nero may have set the fire himself, though the egg of these details is jumbled in history's omelette. Regardless, Nero took advantage of the newly vacated urban land to build the Domus Aurea (Golden House) on Palatine Hill. Its gigantic gardens adorned a thirty-meter bronze statue of the Emperor himself, the Colossus of Nero. The Domus Aurea had 300 rooms, but no sleeping quarters, kitchens, or latrines. It was a narcissist emblem, a sanctuary in which to meditate upon Nero's splendor. Its interior was faced with semi-precious stones and ivory and marble. The exterior was covered, as the name might indicate, in gold leaf. In 65 A.D., another attempt upon Nero's life led to accusations, probably false, that Seneca had participated. Nero ordered Seneca to commit suicide. Seneca denied regicidal conspiracy. Nero persisted. Ever the faithful Roman, Seneca complied.

Seneca's life, as one can see from its context, eroded inner equilibrium. He saw his pupil ascend to power, then descend to megalomania, murder, and madness. Nero savaged Seneca's life, as that of Rome itself. Seneca ended a distinguished career, and his life as well, in ignominy, wrongly condemned.

All of which sets Seneca's advice in context. He advises friend, Serenus, on leading a tranquil life:

---

human members. As Navajo people have long believed, humanity is a "single animated mass of blood, flesh, and bones, of which no member could be touched without all the members suffering." Sullivan and Tifft, "The healing dimension of restorative justice: a one-world body," 2, 11.

> Stop chiding yourself, Serenus. Choose a path and stay on it. Embrace quietude. Avoid pretense. You are yourself; be satisfied. Serve the public, despite whatever shortcomings you suffer. Do nothing to inspire hatred from others. Tend your community. Find something useful to do, and stick with it. Be blunt with yourself; take your measure frankly. Avoid fixations; care about many things. Work sensibly, doing what you do well and comfortably. Live within your means. Tame your tongue. Finish what you start. Choose friends for their goodness; it will rub off on you. They need not be perfect, but ought not to prefer gloom. Money and possessions injure you. Live simply, loving utility, fleeing ostentation. True wealth hides within you. Keep a small library of the best authors. Read them. Laugh at your troubles; bear them silently. Make your life better by solving problems. Die with equanimity. Do nothing that is pointless. Ridicule vices and flee them. Grieve for the misfortunes of others, but not overmuch. Face troubles bravely and simply. Avoid people who hate to no purpose. Spend time alone; spend time with others. Each heals the defects of the other. Alternate work and leisure. Take naps. Get a bit drunk occasionally; being somewhat akimbo sparks creativity. Do these things, Serenus, and you will find tranquility.

Perhaps Seneca helps. Perhaps not. He helps me. **See Epitome 3: Seneca, *Tranquillity*.**

I do not call you to abandon lawful coercion because it is a moral blight, or because it condemns us to the frightful, alienated social landscape we inhabit.[510] I ask for change because coercion at law does not work. **See Epitome 8: Kurlansky, Nonviolence.** Review the outcomes of your litigated cases.[511] See those results from your clients' perspectives. Are your clients flourishing because of your litigation work? I think not. In the social carnage of law, considered from your clients' perspectives, even the winners lose.

Do you agree?

---

[510] Though I could. I do ask you to note the moral contagion inherent in coercion. Coercion leads to further coercion. My request trends toward the utilitarian. Law is not working. Law does not trend toward humankind living in intimate, well-functioning communities. Law aims, instead, to shackle society's unsavory excesses, suspecting that in every person hunkers a savage ingrate slavering for carnage. It is not so.

[511] Review also the outcomes of cases processed in peacemaking modes: facilitative mediation, stakeholder conferences, and stakeholder circles. The results of collaborative law processes also deserve attention. Collaboration is an amalgam of interest-based negotiation and non-coercive lawyering standing upon its core commitment: no recourse to courts. All share a common fundament: facilitated encounter among disputants and other necessary parties. Some researchers of indigenous irenic practices note that Western jurisprudence is vertical and exclusive. One travels up from life to court, then to appeals, then to supremes. Some indigenous adjudications have no judges, call together all involved, insist that all speak and tell their stories, and consensus rules. These alternative approaches share attitudes that are horizontal and inclusive. Yazzie, "Life Comes from It: Navajo Justice Concepts," 177-187.

## STEP TWO
## FIND SUPPORT

To foster amity, an attorney needs support. Irenic practices come in an assortment of flavors: restorative justice stakeholder conferences, facilitative mediation, circles, one-on-one counseling, collaborative law teams, victim offender conferences, and an astounding variety of alternatives and permutations. This book has proposed a change of theory from court-supervised non-litigated approaches (such as those listed above) to an extra-constitutional societal habit of resolving problems by small group Klatching. Most of these various non-litigated dispute structures may be supervised by non-attorneys. The job of attorneys who hope to support amity, is to support the peacemaking of non-law-trained persons. In the end, every conflict is idiosyncratic. Each requires its own approach and recognition. Each requires its own level of process and expertise.

> A PEACEMAKER'S INTIMATE COMMUNITY REPLENISHES THE EMOTIONAL EXHAUSTION THAT AMITY EXACTS FROM ITS HER.

At root, for the peacemaker, any amicable process demands listening, empathizing, bridging, and imagining. Each such effort plunges a peacemaker into a deeply-stressed human system. Listening transmits among brains the thoughts that accompany perceived trauma. Empathizing makes a refuge in one's own emotional life for the troubles of another. Bridging pours emotional foundations and erects a conversational span between once-segregated communicators. Imagining, the most critical, yet most exhausting, component of peacemaking, hears participants' stories afresh, restates and amalgamates them, then conjures a joined path forward for all involved.

Peacemaking is a good. But amity comes at a price. Restoring relationships injures and exhausts its intervenors. To listen, empathize, bridge, and imagine without compensatory sustenance bodes ill for the peacemaker. One needs to heal and replenish what has been given. Many who restore amity suffer secondary post-traumatic stress. One sleeps fitfully. One, if possessed of that measure of neurosis typical of lawyers, worries. So much, it would seem, is at stake. The irenist needs respite. She needs a place to decompress. He needs loving listening and sharing.[512] Considered as a system, peacemaking exports psychic distress from one location to another. Emotional detritus settles upon a peacemaker's

---

[512] Washington's *Rules of Professional Conduct*, as those relate to confidences, client secrets, and privilege may well prevent lawyers from adequately caring for their own psycho-social needs. Exceptions should be created for sharing of anonymized situations with social intimates and therapists. Of necessity, such sharing already occurs. The rules, however, forbid. See Washington Rules of Professional Conduct, Section 1.6 and its associated comments.

equilibrium like a cold, wet blanket. Every person's equanimity is fragile. Every person needs intimate support.

Isolated peacemakers pose a danger to amity. The distressed peacemaker loses track of purposes. She grows ineffective. He spends clients' time and money to diminished effect. Every person who restores amity has limits. Do not risk your own well-being by plunging unsupported into knitting fractured sociality. Pause first to build for yourself a circle of intimate support. Do not depend solely on your significant other. You may overwhelm that person, who is undoubtedly good-hearted. Spread your needs into a group of five to ten persons who support one another, including you. Give what you get. But, before you launch into restoration of amity, find support.

## STEP THREE
## RAISE YOUR VOICE

To foster amity, one unearths within oneself the rudiment of amity. Unless one of life's devastating debilities afflicts us, we have friends.[513] One may trace the impetus toward friendship back into deep psychology to find a root. That subconscious root is amity, our human predilection for friendship. We make friends. We keep friends. We repair damaged friendships. We sport a somewhat undifferentiated willingness to welcome non-threatening strangers into our lives, to collaborate with them on projects of common interest, and to consider making them members of our intimate circle. Synergy with relative strangers distinguishes humans from the remainder of the animal kingdom, more than reason and inventions. Humankind is *homo cooperatio*, the cooperative primate,[514] more than woman the reasoner (*homo rationabile*) or man the tool maker (*homo faber*).

> FIND WORDS, ATTITUDES, AND FEELINGS THAT HELP OTHERS FACE DIFFICULTIES AND CONCILIATE.

Some predicates fray, or even immolate, our amicable attitudes. One interrupts human social amity by dismal moaning, hints of threat, unwanted sexualization, overwork, hunger, thirst, wasting disease, tribalism, war, and a host of other warning signs.

---

[513] Some such afflictions are deep attachment injuries, sociopathy, some forms of drug abuse, and persistent vegetative states. Almost all of us recall a point in time when we knew we stood in the presence of a friend, and were grateful.

[514] Cooperative breeding, in which non-breeder associates assist breeders with care of their offspring, is relatively rare among primates. Neotropical callitrichids, such as tamarins and marmosets, breed cooperatively, as do humans. See Hrdy, *Mothers and Others*, 171ff.

Different predicates enliven amity, opening our hearts to known and unknown others. One buoys infectious friendship by welcoming, affirmation, smiling, laughing, touching, inviting contribution, eating meals, sacrificing for another, offering drink, telling a story that matters, taking emotional risks, and a long list of additional social ease triggers. (Consider the sociological effects of warm cookies.)

What is your role? None can answer but you. Never in fourteen billion years has there been another you. Never in that same time frame has your circumstance previously existed. You will have to invent yourself, for good or ill today, then again tomorrow. Choosing well, you and your practice can become a well-head that gushes amity for the taking, drenching every client and colleague. Choosing otherwise, you can spread fear and anger and foment little wars. You may make of you, your clients, and your colleagues inimical dimwits.

Find your voice. You must be you. Once discovered, raise your voice. The world needs you to act noisily. Because we treat human life so cheaply, we fail to recognize (most days) that we are born into a plenum in which every atom plays its role. And every person.

For what do you cheer?

## STEP FOUR
## PRESUME GOODNESS

To foster amity, one presumes that contenders seek a good outcome. People, even reasonable people, who suffer conflict disagree about acceptable resolutions. A host of confusions, emotional urgencies, power imbalances, superstitions, prejudices, and cognitive pitfalls dog disputants. Where matters languish, rancor often rots into mutual accusations of evil. Amity resists these pressures. One offers deeply-vetted information. One listens. One confronts folly and intolerance. One unmasks confirmation bias and grief over sunk costs. One gives voice to the mute, and stomps genially on the strutting dominator or dominatrix.

> EXPECT GOOD FAITH.
>
> NOT EVERY DISPUTANT SEEKS DESIRABLE OUTCOMES. MOST, THANKFULLY, DO.

It is factually false that all disputants seek good outcomes. Some suffer defects that leave them incapable of recognizing or preferring better rather than worse resolutions. Four percent of humans are sociopathic.[515] Others suffer

[515] Seventy-five percent of sociopaths are male; twenty-five percent are female. **Sociopathy** has suffered numerous name changes. The disorder has been called moral imbecility, psychopathy, and, most recently, anti-social personality disorder. Sociopaths share at least three of seven characteristics: 1) systematic failure to conform to social norms, 2) persistent deceit and manipulation, 3) chartless impulsivity, 4) irritable aggression, 5) reckless disregard for human well-being, including his own, 6) global

narcissistic or borderline personality disorders. Some are habitually violent, or suffer drug-addled hatreds. Amity may mean little, or nothing, to these persons. Two features predominate. Some may, even neurologically, lack the ability to care about others. Others may lack the ability (or desire) to mute their inner noise. Perhaps courtrooms are reserved for persons who so suffer, and their victims.

The vast majority, however, do care. They want a good outcome for themselves, for their loved ones, even for opponents and their affiliates. Most care about our social equities. If Keltner is right, we are (mostly) wired for good. **See Appendix D: Keltner, *Born to Be Good*.** If Keltner is wrong, amity is delusional. We should all duck and find a cave in which to cower and complain.

## STEP FIVE
## SET BOUNDARIES

To foster amity, one sets boundaries for that process. One embraces an image of restored relationships. One asks, What limitations will help us arrive at that destination? The amity-seeking, conflict-fractured group lays out a path to arrive elsewhere, hopefully somewhere better. Some attitudes and actions are encouraged. Others will not be tolerated.

Some boundaries seem universal. No participant gets to threaten others, either in sessions or outside them. None gets to hide information, lie about pertinent matters, or erect bad faith obstructions. All quiet their own cherished outcome, and strive to listen to alternative possibilities. Sobriety is expected. All agree that the result of the amicable process will be compromise, not conquest. Speak quietly; yelling is counterproductive. Silence cannot be used as a weapon. Patience with one another is expected. Errors will be corrected without objection or bad faith advantage-taking. Professionals must be timely paid. Agreements must advantage all parties, and represent a deliberate, information-laden balancing of opposed interests. Respectful exchanges are the

> A WELL-CONCEIVED PROCESS WITH AGREED BOUNDARIES PRESERVES AN AMITY-RESTORING ETHOS.

irresponsibility, and 7) lack of remorse for wrong-doing or injury of others. Stout, *Sociopath Next Door*, 6. Sociopathy has a seventy percent heritability factor, often activated by childhood neglect or abuse. Churchland, *Braintrust*, 41. A person suffering **borderline personality disorder** suffers five or more of these eight signs: unstable and intense interpersonal relationships; impulsivity; extreme mood swings; inability to control anger; suicidal threats or self-mutilation; identity confusions; extreme emptiness; or extreme fear of abandonment. Persons suffering **narcissistic personal disorder** exhibit five or more of these nine signs: grandiose sense of self-importance; preoccupation with fantasies of success and power, beauty, or ideal love; belief that he is special and should associate with similar people of high status; need for excessive admiration; sense of entitlement; exploiting others; complete lack of empathy; envy of others or a belief others are envious of him; or arrogance. Baron-Cohen, *The Science of Evil*, 45, 169, 197-200. Roy Baumeister, perhaps wrongly, asserts: "Evil is socially enacted and constructed. It does not reside in our genes or in our soul, but in the way we relate to other people." Baumeister, *Evil*, 375.

norm. Boundaries may change as we learn about one another, as participants progress toward resolution.

Other boundaries are idiosyncratic. Lights must be dimmed. Food must be, or must not be, served. No dog can bark.[516] The room is a little hotter, or colder, than usual. One participant must go first, because otherwise he may be unable to speak at all. Meetings in mornings, since all fade during afternoon sessions. The local boundaries vary as widely as do the participants. These are not so much procedural rules as accommodations for comfort and caring.

A participant, mid-stream in mediation, once objected, "These boundaries cramp my style. I want to amend them." After listening, we declined. We had agreed on boundaries at inception of our sessions. We can amend our process by agreement, or we can cease our process. Unilateralism is a power grab. Not all acts or words help create amity. Scared people seldom make meaningful peace. Neither do hungry or angry or exhausted ones. Well-conceived boundaries help keep participants on an even keel.

Participants must push amity buttons in their deep psyches if peace is to prevail. The professionals, who are often lawyers, must insist on predicates of peace. To do otherwise incurs the jeremiad; we promise peace without providing any. That is just bad faith "bait and switch."

## STEP SIX
## CRAFT THE EMOTIONS

To foster amity, one crafts the emotional substructure of disputant exchanges. One nudges the limbic systems[517] in the room. All brains hide subconscious triggers that tell us to fear and flee and fight, or relax and relate and rest. Peacemakers hobble "F" triggers and work "R" triggers.

> OF OTHERS, WE KNOW MORE THAN WE CAN EXPRESS.
>
> CREATE THE PREDICATES OF REST, RELAXATION, AND RELATING.

One triggers rest by offering quiet, and by calming oneself. One projects positive emotions and speaks gently. Kindness and courtesy suggest there is nothing to fear in an exchange. Respect and listening indicate interest and openness. Commitment hints that one has set aside short-term and self-interested behavior in the hope of fashioning something better. Food tells us that we will be okay, even nurtured, during an encounter. Being offered a beverage gives nervous people something to do with their hands. People

[516] Possibly a problem at my office, since my dog is convinced she rules the realm.

[517] Mammalian neural developments, located in the several substructures collectively called the limbic system, blanket the brainstem. Limbic structures organize affective social nurturance. The word "affective" describes things relating to or arising from emotions. Primates, including humans share these deep limbic structures with all mammalian life. See MacLean, *Triune Brain*, 1990.

do not eat and drink with cretins. Just melting chocolate in one's mouth may trend toward success in amity.

Few of these facts are spoken in language. They exist for the seeing and feeling. Our faces tell truths that mouths cannot express. Our commitments show in eyes. Our fears excavate facial creases. In the end, our moral judgments emerge from what we have subliminally recognized in the faces of others. Deep in our evolutionary past, a prejudice emerged. We trust higher status individuals to keep peace between us. That, ultimately, is the source of their pre-eminence. Once cooperation has commenced, it elicits compensatory cooperation among participants. Amity is, therefore, contagious.[518] Smidgeons of serenity can sink a surly ship with startling suddenness. A happier vessel may bob to the surface. Embarrassment creates gaze aversion, appeasement gestures, and facial touches. All quash conflict. Smiles reduce stress in smilers and smilees. Laughter is the vocalization of play. It too is contagious, and signals shared purposes. A laugh elicited by another (antiphonal levity) signals friendship. Guffaws relieve grief. So, levity, even teasing, might help. Touches signal trust and cooperation.

Most, but not every, dispute can be handled peacefully. One never knows until she pushes the subliminal "R" triggers, and seeks to restore amity.

## STEP SEVEN
## ASSIST COOPERATION

To foster amity, one helps those who are being helpful. Subtly, more with acts than words, participants in an amicable process teach those less experienced the ropes of friendship. None knows where any given meeting should go, or who will lead it to a good outcome. So, one steps back a bit, listens, and watches. In each successful meeting (which is one that takes tangible steps toward restoring friendship), some participant, or several, do what helps. For them, we are grateful.

> COOPERATE WITH THOSE WHO COOPERATE.

But these supportive folks need supporters. We are individuals with private minds. But we also are collective creatures, and invoke group thinking. Such is one implication of psycho-social interpenetration. If we want amity to prevail, then most participants must recognize the drift of a meeting and get behind the persons who are ushering the team to its good destination. It is so easy, especially in our conflict-addled culture, to sit on the sideline and lob salvos of weaponized innuendo or abject inattention into the midst of a reconciliation process. We must *welcome and*

---

518 Unfortunately, paranoia, anger, and fear are contagious as well.

*embrace* those who choose unhelpful courses. But we need not follow or praise them. These can be politely back-benched. If they inquire, one can instruct.

Cooperation means, quite literally, to work together. Cooperation is shared mentation. People who work together toward an end, even for a short time, develop a shared rubric for words and a joint posture for actions.

## STEP EIGHT
## REVISE THE STORY

To foster amity, one constructs a more-inclusive story. In conflict, there exists an unexplored story that honors the core purposes and values of all parties, what one might call a "conjunctive narrative." But this narrative is hidden, at least to the participants. Instead, each disputer tells a story that supports his desires, often a tale much at odds with that of other disputers. In the parlance of conflict participants, they are at loggerheads.

> UNEARTH A CONJUNCTIVE NARRATIVE.

One retreats to skills. These seem so frail, so puny before the task. **Listening**. Listening is five percent compassion, and ninety-five percent turning down one's own volume. One discovers a quiet place from within, drags it to the surface. Personally, I conjure a simulacrum of serenity from my study before sunrise. In quiet, others can be heard, just barely. **Repeating**, saying again what has been said at the table. Parroting sounds stupid, but keeps clients talking. As information grows, an alternate narrative for the warring parties peeks out. **Curiosity** helps. Few journeys hold wilder rides than distressed humans splattering their fractured meaning upon a conference table. Well-conceived inquiry pries open those floodgates. Clients' laden messages, however, are encoded. **Sympathy** breaks the cipher. Sliding even one foot into a client's worn and smelly shoe opens them up. Common language emerges, glimmers of trust. We begin **re-narrating**, weaving another way to frame their world and their cherished, self-justifying stories. The warp and woof of this new tale encompasses the misery of each, and, on good days, hints resolution without bloodshed or emotional or financial carnage. The shared story can be as simple as the recognition that the opposing party's account tells a story that makes sense, but fails to account for one's own story. The best shared narratives bend the categories in which each party thinks, offering to each a revised normalcy that includes the other. Narrative permutations are enormous in number. The loggerheads perception is ever an illusion.

If antagonists come to share a common tale, no matter how sad a tragedy be recounted, the hard work is done. The conjunctive narrative in place, only drafting and details remain.

## STEP NINE
## BE TOUGH

To foster amity, one must insist upon it. Amity neither grows on trees, nor waits some elusive incantation. Irenea is built. When one builds a garage, expect hammer-crushed fingertips and sunburn. So too peace. Bring a first-aid kit and your best game.

Compassion is never weak. Compassion stands ready to leap into frays, to bark orders, to throw a bucket of cold water on sputtering disputants. A person of great empathy, while feeling the pains of another, must nevertheless stand resolute. One seeks to be kind, but kindness will, when required, pull on a rough glove and do some heavy lifting. The toughness of amity may contradict a speaker. It may growl at bad faith acts. A person of amity must keep the train of amity on its tracks, sweeping aside errant cows and fallen branches. Peace trains must roll to their goals. Obstacles be damned.

> MUSTER MARTIAL MERIT
> TO WAR AGAINST WAR

William James declared himself a pacifist, but was enamored of the martial virtues inculcated by nations facing war—purposeful unity, wincing sacrifice, hard-set jaws, fiery visage, and granite determination. See **Epitome 10: James, "The Moral Equivalent of War."** He said that war will endure until pacifists set themselves to war against war. To end the habit of unrestrained conflicts, one must imbibe the virtues of warmongers, without adopting brutality or a smoldering conscience. Be flinty. Smile, but stand fast. Be open, but do not lose your way. Say what you see, patiently, even gently. But when gentle talk is ignored, pull a tool more blunt from your kit. Move to a hammer. If need be, consider a sledge.

Bloody warriors never doubt their rectitude. Theirs is high aspiration. Nothing less will suffice. Emulate such. Do not coerce, but neither retreat.

For amity to trigger seismic cultural change, its advocates must steel themselves. Be a fist, surely in a velvet glove, but nonetheless clenched. Too much is at stake to tolerate dithering. Find martial grit.

## STEP TEN
## RESOLVE THE RESOLVABLE

FIX WHAT CAN BE FIXED.

To foster amity, one does the possible. It can seem in difficult negotiations that no path forward is open. Stone, Patton, and Heen ("SPH") offer thoughts. Douglas Stone, Bruce Patton, and Sheila Heen wrote *Difficult Conversations: How to Discuss What Matters Most*, a fruit of their labors in the Harvard Negotiation Project. **See Epitome 12: Stone, Patton, Heen, *Difficult Conversations*.**

Difficult conversations are those that make you gulp in contemplation. SPH argue that every such discussion is really three: talk about facts, talk about emotions, and talk about meaning. The fatal temptation lies in defending positions. When parties advocate positions, difficult conversations arrive stillborn. SPH advocate a different approach. One must adopt a learning, not asserting, posture. What do others think? Why do they think those things? Stand in that person's shoes. Inquire. Paraphrase; it will keep them talking. Reframe ugly verbiage as "strong feeling" talk. Summarize to make sure you got their view right. Acknowledge others' feelings and contributions. What would you be feeling? Step up alongside. Experience their experience. Quash feelings of offense. Share how others' actions impacted you. But don't accuse. Assume others well-intentioned, but ignorant of your needs. Identify how each player contributed to the problem. Own your piece of the problem and say so. Describe your own feelings. Don't demand people not feel what they feel. Though feelings change, no one can change their feelings at will. Acknowledge feelings. Apologize, if necessary. SPH advocate exploring how the difficulty is affecting your identity. Avoid denial and hyperbole. Know there is more to you than the criticisms of others. Find a revised, but balanced, view of yourself that includes new information emerging from the difficult conversation. That can be painful. It is not, however, fatal. When you understand all the players, suggest solutions. Hear proposals. Compromise, if appropriate. Adopt a plan of action, if possible. If no common approach is workable, frankly acknowledge that fact. Agree to keep thinking about the problem. Thank people for talking openly.

## STEP ELEVEN
## RESTORE CONNECTIONS

To foster amity, we recognize that none lives alone. Each of us, all of us, are born of others. Gametes collide. In the pain of another, we spill into the world. Teats are suckled, muscles grown. Educations orient us to the communities in which we dwell. We mate, and work, and play with others. We dream and dare in their company. As hair grays and bodies falter, we spew lessons into the minds of youngsters stumbling after us. And we return to the dust of eternity, the ancient, hoary bin which all living things, no longer knowing, share.

Along this common path, events fracture connection. Disease, substances, collisions, broken brains, malice, accidents, rapacity: the varied disruptions of togetherness pile. We begin to feel disconnected. Feeling may become pathological. We may suffer individualism, the conviction that we stand alone against others, who, being aliens, must, occasionally, be disposed. Our individualism infects others, for it is a wasting disease, a social cachexia. Our communities limp.

Ulcers erupt from our disease state. These we recognize as conflicts unresolved, leaking toward vendetta, metastasizing toward war. Bad actors leap to our attention, thrust there by unconscionable ugliness perpetrated on neighbors. These are pimples on reservoirs of pustulous secretions. These severed individuals we treat (often poorly), but fail to dispatch the underlying infection. So, here we stand, limping, sore, frustrated, and uncertain.

You, you sojourner at law, you who considers a twelve-step program to prise you from the inanities of the common law, you ponder what to do. The something that needs doing is this: *reconstitute disrupted communities*. Amity grows where dysfunction does not impair the natural urge of people to build meaningful relationships. Where we fear, none relate. Where we hunger, none relate. Where we suffer disease, none relate. Exigency fractures us, breeds isolation.

To fix communities, endorse the economic mantra *Enough is Best*. Disparage unbridled financial hoarding, whose mantra is ever More is Better.[519] Stop fetishizing billionaires. At least some (and perhaps all) of their wealth springs from raw rapacity much indulged. Fix what stands before you. Do not go hunting for causes. Help your neighbors address their mundane difficulties. Every person's problems lie directly before someone. Help neighbors. Do not rely on government (neither disparage it). Governments aggregate our helpful sentiments, but are prone to aggregate our errors as well, making those misjudgments insuperable.

> COMMUNITIES ARE CONNECTION.
> WHERE ABSENT, BUILD SOME.
> WHERE BROKEN, REFURBISH SOME.

To practice law, stop litigating. Build community, or at least keep colliding people from dismantling theirs. Explain to clients exactly what happens to those who litigate. Inquire about the nature of the dispute. Offer to mediate or find a

[519] Daly, *Steady State Economics*, 2.

mediator. Guide the client through the concerns of opposing parties. Emphasize non-monetary losses in conflict: loss of friendship, lingering anxiety, stressing loved ones, moral compromise, sowing seeds of hatred, the eventual retaliation, reputational damage, and so forth. Understand the client's woe; show them you comprehend their plight. Imagine with the client being friends with opponents. Induce the client to admit that, if friendship proves unattainable, friendliness might be an acceptable fallback posture to seek.

This is the point: Instead of earning a fee throwing gasoline on the conflictual fire, encourage all involved to restore the amicable relations that pre-dated the dispute. Since this activity improves the lives of all involved so dramatically, you will find a way to make a fee from the process. If not, then not. You will have, however, worked to restore amicable relations. And that is an intrinsic good.

## STEP TWELVE
## IMAGINE BETTER

To foster amity, one abandons rusted imagination. "As we have done, so we must do." The creed of fossils. To foster amity, one imagines a world preferable to the outcomes disputants envision. One ushers once-friends toward that better-world and one another. One fabricates, from a web of neurons and possibilities, an alternative that encompasses, but surpasses, those conflicted worlds, those truncated margins, that disputants inhabit.

John Paul Lederach reports, from his lifetime of sorting difficult conflicts, that building resolution to conflicts is creative business, but terribly messy. **See Epitome 14: Lederach, *The Moral Imagination*.** One enters a conflict without much relevant knowledge and vulnerable to the emotions roiling players in the drama. One listens. One probes. One explores complexities, but resists recurrence to polarities. One offers friendship, in hope that it will be reciprocated. Violence lingers at the door, because the parties' understanding of their circumstances are incompatible. If their story prevails, people die or suffer. The stasis is what kills. Where moral stasis prevails, where change cannot be, there death's lure deepens. Moral imagination proves impossible.

> IMAGINE
> WHAT COMBATANTS CANNOT.
>
> TELL A STORY
> THEY CANNOT CONCEIVE.

The peacemaker holds the line for the conflicted parties. There will be no violence. Non-violence prevails by making friends of enemies, but this frequently transpires by antagonists making of their mediator a friend. Having that frail thread in common, some disputants find ways to reach toward one another. For a person's well-being depends upon the security of his enemies.

Lederach reports the role of serendipity in his work. Unexpected intrusions, both events and people, sport unimagined effects. To make peace, one seizes these boons. Combatants share these twists in history, even small ones, and so have discovered something they share, something other than their mutual antipathy. And serendipity surprises. Startled, opponents may drop their battle visages, if only for a moment. That proves to all that a different posture is possible.

Ultimately, a skilled peacemaker works as an artist. She may have acquired skills or academic degrees. But these will help little, if the mediator lacks artistic insight. Artists simplify complex scenes, not so much by excision as by emphasizing critical elements. The peacemaker draws forward what links people, what sets a conflict in a larger context. She diminishes elements that preclude reconciliation until such time as they may be addressed by once-enemies, now seeking amity (or at least non-hatred).

So, we survey twelve steps that law-people, if architects of amity, might pursue. One abandons coercion, finds personal support, raises one's voice, presumes goodness in disputants, sets boundaries, crafts the emotional tenor of the room, assists those open to cooperation, revises the ugly story, finds toughness, resolves what can be resolved, restores human connections, and imagines what others cannot.

By such steps, one may find himself changed and his practice constructive. One may feel better physically and emotionally, and revive a long dormant sense of meaning in life at law. One may reduce her anxiety about courts and judges and opposing counsels. One may find herself offering clients something they want and need, something for which they pray. Then amity-at-law will have infected your inwardness, as it has mine. And that revised interiority will affect others, and they yet others, and so forth.

And, if amity burgeons at law, we will smile and wonder and laugh.
We will be grateful, children of change, ready to work afresh.
Spouses will sigh relief, glad to have us back, intact.
Friends will cherish our heartfelt gratitude.
Dogs will wag; they know amity.
Enmity may wane, and
Friendships wax.
So be it.

∞

## APPENDIX C

### NINE OLYMPIC LORDS

**1.**

Nine lords of our realm in Olympia
Huddled quiet, dark curtains drawn,
    Took an axe to a program
    In ill-conceived pogrom:
"LLLTs, curse you all, and begone."

**2.**

Nine lords of our realm in Olympia
Forgot that the poor cannot play,
    Petty suits cannot be
    Due to high lawyer fees:
"LLLTs, curse you all, do not stay."

**3.**

Nine lords of our realm in Olympia
Sought no word from public or Bar,
    No notice was given,
    So good faith was riven:
"LLLTs, curse you all, and fly far."

**4.**

Nine lords of our realm in Olympia
Heard Wizbah's lament of expense.
    So a million law keeps
    In its pockets so deep:
"LLLTs, curse you all, pay no rent."

**5.**

Nine lords of our realm in Olympia
Suffered lawyers grumbling so loud.
    Lawyer monopoly,
    Undeserved oligopoly:
"LLLTs, curse you all, be much cowed."

**6.**

Nine lords of our realm in Olympia
Set rules convoluted, impaired.
    All the techs struggled
    With rules so befuddled:
"LLLTs, curse you all, and ill-fare."

**7.**

Nine lords of our realm in Olympia
Now wait at their bench on time's ravage
    As practitioners pass
    The program will crash:
"LLLTs, curse you all, error's baggage."

**8.**

Nine lords of our realm in Olympia
Conscience bestirred from the deep
    Wonder with fright
    If dissenters aren't right:
"LLLTs, curse you all, steal our sleep."

**9.**

Nine lords of our realm in Olympia
Might heed the complaints of our throng,
    Repent of their gaff
    And at themselves laugh:
"LLLTs, welcome back, we were wrong."

## BIBLIOGRAPHY


Abel, Richard L. *The Politics of Informal Justice: Comparative Studies*, Volume 2. New York: Academic Press, 1982.

Amsler, Lisa B., Janet K. Martinez, Stephanie E. Smith. *Dispute System Design: Preventing, Managing, and Resolving Conflict.* Stanford, California: Stanford University Press, 2020.

Andersen, William R., "Judicial Selection in Washington—Taking Elections Seriously." *Seattle University Law Review* 33:3 (2010): 605-616.

Apple, James G. and Robert P. Deyling. *A Primer on the Civil-Law System.* Federal Judicial Center, 1995.

Aquinas, Thomas. *Treatise on Law* (being Qs. 90-108 of *Summa Theologica*). Translated by an unstated person. Washington, D.C.: Regenery Gateway, Inc. (1988).

Arendt, Hanah, *Eichmann in Jerusalem: A Report on the Banality of Evil.* New York: Viking Press, 1963.

Aristotle. *Nichomachean Ethics.* Translated by H. Rackham. Cambridge, Massachusetts: Harvard University Press, 1975. Also, Perseus version, H. Rackham, Ed., contained at: https://www.perseus.tufts.edu/hopper/text?doc=Perseus%3Atext%3A1999.01.0054%3Abook%3D5.

Aristotle. *The Politics and The Constitution of Athens.* Translated by Jonathan Barnes, relying upon the Jowett translation. Edited by Stephen Everson. Cambridge, United Kingdom: Cambridge University Press, 2010.

Auerbach, Jerome. *Justice without Law?* Oxford, United Kingdom: Oxford University Press, 1983.

Bacon, Francis. *The Elements of The Common Laws of England* (1629). London: J. Crowder and E. Hemfled, 1803.

Bacon, Francis. *The Works of Francis Bacon: Law Tracts. Maxims of the Law (1596).* London: J. Crowder and E. Hemfled, 1803.

Baron-Cohen, Simon. *The Science of Evil: On Empathy and the Origins of Cruelty.* New York: Basic Books, 2011.

Baumeister, Roy F. *Evil: Inside Human Violence and Cruelty.* New York: Henry Holt and Company, 1999.

Berens, Michael and John Shiffman, "Thousands of U.S. judges who broke laws or oaths remained on the bench." https://www.reuters.com/article/us-usa-judges-misconduct-specialreport/special-report-thousands-of-u-s-judges-who-broke-laws-oaths-remained-on-the-bench-idUSKBN2411WG.

Berman, Greg, and John Feinblatt. *Good Courts: The Case for Problem-Solving Justice.* New York: The New Press, 2005.

Burger, Warren, C.J. "Agenda for 2000 A.D.—A Need for Systematic Anticipation," in *The Pound Conference: Perspectives on Justice in the Future.* St. Paul, Minnesota: West Publishing Co., 1979: 23-35.

Burger, Warren, C.J. "*Isn't There a Better Way?*," A.B.A. J. 68 (1982): 274-277.

*Bible.* Revised Standard Version. Camden, New Jersey: Thomas Nelson & Sons, 1952.

Blackstone, William. *Commentaries on the Laws of England.* Wilfred Prest, Ed. Oxford, United Kingdom: Oxford University Press, 2016.

Block, Peter. *Community: The Structure of Belonging.* San Francisco, California: Berett-Koehler Publishers, Inc., 2008.

Brooks, David, Op. Ed., "The Republican Collapse," *N.Y. Times*, October 5, 2007, at A25.

Brunk, Conrad G. "Professionalism and Responsibility in the Technological Society," 1985 *Conrad Grebel Review*, Waterloo, Ontario, Canada: 60-75.

Burke, Edmund. *Reflections on the Revolution in France.* Edited by Iaian Hampsher-Monk. New York: Cambridge University Press, 2014.

Epicurus. *The Essential Epicurus: Letters, Principal Doctrines, Vatican Sayings, and Fragments.* Translated by Eugene O'Connor. Amherst, New York: Prometheus Books, 1993.

Cardozo, Benjamin N. *The Growth of the Law.* New Haven, Connecticut: Yale University Press, 1924.

Center for Prosecutor Integrity, "Epidemic of Prosecutor Misconduct," Appendix B. http://www.prosecutorintegrity.org/wp-content/uploads/EpidemicofProsecutorMisconduct.pdf.

Churchland, Patricia S. *Braintrust: What Neuroscience Tells Us About Morality.* Princeton, New Jersey: Princeton University Press, 2011.

Cicero. *De Officiis.* Translated by Walter Miller. Cambridge, Massachusetts: Harvard University Press, 2001.

Cloke, Kenneth. *The Crossroads of Conflict: A Journey into the Heart of Dispute Resolution.* California: Janis Publications USA Inc., 2005.

*Code of Hammurabi.* Translated by L. W. King. San Bernadino, California: publisher not identified, 2015.

Coke, Edward. *Reports, Part III.* London: E. and R. Nutt and R. Gosling, 1738.

Cover, Robert, "Nomos and Narrative," *Harvard Law Review* 97:4 (1983): 4-68.

Daly, Herman E. *Steady-State Economics.* Second Edition. Washington D.C.: Island Press, 1991.

D'Amato, Anthony, "Legal Uncertainty," *California Law Review* 71 (2010): 1-55.

Dunbar, Robin I. M. *How Many Friends Does One Person Need?: Dunbar's Number and Other Evolutionary Quirks.* Cambridge, Massachusetts: Harvard University Press, 2010.

Dunbar, Robin. *Friends: Understanding the Power of our Most Important Relationships.* Great Britain: Little, Brown, 2021.

Dworkin, Ronald. *Law's Empire.* Oxford, England: Hart Publishing, 2003.

Extinction Rebellion UK. *Community Assembly Manual*, published by ExtinctionRebellion.UK. Date unspecified. Found at: https://extinctionrebellion.uk/wp-content/uploads/2020/08/Community-Assembly-Manual.pdf.

Frank, Jerome. *Courts on Trial: Myth and Reality in American Justice.* Introduction by Edmond Cahn. New York: Atheneum, 1970.

Frankel, Marvin E. *Partisan Justice: Too Much Fight? Too Little Truth? Equal Justice?* New York: Hill and Wang, 1978.

Freud, Sigmund. *Civilization and Its Discontents.* Translated by Joan Riviere. London: Hogarth Press LTD, 1953.

Freud, Sigmund. *The Future of an Illusion.* Translated by W. D. Robson-Scott. New York: Doubleday Anchor Books, 1953.

Friedman, Lawrence M. *A History of American Law.* New York: Simon and Schuster, Inc., 1985.

Fryer, "Seattle, here's something we haven't tried: A people's assembly," *Seattle Times*, February 26, 2023: Section D1.

Fuller, Lon L, "Legal Fictions," *Illinois Law Review*, XXV, Number 4 (1930): 363-399.

Fuller, Lon. *The Morality of Law.* New Haven, Connecticut: Yale University Press, 1964.

Galanter, Marc and Angela Frozena, "The Continuing Decline of Civil Trials in American Courts," in *Pound Civil Justice Institute, 2011 Forum for Judges*, entitled "The Jury Trial Implosion: The Decline of Trial by Jury and Its Significance for Appellate Courts," 1-28.

Gandhi, Mohandas K. *An Autobiography: The Story of My Experiments with Truth.* Translated by Mahadev Desai. Boston, Massachusetts: Beacon Press, 1957.

Gandhi, Mohandas K. *Non-Violent Resistance (Satyagraha).* Mineola, New York: Dover Publications, Inc., 2001.

Gibbs, James L., "The *Kpelle* Moot," *Africa*, 33 No. 1 (1963), as contained in Aaron Podolefsky and Peter J. Brown, *Applying Anthropology*, Third Edition, 1994.

Gil, David G, "Toward a 'radical' paradigm of restorative justice," in *Handbook of Restorative Justice*, Eds., Dennis Sullivan and Larry Tifft (New York: Routledge, 2008): 499-511.

Glover, Jonathan. *Humanity: A Moral History of the Twentieth Century.* New Haven, Connecticut: Yale University Press, 1999.

Godwin, William. *Enquiry Concerning Political Justice and Its Influence on Morals and Happiness.* Philadelphia, Pennsylvania: Bioren and Madan, 1796.

González, Steven C. and Lisa H. Mansfield, "Working Toward a Just Court," *Washington State Bar News* 43 (June 2021): 38-44.

Graeber, David and David Wengrow. *The Dawn of Everything: A New History of Humanity.* New York: Farrar, Straus and Giroux, 2021.

Graetz, Michael J., "Trusting the Courts: Redressing the State Court Funding Crisis." *Daedalus* 143(3) 2014): 96-104.

Grant, Lamond. "Methodology," in *The Cambridge Companion to The Philosophy of Law*, John Tasioulas, editor (Cambridge University Press, 2020): 17-37.

Greenbaum, Arthur, F., "Judicial Reporting of Lawyer Misconduct," *University of Missouri-Kansas City Law Review* 77:3 (2009): 537-568.

Gutman, David. "Ferguson seeks $2.8M more from Tim Eyman." *Seattle Times*, March 13, 2021.

Haidt, Jonathan. *The Righteous Mind: Why Good People Are Divided by Politics and Religion.* New York: Random House, Inc., 2012.

Hall, Edward T. *Beyond Culture.* New York: Doubleday, 1976.

Halling, Matt. "A Law of No Gods, No Masters—Developing and Defending a Participatory Legal System." 32 *Hastings International and Comparative Law Review* (2009): 237-269.

Hand, Learned. "The Deficiencies of Trials to Reach the Heart of the Matter," *3 Lectures on Legal Topics* (1926): 309-320.

Harrington, Christine B. *Shadow Justice: The Ideology and Institutionalization of Alternatives to Court*. Westport, Connecticut: Greenwood Press, 1985.

Hart, H.L.A. *The Concept of Law*. Oxford: Oxford University Press, 1961.

Hayek, Friedrich A. *The Constitution of Liberty*. Chicago, Illinois: University of Chicago Press, 2011.

Hedeen, Timothy, "Institutionalizing Community Mediation: Can Dispute Resolution "of, by, and for the People" Long Endure?," *Dickinson Law Review* 108 (2003-2004): 265-276.

Higgins,Paul and Mitchell B. Mackinem. *Problem-Solving Courts: Justice for the Twenty-First Century?* Santa Barbara, California: Praeger, 2009.

Hobbes, Thomas. *Leviathan, or The Mattere, Forme, & Power of a Common-Wealth Ecclesiasticall and Civill*. Cambridge, United Kingdom: Cambridge University Press, 2014.

Holmes, Oliver Wendell. *The Common Law*. Boston, Massachusetts: Little, Brown and Company, 1963.

Horowitz, Morton J., "The Conservative Tradition in the Writing of American Legal History," 17 *Am. J. Legal Hist.* 275 (1973): 275 *et seq*.

Hrdy, Sarah Glaffer. *Mothers and Others: The Evolutionary Origins of Mutual Understanding*. Cambridge, Massachusetts: Harvard University Press, 2009.

Jefferson, Thomas. *Writings*. Edited by Merrill D. Peterson. New York: Literary Classics of the United States, Inc., 1984.

Kagan, Robert A. *Adversarial Legalism: The American Way of Law*. Second Edition. Cambridge, Massachusetts: Harvard University Press, 2019.

Kant, Immanuel. *Prolegomena to any Future Metaphysics*. Translated by Paul Carus. New York: The Bobbs-Merrill Company, Inc., 1950.

Kaplan, Richard L., "Economic Inequality and the Role of Law." *Michigan Law Review* 202, Issue 6 (2003): 1987-2006.

Karen, Robert. *Becoming Attached: First Relationships and How They Shape Our Capacity to Love*. Oxford, United Kingdom: Oxford University Press, 1998.

Kelly, Robert L. *The Lifeways of Hunter-Gatherers: The Foraging Spectrum*. New York: Cambridge University Press, 2013.

Keltner, Dacher. *Born to Be Good: The Science of a Meaningful Life*. New York: W. W. Norton & Company: 2009.

Kimmerer, Robin Wall. *Braiding Sweetgrass*. Minneapolis, Minnesota: Milkweed Editions, 2013.

Kimmerer, Robin Wall. *The Serviceberry*. New York: Scribner, 2024.

King, Martin Luther, Jr. *Letter from Birmingham Jail*. London: Penguin Random House, 2018.

Kuhn, Thomas S. *The Structure of Scientific Revolutions*. Chicago, Illinois: University of Chicago Press, 1970.

Lancaster, Brad. *Cull: Choosing Well*. Shoreline, Washington: St. George's Hill Press, 2017.

Lancaster, Brad. *Cull: Epitomes*. Shoreline, Washington: St. George's Hill Press, 2017.

Lansing, Ronald B. *Juggernaut: The Whitman Massacre Trial, 1850*. Ninth Judicial District Historical Society, 1995.

Leidloff, Jean. *The Continuum Concept: In Search of Lost Happiness*. New York: Da Capo Press, 1975.

*Literature of Ancient Egypt*, Third Edition. William Kelly Simpson, Editor. Translated by Robert K. Ritner, William Kelly Simpson, Vincent A. Tobin, and Edward F. Wente, Jr. New Haven, Connecticut: Yale University Press, 2003.

Llewellyn, K. N. *The Bramble Bush: Our Law and Its Study*. New York: Oceana Publications, Inc., 1930.

Lobban, Michael. "The common law mind in the age of Sir Edward Coke," *Amicus Curiae* 33, (2001): 18-21.

Lowell, Josephine Shaw, editor. *Industrial Arbitration and Conciliation: Some Chapters from the Industrial History of the Past Thirty Years*. New York: G. P. Putnam's Sons: 1902.

Luban, David, "The Adversary System Excuse," in *The Good Lawyer: Lawyer's Roles and Lawyers' Ethics*, David Luban, editor, Totowa, New Jersey, Rowman & Allanheld, 1983: 83-122.

Macfarlane, Julie. *The New Lawyer: How Settlement is Transforming the Practice of Law*. Vancouver, British Columbia: UBC Press, 2008.

MacLean, Paul. *The Triune Brain in Evolution*. New York: Plenum Press (1990).

Maine, Henry Sumner. *Ancient Law: Its Connection with the Early History of Society, and Its Relation to Modern Ideas*. Tucson, Arizona: University of Arizona Press, 1986.

Manne, Kate. *Down Girl: The Logic of Misogyny*. New York: Oxford University Press, 2018.

Mansbridge, Jayne N. *Beyond Adversary Democracy*. Chicago, Illinois: University of Chicago Press, 1983.

Matthieson, Peter. *The Tree Where Man Was Born*. New York: Penguin Group, 1995.

Mauet, Thomas A. and Stephen D. Easton. *Trial Techniques and Trials*, Eleventh Edition. New York: Wolters Kluwer, 2021.

McCaslin, Wanda D., Editor. *Justice as Healing: Indigenous Ways*. St. Paul, Minnesota: Living Justice Press, 2005.

McCold, Paul, "The recent history of restorative justice," in *Handbook of Restorative Justice*. Edited by Dennis Sullivan and Larry Tifft. New York: Routledge, 2008: 23-51.

McKinnon, Catharine A. *Toward a Feminist Theory of the State*. Cambridge, Massachusetts: Harvard University Press (1989).

McKnight, John and Peter Block. *The Abundant Community: Awakening the Power of Families and Neighborhoods*. San Francisco, California: Berrett-Koehler Publishers, Inc., 2010.

Menkel-Meadow, Carrie, "Regulation of Dispute Resolution in the United States of America: From the Formal to the Informal to the 'Semi-formal' in *Regulating Dispute Resolution: ADR and Access to Justice at the Crossroads*. Felix Steffek, Hannes Unberath, Hazel Genn, Reinhard Greger and Carrie Menkel-Meadow, eds. Oxford, United Kingdom: Hart 2013, 433-434.

Menkel-Meadow, Carrie, "The Trouble with the Adversary System in a Postmodern, Multicultural World," *William and Mary Law Review* 38 (1996): 5-44.

Mill, John Stuart. *The Subjection of Women*. New York: Penguin Books (2006).

Nader, Laura, editor. *No Access to Law: Alternatives to the American Judicial System*. New York: Academic Press: 1980.

Nelson, Dorothy W, "Alternative Dispute Resolution: A Supermart for Law Reform," *New Mexico Law Review* 14 (1984).

Nelson, Jill, ed. *Police Brutality: An Anthology*. New York: W.W. Norton & Company, Inc: 2000.

Ngomane, Mungi. *Everyday Ubuntu: Living Better Together, the African Way*. London: Bantam Press, 2019. With a foreword by Archbishop Desmond Tutu.

Noll, Douglas. *Peacemaking: Practicing at the Intersection of Law and Human Conflict*. Telford, Pennsylvania: Cascadia Publishing House, 2003.

Panksepp, Jaak. *Affective Neuroscience: The Foundations of Human and Animal Emotions*. New York: Oxford University Press, 1998.

Pazzanese, Christina, "The costs of inequality: Increasingly, it's the rich and *the rest.*" *The Harvard Gazette*, February 8, 2016.

Peters, Christopher J. *A Matter of Dispute: Morality, Democracy, and Law*. Oxford, United Kingdom: Oxford University Press, 2011.

Pfaff, Donald W. *The Altruistic Brain: How We Are Naturally Good*. New York: Oxford University Press, 2015.

Pinker, Steven. *The Better Angels of Our Nature*. New York: Penguin Group, 2011.

Postema, Gerald J, "Philosophy of the Common Law," contained as Chapter 15 of: Coleman, Jules and Shapiro, Scott, *The Oxford Handbook of Jurisprudence and Philosophy of Law*. Oxford, United Kingdom: Oxford University Press, 2002.

Pound, Roscoe. *Interpretations of Legal History*. New York: The MacMillan Company, 1923.

Pound, Roscoe. "The Causes of Popular Dissatisfaction with the Administration of Justice." Lecture presented at convention of American Bar Association, August 29, 1906. Contained in *The Pound Conference: Perspectives on Justice in the Future*, Appendix B (pages 337-353). St. Paul, Minnesota: West Publishing Co., 1979.

Pound, Roscoe. *The Spirit of the Common Law*. Norwood, Massachusetts: The Plimpton Press, 1921.

Pranis, Kay, Barry Stuart, and Mark Wedge. *Peacemaking Circles: From Conflict to Community*. St. Paul, Minnesota: Living Justice Press: 2003.

Pranis, Kay. *The Little Book of Circle Processes: A New/Old Approach to Peacemaking*. New York: Good Books, 2005.

Radin, Margaret Jane, "Compensation and Commensurability," 43 *Duke Law Journal* 56 (1993): 56-86.

Riskin, Leonard L. and James E. Westbrook. *Dispute Resolution and Lawyers* (Abridged Edition). St. Paul, Minnesota: West Publishing Co., 1988.

Röder, Tilmann J., "Informal Justice Systems: Challenges and Perspectives," *Innovations in Rule of Law* 58: (2012): 58-61.

Rothbard, Murray N. *Anatomy of the State*. Middleton, Delaware: BN Publishing, 1974.

Rothstein, Richard. *The Color of Law: A Forgotten History of How Our Government Segregated America*. New York: Liveright Publishing Corporation, 2017.

Russo, Francine, "The Toxic Well of Loneliness," *Scientific American* 318, No. 1 (January 2018): 64-69.

Sachs, Albie, "Truth and Reconciliation," 58 *SMU L. Rev.* (1999): 1563-1578.

Saito, Kohei. *Slow Down: The Degrowth Manifesto*. Translated by Brian Bergstrom. New York: Astra House, 2024.

Schopenhauer, Arthur. *The Basis of Morality*. Translated by Arthur Brodrick Bullock. Mineola, New York: Dover Publications, Inc., 2005.

Schweitzer, Albert. *The Philosophy of Civilization.* Translated by C. T. Campion. New York: Prometheus Books, 1987.

Seneca. "On Tranquillity of Mind," in *Dialogues and Letters*. Translated by C. D. N. Costa. London: Penguin Books, 1997.

Sennett, Richard. *The Uses of Disorder: Personal Identity and City Life*. New York: Alfred A. Knopf, 1970.

Shaw, George Bernard. *The Quintessence of Ibsenism* (1891). Now Completed to the Death of Ibsen. United Kingdom: Constable, 1913.

Shostak, Marjorie. *Nisa: The Life and Words of a !Kung Woman*. Cambridge, Massachusetts: Harvard University Press, 1981.

Snedker, Karen A. *Therapeutic Justice: Crime, Treatment Courts, and Mental Illness*. Cham, Switzerland: Palgrave Macmillan, 2018.

Solomon, Jason and Nicole Smith, "The Surprising Success of Washington State's Limited License Legal Technician Program." White Paper of Stanford Law School, Stanford Center on the Legal Profession, April 2021.

Solzhenitsyn, Aleksandr I. *Letter to the Soviet Leaders.* New York: Harper & Row, 1974.

Spengler, Oswald. *The Decline of the West*, Vol II: *Perspectives of World-History*. Translated (authorized) by Charles Frances Atkinson. London: George Allen and Unwin Ltd.: 1922.

Spiro, Melvin. *Kibbutz: Venture in Utopia.* New York: Schocken Books, 1963.

Spiropoulous, Andrew C. "Just Not Who We are: A Critique of Common Law Constitutionalism," 54 *Villanova Law Review*, No. 2, 181 (2009).

Story, Joseph. *Address Delivered Before the Members of the Suffolk Bar*. Boston, Massachusetts: Freeman & Bolles: 1829.

Strasburger, Larry, H., M.D., "The Litigant-Patient: Mental Health Consequences of Civil Litigation," *Journal of the American Academy of Psychiatry Law* 27, No. 2 (1999): 203-211.

Stuart, Barry and Kay Pranis, "Peacemaking circles: Reflections on principal features and primary outcomes," in *Handbook of Restorative Justice*, Eds., Dennis Sullivan and Larry Tifft. New York: Routledge, 2008: 121-133.

Sullivan, Dennis, and Larry Tifft, "The healing dimension of restorative justice: a one-world body," in *Handbook of Restorative Justice*, Eds., Dennis Sullivan and Larry Tifft. New York: Routledge, 2008: 1-16.

Sward, Ellen E., "Values, Ideology, and the Evolution of the Adversary System," *Indiana Law Journal* 64 (Spring 1989): 301-355.

Taylor, Michael. *The Possibility of Cooperation*. New York: Cambridge University Press, 1987.

Thompson, Mikah K., "Bias on Trial: Toward An Open Discussion of Racial Stereotypes in the Courtroom," 2018 *Michigan State Law Review*: 1243-1307.

Tonucci, Francesco. *City of Children.* Translated by Dessy Vassileva. Delaware, United States: Vernon Press, 2020.

Tremayne, Wendy Jehanara. *The Good Life Lab: Radical Experiments in Hands-On Living.* North Adams, Massachusetts: Storey Publishing, 2013.

United Nations. *Handbook on Restorative Justice Programmes*, Office on Drugs and Crime, November 2006.

Volcansec, Mary L. *Judicial Misconduct: A Cross-National Comparison*. Gainesville, Florida: University Press of Florida, 1996.

Vorrasi, Kenneth M. "England's Reform to Alleviate the Problems of Civil Process: A Comparison of Judicial Case Management in England and the United States," *Journal of Legislation* 30 (May 2004): 360-387.

Wade, Nicholas. *Before the Dawn: Recovering the Lost History of Our Ancestors.* New York: Penguin Books, 2006.

Walzer, Michael. *Spheres of Justice: A Defense of Pluralism and Equality*. Lexington, Kentucky: Basic Books, 1983.

Wilets, Jim and Areto A. Imoukhuede, "A Critique of the Uniquely Adversarial Nature of the U.S. Legal, Economic and Political System and its Implications for Reinforcing Existing Power Hierarchies," University of Pennsylvania Journal of Law and Societal Change 20 (2018): 341-379.

Wilson, Edward O. *The Meaning of Human Existence.* New York: Liveright Publishing Corporation, 2014.

Wittgenstein, Ludwig. *Philosophical Investigations.* Translated by G. E. M. Anscombe. Malden, Massachusetts: Blackwell Publishing Ltd., 2001.

Woolf, Harry, "Civil Justice in the United Kingdom," *The American Journal of Comparative Law* 45 (1997): 709-736.

Yankah, Ekow N. "The Force of Law: the Role of Coercion in Legal Norms," 42 *U. Rich. L. Rev.* 1195 (2008).

Yazzie, Robert, "Life Comes from It: Navajo Justice Concepts," 24 *N.M. L. Rev.* 175 (Spring 1994).

Zakaria, Fareed, "Incarceration Nation," *Time* 179, No. 13 (April 2, 2012): [unable to recover page reference].

Zavos, Harry, "Monetary Damages for Nonmonetary Losses: An Integrated Answer to the Problem of the Meaning, Function, and Calculation of Noneconomic Damages," 43 *Loyola L. A. Law Review* (2009): 193-272.

Zehr, Howard. *The Little Book of Restorative Justice.* New York: Good Books, 2015.

*Zenith Radio Corp. v. Matsushita Elect. Indus. Co.*, 402 F. Supp. 251 (E.D. Pa. 1975).

Zion, James W. and Robert Yazzie, "Navajo peacemaking: Original dispute resolution and a life way," in *Handbook of Restorative Justice*, Eds., Dennis Sullivan and Larry Tifft (New York: Routledge, 2008): 151-160.

Zozula, Christine. *Courting the Community: Legitimacy and Punishment in a Community Court.* Philadelphia, Pennsylvania: Temple University Press, 2019.

## APPRECIATIONS

Every book recounts, in some manner, its author's journey. My trek is replete with intelligent companions and persons of deep moral stature. I name but a few of these wonders of humankind, for I do not wish to compel any to decide, without years of mulling, whether they may agree or disagree with views I express in this book.[520] Nor do I wish to subject them to disparagement from my detractors who might seek to maim them on account of their association with me. Others of my companions, the more famous ones, are gone where go we all. These fear no nastiness. I know these dead companions because they wrote and I read. Not all these deceased speakers are geniuses. All, however, speak of some matter difficult to examine in locations other than their books. Several of these dead-mostly-men, and a few dead-women, I have epitomized for this text, or in others of my works.

Some wonder that I include summaries of others' books in my own efforts. This practice grows from my observation that all adequate thinking arises in colloquy. What you read here (or in any book) is the product of many (probably hundreds) of exchanges between an author and her people, living and dead. For thought is transgenerational, germinating in the remains of the now-dead, flowering in this morning's sun upon a living cerebrum, but seeding a future that is, at present, little else than pregnant speculation. I am most grateful to my companions for their thoughts and our conversations.

In this book, I have spoken ill, directly or obliquely, of the sentiments and preferences of some of my colleagues at law. In so doing, I transgress my mother's dictum: If you cannot say something nice, say nothing at all. I note, for historical accuracy, that Beverly Lancaster, despite her oft-intoned saw, castigated the wrong-doers of her little world in north Idaho with an acutely-whetted tongue. All authors transgress Beverly's command. If nothing needed redress, why would one unsheathe the pen? I am grateful to my mother for courage she inspired by flagellating errant school principals, wayward spouses of her dear friends, drug-addled would-be companions of mine, and, occasionally, me. She was fierce—not always right, but formidable.

As I age, I recognize my debt to you, my reader. Few read difficult books. So, you are an exception and a wonder. You have my appreciation and thanks. My hope is that you found in what I have written the germ of at least a handful of fresh, or at least useful, thoughts.

---

[520] I thank those who consented when I asked to include their names in this book.

## SAINT GEORGE'S HILL PRESS

On St. George's Hill (southwest of London), in 1648, poor people, under the influence of Gerrard Winstanley, tilled and built shacks on public land to feed themselves, when food prices soared during the English Civil War. They called themselves True Levellers, and sought reduction of the financial chasm between the poor and the wealthy. The king sent a representative, who found the group doing no appreciable harm. A local lord felt otherwise, and commissioned thugs to assault the True Levellers. Some were beaten. Their common meal house was burned. Leaders were tried; the judge refused to let them speak in their defense. The True Levellers, dubbed Diggers by opponents, abandoned their plots for less hostile locations. In the twenty-first century, St. George's Hill is home to an exclusive gated and closely-guarded community, consisting in 450 mansions with tennis club and golf course amenities. St. George's Hill claims to be the premier private residential estate in Europe, close to London and Britain's most desirable private preparatory schools. The median price of a residence on St. George's Hill exceeds £3,000,000. St. George's Hill, then, is the dirt upon which clash desperate diggers and entrenched elites, a metaphor barely metaphorical.

Made in the USA
Monee, IL
03 November 2025

32579531R00203